The Twenty-First Century and Its Discontents

The Twenty-First Century and Its Discontents

How Changing Discourse Norms Are Changing Culture

Edited by
Jack Simmons

LEXINGTON BOOKS
Lanham • Boulder • New York • London

Published by Lexington Books
An imprint of The Rowman & Littlefield Publishing Group, Inc.
4501 Forbes Boulevard, Suite 200, Lanham, Maryland 20706
www.rowman.com

6 Tinworth Street, London SE11 5AL, United Kingdom

Copyright © 2020 The Rowman & Littlefield Publishing Group, Inc.

Chapter 1: "The Outsourcing of Ethical Thinking" previously appeared in the *Journal of Human Values*, Volume 24, Number 2, May 2018.

All rights reserved. No part of this book may be reproduced in any form or by any electronic or mechanical means, including information storage and retrieval systems, without written permission from the publisher, except by a reviewer who may quote passages in a review.

British Library Cataloguing in Publication Information Available

Library of Congress Cataloging-in-Publication Data

Names: Simmons, Jack, 1964– author.
Title: The twenty-first century and its discontents : how changing discourse norms are changing culture / Jack Simmons.
Description: Lanham : Lexington, 2020. | Includes bibliographical references and index. | Summary: "Philosophers and political theorists tackle the question of cultural transformation in the twenty-first century and the role discourse norms play in producing cancel culture, a counter-sexual revolution, racism and a toxic politics that has left the nation feeling vulnerable and angry"—Provided by publisher.
Identifiers: LCCN 2020039727 (print) | LCCN 2020039728 (ebook) | ISBN 9781793607997 (cloth) | ISBN 9781793608017 (pbk) | ISBN 9781793608000 (epub)
Subjects: LCSH: Social change. | Sex role. | Racism—Political aspects. | Political culture.
Classification: LCC HM831 .S56 2020 (print) | LCC HM831 (ebook) | DDC 303.4—dc23
LC record available at https://lccn.loc.gov/2020039727
LC ebook record available at https://lccn.loc.gov/2020039728

Contents

Acknowledgments — vii

Introduction — 1

PART 1: INSTITUTIONAL DISCOURSE — 13

1. The Outsourcing of Ethical Thinking — 15
   Erik Nordenhaug and Jack Simmons

2. The Diversity of "Diversity": Support for Differing Conceptions of Diversity on the University Campus — 39
   Kenneth B. McIntyre and Stacy G. Ulbig

3. Undermining Communicative Action in the Medical Encounter: Informed Consent, Compelled Speech, and Promises to Pay — 65
   Leigh E. Rich

4. The Rebirth of Canonical Love — 107
   Jack Simmons

PART 2: TRIBAL DISCOURSE — 133

5. The Social Justice Discourse Ethic: Contours and Causes — 135
   Robert Gressis

6. Dealing with the Devil: Objectification of Counter-Partisans and Political Compromise — 167
   Stacy G. Ulbig

7   From "Post-Racial America" to #BlackLivesMatter:
    Rethinking Race for the Twenty-First Century   205
    Elizabeth Butterfield

PART 3: THE PANDEMIC   **229**

8   Lessons from the Death Zone: What Jon Krakauer's
    Into Thin Air Can Teach Us about the COVID-19
    Pandemic and Why We May Be Doomed to Repeat It   231
    Leigh E. Rich

9   Strategic Discourse in the Time of the Coronavirus   263
    Robert Gressis

Index   275

About the Contributors   281

Acknowledgments

I would like to thank my wife Katherine for her patience and devotion, and my children Savannah, Mary, and Gus for their support and affection. I would also like to thank Dolores Rogge for being my mother and enduring the slings and arrows of that enterprise with grace and courtesy.

The colorful and sometimes dreadful character of 2020 made writing and collecting chapters on contemporary issues particularly challenging, and I would like to thank my contributors for their energy and effort in creating a collection that reflects the spirit of the times.

Additionally, I would like to thank my Georgia Southern undergraduate research team: Kara Brown, Alexis Chessher, Zakary Davis, Adam Deal, Brandon Ellershaw, Zach Graham, Noah Hendrix, Caleb Kirby, Marcus Leach, Beverly Leitelt, Jonathan Martin, Eli Neumann, Thomas Reeves, Charles Robertson, Miranda Smith, Carter Smith and Bronte Wright.

Introduction

In what might best be described as prescient, Jane Flax suggested in 1987 that having grown old, Western culture is in the middle of a fundamental transformation.[1] We hear this sentiment echoed in the vernacular. The phrases "the new normal" and "in these uncertain times" regularly introduce all forms of public discourse as the twenty-first century brings catastrophe after catastrophe. In addition to the acute crises such as 9/11, the wars in the Middle East, the great recession, and COVID-19, the backdrop of global warming, toxic masculinity, the glass ceiling, rape culture, illegal immigration, police brutality, institutional racism, hurricanes, flooding, drought maintains a perpetual sense of social fragility and vulnerability. Because many of the contemporary issues reflect public concerns from the 1960s to 1970s, such as racism, sexism and homophobia, we might view twenty-first-century discontent as a revisiting of unfinished business from culture wars, but I think that Flax is correct. The history of all previous societies may be class conflict, but that doesn't mean the conflicts are always the same. The culture wars that inspired vigorous conflict over ideas and the social contract transformed into identity wars that emphasize tribal character and a conflict over access to social resources.

The culture wars post–World War II reflected an American exceptionalism and optimism, sparked in large part by the nation's ascendency to the status of global superpower. If America could tame Western civilization's greatest enemies, the Axis powers, surely it could cure its internal problems. But in the twenty-first century, the optimism faded. The cause of our pessimism remains unclear. Perhaps it is the growing dangers described above, though they do not appear more perilous than the post–World War II threat of nuclear war. Perhaps it is twenty-first-century technology that offers us incessant coverage of these dangers through a mass, social media that contributes to the new anxiety. Diagnosing the cause of contemporary fear remains difficult, but few have failed to recognize the anxiety and its manifestation in social discourse.

Despite her clairvoyance, Flax may have undershot her mark. She rightly anticipates the rise of postmodernism and sees that change as informed by the Holocaust, atomic bomb and Vietnam War, but in her twentieth-century optimism, imagined a postmodernism that would offer a new pluralism. Instead, the demise of modernity gave rise to a pseudo-pluralism that generated powerful ideologies, corporatism, and class divisions that resemble a return to medievalism. With the decline of modernism, the veneer of American exceptionalism and optimism wore off leaving only fear and disappointment at our failure to live up to that exceptionalism. We see the new national character on display in the retreat from personal autonomy (e.g., the dominance of corporate culture, sexual consent rules, and limits on women's reproductive rights), cancel culture (e.g., intolerance for unapproved speech and art), tribalism (emphasis on group identity), and anti-intellectualism (e.g., denial of climate change and vaccine efficacy). Intellectual postmodernism, intended to inspire cultural pluralism by neutralizing monolithic notions of the American dream, gave rise to a postmodernism discourse that emphasizes strategic discourse (aimed at achieving some goal) rather than shared understanding. The decline of shared understanding gave rise to a new Manicheanism, which divides people into good and evil, replaces values debate with rules, and makes compromise difficult. In this collection, the authors look at the role of changing discourse norms in twenty-first-century cultural changes.

POSTMODERN DISCOURSE

If there is a cultural manifestation of the twenty-first century, the evidence points to a distortion of public discourse. This distortion has two components. The first is the emphasis on language in the twenty-first century, which appears to be a product of postmodernism and communication technology. Postmodernism brought the philosophical linguistic turn (often associated with Ludwig Wittgenstein and Ferdinand de Saussure) into popular culture, shifting our focus from material to symbolic/linguistic culture, and the most significant technological advances of the early twenty-first century have involved communications technology (mobile devices for texting, social media and instant access to the global Internet). These developments magnified the effect of discourse norms on the society.

This second component is that the fashionable form of postmodern thinking created a cultural paradox: the distrust of ideology and the reliance on ideology. The postmodern suspicion of grand narratives arose out of the realization that the universal norms expressed in enlightenment values concealed oppressive political hierarchies and hidden agendas (e.g., racism, sexism, xenophobia, and homophobia). By deconstructing and revealing those biases, postmodernists hoped to provide intellectual space for a plurality of narratives and modi vivendi. At this stage, the postmodernist thinkers borrowed from the enlightenment in recognizing the need for a marketplace of ideas, a marketplace that would allow a diversity of ideas to be heard and the best ideas to guide culture. This need popularized the work of discourse theorists like Jürgen Habermas, Johanna Meehan, John Rawls, and Jane Flax. Discourse ethics promised a context in which intersubjective communication, aimed at shared understanding and community formation, replaces strategic, goal-oriented discourse. Under communicative discourse conditions, all participants enjoy an equal opportunity to speak, and no veto power is granted to specialized experts. But discourse ethics could not contend with the development of the technocratic society and the associated corporate ideologies.

The rise of grand organizational systems (e.g., the financial industry, the medical industry, the communication system, and the educational system) created a massive technocracy that permeated communal life and became necessary for the regular functioning of society. In 2008, we discovered that the financial organizational system and auto industry was too big to fail. In the twenty-first century, individuals may still fail, but organizational systems cannot, because if they do, they take us all with them. This means that individuals must ultimately serve the grand organizational systems, enterprises that exist for the sake of designated goals. Because those enterprises must be sustained, we shaped social intercourse to serve the strategic goals of those enterprises. In this way, corporate interests captured social discourse and bent the marketplace of ideas to reflect those interests. James Carville's 1992 quote, "It's the economy, stupid," neatly anticipated twenty-first-century thinking: that all public debate would ultimately reference the grand organizational systems upon which we depend. Carville's point is that all problems are financial problems, which may ultimately be true, though this is not the conclusion arrived at here. In this collection, we see how the organizational apparatus that sustains educational and health care spawns public and private discourse norms that serve their strategic interests. The resulting technocracy, a society determined by the algorithms of organizational systems, undermines free will, replaces meaning creation with system maintenance and quite naturally results in nihilism. Contributors to this collection address the problem of technocracy in the section: Institutional Discourse.

This nihilism has birthed a savage identity politics and corresponding cancel culture. Identity politics generated discourse norms designed to validate new modes of being in the world, centered around distinct socially recognized characteristics that allowed for corporate identity: identity based on ethnicity, gender, profession, religion, political party, generation, and so on.

Maintaining these corporate identities requires an ideology. The proliferation of corporate identities might have resulted in an explosion of pluralism, but instead, it resulted in cancel culture, in which the validation of one identity group requires the invalidation of others, which too may have its intellectual foundations in de Saussure semiotics. In the culture wars of the twentieth century, women's sexual liberation complemented men's sexuality, but in the twenty-first century, women's liberation means liberation from toxic masculinity, which requires the designation of a previously normal way of life as toxic.

Cancel culture may be the result of the linguistic turn in the age of nihilism. In the face of our own meaninglessness, only words continue to mean anything, and their meaning is derived not by reference to some fixed reality, but rather in relation to other words that represent a negation of their meaning. "White" is only white in so far as it is not "black." "Heterosexual" only signifies not being homosexual. The validity of a new identity cannot be grounded on positive characteristics but is instead grounded on the negative attributes of others. Hence, ethnic identity relies on the shared experience of racism, rather than "Black is beautiful," and gender identity on the shared experience of misogyny, rather than Rosie the Riveter's "We can do it," religious identity on bigotry, rather than salvation, and so on. To express an identity in the postmodern political environment involves an ideological rejection and cancelation of some other, designated identity. Mussolini preached that war brings people purpose; we have replaced war with negation.

Corporatism and tribalism require powerful ideological commitments, both regularly on display on university campuses across the country. On the Statesboro branch of my own institution, Georgia Southern University, several students burned the book of invited speaker Jennine Capó Crucet in the fall of 2019, accusing her of racism for her talk on her experience "among the whites." The local, national and international press accused the students of racism for having desecrated the book of a Latina author talking about race and white privilege. Calls came from all quarters demanding that the students be expelled, and the Georgia Southern University faculty found themselves embroiled in the controversy, their students equated with Nazis for their book burning and the institution described as a haven for racists. The university president came under fire for suggesting that although book burning did not align with the values of the institution, the action was protected under the First Amendment, hence, the students could not be expelled.

Given that the students burned their own books, after hearing the speaker's ideas, and made no effort to remove the books from general circulation, the comparison to Nazi book burnings does not hold up. The students' behavior more closely resembles Martin Luther's burning of the papal bulls. Because the bulls were Luther's property, and his action made no effort to remove the bulls from circulation, historians view Luther's action as symbolic protest; like anti-war protesters burning an American flag, or athletes taking a knee during an anthem to protest racism. The inelegant and inaccurate comparison of the students to Nazis achieved the strategic goal—to identify the student protestors as "other," to declare that they are not "one of us," and attempt to deny them access to educational resources.

At the faculty senate meetings during this crisis, it became clear to me that the driving force behind the general outrage was embarrassment. The faculty at Georgia Southern University felt guilty by association with the students and wished to send a clear message: we are not Nazis; we are not racists. Similarly, Jennine Capó Crucet made it clear to the students in the audience that she was not like them, that she was a victim of the institutional racism which benefitted them.[2] The students burned her book to show that they were not like her, that her diagnosis of their inherent racism based on the color of their skin was itself racist. And the intellectual community, readers and writers of books, called the students Nazis because they burned books. We were all embarrassed to be associated with some designated, bigoted, other.

Perhaps better than any other twenty-first-century idea, institutional racism highlights the collision of organizational determinism and the politics of identity. Institutional racism suggests that individuals, despite their personal sentiments, reflect the racism inherent to the organizational systems and institutions that sustain culture. No individual can undo their own racism by changing their opinions or their behaviors. Institutional racism was made clear and distinct in the flaccid response to the book-burning crisis at Georgia Southern University. The university's faculty and administration could do little other than accept Crucet's cancelling of her scheduled appearance on the Savannah campus of Georgia Southern University, sixty miles away from where the book burning occurred. While the university president claims to have shared the faculty's disapproval of the behavior, the University System of Georgia attorneys vetted and tailored his public statement to protect the interests of the $2.4 billion/year public higher education enterprise: neither condemning nor condoning the actions, nor offering a nuanced affirmation of higher education as a conduit for all forms of social discourse: a marketplace of ideas. Faculty too were warned not to express opinions about the event if they were representing the university in any way. The university system cannot risk its organizational stability addressing the values and interests of individuals, nor embroil itself in the social discourse of community and identity. Ultimately, the university adopted several organizational approaches to institutional racism: hiring a new administrator for the office of diversity, organizing meetings through the diversity office to discuss institutional racism (supporting the idea that racism is unconscious and that individuals have no control over it), and promising to include more diversity training to students and faculty. These responses reflect organizational standards for dealing with institutional racism and each approach aims to shape behavior to support the institutional goals. It is difficult not to notice the irony of an institutional response to institutional racism, and that it was the university's diversity training (assigning the Crucet book to freshman and inviting her to campus) that inspired the campus crisis.

In the nihilism of institutional determinism and the crisis of identity, we bind ourselves dogmatically to ideologies that offer some semblance of meaning. Burning a book on a barbeque grill fails to rise to the level of Kristallnacht, concentration camps, or the invasion of Poland, but Nazism represents evil in the vernacular, and we deemed the book burning evil. The comparison was lazy and reflects a postmodern Manicheanism, rejecting nuanced reason in favor of corporate ideology and dogma.

Medieval theologian Saint Ignatius of Loyola neatly characterized an overpowering ideology; "What seems to me white, I will believe black if the hierarchical Church so defines."[3] The scientific revolution reversed this, placing reason and empirical evidence over ideology, and although America has always harbored a well-documented anti-intellectual streak, American pragmatism and a Cold War generally tipped the scales in favor of the rationalists and empiricists through the latter half of the twentieth century. Twenty-first century fear and nihilism tipped the scales back in favor of ideologues. Many Americans now reside in dogmatic fortresses that trump even empirical science and reason. Ideological attacks on climate scientists (advising a reduction in carbon emissions) and epidemiologists (advising social distancing to reduce contagion) have become commonplace, and climate scientists and epidemiologists are now often linked and criticized for having strategic agendas associated with elitist values. Postmodern discourse theory, intended to neutralize the strategic rationality of enlightenment ideologies, replaced them with the strategic rationality of contemporary ideologies (corporatism and identity politics), signaling a potent return to a pre-enlightenment perspective: everything is ideology.

The collection is broken into three parts. The first section, *Institutional Discourse*, addresses the incursion of strategic, means–end reasoning into our lives through institutional norms. Given that institutions exist for some designated purpose, it may seem quite natural for them to practice means–end reasoning, but in these chapters, the authors illustrate how institutional goals creep into and shape aspects of our lives traditionally considered the realm of the personal, the private, the intellectual and the confidential.

In the first chapter in this section, Erik Nordenhaug and I point to the outsourcing of ethical thinking as a way in which methodical thinking and institutional structures channel, replace, and transform individual moral agency. Using the example of Pinocchio, we illustrate how the process of becoming human traditionally involved the development of an internal moral voice, replacing the external moral guidance of the cricket (adult moral authority). To possess human moral agency is not simply doing as you are told, but rather developing an autonomous sense of right and wrong. Through ethics trainings, generally provided by online, ethics courses, declarations of core values and employee policy manuals, institutions systematically redefine ethics as a mode of being in the world that serves institutional systems by increasing worker efficiency and limiting corporate liability. Access to employment opportunities increasingly requires employees to accept greater institutional oversight inside and outside the workplace. Our analysis of institutional ethics reveals the larger phenomenon of how technologies and technological systems increasingly mediate ethical thinking and ethical behaviors thereby undermining the meaning of human moral agency. Human agency can no longer be analyzed independently of the agency and influence of the technological systems and technological thinking.

Not only do institutional goals distort our understanding of ethics and moral agency, means–end rationality distorts the institutional goals themselves by narrowly focusing on politically fashionable aspects of those goals. Decrying the politicization of universities might well constitute a cottage industry of its own, and the suggestion that universities were ever free of politics requires a level of naïveté reserved for a faithful remnant. McIntyre and Ulbig examine the purpose of higher education and the twenty-first-century notion of diversity and conclude that both strive to construct open discourse conditions that facilitate the free exchange of ideas and ultimately greater open-mindedness about ourselves and other people. Unfortunately, the focus on identity-based diversity distorts intellectual diversity. This distortion hinders the development of open discourse conditions and the free exchange of ideas. The current prosecution of the diversity mission is, with apologies to Allan Bloom, closing American minds, increasing levels of intolerance and fanaticism in the student body.

Leigh E. Rich and I tackle the problem of institutionalized consent. In the marketplace of ideas, the goal of discourse is not a particular outcome, but rather an agreement, arrived at through the persuasive power of reason alone (what Habermas calls the compulsionless compulsion). This agreement is the basis of consent. When we worry about the validity of consent, we worry about whether the persuasion was compulsionless, or whether it was compelled. A compelled consent is no consent at all.

In contemporary medicine, institutional goals distort informed medical consent such that we now understand consent in the health care encounter as the patient's signature on a contract that superficially addresses autonomous decision-making while limiting the medical liability of the physician and health care organization. Although most health care providers have good intentions, to uphold the tenets of informed consent, they often lack the training and time to carry out such communicative discussions in practice. Thus, the task becomes "obtaining" a patient's consent or even "consenting a patient," rather than reaching consensus with a patient. Moreover, in the U.S. health care system, the responsibility for payment ultimately resides with the patient, and patients (except in certain circumstances such as emergencies) are asked to sign financial responsibility forms before they reach an examination room or see a doctor. Refusing to consent to such conditions likely means the patient will receive no health care, but how can patients agree to be financially responsible for all charges before they know what diagnoses or treatments are appropriate? Patients often do not know what they will owe even after tests and treatments are administered, and nowhere in the informed consent process is a requirement to disclose and discuss financial risks and consequences (as this likely would be impossible in the fragmented, multiple-payer system that exists in the United States). The misperception of informed consent by both providers and patients within a health care encounter—as well as the blind financial contracts to which patients must agree—distorts the idea of informed consent, which hinges upon the conversations between the patient and physician and implies that both reach a shared understanding of the nature of the illness, the possible remedies, and the best path forward for that particular patient and his or her lifeworld. Rich unravels the history of medical consent and helps us to understand how we arrived at this point and why informed consent in practice remains so challenging.

Like informed medical consent, sexual consent implies a personal agreement between two people, but in following Title IX guidelines, colleges and universities across the country adopted institutional standards that dictate the conditions of interpersonal discourse and sexual consent for the sake of reducing sexual assault. This means–end approach to discourse and sexual consent closely mimics twelfth-century canonical standards, when the Catholic Church imposed new standards on marriage and sexual behavior to attenuate the danger women face in a society of toxic masculinity. In this chapter, I show how the 2014 Title IX guidelines to reduce sexual assault on college campuses, mimic the medieval, canonical effort by: recognizing the need to address the imbalance in social power between men and women, describing masculine sexual norms as toxic, condemning sexual passion, insisting on rational sexual behavior, codifying rational sexual behavior, and launching a public information campaign to change the norms of sexuality. Both the medieval and contemporary approaches dismiss the romantic conception of love, which glorifies passion and autonomy, as part of rape culture, and insist that valid sexual behavior involves the identification of the sexual goals of all participants and the application of institutionally authorized criteria for establishing agreement on the goals and pursing them. In this way, means–end reasoning regulates even the most intimate human dynamics.

In the second section, *Tribal Discourse*, the writers study the way discourse norms shape political identity, and how political identity shapes discourse norms. Robert Gressis and Stacy Ulbig tackle the social justice movement and how contemporary discourse norms around these movements stifle compromise and progress. In "The Social Justice Discourse Ethic," Gressis unpacks the discursive assumptions underlying contemporary social justice discourse and its perception of politics as a struggle between dominant and oppressed groups. Conceptualizing the struggle this way justifies creating unequal discourse conditions. Phrases like "gaslighting," "victim-blaming," "systemic violence," "emotional labor" and "himpathy," aim to neutralize the effects of the dominant cultural discourse on oppressed people and invalidate any opposition. Gressis uses a key premise of social justice advocates, that people are likely to adopt beliefs that allow them to rationalize their own power, to demonstrate that social justice discourse norms are used strategically rather than for mutual understanding, and therefore primarily serve the needs of the social justice activists rather than the oppressed populations they claim to champion.

Ulbig suggests that people now adopt political parties as identity markers, making political compromise and shared governance very difficult. Strong identification with an ethnic or racial group often causes favoritism toward members of that group and intolerance, disrespect and violence toward people outside the group. As we have begun to identify personally with political groups, such as Republican and Democrat, the result is that we react toward the opposition political party with the sort of animosity traditionally reserved for racial or ethnic hatred. Consequently, a "get out the vote" effort by Democrats manifests as an attack on Republican voters by Republicans. If identity is tied to the Republican Party, and that party is out of power in your state, you feel powerless, your way of life threatened. In an environment in which personal identity is tied to political affiliation, political disputes transform debates regarding the proper scope of government to existential threats. Ulbig uses empirical data to demonstrate the growing divide in American culture and the tendency to identify political opponents as the other, as the enemy. She explains that "politics at both the elite and mass level have become the battleground for a zero-sum game in which both sides feel that conceding any ground to their opponents represents not just practical, political horse-trading, but an unthinkable act of negotiation with immoral, and somehow less than human, others."

Optimistic declarations that the election of Barack Obama in 2008 signaled the beginning of a post-racial America now appear premature to most scholars, and the rise of American tribalism may represent a cultural riposte to unifying visions of the nation. Elizabeth Butterfield argues that race still matters in America but agrees with Lucius Outlaw that this might not be such a bad thing after all. She acknowledges that since Obama's election, the nation is experiencing a heightened awareness of racism (e.g., BlackLivesMatter and attention to high incarceration rates of black men), a rise in white supremacist violence, discussions of white privilege, and a recognition of the fluidity of racial categories, but she does not see the erasure of racial identity as the solution. Butterfield deconstructs the dream for a colorblind future and deploys Jean-Paul Sartre's framework for understanding human "freedom in situation" to reconceptualize racial identity as both real (culturally) and not real (biologically). She argues that in order to understand racial identity in a way that is both accurate and useful, what we need is the virtue of patience to sit with complexities and ambiguities. This will allow us to address structural racism, preserve the dignity of ethnic culture, and neutralize the distortions caused by generalizations about race and identity. In this way, Butterfield rejects a discourse governed by instant messaging, 140-character ideologies and means–end reasoning, and calls for a dialectical reasoning capable of accommodating the ambiguous reality that: we are all the same, and we are all different.

It is worth nothing that this collection was completed during the COVID-19 pandemic, with at least one of the contributors under quarantine. The final section, *The Pandemic*, provides an acute perspective on means–end rationality and strategic discourse. Rich suggests that comparisons to other pandemic responses are likely misleading, and instead uses a more contemporary model, associated with mountaineering, to reveal how communicative norms left the United States ill-equipped to manage the spread of COVID-19. Rich points to the difficulty of preparing for future crises, the dangers of the "every man for himself" mindset, and the challenge of moral courage in the face of distress, as keys to understanding how the United States, with significant forewarning, failed to prepare for the COVID-19 pandemic.

Although somewhat behind the rest of the industrialized world in pandemic preparation, the United States leads the world in protests against health measures, and at the time this book is being written, support and opposition to the pandemic response tends to fall on political lines. Gressis breaks the American cultural landscape into four political groups and explains the American response to COVID-19 along these lines. That the response to a deadly pandemic would correspond to political ideologies so neatly reveals the extent to which American culture remains ideologically driven—that ideological concerns outweigh health concerns. Gressis offers us examples in which different ideological groups, including the Center for Disease Control, dissembled, lied, or acted in bad faith during the pandemic in order to achieve some strategic end: economic health, freedom, social justice, social control.

The proliferation of deception, and the ease with which we discover it, helps explain the lack of trust across the American ideological spectrum and the general nihilism that has befallen the nation.

At the completion of this work, COVID-19 infection rates in the United States, the wealthiest nation in the world, remain significantly higher than most industrialized nations, begging the question: have our new discourse norms left us unprepared for the challenges of the twenty-first century?

NOTES

1. Jane Flax, "Postmodernism and Gender Relations in Feminist Theory," *Signs* 12, no. 4 (1987).

2. In a twist of serendipity, the outgoing president of the University of Nebraska, where Crucet works, noted that faculty intolerance of conservative ideas on the Nebraska campus might make it hard to be a conservative student.

3. Saint Ignatius of Loyola, *Rules for Thinking with the Church, in Spiritual Exercises*, trans. Ludovico J. Puhl, SJ (Chicago: The Newman Press, 1951), http://spex.ignatians-pirituality.com/SpiritualExercises/Puhl#c31-1234, accessed October 14, 2020.

Part 1

INSTITUTIONAL DISCOURSE

Chapter 1

The Outsourcing of Ethical Thinking

Erik Nordenhaug and Jack Simmons

Carlo Lorenzini (1826–1890), author of *Pinocchio*, once symbolized moral development in the image of a wooden puppet boy who became human through the painful process of internalizing the nagging cricket voice of conscience. In 1940, the nagging cricket voice of moral reasoning from Lorenzini's ideal was transformed into the lively, flamboyant voice of Jiminy Cricket in Walt Disney's remake of *Pinocchio*. Jiminy Cricket, as an idea in text or a character on screen, represents the externalized voice of moral reasoning that is generally foisted upon children by adults. For Lorenzini, it is the internalizing of this moral voice that humanizes us. Our concern here is that in our methodically bound culture as a whole, the teaching of rules, codes, policies, professional procedures as well as the existence of ethics committees and legal advisors are becoming the externalized and institutionalized Jiminy Crickets of society, replacing the internal voice of moral reasoning in the individual. In other words, methodical, professional reasoning is swallowing up another type of reasoning that is related to being a unified, whole human being. Methodical reasoning is the quest for the one most efficient way in every field of human activity (including moral activity) though the full implications of this definition depend on other complex arguments offered later in the text. While our thesis focuses on one type of reasoning replacing another type of reasoning, we have attempted to ground this shift using examples from the health professions, sports, and higher education. By offering these illustrations, we do not mean to suggest that our thesis will be proven or disproven by empirically observable practices alone, only that such practices arguably serve as indicators of a deeper phenomenological shift in what is now being perceived as "ethical thinking." In this chapter, we will (1) identify the phenomenological form of this trend and its unique manifestation in various professions and medical ethics and (2) show how this form leads us into two common fallacies: equivocation and the fallacy of composition.

For example, Hurricane Katrina in 2005, physicians and health care professionals found themselves stranded in Memorial Hospital in New Orleans with many ill patients. The physicians infamously ordered that some of the patients receive lethal levels of narcotics so that the physicians, health care professionals, and some of the patients could leave. In her book *Five Days at Memorial*, Sheri Fink describes the inadequacy of institutional mechanisms for addressing extraordinary professional and institutional challenges.[1] We do not believe that this acknowledgment of the inadequacy of institutional mechanisms is unique to the health professions, but that the problem in medical ethics is a symptom of a general trend in professional ethics. Our primary aim is to diagnose the current trend in thinking that weakens the development of moral reasoning in medical ethics courses, medical ethics guidelines, and the practice of medicine as a whole and in other professions. A diagnosis is the first step toward a treatment and no less a step forward even if a treatment is not completely in sight. The goal is thus not to solve any empirically observable moral problems, since the very thought of "ethics" as limited to "moral problem-solving" is evidence of how the methodological type of reason is already excluding other ways of experiencing "ethical thinking."

METHODOLOGICAL REASONING

Methodological reasoning transforms our understanding of professionalism and ethics. Today, the ideal of professionalism efficiently encourages students and clinicians in the health professions to avoid the difficult process of internalizing moral reasoning (while still achieving the desired effect of moral behavior) by following prescribed protocols and procedures that come from hired cricket voices of moral reasoning emanating from professional standards boards, ethics offices and committees, and legal departments. For the most part, what is called the "teaching of ethics" in health care (and other industries) reduces to the lesson that professional standards, codes, policies, rules, and the established procedures of institutions and professions must be followed while on the job. In this way, the professionally trained clinician, performing her duties within the range of policies and codes that regulate professional conduct, is characterized as behaving ethically without having internalized a non-methodological rationality capable of producing or discovering moral standards or applying those standards to new situations. As long as she follows the rules and procedures laid out by the professions, then one is "professional," regardless of one's moral judgments or one's lived human obligations. Professionalism is becoming a substitute for humanism and its accompanying ethical consciousness, despite the ostensible belief that we are always human even while being professional. "Being human" is not equivalent to simply having the biology or anatomy of a member of the species *Homo sapiens*. Our concern in this article focuses on the phenomenology of the internal nonphysical (and therefore, empirically unobservable) ethical dimension of "being human" and how the meaning and valuing of this dimension is changing in our highly professionalized, technological culture.

Where once the term "profession" described a "calling" to publicly proclaim vows, now a "profession" is predominantly thought of as having a body of specialized knowledge and methods at one's disposal to make a living. "Professionalism" in the modern world refers to some kind of expertise at a skill and "professional" to being a technical expert or "technician" at something. By "technician" we mean someone who applies a specific set of techniques and methods affirmed by the body of knowledge they "profess" to follow. But more than just the skill, "professionalism" was thought to include the "judgment" that allowed one to perform the skill. Beyond that, "professionalism" was associated with the "character" that led to the "judgment" which expertly practiced a skill.

In medicine, the definition of professionalism is extended to include the use of emotions and values in one's practice as indicated by Hundert's definition: "Professional competence is the habitual and judicious use of communication, knowledge, technical skills, clinical reasoning, emotions, values, and reflection in daily practice for the benefit of the individual and community being served."[2] This suggests it is no longer the individual as human who emotes and values, but the individual as expressing the attributes of a profession who "with professional competence" uses emotions and values. This begs the question: what does it mean to be professionally emotional? What are professionally competent uses of emotions and values? Nearly all the terms we once used to define aspects of what it meant to be "human" and a "person" in general (like "communication," "knowledge," "emotions," and "values") are becoming associated with what it means to be "professional" or "professionally competent."

Philosophers reflecting on technology now observe how a specific kind of "technological" thinking, or what we call "methodological reasoning," is transforming human consciousness and its relation to ethics and ethical behavior. Gernot Böhme in *Invasive Technification* raises two important questions regarding the "caring professions" (which include the medical professions).

> Two vital questions arise: first, whether the dominant position of scientific knowledge within contemporary society is leading to a decay of other forms of knowledge, and, second, whether there are types of problems, and types of

human need, that scientific or technical knowledge is particularly ill suited to address. The dominant position of technoscientific knowledge in contemporary society implies a belief that this particular form of knowledge has the last say in establishing all matters of fact, and in solving problems of all kinds.[3]

The "technoscientific knowledge" to which Böhme refers here is the product of a methodological reasoning, and the phrase "solving problems of all kinds" is intended to include ethical problems as well as the quest for the most efficient solution (since solutions that work will methodically be compared to discover which one works best). His concern and ours is that this "technical" or professional knowledge produced by a certain type of reasoning is "particularly ill suited" to address what is traditionally called ethical thinking.

Böhme observes further that what we think of as our "everyday life" and everyday thinking are being transformed into a "technical" way of life and thinking.

The external preconditions of everyday life, transformed over time into technical preconditions, have such a powerful effect on behavior that individuals can progressively feel themselves absolved of ethical constraints. In tandem with a growing luxury economy, this leads to a waning of the puritan ethic and a substitution of technical norms for moral norms. Cases in point are the replacement of a traditional handicraft ethics and business ethics by quality control, obligatory declarations and government supervision. A further case in point is the obsolescence of virtues such as thrift on the part of consumers. The standard example of technical norms taking the place of their ethical forerunners is the redundancy of traditional sexual morality as a result of the industrialized provision of effective means of birth control.[4]

By "technical preconditions," he means the kind of methodological reasoning promoted in the contemporary professions. The technical, the methodical and technique merge and preempt more spontaneous, traditional and organic forms of rationality that evolve and function over time without conscious comparison of which works the "best" in some absolute quantitative sense. It should be noted that "quality control" is in the modern world defined in terms of quantities. If a number cannot be assigned to "quality control" variables, it is not "quality" control at least not according to the usual methodological reasoning. But the more philosophical problematic point Böhme asks: Are we still thinking about qualities (moral or human) if we must always substitute or even link quantities to them? Methodological reasoning requires this substitution.

In 1991, Alvin Weinberg makes a similar point using a different vocabulary in "Can Technology Replace Social Engineering?"

> The resolution of social problems by the traditional methods—by motivating or forcing people to behave more rationally—is a frustrating business. People don't behave rationally; it is a long, hard business to persuade individuals to forgo immediate personal gain or pleasure (as seen by the individual) in favor of long-term social gain. And indeed, the aim of social engineering is to invent the social devices—usually legal, but also moral and educational and organizational—that will change each person's motivation and redirect his activities along ways that are more acceptable to society.[5]

By "traditional methods," Weinberg means using appeals to the range of deontological, utilitarian and virtue ethics views as a motivator to being more rational. Social engineering, as Weinberg describes it, results from the transformation of social and moral problems into technical problems that are solvable, or at least manageable, by a type of reason suited to finding the most efficient method for achieving a desired behavior.

We interpret Weinberg's reference to invented "social devices" to include "professions" and "professional ethics," both of which are inventions of methodological reason "that will change each person's motivation and redirect his activities along ways that are more acceptable to society." We might describe the quote above as the goal of "professional ethics" but not the goal of ethics in the traditional sense of producing good people who morally reason non-methodically.

The idea of an invented "moral device" suggested by Weinberg requires further reflection, since the conjunction of "moral" and "device" suggests a new use of the word "morality." One example of an "invented moral device" is a policy awareness test, which is being called an "ethics test" by many institutions and systems throughout the country. In the University System of Georgia (USG), an Ethics Training course is required of all faculty, including those who will then be asked to teach medical ethics. Hosted on the *Building a Better U* website, faculty are asked fifteen questions concerning Board of Regents policy. The following true/false question nicely demonstrates the methodological reasoning externalized in an ethics policy and imposed upon faculty:

> Compliance with laws, rules and regulations governing USG institutions is both a legal and an ethical mandate. The risks associated with non-compliance can be significant. Significant risks include: loss of reputation, loss of external funding, financial penalties, loss of accreditation and potential criminal prosecution.[6]

The "true" statement suggests that ethics involves compliance with rules and offers specific punishments to motivate that compliance. In order to humanize the training, several videos are provided that show human resources experts discussing the ethical cases covered in the course. In this way, the ethics training outsources the ethical discourse to people identified as professionals.

The final question of the exam prompts faculty to "affirm that I will abide by the policies, rules and guidelines presented in this training on behalf of the Board of Regents of the University System of Georgia."[7] Following a national trend to require ethics training courses (moral devices), the University System of Georgia, which includes the Medical College of Georgia in Augusta, requires faculty to accept this externalized, methodological reasoning, engineered both to manage their behavior and reduce liability for the system. When ethics is identified with system risk reduction, methodological reason is at work.

Whether this approach to ethics training affects compliance is not our concern. Our position is that compliance training is not ethics training. However, these tests are "invented moral devices" that over time alter our motivations and thinking about ethics and redirect our activities. These "ethics tests" would also qualify as what Böhme calls "obligatory declarations" (mentioned on page 18). People must now make "obligatory declarations" that substitute for actual moral thinking and discussion. We are motivated to use the newly invented moral device because our jobs require it. That is not traditional ethical motivation, but it does reflect Weinberg's meaning of "social engineering," which includes moral engineering.

The result of such "social engineering," as Böhme indicates in the following example regarding population growth, is ultimately a new kind of morality.

> When, at the start of the nineteenth century, Malthus expressly appealed to individual morality in the hope of halting the runaway growth of the population, his appeal alone was an indication that an era of history had come to an end. Today, the Malthusian social goal, a lower birth rate, is something that can be reached directly by technological mean—in this case contraceptive technology. Yet the complex consequence of that simple fact is that the greater part of sexual morality has become superfluous. . . . My point is that as a result of technological development, morality in the future will be a different kind of morality. Stripped of its social function, morality will become a kind of luxury.[8]

Ethical standards are being reduced to technical standards because one type of reasoning is in the process of reinterpreting and rethinking another type of reasoning. The "outsourcing" of ethics is a metaphor to illustrate how methodological reasoning is replacing and transforming ethical reasoning. To avoid misunderstanding given the already ubiquitous affirmation of the value of methodological reasoning, we are not claiming methodological reasoning is simply "bad" and should be avoided. We are well aware of its usefulness, efficacy, and power, but less aware of its meaning and its moral effects. Our observations suggest only that when methodological reasoning becomes a totalizing form of consciousness, unavoidably pushing aside all other forms of reasoning, then and only then does methodological reasoning become the worrisome phenomenon we are describing.[9]

It is part of our thesis that the technical way of thinking, a technical methodical rationality, is appropriating and transforming the meaning of ethical thinking, a non-methodical rationality. Methodological reasoning is more easily "externalized" in institutional procedures and policies because of its objective character. Non-methodical reasoning is not reducible to techniques, policies, and codified standards, nor is it capable of being "institutionalized" precisely because it remains only attributable to humans (not systems, not institutions, and not machines all of which are circumscribed by method and technique).

Our claim that "professionalism is becoming a substitute for humanism" means external, technical, methodological thinking is being identified more with rationality than internal, non-methodological reasoning. Methodological rationality is rule-based in much the same way Descartes presented his rules for rightly conducting reason in *Discourse on Method*. Because his and all methods can so clearly be written out in a series of steps, such rationality lends itself to being "exported" from the human mind to software programs, laws, codes, regulations, and policies that govern how programs, cities, states, institutions, and professions function at the collective level. While we all know that humans are necessary for an institution to run, we also know that any individual human or specific group of humans is not necessary for the continued existence of an institution, corporation, or profession. The profession of philosophy appears to function just fine without us, a couple of individual philosophers. Should any one of us no longer be employed at our university, we know it will continue to function more or less as it did before and following the same regulations and rules more or less as it did before. Looking at institutions at this level, we must acknowledge a kind of methodological rationality embodied in the institutional procedures and operations that functions more or less independently of the agency of individual moral human beings (keeping in mind that the professional human being *qua* professional is ideally a technician following the techniques and codes established in the profession). Humans may have created methodological reason, but that doesn't mean they can uncreate it after imparting it to organizational structures that manifest that methodological reason collectively and *to some degree* independently of the humans who participate in the institutions and professions.

There is a circularly reinforcing relation between human and institution or human and profession that is difficult to see, much less describe. But using the idea of "methodological reason" both internal to and external to the human mind helps illustrate the circularity of a form of reasoning both "inside" and "outside" the human. A human being, let's say Descartes, creates in his thinking "the method" for reasoning our way to the truth and writes the method down in a series of steps and procedures for all to see and think about. Then "the method" as a form of reasoning spreads to other humans, who now want to build "the method" into their institutions, disciplines, nations, and professions. Laws, constitutions, rules, codes, policies, governmental procedures, and a multitude of other techniques are now written into the founding documents and manuals that in effect program the parameters or how each nation, institution, and profession should function ideally and independently of any given morally good or bad human beings. At this point, an "internalized" form of methodological reason in a few individual humans has been exported or "externalized" into an institution endowing it with a built-in rationality consisting of required procedures and methods for anyone wishing to participate in said institution. If "rationality" is too anthropomorphic a quality to assign to an institution, as critics might argue, then we are prepared to call it "an institutionally built-in, rationally-defined series of procedures any member of the institution must follow in order to participate in that institution," but this description becomes unwieldy and no more accurate than anthropomorphically attributing the characteristic of "rationality" to our institutions.

We find this built-in reasoning in the health care professions, in courses specifically designed to train health care students in ethical reasoning and in the educational materials employed in that training. The health professions widely recognize four grounding principles that guide decision-making: autonomy, beneficence, nonmaleficence, and justice. While these are all fairly straightforward principles that are easy enough to learn, John Stuart Mill reminds us that "[t]here exists no moral system under which there do not arise unequivocal cases of conflicting obligation."[10] In other words, methodological reasoning is not sufficient to the task of ethical thinking. Problems will arise in which the professional's obligation to nonmaleficence conflicts with her obligation to justice. Ethical reasoning ultimately requires a carefully developed, non-methodological, internalized reasoning: the goal of humanism. It is with this humanist idea in mind that Martha Nussbaum suggests:

> Our moral duties are not always simple, and may . . . impose conflicting demands on the well-intentioned person who wishes both to behave honestly and to prevent harm to others. Morality, it seems, needs to recognize the existence of such conflicts and to learn to think well about them. We are, in addition, urged [by Plato] to think hard about the whole question of a morality based on rules and principles: can such a morality be adequate to the complex contingencies of life? In order to encourage well-considered policy and practice in the

profession, medical schools and law schools are increasingly supplementing their technical education with courses in ethics that pose just such questions and show students how difficult and how urgent they are.[11]

Some rules and policies are superior to others, and one rule more applicable at a given time than another, but distinguishing the superior rules and more applicable rules is precisely the sort of thing that is necessary in situations that we describe as ethically challenging. An approach to biomedical ethics that encourages methodological reasoning is unlikely to develop an internalized reasoning capable of tackling the whole question of a rule-based morality that Nussbaum sees as critical to true ethical thinking.

Once the institutions that sustain the health care industry have built methodological reasoning into their professional courses and textbooks, those institutions will tacitly and systematically require that all humans conform to those methods if they want to participate or work in that institution. In this way, institutionally externalized methodological reasoning now circularly reinforces itself through professional ethics necessary for participation in a profession. Unlike Lorenzini's ideal of becoming human by internalizing the cricket voice of conscience, modern professions externalize, institutionalize, and thus outsource the moral voice in various types of professional ethics standards, codes, policies, procedures, and exams.

EQUIVOCATION

This new notion of professional ethics creates a perpetual equivocation by confusing externally motivated ethics with the development of internal, non-methodological moral reasoning described in classical ethics. This equivocation makes the discussion and teaching of internal moral reasoning more difficult, if not a lost cause, for "professionals" training for a job.

We learn from Plato and Aristotle that the study of ethics began with the study of virtue. The Greek word for virtue, *Aretê*, is best translated as "excellence," though "virtue" is also a common translation of the term. In their discussions and illustrations of the meaning of "excellence" or "virtue," they would use a phrase like "the virtue of medicine" alongside their descriptions of "the virtue of a doctor" as a human being. Then there is the virtue or excellence of "ruling well," conjoined with their description of the excellence of the ruler being a good example of a human being. In this way, these ancient thinkers both acknowledge there are virtues of art, crafts, disciplines, and what we might call "professions." For example, there would be a virtue of dentistry as a profession just as they acknowledged a virtue of horsemanship as an art. But it is absolutely essential to remember that no description of the virtue of medicine would or even could occur for Plato and Aristotle without simultaneously describing the virtue of the human being practicing the art of medicine.

In modern discourse, we hardly know how to articulate this Platonic-Aristotelian point except perhaps in our preference that we prefer intelligent, sympathetic and caring individuals to be directly involved in important decision-making processes. Henry K. Beecher is known in scholarly circles for his 1966 article documenting lapses in ethics for numerous research projects conducted by professional scientists. His article prompted changes in research practices and influenced the federal government to consider various implementations of "informed consent." Nevertheless, Beecher

> expressed scepticism that "consent in any fully informed sense" was obtainable. Rather than formal rules for human experimentation, Beecher argued that the presence of an intelligent, informed, conscientious, compassionate, and responsible investigator offered the best protection for human research subjects. For the same reason, Beecher was not an advocate of the mechanism of the ethical review committee, now a fixture in health research.[12]

Beecher sensed that ethical lapses in research practices would likely not be prevented by substituting mechanisms like ethical review committees or even consent forms to fill out because he could not affirm the presence of moral reasoning in the review process without reference to the intelligent, conscientious, responsible investigator.

In other words, Beecher appears to lean toward Aristotle's affirmation that you could not possess any single professional virtue without possessing what Aristotle would call "moral virtue" as a human being (i.e., the whole package of traits Beecher affirms above). Plato and Aristotle tended to use what we might call "professional excellences" or perhaps even "practical virtues" (which is one translation of Aristotle's category) as analogies to illustrate and demonstrate the importance of "moral virtue" possessed as a whole by a human being who was more than simply a "professional" practicing his art. There is more to say about this excellence of moral reasoning as a human being, but for our purposes here, we emphasize that, for those ancient ethicists, performing any professional activity well—meaning with excellence or virtue—necessarily entailed as a prerequisite the possession and excellent use of an internal moral reasoning and judgment that we possess only as human beings, not as trained professionals following methods, guidelines, policies, and standards set by committees of professionals. For Plato and Aristotle, it would be inconceivable for one to be professionally good at something without being also a good human being.[13]

Professional ethics tends to focus on being good at something which is more easily trained into individuals by following a kind of reasoning externalized in rules, methods, procedures, and standards. We see this externalized training in the development of professional football players. Coaches follow established training regiments to produce excellence on the field, but as the newspapers constantly remind us, professional excellence at coaching football does not always translate into moral excellence off the field. Being an excellent human, the original meaning of ethics is not reducible to rules, methods, or procedures. Ethics, which has to do with the individual's character, is embodied in a kind of reasoning that can be observed and discussed, though never converted into a code or method (technique).[14]

Our contention is not that ethics requires the elimination of rules or that society would benefit by an elimination of codified law. Nevertheless, conformity to a set of rules and principles in professional ethics figures so significantly in the discussion of ethics that the term ethics now has two, divergent meanings, but is generally used without recognition of that divergence: hence the equivocation.

Though there are a variety of intellectual voices over the course of our history who illustrate the emergence of ethics based on professional practice independently of ethics based on being an excellent human being, we will only mention two influential thinkers who set us on the path to modern professionalism—Niccolo Machiavelli and Thomas Hobbes.

This ancient distinction between ethical virtues of being and professional virtues of practice is sharply separated in the work of Machiavelli, who reminds us that some immoral acts (severe cruelty) may be virtuous for a prince when necessary for the professional practice of maintaining the security of the nation, but in no way make the prince a virtuous human being. Machiavelli writes: "Those [severe cruelties] can be called well used (if it is permissible to speak well of evil) that are done at a stroke, out of the necessity to secure oneself."[15] The cruelties are necessary from the standpoint of professional politics, but they are still ethically evil. Hence, Machiavelli avoids the equivocation on the term "ethics" or "virtue" by severing the connection between the virtue associated with a professional activity and what may be deemed ethical and unethical.

A hundred and twenty years later, Hobbes extends the sharp division Machiavelli started by cutting up the definition of "personhood" itself. In the *Leviathan*, Hobbes proposed the following definitions for what it means to be a "person" in modern society based on the social contract.

> A person, is he whose words or actions are considered, either as his own, or as representing the words or actions of an other man, or of any other thing to whom they attributed, whether Truly or by Fiction. When they [the words] are considered as his owne, then is he called a *Natural Person*; And when they are considered as representing the words and actions of an other, then is he a *Feigned* or *Artificiall person*.[16]

How many professionals have felt that their words are not their own? When a faculty member repeats a university policy in answer to a student's question, the words are not her own. When a judge repeats the law to a courtroom, the words are not her own. When presidential candidates represent the words of their speechwriters, who further represent the words of ideologies, parties, polls, and studies of the public's reactions to words, those words are not their own. This is not an accusation of plagiarism but, rather, "artificial personhood." Our entire society, which is itself an artificial person, is composed of what Hobbes called "Feigned or Artificiall" persons whose words are not their own. But to say this as bluntly as Hobbes does is offensive to our usual self-image that we are ourselves and that our words are our own, so we soften the blow and compartmentalize the "Artificial person" under the far more modern and ethically positive category of the "professional," who by definition as a "professional" must represent the latest words, standards, and methods of the profession.

This "representing the words and actions of an other man or thing" is precisely what we are calling a kind of external, outsourced moral reasoning that is not really *our own*, but represents institutional and professional interests—not those of an "excellent human being" who lives an internal, integrated sense of moral reasoning and whose un-compartmentalized and unprofessionalized unity of being cannot comprehend his words and actions as not being his own. Our point here is not to argue that our words must always be our own; rather, we observe that our current methodological structures and externalized moral codes are continually and forcefully pushing our own words and voices to the margins of our consciousness while in our professional roles. This tendency over time is having unforeseen effects on our identity and moral sensibilities.

The equivocation we point to is thus based on a separation of what was once impossible to imagine separately—doing good and being good. Today, we regularly acknowledge "professionals" who perform their activities well and are not being human well. We have presidents, actors, sports figures, coaches, doctors, priests, and preachers who all fit this category. The word "ethics" in the professional sense does not indicate the same thing as the word "ethics" when used in the classical sense. When we discuss or teach professional ethics, we hope to generate good behaviors. When we discuss or teach ethics, we hope to generate good people.

FALLACY OF COMPOSITION

To demonstrate how a discussion of professional ethics might lead to the fallacy of composition, some reflection on the larger issue of the relation between the individual and the institution and between the individual and the profession is instructive. Modern society has already conceded an answer with little reflection or analysis to what is arguably the most important moral question of the twenty-first century: Can institutions and corporations be moral? While it is clear that we make moral judgments about institutions such as "Walmart is immoral," "Memorial Hospital treats its patients fairly," or "BP is a morally responsible corporation," the moral status of the subject of these sentences is problematic. Is Memorial Hospital a moral agent? Is BP as an institution capable of feeling sympathy, the bite of conscience, or even the slightest remorse? Is Walmart capable of moral thinking, Aristotelian "phronesis," or the good will capable of giving the categorical imperative to itself and following it? These questions are rarely asked, much less answered, because we tend to assume that as long as the humans who make up such institutions are being moral, or at least trying to be moral, then the institutions are also moral to whatever degree its individual participants are. Our society's affirmation that institutions can be moral (i.e., can be "good" in the moral sense) appears to be founded on the fallacy of composition, which mistakenly reasons that because each of the parts—in this case, the individual humans—has some particular property, like the ability to be moral or immoral, then it must follow that the whole—the institution—containing those parts also has that same property: the ability to be moral or immoral.

In the United States and nearly all other Western countries, this composition fallacy of misplaced moral properties is concretely expressed in laws that affirm and uphold the legal fiction of corporate personhood. Ever since Thomas Hobbes referred to government as an "artificial person," the tradition of regarding governments, institutions, and corporations as "artificial persons" expanded until law itself eventually acknowledged that the Fourteenth Amendment to the U.S. Constitution applies to both living human beings and nonliving artificial beings such as corporate institutions. Chief Justice John Marshall in the 1819 landmark case *Dartmouth College v. Woodward* affirmed the majority opinion that "a corporation is an artificial being, invisible, intangible and existing only in contemplation of law."[17]

For a detailed account of the corporate journey toward "personhood" in early American history, Thom Hartmann's *Unequal Protection: How Corporations Became "People"—And How You Can Fight Back* (2010) beautifully elaborates the theme.

> The modern corporation is neither male nor female, doesn't breathe or eat, can't be enslaved, can't give birth, can live forever, doesn't fear prison, and can't be executed if found guilty of misdoings. It can cut off parts of itself and turn them into new "persons," can change its identity in a day, and can have simultaneous residences in many different nations. It is not a human but a creation of humans.

Nonetheless, today a corporation gets many of the constitutional protections America's Founders gave humans in the Bill of Rights to protect them against governments or other potential oppressors.[18]

Our simplistic account of the corporate progression below attempts to extend Hartmann's analysis in two small ways (a) by pointing out some previous philosophical seeds in Hobbes which triggered the developments in early American history he describes and (b) by affirming the journey of the corporation is not over. Hartmann's cogent and well-argued thesis affirms "the ultimate manifestation of corporate power—*corporate personhood*"[19] because he is concerned with the political threat to democratic freedom entailed in this manifestation of power. While we agree on the threat, we take issue primarily with the word "ultimate" because power never finds ultimate expression period. By definition, corporate power will once reaching a certain level of personhood want more. Corporate responsibility? Corporate goodness and corporate conscience perhaps? How about a corporate soul which no doubt would entail additional reflection on a corporate afterlife? If that is too far, how about corporate ownership of souls? Our argument affirms that the widespread acknowledgment of "corporate personhood" itself involves a transformation of human moral agency itself, meaning regular persons are also transformed by the existence of "corporate personhood." If human moral agency is transformed, perhaps undermined, by a certain kind of thinking and being occurring in the context of corporate environments, then what meaning could politics, which presupposes moral agency, ever hope to bring to democratic freedom?

Given the long American legal tradition Hartmann describes of the journey toward treating corporate institutions as "persons," it follows that people would think of these "artificial persons" as moral or immoral, having already understood that such "persons" could be found "guilty" or "not guilty" in a court of law.

The historical progression is this: First, there are intellectuals, like Hobbes, thinking of institutions as "persons." Second, there are judges and lawyers legally treating institutions as "plaintiffs and defendants" in courts throughout the land. Third, the assertion of "rights" for corporations[20] And now there is a desire and hope to make institutions and corporations "moral."[21] This goal is but an extension of the long-standing tradition and fallacy of legally treating corporations as "artificial persons."

To continue with the fallacious metaphor that corporations are "artificial persons," would we not eventually wonder if these "artificial persons" also had "souls"? Would we not want these artificial persons to be capable of distinguishing good and evil as living persons do? Would we not hope that these artificial institution-beings felt a deeper calling to be "good" like so many other living persons? These may seem far-fetched concerns, but in a discussion of the morality and legality of the Patient Protection and Affordable Care Act of 2010 (affectionately termed ObamaCare) that required faith-based organizations to provide insurance to its employees that covered birth control, Michael Gerson reminded listeners that "[i]nstitutions have rights, not just individuals," demonstrating the extent of the fallacy of composition and leaving us to wonder whether an institution might have its own moral voice independent of the individuals associated with it.[22]

Literature in medicine supports our concern that the commitment to professionalism often usurps the commitment to the internalized, non-methodical characteristics of moral reasoning. In a 2011 *Journal of Bioethical Inquiry* article, in which Cameron Stewart analyzes the important issue of "futility determination," the subtle shift from ethics to professionalism is illustrated, as well as the tension between the two. Determining futility is relevant in handling medical cases where families demand treatments that the medical profession "feels" are "futile."[23] The problem Stewart focuses on is: who or what gets to determine the definition of "futility"? The profession, a combined professional-legal procedure, or individuals? Stewart's reasonable conclusion is that a combined professional-legal procedure is the "least bad" approach to defining "futility," but that is not our interest here. The personified style and tone in which scholars now discuss "professions" resembles that same personification of "corporations" in legal discourse. Here are a few samples from Stewart's article:

> [F]amilies [were] demanding treatments the medical *profession did not feel* could be provided.
>
> According to this logic, the medical *profession should control* the concept of futility because *as a profession*, medicine controls the concept of treatment and healthcare.
>
> Professionalism necessarily requires some form of *ingrained ethic of care*, of protection for patients and the public at large. . . . This has been described as the "higher aim of professionalism." The key value underlying professionalism is therefore *public trust*.[24]

Just where we would normally use and discuss the autonomous human "we" who should "feel," "control," "care," and "have an ethic," instead the "it," the profession, takes on these functions. The term "profession" has become a placeholder for the source of both moral and technical decision-making. Who is this "profession" that "it" can make decisions? How do professions "care" or have an "ethic of care"? How do professionals *qua* professionals "care" when being "professional" means following the discipline, methods, and procedures of one's profession precisely when they conflict with one's human sympathetic, caring judgments? How do we act when faced with the conflicting needs of our patients? "Caring" should involve us as humans primarily, not as "professionals" that implies following with detached objectivity all the knowledge, procedures, codes, and standards of the profession.

There is no such category as being "professionally human," but we do hear a great deal about humanizing the professions and even giving the professions an "ingrained ethic of care." Ultimately, the humanizing of professionalism requires *it* to "think morally" and develop "an artificial moral conscience" that stands independently of our individual moral sensibilities.

As noted above by Stewart, the key value of "professionalism" is "public trust," which means that "professionalism" personified wants us to trust *it*. Never mind that achieving the "key value of public trust" is frequently in tension with and certainly not identical to the "higher aim" of an "ethic of care" (given that "public trust" depends on "public perceptions" that are for the most part created by media techniques and need not correspond with the reality of an "ingrained care").[25] The more revealing implication is how the quality of trust is now being attributed to and demanded by the abstraction called "profession," which pretends to be a "person" with which we can have a trusting, caring, and moral relationship.

The verbal shift from the "human-we" to the "professional-it" that is made effortlessly now in our thinking represents and accommodates the outsourcing of ethical thinking. Here is a typical example from Stewart's journal article: "Like every profession, the medical profession makes mistakes. Like every profession, there will be people who engage in outlying, and sometimes outrageous, behavior."[26] Notice the interchangeable substitution of "people" for "profession" and "profession" for "people" based on the composition fallacy of misplaced moral properties.

CONCLUSION

We accept that best practices and reasonable policies ensure efficacy of a profession. But these policies should not be confused with ethics, and when they are, they leave the professionals and their clients at risk. Nussbaum warns us that these codes and rules may not be adequate to the complex contingencies of life. When those rules fail us, and they necessarily must, it is then and perhaps only then that we will truly feel in want of a sophisticated, internal moral voice, and this is precisely the voice that is being neglected.

The modern use of "professional ethics" commits the fallacy of composition by granting a profession what is an inherently internal, rational process associated with the development of the individual: moral reasoning. While individuals in a group participate in moral reasoning, there is no genuine sense in which the American Medical Association, BP, or any given university participates in moral reasoning. At best, individuals in those institutions discuss ethics and develop rules based on those discussions, but the corporate validity of these rules as ethics could only apply to those individuals robustly involved in the discussion. Such discourses cannot be understood to generate norms that have ethical implications for those uninvolved in the ethical discourse, unless we accept that our ethics have been outsourced.

In conjunction with the fallacy of composition, the equivocation that now substitutes professional excellences for human excellences, ultimately creates, under the heading of "professional ethics," an anti-ethic through which individuals learn to become "professional" and "artificially moral" by reasoning only as far as the professional rules, policies, procedures, standards, lawyers, and ethics committees direct. The profession attempts to guarantee appropriate behavior through rules and standards, rather than addressing the internal ethical transformation of the individual, and conceals this usurping of the individual's ethical autonomy through an equivocation: conflating professional excellence with individual virtue. In this way, the discussion and teaching of professional ethics threaten to undermine the development of ethical persons and replace them with wooden puppet-policy-partisans. Our concern is that this gradual transition is occurring without a robust discussion of the relative merits of an ethical education and behavior modification. It is our hope that this chapter will help identify the trend and initiate the debate.

ADDENDUM: THE "OUTSOURCING OF ETHICS" TO WHERE?

When using the metaphor "outsourcing of ethics" to describe how technological systems are transforming both theoretical ethics and the phenomenological experience of ethics in technological environments, the thesis that ethical thinking is being moved "from" the individual "to" collective systems is unavoidable. Such a metaphor necessarily heightens emphasis on the individual self as the long-standing source of agency and the individual's felt loss of that agency when moral thinking is "outsourced." From the individual pole of moral experience in technological environments, something is being transformed and/or lost, but this suggests that from the collective environment pole of describing ethics, something is being gained and appropriated by a system.

If ethical thinking is being "outsourced" from individual humans, then presumably the functions of such thinking can also be "insourced" and internalized by systems. Consequently, the following unusual corollary to the "outsourcing of ethics" thesis appears to follow: systems can appropriate and internalize the functions of ethical thinking, if not the self-consciousness and conscience of ethical thinking.

Surely, discussions among programmers regarding the most "moral" computer codes and algorithms to embed in self-driving automobiles is evidence of an ongoing transformation of ethics into something that can be built into devices and systems. The programming of autonomous automobiles will have to cause the car to stop, swerve right or left, or accelerate when all predictable outcomes suddenly yield collision with human life. Will the algorithm be weighted to preserve driver over pedestrian when likelihood of damage to both is statistically predictable by the software? Even if thinking, consciousness, and decisions are words we are not yet willing to attribute to the self-driving automobile, moral consequences of the algorithms running the self-driving system are unavoidable. Some type of "decision" or even "agency" needs to be discussed in relation to this system, especially when neither the car nor the programmers (assuming the audited code is performing as designed) are likely to be arrested when that car kills a pedestrian (as one already has).

The self-driving car is an analog to the self-directing system or institution that is similarly operating according to system/institutional "software" in the form of rules, policies, and regulations that participating professionals must follow if they are to remain employed professionals. The methodological reasoning of committees and committee members taught by systems is the humanly internalized algorithm similarly performing as the software of the self-driving car and having similar moral implications.

In what ways can morality, moral action, moral design, and moral agency be embedded in systems? Living in large-scale systems that channel thoughts, decisions, and behaviors in statistically predictable and predetermined ways requires considerable reflection about if and how systems can be moral (independently of the moral agency and moral concerns of the individuals who professionally participate in and develop those systems). The morality of systems must be explored and discussed independently of the ethical views of the individual officers (CEOs and the like) presumed in charge and presumed responsible for the organization. We say "presumed" given the legal separation of the corporate fictitious person called the "corporation" and its responsibility and the individual CEO's responsibility. *In cultural and ethical discussions*, we appear to hold the CEO-individuals in charge responsible for their organization-systems, but *in law* the corporate system is with few exceptions litigated independently of those individuals in charge, indicating a long-standing ambiguity regarding the moral responsibilities of systems.

Interesting explorations of this "outsourcing" of moral functions to technological artifacts and systems have occurred by both phenomenological and post-phenomenological philosophers of technology such as Peter-Paul

Verbeek and Don Ihde, who argue that things, artifacts, and devices have designed-in moralities and even a type of agency continually negotiated in relation to the humans using them.[27]

Though there are divisions within the field of the philosophy of technology between self-proclaimed post-phenomenological empirical-turn thinkers like Verbeek and Ihde and the ontological-phenomenological approaches to technology represented by Heidegger, all of these thinkers are unified in affirming that technology is embodying morality and some form of agency that is fully or largely independent of and/or interdependent with the individual moral agency presupposed by the usual deontological, utilitarian, and mixed-deontological ethical theories. The significant differences among many of these thinkers cluster first around definitions of technology—as things/artifacts (Ihde/Verbeek), as social-environment and system (Jacques Ellul), as a form of life and political artifacts (Langdon Winner), or as an enframing mode of being (Martin Heidegger/Albert Borgmann). Nevertheless, across these divides and others, nearly all these critical philosophers of technology are affirming a challenge to our most basic notions of moral agency and the efficacy of all ethical theories presupposing autonomous human moral agency. Certainly some approaches border on deterministic denials of human moral agency and autonomy altogether, whereas others describe a transformation of human autonomy into a hybrid form of agency emanating from both artifact and technologically mediated human tool-user.[28]

Our "outsourcing" thesis is intended to point to an underlying agreement common to these critical approaches to philosophy of technology—nearly all current ethical theories presuppose an understanding of human agency and autonomy that does not exist in the twenty-first century, precisely because technology, however defined on the spectrum from devices to modes of being, is now recognized to have some type of moral agency. The morality of things and systems may not leave sufficient moral room for human agency to be effective—especially if this moral agency of systems is never discussed. In short, human autonomy ain't what it used to be, if it ever was, and consequently the institutional discourse and training in ethics as well as ethical theory itself must be rethought in the context of technological moral intervention.

NOTES

1. Sheri Fink, *Five Days at Memorial* (New York, NY: Random House, 2013).

2. R. M. Epstein and E. M. Hundert, "Defining and Assessing Professional Competence," *The Journal of the American Medical Association* 287, no. 2 (2002): 226–35.

3. Gernot Böhme, *Invasive Technification: Critical Essay in the Philosophy of Technology* (New York, NY: Bloomsbury, 2012), 44.

4. Ibid., 5.

5. William T. Thompson, ed., *Controlling Technology: Contemporary Issues* (New York, NY: Prometheus Books, 1991), 42.

6. University System of Georgia [USG], *EthicsTraining*, 2014, http://buildingabetteru2.skillport.com, accessed May 23, 2014. By the lack of acknowledgement of (a) the inevitable conflict among the "laws, rules, and regulations" created at various levels and (b) the inevitable conflict between legal and ethical mandates, it is implied in the professional world that legal and ethical mandates are *only* embodied in "laws, rules, and regulations." Both (a) and (b) would require some type of reasoning that extends beyond these mandates to mediate.

Note also the strange audience that these statements are intended for. While individual employees are required to agree, the "significant risk" of "loss of accreditation" is a risk for the system or an institution, not for the individual employee whose earned degrees presumably would not be revoked in cases of non-compliance. This test addresses us as abstract, artificial "professional members" of a system, not as concrete individual humans whose reasoning is capable of transcending and mediating the variety of conflicts regularly experienced among the laws, regulations, and ethical rules.

7. Ibid.

8. Böhme, *Invasive Technification*, 24.

9. While we are not metaphysically arguing that the essence of methodological reasoning necessarily requires that it become totalizing in all environments, we are arguing that when methodological reasoning lives, moves, and has its being in external institutions and environments originally created by methodological reasoning, then—in these internally and externally self-justifying environments—methodological reasoning unavoidably becomes a totalizing form of consciousness excluding all others.

10. John Stuart Mill, *Utilitarianism* (New York, NY: Macmillan Publishing Company, 1957), 32.

11. Martha Nussbaum, *Cultivating Humanity: A Classical Defense of Reform in Liberal Education* (Cambridge, MA: Harvard University Press, 1997), 25.

12. Jon Harkness, Susan E. Lederer, and Daniel Wikler, "Laying Ethical Foundations for Clinical Research," *Bulletin of the World Health Organization* 79, no. 4 (2001): 366.

13. Aristotle, *Nicomachean Ethics*, trans. T. Irwin (Indianapolis, IN: Hackett Publishing, 1999).

14. Aristotle's "golden mean between extremes" is not a rule or method, but more of a description of how an excellent human being blends their internal moral reasoning with emotions of various types and degrees and in various situations.

15. Nicholas Machiavelli, *The Prince*, trans. H. Mansfield (Chicago, IL and London: The University of Chicago Press, 1985), 37–38.

16. Thomas Hobbes, *Leviathan* (New York, NY: Penguin Classics, 1985), 217.

17. *Dartmouth College v. Woodward*, 17 U.S. 518, 1819, http://supreme.justia.com/cases/federal/us/17/518/case.html, accessed May 23, 2014.

18. Thom Hartmann, *Unequal Protection: How Corporations Became "People" – And How You Can Fight Back* (San Francisco, CA: Berrett-Koehler Publishers, 2010), 9.

19. Ibid., emphasis is Hartmann's.

20. *Burwell, Secretary of Health and Human Services, et al. v. Hobby Lobby Stores, Inc., et al. No. 13–354*, http://www.supremecourt.gov/opinions/13pdf/13-354_olp1.pdf, accessed May 23, 2014.

21. Peter A. French, "The Corporation as a Moral Person," *American Philosophical Quarterly* 16, no. 3 (July 1979): 207–15.

22. Micheal Gerson, "Politics and Faith Collide in Contraceptive Debate," *NPR's Talk of the Nation*, February 14, 2012, http://www.npr.org/2012/02/14/146875969/catholics-split-on-contraceptives-and-health-care, accessed May 23, 2014.

23. Cameron Stewart, "Futility Determination as a Process: Problems with Medical Sovereignty, Legal Issues and the Strengths and Weakness of the Procedural Approach," *Journal of Bioethical Inquiry* 8, no. 2 (2011): 156. Even our scholarly analyses of "professions" tends to require terms, like "feel" once reserved for living non-artificial persons.

24. Ibid., emphasis added. Parenthetical notes are Stuart's and it should be noted that Stuart does not completely agree with his cited sources, but his writing style too exhibits a similar personification of "professions."

25. Consider the volume and price of advertising that companies and institutions purchase to generate "public trust" in the general character of their institution rather than their product. BP reminds us that they are environmentally conscious. Miller beer reminds us that they care about their community.

26. Ibid., 157. Our thesis suggests that the proper pronoun is not the misleadingly reassuring "we" doing our ethical thinking, but the "professional-it" which vampire-like acquires the very moral autonomy that modernity attributes to mankind. In other words just where we would use the morally autonomous "we" deriving from the modern conviction in autonomous human beings come of age and capable of giving themselves a teleology, we are now referring to institutional structures, like "professions," that are doing our ethical thinking for us.

27. See Peter-Paul Verbeek, *The Morality of Things* (Bloomington, IN: Indiana UP, 2001) for most interesting description of the "moral agency" of things and a new type of "hybrid" human agency.

28. Heidegger and Ellul are frequently interpreted as affirming highly deterministic views of technology which fully deny human autonomy. Admittedly, their specific works on technology, Jacques Ellul, *The Technological Society*, trans. J. Wilkinson (New York, NY: Vintage Books, 1964) and Martin Heidegger, "The Question Concerning Technology," in *Martin Heidegger: The Question Concerning Technology and Other Essays*, trans. W. Lovitt (New York, NY: Harper Torchbooks, 1977), 3–35 are easily interpreted in strongly deterministic ways *only when taken in isolation from the rest of their writings*. Verbeek's and perhaps Borgmann's views would tend in comparison to be much less deterministic and yet both of their views still require rethinking what is meant by "human autonomy" and "human agency" just as Ellul's and Heidegger's views require.

BIBLIOGRAPHY

Aristotle. *Nicomachean Ethics*. Translated by T. Irwin. Indianapolis, IN: Hackett Publishing, 1999.

Associated Press. "State Ethics Commission Chief Received Salary Increase." *Savannah Morning News*, September 21, 2013.

Bell, J., I. Hays, G. Emerson, et al. "Report of the Committee Appointed Under the Sixth Resolution, Adopted by the National Medical Convention Which Assembled in New York, in May, 1846." In *Association Medical Journal, Edited for the Provincial Medical and Surgical Association*, edited by J. R. Cormack, 777–782. London: Thomas John Honeyman, 1854. books.google.com/books?id=dRVAAAAAcAAJ.

Böhme, Gernot. *Invasive Technification: Critical Essay in the Philosophy of Technology*. New York, NY: Bloomsbury, 2012.

Borgmann, Albert. *Technology and the Character of Contemporary Life*. Chicago, IL: Chicago UP, 1984.

Burwell, Secretary of Health and Human Services, et al. v. Hobby Lobby Stores, Inc., et al. No. 13–354, 2014. http://www.supremecourt.gov/opinions/13pdf/13-354_olp1.pdf.

Dartmouth College v. Woodward, 17 U.S. 518, 1819. http://supreme.justia.com/cases/federal/us/17/518/case.html. Accessed May 23, 2014.

Ellul, Jacques. *The Technological Society*. Translated by J. Wilkinson. New York, NY: Vintage Books, 1964.

Epstein, R. M., and E. M. Hundert. "Defining and Assessing Professional Competence." *The Journal of the American Medical Association* 287, no. 2 (2002): 226–235.

Fink, Sheri. "During Katrina, 'Memorial' Doctors Chose Who Lived, Who Died." *NPR's Morning Edition*, September 10, 2013. http://www.npr.org/templates/transcript/transcript.php?storyId=220687231. Accessed May 23, 2014.

Fink, Sheri. *Five Days at Memorial*. New York, NY: Random House, 2013.

French, Peter A. "The Corporation as a Moral Person." *American Philosophical Quarterly* 16, no. 3 (July 1979): 207–215. http://www.jstor.org/stable/200099760. Accessed June 28, 2018.

Gerson, Michael. "Politics and Faith Collide in Contraceptive Debate." *NPR's Talk of the Nation*, February 14, 2012. http://www.npr.org/2012/02/14/146875969/catholics-split-on-contraceptives-and-health-care. Accessed May 23, 2014.

Heidegger, Martin. "The Question Concerning Technology." In *Martin Heidegger: The Question Concerning Technology and Other Essays*, translated by W. Lovitt, 3–35. New York, NY: Harper Torchbooks, 1977.

Hobbes, Thomas. *Leviathan*. New York, NY: Penguin Classics, 1985.

Ihde, Don. *Technology and the Life-World: From Garden to Earth*. Bloomington, IN: Indiana UP, 1990.

———. *Postphenomenology: Essays in the Postmodern Context*. Evanston, IL: Northwestern UP, 1993.

Lane, David. *Personal Correspondence, e-Mail*, Systemwide Deputy Compliance Officer, University of California, September 18, 2014.

Machiavelli, Nicholas. *The Prince*. Translated by H. Mansfield. Chicago, IL and London: The University of Chicago Press, 1985.

Mill, John Stuart. *Utilitarianism*. New York, NY: Macmillan Publishing Company, 1957.

Nussbaum, Martha. *Cultivating Humanity: A Classical Defense of Reform in Liberal Education*. Cambridge, MA: Harvard University Press, 1997.

Public Health Leadership Society. *Principles of the Ethical Practice of Public Health*, 2002. http://www.apha.org/NR/rdonlyres/1CED3CEA-287E-4185-9CBD-BD405FC60856/0/ethicsbrochure.pdf. Accessed May 15, 2014.

Stewart, Cameron. "Futility Determination as a Process: Problems With Medical Sovereignty, Legal Issues and the Strengths and Weakness of the Procedural Approach." *Journal of Bioethical Inquiry* 8, no. 2 (2011): 155–163.

Thompson, William T., ed. *Controlling Technology: Contemporary Issues*. New York, NY: Prometheus Books, 1991.

University System of Georgia [USG]. *EthicsTraining*, 2014. http://buildingabetteru2.skillport.com. Accessed May 23, 2014.

Verbeek, Peter-Paul. *The Morality of Things*. Bloomington, IN: Indiana UP, 2001.

Winner, Langdon. *The Whale and the Reactor: A Search for Limits in an Age of High Technology*. Chicago, IL: Chicago UP, 1986.

Chapter 2

The Diversity of "Diversity"

Support for Differing Conceptions of Diversity on the University Campus

Kenneth B. McIntyre and Stacy G. Ulbig

Our chapter is intended, first, to examine briefly the connections between three different conceptions of diversity and the purposes of a liberal arts university education, and, second, to offer an introduction to the current empirical research on the matter and some thoughts about ways to move forward. We are only concerned with the relationship of the three kinds of diversity with liberal arts education, so what we say about diversity in this context does not necessarily apply to the relationship between the different conceptions of diversity examined and vocational education, primary education, the social sphere, the political community, and so on. The three conceptions of diversity we will be examining are as follows. First, there is intellectual/epistemological diversity and values related to it like freedom of speech, academic freedom, and so on. Second, there is viewpoint diversity or moral pluralism and its values like tolerance (meaning, of course, putting up with things that we don't like) of differences and freedom of association. Third, there is identity group diversity and its values such as promotion and protection based upon racial, ethnic, or sexual characteristics, the suppression of unpopular opinions, the suppression of academic freedom, intolerance, and the suppression of freedom of association. The first two might be considered as different versions of liberal diversity and the latter a particular version of illiberal or antiliberal diversity. The first one is integral to the success of a university liberal arts education. The second one doesn't necessarily interfere with the success of such an education, and may become necessary in certain circumstances. The third one, however, is in direct contradiction to the purpose or purposes of a liberal arts education. Unfortunately, most university diversity programs focus almost solely on the third type of diversity, though such programs often give attention to the second type (i.e., viewpoint diversity and moral pluralism). The first type is rarely addressed at all by university diversity programs, and the ideological or programmatic character of the third type of diversity has tended to undermine attempts by faculty and others concerned about academic quality to refocus attention on diversity in academic programs (e.g., support for philosophy, religion, and anthropology departments instead of support for so-called social justice issues). The partisan ideological nature of the third type of diversity has also led to a significant increase in intolerance of the first two types of diversity on the part of students.

LIBERAL ARTS EDUCATION AT THE UNIVERSITY

As mentioned, we are not interested in questions about diversity in any or every form of social life, but, instead, are focused specifically on the idea of diversity as it pertains to liberal arts education at the university. So, what does the term "education" in "liberal arts education" mean?[1] The term "education" is, of course, a noun, but most of its cognate terms do not have the same form as it does (e.g., training, teaching, learning, tutoring, schooling). Its etymology reveals it to be directly related to a Latin term which meant raising, rearing, bringing up, or leading out, but its current usage suggests several other alternatives, including both the systematic instruction and training given to young people in preparation for adulthood and the cultivation of the qualities necessary to human flourishing. The participial form of education, "educating," doesn't function the same way as the participial forms of some of its cognates, either. For example, we can say, "I was learning math from my teacher or I was teaching Latin to my students," but not "I was educating geometry to my student or from my teacher." The direct object of "educating" is a person, whereas the direct object of "teaching" is usually a subject, which along with the traditional dictionary definition and etymology suggest that education concerns the whole human being in some way instead of a narrow focus on a subject or skill. Further, the way that we use the term "educated" and its contrary "uneducated' is distinct from the way that we use the terms "trained" or "taught" and their contraries. The term "uneducated" is commonly understood as a comprehensive condemnation, whereas the terms "untrained" or "untaught" often refer to a situation in which a person can do an action "x" well (e.g., playing the piano) without having been under instruction from a teacher. So, it appears that education is distinguished from training, learning, and other such terms by both its generality and its relation to the whole person.

Thus, education is quite different from training, but what is the *differentia* of university education? Ideally, university education is distinguished from primary education by its emphasis on the development of the critical intellect in all of its manifestations. University education offers an initiation into a variety of ways of understanding and explaining the world, and promotes the development of such various ways of understanding. Primary education, on the other hand (and, to use a trite and not always helpful metaphor) is concerned with the acquisition and development of the tools of understanding. Primary education provides the conditions which make university education possible, though this is not the only purpose of primary education. A university education at its best is an education by connoisseurs or experts, while primary education usually involves teachers without the same level of accomplishment and often with little in the way of qualifications at all. The blurring of the distinction between primary and university education has almost certainly come at the expense of university education, with many faculty, administrators, and students viewing the university as, more or less, the thirteenth through the sixteenth grades. Nonetheless, the distinction between primary and secondary education is not central to the current argument.

A further distinction is needed between liberal education and vocational training, and an initial point of departure is that vocational training is considered practical, or useful, while liberal arts education is understood to be intrinsically valuable. The practical nature of vocational education suggests that it is valued primarily instrumentally. So, Bob studies accounting, Julie apprentices to a plumber, Becky goes to law school, Bill learns carpentry, and Rhett goes to med school because they know that accountants, plumbers, lawyers, carpenters, and doctors are valued by the community at large and, thus, skills in these practices are instrumentally useful in providing each with the opportunity to pursue other noninstrumental values. It is, of course, not necessarily the case that these various individuals do not value their vocations in noninstrumental ways, as well. However, it is not necessary and many would say irrelevant to the practice of being a good accountant, plumber, and lawyer, to know almost anything about the history, philosophy, or aesthetics of such practices. In contrast, the liberal arts have traditionally been valued primarily, not because of some instrumental utility that they might provide, but because they are objectively and exemplary excellences in themselves.[2] The usage of the term "liberal" to modify the term "education" is older than the political use of the term, and so, at least, historically, the contrast here is not with conservative or socialist or fascist or communist education. Indeed, one of the most confusing aspects of the political use of the term "liberal" has been that it is read in a political or ideological way even when there is no specific political or ideological context to its use. Nonetheless, when the term is used to modify "education" or "arts," as in "liberal arts," its contrary has nothing to do with contemporary political parties. Instead, the contrast is between, on the one hand, an education which is suitable for a human being no matter what his or her practical interests or necessities might be and a subject matter which is intrinsically valuable and suitable to such a general study, and, on the other hand, a training in a specific trade, craft, or profession designed to qualify a person to engage in said trade, craft, or profession in order to satisfy her practical needs. Thus, the contrast is between liberal and servile education. Servile education is clearly defined as training for the purposes of working for wages, though, as mentioned above, it is reasonable for the well-trained plumber, carpenter, doctor, or lawyer to develop an intrinsic interest in her work aside from the purely pecuniary one. The preferred term these days is "vocational" and/or "professional education" or "training," but the contrast remains the same. In fact, there remains a residue of redundancy in the term "liberal education" insofar as both terms contrast with the banausic or utilitarian concern with learning something in order to make a living, and, though we do now speak of vocational or professional education, the locution "liberal training" remains an infelicitous one.

What distinguishes a liberal education from other sorts of education, specifically vocational training is that it involves an initiation into the various nonpractical explanatory languages which human beings have developed over the last few thousand years in their various efforts to make themselves and their world intelligible. These languages are plural and what they share is an explanatory logic which distinguishes them from the language of desire, aversion, approval, disapproval, justification, and recommendation that characterizes the practical world.[3] These explanatory languages, which manifest themselves in the various disciplines associated with liberal arts education, are themselves relatively autonomous and, thus, there is no architectonic science which orders all the others nor is there even a hierarchy of "sciences." The relationship between these various kinds of explanatory discourse is conversational and non-teleological.[4] A liberal education is then an initiation into an inherently plural world of more or less intelligible explanations. Each language has its own logic of explanation, which has emerged historically from within the practice of the language itself. Each language is also a living language insofar as any conclusions that have been reached are understood not as doctrines to be accepted but as invitations to further inquiry. Thus, liberal education, unlike vocational training, cannot be said to issue in a finished product, but might be understood to offer an alternative way or series of alternative ways of conceiving ourselves and our relationship to the world which can neither be reduced to our practical needs and desires nor to a single monistic unity.[5]

DIVERSITY AND LIBERAL ARTS EDUCATION

So, what is the connection of the three different conceptions of diversity with university liberal arts education? First, epistemological diversity of the pluralist type mentioned in the previous section involves the claim that there is no single mode or method of explanation to which all others can be reduced, so it is of primary importance that liberal education manifest a commitment to offering a variety of disciplinary options for students. Thus, it should be clear that intellectual/epistemological diversity is central to liberal education. The different disciplines manifest a great variety of approaches to understanding the world. For example, a student interested in studying the work of William Faulkner can find aesthetic explanations in the English Department that deal with Faulkner's use of the stream of consciousness, historical explanations in the History Department that place him as an example of an American modernist or that can address his place in Southern history, sociopolitical explanations in the Sociology and Political Science Department that treat him as a type of faded Southern gentleman, and, of course, the Philosophy Department might offer examinations of the logical character of Faulknerian arguments. Beyond this, the practically minded might read Faulkner in order to make moral judgments about his novels. So then, the various modes of knowing, including the scientific, historical, theological, aesthetic, practical, are all constituted by different presuppositions and make use of a variety of methods which are neither interchangeable nor reducible to each other. Universities which are cutting philosophy programs or that don't offer religion (not theology) or anthropology or all of the natural sciences are failing their liberal arts mission in that they are not epistemologically diverse.

Another danger is that some of those who speak one of these languages might claim that it is the only true language, and try to suppress the other languages. Though the natural sciences have appealed to many who would claim that all knowledge can be reduced to one modal or methodological system, the most likely suspect to engage in this epistemological imperialism today is a proponent of the notion that education must be in service of the language of practice. These claims come from two different political directions, and I will return to this in the last section of this part of the chapter. On the one hand, there are those who want to vocationalize all forms of education. The vocationalist would subordinate liberal education to questions about making a living or "growing (*sic*) the economy," and the numbers of those both inside and outside the university who support such a notion have increased dramatically as the number of students entering university purely for instrumental or vocational reasons has gone up exponentially.

On the other hand, there are those whose primary practical purpose is to politicize liberal education, and ideological politicization has largely displaced the danger to liberal education posed by religion over the past century. Here the professor is understood as prophet and proselytizer, the students are potential converts or acolytes, and liberal education is conceived as producing virtuous citizens, whether these be communists, fascists, social democrats, neoconservative patriots, or social justice warriors.

In order to offer an example of this problem, we might return to the distinction between liberal education and vocational training. As mentioned above, the latter is concerned with preparing an individual with marketable skills. It is necessarily practical and present-centered (e.g., it is not necessary to know the history of engineering to be a good engineer or to know the aesthetics of accounting to be a good accountant). Vocational training engages in education in the world of practice but it is focused on the world of a particular practice, and the language of practice generally. Liberal arts education, on the other hand, involves the notion of developing the fully human individual who is able to think for herself (or, at least, with developing individuals who are interesting at cocktail parties). Liberal education deals with explanatory languages, not recommendatory. For example, though science can be used in a practical way by being converted into technology and history can be reduced to a series of Manichean moral lessons, in being reduced, the former is no longer academic science and the latter is no longer academic history. The grave danger of reducing the languages of explanation (e.g., history, science, aesthetics) to the languages of recommendation is especially tempting in the humanities and the social sciences because they concern human actions, which are always susceptible of approval and disapproval. Here, art becomes either entertainment or propaganda; history becomes either journalism or myth; science becomes either technology or the equivalent of Lysenkoism; and philosophy becomes either advertising or ideology.

The second version of diversity under consideration here is "viewpoint" or "moral" diversity and it is connected with the notion that there is not a single, general, universally valid version of what makes for a good human life.[6] Values are both incompatible (i.e., there are multiple things that humans value and that are valuable, and these things do not form a coherent whole, but often conflict with each other) and incommensurable (i.e., values are not completely comparable according to a single metric, whether that be pleasure, preference satisfaction, or a hierarchy of rules). If this is so, then there is no reason that a multiplicity of moral and nonmoral values should undermine the primary mission of the university, especially if the claims of epistemological pluralists are accepted as valid. The commitments of the zither player and zipliner, the funambulist and the flower arranger, and the yoga enthusiast and the yo-yoer can all be accommodated within a university community, as long the persons with such commitments acknowledge that their particular interests ought not to be allowed to trump the similar interests of others or the educational mission of the university. More importantly, the personal projects and commitments of the various students, faculty, and administrators whether they be promoting the Gospel of Jesus or the Gospel of Social Justice, whether they concern environmental preservation or entrepreneurial innovation, ought to be of secondary concern to the primary educational mission of the liberal arts university. Of course, for many, if not most, students, faculty, and administrators, their projects and commitments will include contributing to the preservation and flourishing of liberal education.

Universities, here, are not understood as completely distinct from other institutions in a pluralist society. However, all versions of the good life are not equally conducive to the purposes of the university. For example, the zeal of the ideological partisan or the fundamentalist hedge preacher are inimical to the purposes of liberal arts education and, though we are not concerned with vocational training, they are also irrelevant to most of the forms of it. There are seminaries where such commitments are central, if required, for the success of the institution, but universities are not seminaries. Thus, the relevance of viewpoint/moral pluralism diversity is not always clear, but, in certain circumstances (e.g., when a group of faculty or administrative officials attempts to prescribe ideological uniformity for the university community), the emphasis on viewpoint diversity becomes a matter of urgency.

Finally, the third type of diversity is identity group diversity which consists of the notion that various groups have inherent qualities that enhance university education, though this is rarely explicitly argued in terms of the specific qualities, and that diversity is understood in terms of some vague notion of representation.[7] The groups to be represented are often, but not always, considered in terms of their victimhood or grievance, and the claim is that mere membership in a group assures the possession of certain admirable qualities.[8] Sometimes this grievance status is based upon claims about historical treatment, but, more often, it is a manifestation of a certain kind of practical ideological commitment derived from a farrago of Marx, Freud, Foucault, and Marcuse.[9]

This third type of diversity then manifests itself in two different forms when dealing with liberal arts education. In the first, an argument is made that certain groups of individuals have discrete qualities as members of their particular group that have been "underrepresented" in student bodies, in the faculties, and among the administrators of universities and that these qualities would somehow improve university life. There is almost no empirical evidence that this is so, but this particular version of identity group diversity does misconceive the ideal character of liberal arts students and faculty.[10] Such students and faculty are individuals engaged in the common practices of disinterested scholarship, and, thus, not properly understood to be "representing" racial, ethnic, sexual, or other nonacademic groups. This type of diversity is not directly antithetical to liberal education, but its focus on nonacademic considerations does suggest that it has nothing positive to contribute to liberal education.

The second group couples claim about the special characteristics of certain sorts of groups with claims about the centrality of the oppression of such groups to university life. According to this latter version, the university is itself corrupt because of its historical mistreatment of certain groups and the university must reform itself in order to cater to the special needs of such grievance groups. These arguments are generally couched in the neo-Marxist language of the hermeneutics of suspicion, and consist of the claim that the traditional defense of liberal education as a disinterested quest for the most adequate explanation of the subjects studied or, as here, an initiation into the variety of explanatory languages created by human beings is merely a mask that hides the fact that the powerful continue to oppress the grievance group or groups in question. This sort of diversity insists that liberal education is an impossibility given that the world is, in its actuality, not a plural world, but a world defined in the purely practical terms of power relations.

This highly politicized version of diversity then reduces the modal variety of conceptions of the world associated with epistemological diversity and the various versions of the good life exemplified in the claims of moral pluralism diversity to simplistic arguments about oppressors and oppressed.[11] Thus, identity group diversity consists of a radical repudiation of the entire educational mission of the university. The primary argument in favor of this third type of diversity is that people should be treated, first and foremost, as members of insular racial, ethnic, sexual groups, and that attention to these group identities outweighs other considerations, like considerations related to the purpose of the university. So, considerations of the intelligence, preparedness, and desire of individual students in admission decisions and of individual faculty in hiring and promotion decisions are irrelevant or, at best, secondary for the proponents of this third type of diversity. And, insofar as the university is an institution devoted to the pursuit of a variety of ways of understanding and explaining the world and ideologies are not concerned with explanation but with recommendation and partisan action, then the conflation of university education with ideological indoctrination means the destruction of the historical character of universities. Indeed, there is no obvious connection between this kind of bean-counting diversity and university education at all, and there is little to commend the notion that having a variety of individuals whose primary qualification is being a member of a supposedly "under-represented" group (whether a "grievance group" or not) improves university education. As suggested, instead, this version politicizes university education by reducing the explanatory languages to languages of recommendation (and of a rather specific ideological stripe) and directs vocational education away from training in a specific practice to a concern with characteristics irrelevant to expertise.

THE CLASH OF IDENTITY AND VIEWPOINT DIVERSITY ON THE MODERN UNIVERSITY CAMPUS

Since an openness to and toleration of opposing opinions have long been a hallmarks of higher learning, we might expect colleges and universities to be places that counter the partisan hatreds that pervade much of the rest of society. And, in fact, researchers have long documented the connection between higher levels of education and lower levels of prejudice.[12] Education shows a connection with higher levels of tolerance for racial and ethnic minorities, immigrant groups, religious outgroups, sexual minorities, the obese, the homeless, and the disabled.[13] Further, there is some evidence that levels of symbolic racism among students declined between their first and last years in college.[14] These findings have generally been based on arguments that education, either through knowledge or cognitive competence, socializes people to be more tolerant of those who differ from them.[15] This finding may be encouraging for those who support conceptions of diversity centered on group identities, but when it comes to viewpoint diversity the relationship between tolerance and contemporary higher education looks somewhat different. Nearly a decade ago, students reported that their peers were arrogant, believed "they [were] always right," and had no respect for views different from their own.[16] More recently, Henry and Napier documented a connection between higher levels of education and higher levels of ideological prejudice, from both the left and the right. But this does not appear to have always been the case.[17] Examining longitudinal trends, researchers have documented a decline in support for the expression of conflicting opinions on the college campus among those who entered college since the late 1980s. College students in the millennial generation (those born in the 1980s and early 1990s and entering college early in the twenty-first century), and especially those in the iGen/Gen Z cohort (born since the about 1995 and entering college in about 2013), report being less willing to let a controversial speaker express opinions on the college campus.[18]

And in recent years, university students report feeling less comfortable speaking up inside or outside the classroom for fear of suffering negative judgments from friends or retaliation from professors.[19] In fact, a 2017 survey of American college students revealed that slightly more than half of those interviewed (54 percent) agreed that they had stopped themselves from sharing an idea or opinion in class at some point since beginning college.[20] Almost one-third of students (29–30 percent) have self-censored themselves in class because they felt their ideas were politically incorrect and because they thought their words might be considered offensive to their peers. So while contemporary conceptions of diversity may be improving cultural appreciation for identity diversity, they do not seem to be promoting tolerance for viewpoint diversity.

Many argue that intolerance of conflicting opinions began with changes in the culture of higher education that occurred in the late 1980s and 1990s.[21] During that era, those in higher education engaged in debates about whether derogatory speech on college campuses, especially but not limited to that targeting racial minorities, merited First Amendment protections.[22] In response, many colleges and universities adopted speech codes that sought to regulate and punish offensive speech, prompting some to claim that college campuses were becoming "islands of repression" where the expression of unpopular ideas was verboten.[23] Many contended that "the range of ideas circulating in the academy [had] narrowed and American universities [had] grown increasingly intolerant toward dissenting voices."[24] Others defended the speech codes as necessary to combat serious incidents of racial harassment and to protect the right of minority groups to fully engage in campus activities.[25] The argument was that without the codes in place, "universities may become hostile educational environments in which some students are deprived of an equal opportunity to thrive."[26] Though the courts eventually struck down many of the speech codes as conflicting with constitutional protections of free speech, university administrators continued to be supportive of restricting the airing of unpopular, and potentially hurtful, speech on their campuses.[27] In fact, estimates suggest that between one-third and one-half of colleges and universities in the United States have regulations against group-targeted speech.[28]

While much of the support for campus speech code policies promulgated in the 1980s and 1990s came from political progressives, the left has not been alone in supporting regulations on the boundaries on free expression in the academy. In the wake of recent episodes of campus unrest, supported by conservative policy groups, legislative and executive officials in at least three states have successfully implemented laws outlining punishments for campus protest activities. Arizona prescribes a half-year jail term for "protestors who stop traffic headed to political rallies."[29] North Carolina prohibits "protests and demonstrations that materially infringe upon the rights of others to engage in and listen to expressive activity."[30] A Board of Regents of the University Wisconsin policy provides that "students found to have twice engaged in violence or other disorderly conduct that disrupts others' free speech would be suspended. Students found to have disrupted others' free expression three times would be expelled."[31] At the same time, a number of efforts aimed at protecting campus free speech have found bipartisan support. Several of these efforts, in states including Arizona, Colorado, Missouri, Tennessee, Utah, and Virginia, take aim at free speech zones that many from the left and right alike view as overly restrictive of speakers sympathetic to their own political leanings.[32] Tennessee's law, which found strong bipartisan support, goes further and explicitly prevents administrators from rescinding invitations to speakers. In fact, as students and faculty returned for the 2019–2020 academic year, at least seventeen states had enacted laws targeted at campus speech.[33] In an instance of both progressives and conservatives claiming cover from free speech appeals, conservatives pointed to progressive protests of a University of Nebraska-Lincoln sophomore student's recruitment for a conservative student group.[34] The university relieved a graduate student lecturer of her teaching duties for being among the protestors who accused the undergraduate of advocating white nationalism and having KKK leanings. Appealing to free speech supporters, the university argued that the lecturer was "not representative of a university where the robust free exchange of ideas takes place 24 hours a day, seven days a week." In an ironic turn, the Foundation for Individual Rights in Education (FIRE), which investigated the incident with the encouragement of conservative state lawmakers, ultimately requested that the university reinstate the graduate student lecturer since the free expression of her political opinions merited speech protections. As this case strikingly illustrates, threats to viewpoint diversity can emanate from any quarter, and sometimes from several at once.

Whether springing from the left, the right, or both, some claim that the change in campus culture that resulted from the speech code debates and governmental regulation of campus speech has created an "illiberal" dynamic in which students seek to silence rather than engage with those holding opposing viewpoints.[35] Studies show that more than half of college students surveyed falsely believe that hate speech is not protected by the First Amendment and that those with higher levels of education tend to exhibit more ideological prejudice than those with less education.[36] Further, there is some evidence that the relationship between educational attainment and intolerance of differing viewpoints changed in important ways after the speech code debates of the late 1980s. More recent college students express more support for "blasphemy laws" (laws mandating punishment for insulting or disrespectful speech). Almost half of twenty-first-century students favor such laws in contrast to about one-third of students of the Baby Boom era.[37] Likewise, Chong reported that among students educated before 1986, those who expressed support for multiculturalism tended to be more tolerant of a person who purported that blacks were genetically inferior.[38] However, for students educated after that time, the opposite was the case. Such findings comport well with empirical findings that support for an open marketplace of competing ideas on college campuses is waning, especially when such sentiments might be viewed as offensive or hurtful to an identity group. For instance, Stevens and Haidt found that in just one year support for an "open learning environment" in which students are exposed to all types of speech and viewpoints over a "positive environment" in which certain speech or expression is prohibited shrank by about 15 percent.[39] Similarly, Villasenor found that about half of the post-millennial college students he studied felt that silencing a speaker they find offensive was acceptable and preferred a campus environment that shelters them from offensive views.[40] On the whole, the contemporary American academy seems to be less of a "place to 'find oneself' and learn from others" than "a place where *already-formed* citizens clash, stay with like-minded others, or avoid politics altogether."[41] Thus, it seems that not all forms of diversity fit comfortably on the contemporary university campus.

INVESTIGATING SUPPORT FOR DIVERSITY ON THE UNIVERSITY CAMPUS

As a preliminary investigation into support for differing conceptions of diversity on the university campus, we analyzed survey data which had been previously collected by the Gallup/Knight Foundation.[42] We specifically investigated support for campus free speech with the expectation that those who had been exposed to university culture longer would be less supportive of free speech. Further, we expected that students who were members of groups who have been targets of group identity diversity policies and protections, as well as those holding established political beliefs, would be especially opposed to a fully open exchange of viewpoints. We take the Stanton Foundation's Free Speech Index (FSI) as a crude measure of support for viewpoint diversity. The additive index combines responses to fourteen survey items focused on free speech issues related to the restriction of certain forms of speech on the college campus.[43] The index comprises five different aspects of campus expression: (1) affirmation of policies that prohibit speech or expression that might be offensive to some groups of students; (2) support for student protest behavior targeting controversial speakers; (3) endorsement of enforced speech codes and speech zones; (4) prioritization of inclusivity and protection for diverse groups over protection of free speech rights; and (5) assent for limiting First Amendment protections for hate speech. The index conceptually ranges from zero to fourteen with lower values indicating support for speech restrictions and higher values representing support for free speech.

The sample of students examined here showed a good deal of variability on the FSI, with additive scores ranging from 1.83 to 13.50 and averaging about 7.82, give or take almost 2 index points. Overall, about half the respondents preferred free over restricted speech about eight times out of fourteen. An initial look at support for free speech across the class ranks reveals little difference between the attitudes of those new to the campus environment and those who have been there longer. As the first set of rows on table 2.1 illustrate, freshman through senior students report very similar levels of support for free speech on campus.

Table 2.1 Support for Free Speech on Campus

	Mean	Std. Dev.	Minimum	Median	Maximum
Class Rank					
Freshman	7.80	1.94	1.83	8.00	12.66
Sophomore	7.85	2.13	2.00	8.00	13.00
Junior	7.84	1.92	2.16	8.00	13.50
Senior	7.79	1.96	2.33	7.66	13.00
Partisanship					
Democrat	7.19	1.91	2.16	7.16	12.33
Independent	8.04	1.88	1.83	8.16	13.50
Republican	8.88	1.83	4.33	9.16	13.00
Ideology					
Very Liberal	6.49	2.01	1.83	6.34	11.50
Liberal	7.30	1.88	2.00	7.50	13.00
Moderate	8.24	1.75	2.33	8.16	13.50
Conservative	8.69	1.81	3.66	8.16	13.00
Very Conservative	9.56	1.76	4.16	9.66	13.00
Gender					
Female	7.37	1.92	2.33	8.50	13.50
Male	8.40	1.91	1.83	7.50	13.00
Race/Ethnicity					
Black	7.20	1.85	2.33	7.16	12.00
Hispanic	7.81	1.92	1.83	8.00	13.00
Asian	7.42	1.87	2.33	7.50	13.50
Other	8.34	1.70	4.00	8.44	10.66
White	7.99	2.01	2.00	8.16	13.00

Notes: Cell entries are values on the 14-point Free Speech Index. See Appendix A for details on this measure.

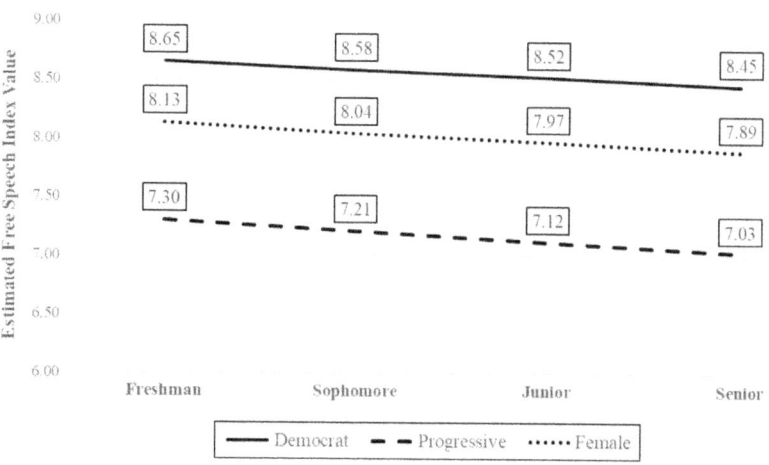

Figure 2.1 Support for Campus Free Speech by Class Rank.

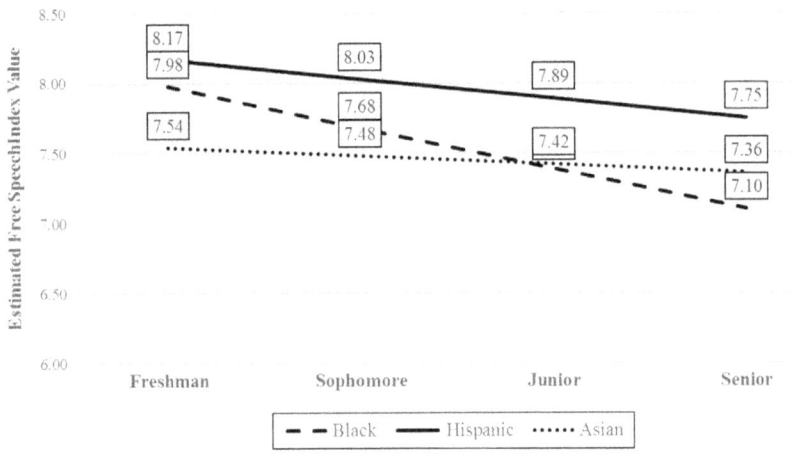

Figure 2.2 Support for Campus Free Speech by Class Rank and Race/Ethnicity.

The same cannot be said about attitudes across the political spectrum or for students of different sexes, races, and ethnicities. Students who self-identified as Republican and ideologically conservative expressed more support for free speech than did their self-acknowledged Democratic and liberal (progressive) counterparts. Those in the center (partisan Independents and ideological moderates) fell in between. Somewhat ironically, then, it appears that "liberal" American students hold attitudes that are more antithetical to a truly liberal education. Due to this contradiction, and in an attempt to avoid confusion, we will henceforth refer to such "liberal" American students as "progressive," reserving the term "liberal" to its classical meaning of openness to epistemological and viewpoint diversity. Similar results emerge across gender (sex) and racial/ethnic groups. Men reported higher levels of support for an open speech environment than women. In fact, men score, on average, more than one full point (or about 7 percent) higher than women on the 14-point scale. Similarly, white students averaged a higher level of support for free speech on the college campus than did black or Asian students, and marginally more than Hispanic students.[44] Taken together, this summary look at openness to viewpoint diversity suggests that left-leaning political attitudes and minority group status appear to be associated with lower levels of support for diversity of expression on the university campus, but that time spent in the campus environment does not. At the same time, it appears that exposure to the modern campus culture does little to inculcate a respect for viewpoint diversity.

To further investigate the relationship between exposure to the modern university environment and support for viewpoint diversity, we next conducted a series of multivariate regression equations taking the individual-level characteristics presented above as predictors of support for a campus open to the free exchange of ideas.[45] The first of these models, presented in table 2.2, confirms the null relationship that class rank had with endorsement of speech diversity, as well as the associations between partisanship, political ideology, sex, and race. Students identifying as partisan Democrats and ideological progressives, along with black and Asian students, report significantly lower levels of support for free expression on campus than Republican and conservative identifiers, and white students.

The failure of the class rank measure to show an association with attitudes about open expression might suggest that concerns that contemporary campus culture prioritizes identity group diversity over intellectual/epistemological and viewpoint/moral pluralism are misplaced. After all, if students who have had longer exposure to campus culture are no less supportive of free expression than those who have not been exposed as long, perhaps the academy is not in as much peril as some claim. We urge caution in taking such a view for two reasons, however. First and foremost, the lack of an association between time spent at university and support for free expression suggests that the contemporary college experience is not necessarily instilling the critical intellect that distinguishes a university education from primary or vocational education. As we have argued, one of the primary goals of a liberal arts education is to produce students who appreciate a variety of ways of understanding and explaining the world. An institution that graduates students no more open to such diversity than when they matriculated can hardly be held as successful. A second, more technical, point involves the specification of the first statistical model presented. The insignificant class rank coefficient does not capture the differential ways in which campus culture might affect students from different identity groups. If it is the case that university priorities for identity group diversity conflict with, and perhaps impede, the development of an appreciation for intellectual and viewpoint diversity, then we should not expect all students to react in the same manner to campus environments that prioritize the former over the latter. When campus climates prioritize identity group diversity and protections over other forms of diversity, it is those who champion identity group protections out of self-interest or sympathy who would be more open to sacrificing epistemological and moral diversity. After all, the safe space, trigger warning, microaggression, and bias response team policies instituted at universities were meant to protect members in these groups so that they could have equal access to the educational opportunities on campus. For students remaining unprotected by such policies, though, there can be little benefit from squelching free expression of ideas. Thus, we next test to see if students in protected racial/ethnic and gender identity groups as well as those sympathetic to them (i.e., Democrats and Progressives) who have spent more time on the college campus express less support for the free expression of ideas.

The remaining models presented on table 2.2 explore the interactive effects between individual-level student characteristics and time spent in the campus environment. The second model tests for the possibility that Democrats who spend more time on campus might become even less supportive of campus free speech the longer they are exposed to contemporary university policies. The results largely confirm this expectation. Substantively, Democratic identifiers who are in their senior (fourth) year on campus express levels of support for viewpoint diversity that are about 0.20 points (about 1.4 percent) lower on the 14-point Free Speech Index than do Democratic identifiers who are new to the college environment (see figure 2.1). Similar effects are predicted for Progressive students, with fourth year Progressive students showing about 1.9 percent less support for viewpoint diversity on campus (see figure 2.2). Further, the predicted effects of exposure to contemporary campus culture appears to exert an even stronger influence on the attitudes of students comprising identity groups that campus policies and administrators often champion. Female students who are further along in their university studies express less support for open expression than do their female counterparts who are earlier in their university careers. The predicted effects for female students are similar to that of Democratic and Progressive students; freshman female students express about 1.9 percent more support free expression on campus than do their senior colleagues (see figure 2.2). Though these substantive effects are not especially hefty, the mere fact that students become *less* rather than more supportive of the free exchange ideas the longer they spend on the university campus does not bode well for the future of liberal education in America.

Among all of the identity groups examined here, though, the modern campus climate seems to especially impact black college goers. Among this group of students, those who are seniors express about 6.3 percent less support for the items comprising the Free Speech Index than their freshman brethren (see figure 2.2). In fact, in just their first year on campus, black students' support for campus free expression is estimated to drop by about 2 percent (an amount roughly equivalent to the total predicted impact of campus culture on Democratic, Progressive, and female students). While Hispanic students' speech diversity attitudes also decline over their college years, the predicted decline is about half as large as that for black students—about a 3 percent decline in support for viewpoint diversity on campus across four years (see figure 2.2). For their part, Asian students bring more restrictive speech views with them to college, and the contemporary campus culture does little to change them (see figure 2.2).

Table 2.2 Student Characteristics and Support for Campus Free Speech

	I.	II.	III.	IV.	V.
	B (s.e.)	B (s.e.)	B (s.e.)	B(s.e.)	B (s.e.)
Student Class Rank (Fr., So., Jr. Sr.)	0.004	0.082	0.044	0.099 **	0.135 ***
	(0.027)	(0.042)	(0.041)	(0.040)	(0.035)
Democrat	-0.292 ***	0.084	-0.298 ***	-0.288 ***	-0.283 ***
	(0.081)	(0.175)	(0.081)	(0.081)	(0.081)
Republican	0.225 **	0.492 **	0.239 **	0.234 **	0.255 **
	(0.102)	(0.212)	(0.103)	(0.102)	(0.102)
Female	-0.835 ***	-0.836 ***	-0.837 ***	-0.382 **	-0.856 ***
	(0.065)	(0.065)	(0.065)	(0.154)	(0.065)
Hispanic	-0.006	0.009	-0.002	-0.007 0.944	0.665 ***
	(0.095)	(0.095)	(0.094)	(0.094)	(0.208)
Black	-0.463 ***	-0.481 ***	-0.468 ***	-0.502 ***	0.619 **
	(0.115)	(0.115)	(0.115)	(0.116)	(0.254)
Asian	-0.559 ***	-0.561 ***	-0.543 ***	-0.553 ***	-0.049
	(0.106)	(0.106)	(0.106)	(0.105)	(0.255)
Other Race	-0.279	-0.261	-0.333	-0.283 0.229	1.596 ***
	(0.236)	(0.236)	(0.237)	(0.236)	(0.480)
Progressive	-0.844 ***	-0.845 ***	-0.504 ***	-0.857 ***	-0.866 ***
	(0.081)	(0.081)	(0.174)	(0.081)	(0.081)
Conservative	0.411 ***	0.423 ***	0.217	0.337 ***	0.393 ***
	(0.103)	(0.103)	(0.222)	(0.103)	(0.102)
Democrat χ Class Rank	---	-0.146 **	---	---	---
		(0.061)			
Republican χ Class Rank	---	-0.109	---	---	---
		(0.078)			
Progressive χ Class Rank	---	---	-0.132 **	---	---
			(0.060)		
Conservative χ Class Rank	---	---	0.073	---	---
			(0.079)		
Female χ Class Rank	---	---	---	-0.179 ***	---
				(0.055)	
Black χ Class Rank					-0.426 ***
					(0.089)
Hispanic χ Class Rank	---	---	---	---	-0.275 ***
					(0.079)
Asian χ Class Rank					-0.195 **
					(0.087)

(Continued)

Table 2.2 Student Characteristics and Support for Campus Free Speech (*Continued*)

	I.	II.	III.	IV.	V.
	B (s.e.)	B (s.e.)	B (s.e.)	B(s.e.)	B (s.e.)
Other Race χ Class Rank	---	---	---	---	-0.789 ***
					(0.178)
Constant	8.826 ***	8.627 ***	8.725 ***	8.592 ***	8.505 ***
	(0.100)	(0.129)	(0.125)	(0.123)	(0.114)
Adjusted R-squared	0.184	0.185	0.186	0.187	0.195
Number of Cases	3009	3009	3009	3009	3009

Notes: Dependent variable is the Free Speech Index (ranges 1.83–13.50). Cell entries are OLS regression coefficients and standard errors. ***$p \leq 0.001$; **$p \leq 0.05$ (two-tailed).

Taken together the analyses we present here suggest that contemporary American universities are doing little to instill a respect for healthy discussion on campuses across the nation. It might indeed be the case, that "the safe space, trigger warning, and microaggression movements that have emerged at many colleges are making it more and more difficult to have open discussions about controversial topics."[46] Our analyses here suggest that for students on the political left and those who are members of some protected classes of students, time spent on a university campus seems to impart disapprobation for the expression of a diverse set of viewpoints on the campus quad. Though our findings do not illustrate it, there are challenges to viewpoint diversity from the other end of the political spectrum as well. In the past year, the University of Georgia sought guidance from the state's Republican attorney general about investigating a graduate student who made a social media post about "crappy white people," the Georgia Southern campus witnessed a book burning by conservative students who took offense at an author's portrayal of all white people as privileged, and a community college adjunct instructor came under fire because of online posts sympathetic to the Antifa movement.[47] Republican lawmakers have also reportedly threatened universities with budget cuts due to concerns about reading assignments that were viewed as "obscene," a professor's T-shirt that displayed a message critical of President Trump, faculty members' deprecatory remarks about Republican officeholders, and the potential for anti-Israeli remarks to arise in campus discussions of the Middle East.[48]

IMPLICATIONS

Whether responding to pressures from the left or the right, campus environments demanding only particular approaches to learning or the expression of only certain beliefs in university education gravely compromise the true value of liberal arts education. Unfortunately, our evidence suggests that administrative practices at modern American universities may indeed be adverse to the core meaning of a liberal arts education. Somewhat ironically and inimically, American universities "[i]n attempting to combat intolerance, . . . have become intolerant."[49] The findings presented here suggest that the continued creation and enforcement of campus policies championing the promotion and protection of certain groups of students over others, and the simultaneous neglect of intellectual and moral diversity, will likely come at the cost of viewpoint and epistemological diversity. Restrictions on the domain of allowable viewpoints and constraints on what counts as acceptable epistemological approaches to university education severely hinder student exposure to a diversity of approaches to understanding and explaining the world in which they live, and makes the educator's job of fully nurturing the critical intellect of students exceedingly difficult.

APPENDIX A: MEASURES AND CODING

Free Speech Index (FSI): Additive index of the 14 items listed below. Ranges from 1.83 – 13.50. Mean = 7.82, std. dev. = 1.98; median = 8.

Preferred Learning Environment: Roughly half of respondents answered question (a), and the other half answered (b). If you had to choose, do you think it is more important for colleges to:

1a. Create a positive learning environment for all students by prohibiting certain speech or expression that are offensive to certain groups, OR Create an open learning environment, where students are exposed to all types of speech and viewpoints, even if it means allowing speech that if offensive or biased against certain groups of people.
1b. Protect students by prohibiting speech they may find offensive or biased, OR Allow students to be exposed to all types of speech even if they may find it offensive or biased.

Opinion on Campus Policies Restricting Speech and Expression: Do you think colleges should or should not be able to establish policies that restrict each of the following types of speech or expression on campus? How about . . .

2. Expressing political views that are upsetting or offensive to certain groups.
3. Using slurs and other language on campus that is intentionally offensive to other groups.

Opinion on Student Protest Behavior: Do you think each of the following actions that could be taken by college students are always acceptable, sometimes acceptable, or never acceptable? How about . . .

4. Shouting down speakers or trying to prevent them from talking.
5. Engaging in protests against speakers.
6. Denying the news media access to cover a protest or rally on campus.
7. Distributing pamphlets or literature on controversial issues.
8. Engaging in sit-ins or similar attempts to disrupt operations in campus buildings.

Opinion on Campus Speech Codes and Speech Zones: Next, please say whether you favor or oppose each of the following actions taken by colleges.

9. Establishing a free speech zone, a designated area of campus in which protesting or distributing literature is permitted, usually with preapproval.
10. Instituting speech codes, or codes of conduct that restrict offensive or biased speech on campus that would be permitted in society more generally.
11. Disinviting speakers because some students are opposed to the invitation.

Importance in a Democracy: Inclusive Society and Free Speech Rights:

12. How important do you consider protecting citizens' free speech rights to be in our democracy—extremely important, very important, moderately important, or not that important?
13. If you had to choose, which do you think is more important? Promoting an inclusive society that is welcoming to diverse groups, OR protecting citizens' free speech rights.

Hate Speech and the First Amendment:

14. Do you think hate speech is a form of expression that should or should not be protected by the First Amendment?

Student Class Rank: 1 = First Year/Freshman; 2 = Second Year/ Sophomore; 3 = Third Year/Junior; 4 = Fourth year or higher/ Senior

Partisanship: Dichotomous (dummy) variables for self-identified Democrats and Republicans. Strong, weak, and leaning partisans = 1, pure independents, other party identifiers = 0.

Ideology: Dichotomous (dummy) variables for self-identified progressives (liberals) and conservatives. Ideologues = 1; moderates = 0.

Gender: Dichotomous (dummy) variable for female respondents (female = 1; male = 0)

Race/Ethnicity: Four dichotomous (dummy) variables for black, Hispanic (non-white/non-black), Asian, and Other race (American Indian or Alaska Native, Native Hawaiian or Pacific Islander) respondents. Black = 1, non-Black = 0; Hispanic = 1, non-Hispanic = 0; Asian = 1; non-Asian = 0; Other race = 1, not Other race = 0. White respondents represent the excluded category.

NOTES

1. Our discussion of the character of liberal arts education is greatly indebted to the following writers and works: John Henry Newman, *The Idea of a University*, ed. Martin J. Svaglic (Notre Dame, IN: University of Notre Dame Press, 1982); T. S. Eliot, *Essays Ancient and Modern* (London: Faber and Faber, Ltd., 1936); T. S. Eliot, *To Criticize the Critic and Other Writings* (London: Faber and Faber, Ltd., 1965); F. R. Leavis, *The Critic as Anti-Philosopher*, ed. G. Singh (Chicago, IL: Ivan R. Dee, Inc., 1982); Joseph Pieper, *Leisure: The Basis of Culture*, trans. Alexander Dru (Indianapolis, IN: Liberty Fund, 1998); Herbert Butterfield, *The Universities and Education Today* (London: Routledge & Kegan Paul, 1961); Michael Oakeshott, *The Voice of Liberal Learning* (Indianapolis, IN: Liberty Press, 2001); Antony Flew, *Sociology, Equality and Education: Philosophical Essays in Defense of a Variety of Differences* (New York, NY: Harper and Row, 1976); Jaroslav Pelikan, *The Idea of the University: A Reexamination* (New Haven, CT: Yale University Press, 1992); Kenneth Minogue, *The Concept of a University* (London: Transaction Publishers, 2005); and Stanley Fish, *Save the World on Your Own Time* (Oxford: Oxford University Press, 2008).

2. For insightful treatments of intrinsic value and perfectionist values (the values of excellence), see, among others, Thomas Nagel, "The Fragmentation of Value," in *Mortal Questions* (Cambridge: Cambridge University Press, 1979), 128–41; Susan Wolf, "Good-for-Nothings," in *The Variety of Values: Essays on Morality, Meaning, and Love* (Oxford: Oxford University Press, 2015), 67–85; John Kekes, *Enjoyment: The Moral Significance of Styles of Life* (Oxford: Clarendon Press, 2008), 21–136; and G. H. von Wright, *The Varieties of Goodness* (London: Routledge & Kegan Paul, 1963), 86–113.

3. For accounts of the kind of epistemological pluralism that I am describing here, see Amelie Rorty, "Varieties of Pluralism in a Polyphonic Society," *The Review of Metaphysics* 44 (1990): 3–20; the special issue of *The Monist* 73 (1990): 335–478; R. G. Collingwood, *Speculum Mentis, or The Map of Knowledge* (Oxford: Clarendon Press, 1924); Michael Oakeshott, *Experience and Its Modes* (Cambridge: Cambridge University Press, 1933); and John Kekes, *Pluralism in Philosophy: Changing the Subject* (Ithaca, NY: Cornell University Press, 2000).

4. Michael Oakeshott uses term "conversation" to describe the interaction between speakers of the language of science, history, religion, art, and practical life. Michael Oakeshott, "The Voice of Poetry in the Conversation of Mankind," in *Rationalism in Politics and Other Essays: New and Expanded Edition* (Indianapolis, IN: Liberty Fund, 1991), 488–541.

5. Oakeshott notes that liberal education offers "the opportunity to exercise, and perhaps to cultivate, the highest and most easily destroyed of human capacities, what Keats called "negative capability"—when a man is capable of being in uncertainties, mysteries, doubts, without any irritable racing after fact and reason—an opportunity to practice that "suspended judgment" of which the "neutrality" of liberalism is so pale a shadow. And all this, not in an intellectual vacuum, but surrounded by all the inherited learning and literature and experience of our civilization." Michael Oakeshott, "The Universities," in *The Voice of Liberal Learning* (Indianapolis, IN: Liberty Press, 2001), 148.

6. For discussions of value or moral pluralism, see, among others, Joseph Raz, *The Morality of Freedom* (Oxford: Clarendon Press, 1986); Michael Stocker, *Plural and Conflicting Values* (Oxford: Clarendon Press, 1990); Martha C. Nussbaum, *The Fragility of Goodness: Luck and Ethics in Greek Tragedy and Philosophy*, Updated Edition (Cambridge: Cambridge University Press, 2001); Annette Baier, *Postures of the Mind: Essays on Mind and Morals* (Minneapolis, MN: The University of Minnesota Press, 1985); Edmund L. Pincoffs, *Quandaries and Virtues: Against Reductivism in Ethics* (Lawrence, KS: The University Press of Kansas, 1986); Stuart Hampshire, *Innocence and Experience* (Cambridge, MA: Harvard University Press, 1989); Isaiah Berlin, "Two Concepts of Liberty," in *Liberty*, ed. Henry Hardy (Oxford: Oxford University Press, 2002), 166–217; John Kekes, *The Morality of Pluralism* (Princeton, NJ: Princeton University Press, 1993); Charles Larmore, *Patterns of Moral Complexity* (Cambridge: Cambridge University Press, 1987); and Bernard Williams, *Ethics and the Limits of Philosophy* (Cambridge, MA: Harvard University Press, 1985).

7. See, among others, the collection edited by Steven Vertovec titled *Routledge Handbook of International Diversity Studies* (New York, NY: Routledge, 2015). See also Peter Wood, *Diversity: The Invention of a Concept* (San Francisco, CA: Encounter Books, 2003).

8. For a sampling of arguments suggesting that membership in a specific community ought to result in special consideration, see Kimberlé Crenshaw and Gary Peller, eds., *Reaffirming Racism: The Faulty Logic of Colorblindness, Remedy and Diversity* (New York, NY: The New Press, 2016).

9. For the connections between various forms of critical theory which support identity group diversity and Marx, Freud, Foucault, and Marcuse, see, among others, Mike Cole, *New Developments in Critical Race Theory and Education: Revisiting Racialized Capitalism and Socialism in Austerity* (New York, NY: Palgrave Macmillen, 2017); Tim Dant, *Critical Social Theory* (London: Sage, 2003); Fred Ruch, ed., *The Cambridge Companion to Critical Theory* (Cambridge: Cambridge University Press, 1994); Stuart Sim, ed., *The Edinburgh Companion to Critical Theory* (Edinburgh: Edinburgh University Press, 2016) especially the section on critical race theory, 196–229, gender, 235–250, and feminism, 290–323; Banu Bargu and Chiara Bottici, eds., *Feminism, Capitalism, and Criticism* (New York, NY: Palgrave Macmillan, 2017); and Dianna Taylor and Karen Vintges, eds., *Feminism and the Final Foucault* (Urbana, IL: The University of Illinois Press, 2004). For an insightful and prescient account of the use of Marx and neo-Marxists like Gramsci

and the various members of the Frankfurt School, especially Marcuse, by those who have played a role in the development of identity group diversity, see Paul Gottfried, *Multiculturalism and the Politics of Guilt: Toward a Secular Theocracy* (Columbia, MO: The University of Missouri Press, 2004) and Paul Gottfried, *The Strange Death of Marxism: The European Left in the New Millennium* (Columbia, MO: The University of Missouri Press, 2018).

10. There have been a variety of arguments that moral pluralism and viewpoint diversity do produce better results in certain sorts of decision-making circumstances. For example, Aristotle suggested that great banquets are enriched by a variety of contributions from different individuals and groups. Other activities where a diversity of viewpoints might improve decisions are electoral procedures such as voting, making tactical and sometimes even strategic decisions, "brainstorming," and throwing an entertaining party. However, these claims concern moral, value, or viewpoint diversity, not racial, ethnic, or sex diversity. The latter three are sometimes used as a proxy for the former three, but the assumption that they are proxies certainly seems tinged with racism and sexism. For a recent defense of the epistemic argument for democracy, see Hélène Landemore, *Democratic Reason: Politics, Collective Intelligence, and the Rule of the Many* (Princeton, NJ: Princeton University Press, 2013).

11. For instance, Ibram X. Kendi writes that "there is no such thing as a nonracist or race-neutral policy … If discrimination is creating equity, then it is antiracist. If discrimination is creating inequity, then it is racist … Every policy in every institution in every community in every nation is producing or sustaining either racial inequity or equity between racial groups." Ibram X. Kendi, *How to Be an Antiracist* (New York, NY: Random House, 2019). Kendi's proposal to remedy this problem manifests his totalizing ideology, and would destroy any independent purpose that liberal education might pursue. His proposal, which was a contribution to *Politico*, an online website devoted to political issues in the USA, is as follows: "To fix the original sin of racism, Americans should pass an anti-racist amendment to the U.S. Constitution that enshrines two guiding anti-racist principals: Racial inequity is evidence of racist policy and the different racial groups are equals. The amendment would make unconstitutional racial inequity over a certain threshold, as well as racist ideas by public officials (with "racist ideas" and "public official" clearly defined). It would establish and permanently fund the Department of Anti-racism (DOA) comprised of formally trained experts on racism and no political appointees. The DOA would be responsible for preclearing all local, state and federal public policies to ensure they won't yield racial inequity, monitor those policies, investigate private racist policies when racial inequity surfaces, and monitor public officials for expressions of racist ideas. The DOA would be empowered with disciplinary tools to wield over and against policymakers and public officials who do not voluntarily change their racist policy and ideas." https://www.politico.com/interactives/2019/how-to-fix-politics-in-america/inequality/pass-an-anti-racist-constitutional-amendment/.

12. Gordon Allport, *The Nature of Prejudice* (Cambridge, MA: Addison-Wesley, 1954).

13. See P. J. Henry and Jaime L. Napier, "Education is Related to Greater Ideological Prejudice," *Public Opinion Quarterly* 81, no. 4 (2017): 930–42.

14. James Sidanius, Shana Levin, Colette van Laar, and David O. Sears, *The Diversity Challenge: Social Identity and Intergroup Relations on the College Campus* (New York, NY: Russell Sage Foundation, 2008). John Sides, "Your Do-Nothing Congress (in One Graph)," *Washington Monthly*, September 21, 2012.

15. For arguments that knowledge gains increase tolerance, see Anders Todal Jenssen and Heidi Engesbak, "The Many Faces of Education: Why Are People with Lower Education More Hostile toward Immigrants Than People with Higher Education?" *Scandinavian Journal of Educational Research* 38 (1994): 33–50. Evidence for cognitive competence leading to heightened tolerance of differing others can be found here: Lawrence Bobo and Frederick C. Licari, "Education and Political Tolerance: Testing the Effects of Cognitive Sophistication and Target Group Affect," *Public Opinion Quarterly* 53 (1989): 285–308; Norman H. Nie, Jane Junn, and Kenneth Stehlik-Barry, *Education and Democratic Citizenship in America* (Chicago, IL: University of Chicago Press, 1996); Henry and Napier, "Education is Related to Greater Ideological Prejudice," 930–42; Héctor Carvacho, Andreas Zick, Andrés Haye, Roberto Gonzáles, Jorge Manzi, Caroline Kocik, and Melanie Bertl, "On the Relation between Social Class and Prejudice: The Roles of Education, Income, and Ideological Attitudes," *European Journal of Social Psychology* 43 (2013): 272–85.

16. Susan Herbst, *Rude Democracy: Civility and Incivility in America* (Philadelphia, PA: Temple University Press, 2010), 109–11.

17. Henry and Napier, "Education is Related to Greater Ideological Prejudice," 930–42.

18. Jacob Poushter, "40% of Millennials OK with Limiting Speech Offensive to Minorities," *Pew Research Center Fact Think*, November 20, 2015 and John Sides, "The 40-Year Decline in the Tolerance of College Students, Graphed," *Washington Post*, March 9, 2017. The Millennial generation typically includes those born in the 1980s and early 1990s and entering college early in the twenty-first century, while those in the iGen (sometimes also called Gen Z) cohort have been born since the about 1995 and started entering college in about 2013.

19. Sean Stevens and Jonathan Haidt, "The Skeptics are Wrong Part 1: Speech Culture on Campus is Changing," *Heterodox Academy*, March 19, 2018a. See also Erwin Chemerinsky and Howard Gillam, *Free Speech on Campus* (New Haven, CT: Yale University Press, 2017).

20. Kelsey Ann Naughton, *Speaking Freely: What Students Think about Expression at American Colleges* (Philadelphia, PA: Foundation for Individual Rights in Education, 2017).

21. Dennis Chong, "Free Speech and Multiculturalism In and Out of the Academy," *Political Psychology* 27, no. 1 (2006): 29–54 and Sides, "The 40-Year Decline in the Tolerance."

22. Chong, "Free Speech and Multiculturalism," 29–54; Charles R. Lawrence III and Gerald Gunther, "Speech that Harms: An Exchange," *Academe* 76, no. 6 (1990): 10–14; M. Matsuda, C. Lawrence, R. Delgado, and K. Crenshaw, eds., *Words that Wound : Critical Race Theory, Assaultive Speech, and the First Amendment* (Boulder, CO: Westview Press, 1993); S. Walker, *Hate Speech* (Lincoln, NE: University of Nebraska Press, 1994).

23. For information on speech codes, see: M. Heumann and T. W. Church, eds., *Hate Speech on Campus* (Boston, MA: Northeastern University Press, 1997); Steve Kolowich, "State of Conflict," *The Chronicle of Higher Education*, April 27, 2018; T. C. Shiell, *Campus Hate Speech on Trial* (Lawrence, KS: University Press of Kansas, 1998); Walker, *Hate Speech*. Per the potentially repressive effects of such codes, refer to D. D'Souza, *Illiberal Education: The Politics of Race and Sex on Campus* (New York, NY: Free Press, 1991).

24. Chong, "Free Speech and Multiculturalism," 29–54.

25. Heumann and Church, *Hate Speech on Campus*; R. Delgado, "Words that Wound: A Tort Action for Racial Insults, Epithets and Name-calling," *Harvard Civil Rights-Civil Liberties Law Review* 17 (1982): 133; R. Delgado, "Campus Anti-Racism Rules: Constitutional Narratives in Collision," *Northwestern University Law Review* 85 (1991): 343; C. MacKinnon, *Only Words* (Cambridge MA: Harvard University Press, 1993); M. J. Matsuda, "Public Response to Racist speech: Considering the Victim's Story," *Michigan Law Review* 87 (1989): 2320–81.

26. Chong, "Free Speech and Multiculturalism," 29–54.

27. Kolowich, "State of Conflict."

28. Chong, "Free Speech and Multiculturalism," 29–54; A. R. Korwar, *War of Words: Speech Codes at Public Colleges and Universities* (Nashville, TN: The Freedom Forum First Amendment Center, 1995).

29. Arizona HB 2548 (see also HB 2516).

30. North Carolina Restore Campus Free Speech Act (SL 2017-96).

31. University of Wisconsin Regent Policy Document 4–21, "Commitment to Academic Freedom and Freedom of Expression."

32. Arizona HB 2615, Colorado SB 21, Missouri SB93, Tennessee SB 723, Utah HB54, and Virginia HB 1401.

33. Jeremy Bauer-Wolf, "Free Speech Laws Mushroom in Wake of Campus Protests," *Inside Higher Ed*, September 16, 2019.

34. Rick Ruggles, "UNL Sophomore Says She was Berated and Intimidated While Trying to Recruit Students for Conservative Group," *Omaha World Herald*, August 30: 107; Rick Ruggles, "Lecturer Accused of Harassing Conservative Student Will No Longer Work at UNL; 2 PR Officials Also Out," *Omaha World Herald*, November 19, 2017; Rick Ruggles, "UNL Under Fire From National Groups for Punishing Lecturer After Clash with Conservative Student," *Omaha World Herald*, December 18, 2017; Tyler Coward, "FIRE asks University of Nebraska-Lincoln to Reinstate Graduate Student," *FIRE*, December 11, 2017.

35. D'Souza, *Illiberal Education*; Frank Furedi, *What's Happened to the University? A Sociological Exploration of Its Infantilisation* (New York, NY: Routledge, 2017); Stevens and Haidt, "The Skeptics are Wrong Part 1."

36. John Villasenor, "Views Among College Students Regarding the First Amendment: Results from a New Survey," *Brookings Institution*, September 18, 2017; Henry and Napier, "Education is Related to Greater Ideological Prejudice," 930–42.

37. Stevens and Haidt, "The Skeptics are Wrong Part 1."

38. Chong, "Free Speech and Multiculturalism," 29–54.

39. Stevens and Haidt, "The Skeptics are Wrong Part 1."
40. Villasenor, "Views Among College Students Regarding the First Amendment."
41. Herbst, *Rude Democracy*, 111.
42. The Knight Foundation, along with the American Council on Education, the Koch Foundation, and the Stanton Foundation commissioned a survey about college students' thoughts on the First Amendment. Gallup conducted the survey, which included 3,014 full-time four year students enrolled at colleges in all four U.S. census regions, in the fall semester of 2017.
43. See Appendix A for details on all index items.
44. Only those identifying as an "other" race (American Indian or Alaska Native, Native Hawaiian or Pacific Islander) rated an average score higher than the subsample of White students.
45. Multivariate regression is a statistical technique that enables estimation of the effects that key causal factors (time at university, and socio-demographic and political identities) have on the response factor (support for an open learning environment). Though regression estimates cannot offer deterministic predictions, they can offer some probabilistic insight into the correlative relationships between causal and response variables.
46. Clay Routledge, "We Champion Racial, Gender and Cultural Diversity – Why not Viewpoint Diversity?" *Scientific American Blog Network*, October 24, 2017.
47. Daniel Burnett, "A Closer Look at Georgia Southern's Response to Students' Book Burning," *FIRE*, October 18m, 2019; Shikha Dalmia, "The Left-Wing Threat to Campus Free Speech is Abating. The Right-Wing Threat Is Not," *The Week*, September 16, 2019; Colleen Flaherty, "Pro-Antifa Professor Out in Iowa," *Inside Higher Ed*, August 26, 2019.
48. Dalmia, "The Left-Wing Threat to Campus Free Speech is Abating"; Jeffrey Sachs, "Campus Free Speech, Under Threat from the Right," *ARC Digital Media*, September 3, 2019.
49. Kira Barrett, "Walking on Eggshells – How Political Correctness is Changing the Campus Dynamic," *The Sophian: the Independent Newspaper of Smith College*, September 22, 2016.

BIBLIOGRAPHY

Chong, Dennis. "Free Speech and Multiculturalism In and Out of the Academy." *Political Psychology* 27, no. 1 (2006): 29–54.

Herbst, Susan. *Rude Democracy: Civility and Incivility in America.* Philadelphia, PA: Temple University Press, 2010.

Chapter 3

Undermining Communicative Action in the Medical Encounter

Informed Consent, Compelled Speech, and Promises to Pay

Leigh E. Rich

Within medicine, informed consent typically is understood as a modern idea, although one that has ancient roots in philosophy and perhaps even in practice. It is a concept carved from multiple disciplines and whose complex medical, legal, and ethical implications have expanded over time. While patients and, at times, even health care practitioners may mistake the *document* one signs prior to a procedure as "consent," such paperwork primarily serves bureaucratic and legal purposes that mark the completion of an institutional protocol. Rather, informed consent is the *dialogue* between a provider and a patient—throughout the course of a treatment and sometimes across multiple conversations and interactions—in which the parties attempt to reach a shared understanding. For the patient, this may mean the nature and risks of a proposed therapy and its consequences and alternatives; for the provider, the concerns and constraints unique to that patient. The signed piece of paper merely provides a (rather flimsy) form of evidence that such conversations took place. Thus, if understood and carried out correctly, informed consent could occur without any documentation at all, as it exists in the "linguistically mediated interaction . . . of subjects capable of speech and action who are now *situated in the world*."[1] In this way, informed consent is an exercise in Jürgen Habermas' communicative action, where "the goal of communication is not to understand a spoken utterance per se, but *to reach an understanding about what was said*."[2]

Unfortunately, in studies of actual clinicians (as well as fictional dramatizations), informed consent is often still seen as too complicated, unachievable, or a box to be ticked before the "real action" occurs, rather than a process that unfolds along with and essential to the medical encounter. Despite six decades since the term "informed consent" appeared in law and then was fleshed out in bioethics, the concept remains stunted in practice, with even cultural depictions reflecting an ongoing misunderstanding of what "consent" means or what occurs when one "consents." For example, in the second episode of the television show *House M.D.*, neurologist Dr. Eric Foreman tells the parents of a teenage patient: "Look, I'm sorry. I can explain this as best I can, but the notion that you're going to fully understand your son's treatment and make an informed decision is, is kind of insane. Here's what you need to know. It's dangerous. It could kill him. You should do it."[3] In framing informed consent as information a doctor must provide to a patient and a form to be completed and signed, the modern health care system obscures the communicative nature of informed consent and reshapes it into something tactical.[4]

This is due, in part, to the ways in which health care providers are trained, with more emphasis on laboratory sciences and less on communication and the humanities, and how health care organizations operate in the provision of technical, expensive, and scarce life-altering resources. But we also have misunderstood, especially in the United States, fundamental aspects of consent and autonomous decision-making. Neither can occur without mutual understanding between provider and patient of the topic at hand, achieved through intersubjective discourse and the "'unforced force' of the better argument"[5] rather than coercive authority (even when well intentioned) aimed at an instrumental end. No practitioner, of course, would think to skip the paperwork today (much to the relief of legal counsel, whose shock at such behavior might necessitate medical attention in and of itself), as the consent form serves a strategic function for the medicolegal system: a concrete reminder of a practitioner's duties and a physical record should a dispute emerge. This is not surprising, since the informed consent process known today grew out of civil and criminal cases in medical care and research, beginning in the early twentieth century and following World War II, along with the rise of bioethics as a professional discipline in the wake of the Nuremberg trials, physician-led articles,[6] civil rights, and the 1972 Associated Press exposé that ended the four-decade Tuskegee syphilis study.[7] These events, particularly those related to medical experimentation, prompted congressional action and the passage of the National Research Act in 1974, which established a commission that, by the end of the decade, produced *The Belmont Report* outlining ethically grounded federal guidelines to protect human subjects, including the need for informed consent.[8] Philosopher Tom Beauchamp was drafted by the commission to write the report, focusing on three basic principles it had identified at a conference in 1976, but early drafts were deemed "too philosophical" for the commission's purposes and "had to be pared back so that someone who was not a philosopher would be able to sustain interest."[9] Much of Beauchamp's scholarly thinking, however, and his references "to great classical philosophers" that ended up on "the [commission's] cutting room floor" found a home in the book he was simultaneously writing with philosopher and theologian James Childress.[10] Published roughly at the same time, *Principles of Biomedical Ethics*—which both influenced and was influenced by *The Belmont Report*—speaks not only to medical research but also to medical care and has become a "bible" of ethical medical practice.[11]

Weaving together philosophy, scientific data, and case-based examples, Beauchamp and Childress' *Principles* delineates the underpinnings of informed consent as well as description and prescription for operationalizing it.[12] Their book, along with court rulings described in judicial opinions, has since shaped the education and training of health care providers in what informed consent is, its importance, and its application. Interestingly, what Beauchamp and Childress paint as the ideal (though it might have been impossible to connect at the time) echoes the work of German philosopher Jürgen Habermas and his 1981 *Theorie des kommunikativen Handelns* (*The Theory of Communicative Action*), and even courts, in their dicta, have sometimes serendipitously intimated a Habermasian approach.[13] Yet, despite four decades since *Principles* was first published, the recently updated eighth edition makes no mention of Habermas (nor do judges or other political leaders, although they may lack such philosophical foundations).[14] While the reasons for this gap are not readily clear, making the similitude explicit—for both providers and patients—might improve our understanding and practice of informed consent as communicative, rather than strategic. Unfortunately, although Beauchamp and Childress do caution against goal-oriented and formulaic approaches, health care providers (and even their professors and superiors) and the everyday citizen are not likely to have read *Principles*, let alone Habermas, and in the twenty-first century informed consent often continues to be misconstrued as an objective task to complete (providers must "get the patient's consent" before a procedure) or a one-sided conversation focused on the delivery of medical information ("Did the patient consent?"), suggesting something that is uniform and passive. When viewed through the lens of communicative action, however, "consent" becomes more readily understood as "consensus"—as in, "Did the patient and provider reach a consensus?" or "Did you reach a consensus with the patient?"—and more along the lines of what informed consent is supposed to be.

Discussing informed consent as an exercise in communicative action also serves to reveal aspects of the U.S. health care system that undermine communicative rationality for something more strategic in the name of bureaucratic efficiency. This can be seen in just a few examples, such as compelled speech laws, especially in relation to abortion, where a legislatively designed strategy intentionally disrupts shared understanding, or the financial responsibility forms patients sign before they ever reach the exam room. Cost tends not to be included in informed consent conversations, yet a promise to pay typically must be made before obtaining care, much to the detriment not only of patients but also the sustainability of the health care system as a whole.

If medical education and modern culture highlighted a Habermasian approach within the medical encounter, truer engagement in informed consent might be achieved.

COMMUNICATIVE VERSUS STRATEGIC ACTION

With strategic action, the aim of a person or an agent engaged in a speech act is goal oriented. It does not matter whether the listener or other participant understands why the expression or request is being made, or whether there are valid reasons supporting it, but that the desired outcome is achieved. For example, in an earlier, more paternalistic era in health care, doctors sometimes withheld the true description of a diagnosis or procedure under the guise of medical authority—that the professional clinician knew best and a patient who lacked such knowledge and experience either couldn't understand or would object. An ignorant or fearful patient might opt for a path that, per clinical expertise, undermined his or her health. Such strategic action was at the heart of a case near the turn of the twentieth century involving Mrs. Parmelia J. Davis, a married woman around the age of forty and a mother of four who had been suffering increasing epileptic seizures for more than a decade.[15] Treatment was sought from Dr. Edwin H. Pratt, a physician of a Chicago sanitarium where Mrs. Davis had been taken. Despite the fact that Mrs. Davis' "mind, except during the periods immediately following these attacks, was normal," Dr. Pratt did not explain the extent of the two operations he performed as part of her treatment and failed to obtain consent for the second surgery that "remov[ed] her ovaries and uterus."[16] In the lawsuit that followed, he testified that he "told Mrs. Davis just enough about her condition" and "worked her deliberately and systematically, taking chances which she did not realize the full aspect of, deliberately and calmly deceiving the woman; that is, I did not tell her the whole truth."[17] In other words, as historian and legal scholar Paul A. Lombardo explains, "he intentionally deceived Mrs. Davis so that she would comply" and "excused his actions with the assertion that she was insane . . . and the [hysterectomy] was a treatment for her condition."[18] Mrs. Davis, through her husband, prevailed in court, based on "trespass to the person" in a nonemergency situation (and today it's also clear why the gender-biased, scientifically unfounded operations would do nothing to improve her health). Dr. Pratt, however, argued that, at least in his medical opinion, no harm necessitating an award for damages had occurred.[19] At the trial level, his attorney asserted that "the employment of the physician or surgeon gives him implied license to do whatever in the exercise of his judgment may be necessary."[20]

Communicative action, on the other hand, seeks shared understanding. This occurs within an interpersonal relationship where subjects reach an understanding about a situation and coordinate "their plans of action"[21] through the expression of criticizable validity claims—about the world, cultural norms, and themselves—that both parties come to accept after dialogue and debate and "based on the 'unforced force' of the better argument."[22] In this "mutual deliberation," the parties involved "are respected as equal, valuable, and knowledgeable contributors,"[23] and the "speakers-hearers simultaneously establish communication at *both* levels: at the level of intersubjectivity, where the subjects talk with one another, and at the level of the objects (or states of affairs) *about* which they communicate."[24] It is a "discursive rationality" where the speaker implicitly offers a guarantee that the claims he raises are credible and can, if needed, be redeemed. In this dialogue where (directly or not) the hearer questions and the speaker defends a claim, both parties come to "know *what makes it acceptable*. A speaker, with a validity claim, appeals to a reservoir of potential reasons that he could produce in support of the claim."[25] In *The Theory of Communicative Action*, Habermas explains that it "is the credibility of this guarantee," along with a mutual respect among the participants, "that facilitates coordination" through a shared understanding of the issue at hand and, to some extent, the world.[26] In communicative versus strategic action, claims that cannot be defended are unmasked and, if the breach is minor, may be clarified through "everyday speech" or, if more serious, face a deeper examination through a critical discourse.[27] This type of "rationality" was absent in the medical encounter with Mrs. Davis, as Dr. Pratt relied on his professional authority, his social (and nonepileptic mental and male) status, and the growing power of an allopathic medical discipline (that was becoming progressively positivistic and laboratory-based) to "justify" his "deliberately and systematically" deceptive assertions and actions as best for his patient. He knew that his claims—such as what operations were to occur and when—were unredeemable and provided only a simulacrum of an implicit guarantee. There was no "equal hermeneutic footing"[28] or "practice of argumentation"[29] between physician and patient. Mrs. Davis was diseased, he was not. He was a doctor, she was not. Instead of engaging in what Habermas admits is "a demanding form of communication"[30]—and one that could have prevented the ensuing bodily trespass and dehumanizing harms (even if, especially at that time, it may not have altered the course of treatment)—Dr. Pratt resorted to a medical gaze that, as Michel Foucault describes in *The Birth of the Clinic*, seeks to communicate with the disease rather than the patient.[31] "This trend towards objectivization, which began with the *modern natural sciences*" and became the foundation of Western biomedicine, "approaches the idea of impartial judgement by *eliminating* the lifeworld qualities of the everyday world" and "seems to boil down to the assumption that a radical, scientistic form of naturalism has the last word."[32] The Foucauldian *regard* frames a patient's "lifeworld" as but distracting ephemera to be factored out of the medical encounter and duly placed in parentheses, while Habermas diagnoses this "decoupling of system and lifeworld" as itself pathological.[33]

Communicative action involves more than just redeemable empirical claims. Habermas identifies three types of speech acts that, in addition to constatives (something that can be judged according to truthfulness), include regulatives and expressives—claims judged according to the normative "rightness for what is done" and the "sincerity for what is expressed."[34] Uttering a claim comes with a concomitant responsibility to assure that what is said aligns with one's "inner, outer, and social worlds":

> For any speech act oriented towards mutual understanding, there is a presumed fit of *sincerity* to the speaker's inner world, *truth* to the outer world, and *rightness* to what is inter-subjectively done in the social world. Naturally, these presumptions are defeasible. Yet, the point is that speakers who want to reach an agreement have to *presuppose* sincerity, truth and rightness so as to be able to mutually accept something as a fact, valid norm, or subjectively held experience.[35]

The case of *Pratt v. Davis* provides examples here as well. Dr. Pratt, by his own admission, lacked sincerity in his speech toward both his patient and her husband. Not only did he intentionally deceive Mrs. Davis, he informed Mr. Davis, when he first brought his wife to the sanitarium, that the initial surgery "would be a trifling one" (though he "then told Davis, in substance, that two operations might be necessary").[36] Although Mr. Davis requested that the surgeon "do as little as possible," Dr. Pratt later engaged in a second and invasive operation without either Mrs. or Mr. Davis' consent.[37] While the American Medical Association's original 1847 *Code of Ethics* condones some of Dr. Pratt's behavior, including deceptive language and the downplaying of an illness or treatment in order to "minister . . . hope and comfort to the sick," it highlights how a physician's "mind ought also to be imbued with the greatness of his mission, and the responsibility he habitually incurs in its discharge," and that "[e]very case . . . should be treated with attention, steadiness, and humanity."[38] This includes "not fail[ing], on proper occasions, to give to the friends of the patient timely notice of danger, when it really occurs; and even to the patient himself, if absolutely necessary."[39] Similarly, the Hippocratic Oath, which once "preclude[d] physicians from including patients in medical decisionmaking"[40] and demanded "concealing most things from the patient,"[41] advises practitioners to "abstain from whatever is deleterious and mischievous."[42] Physicians should be genuine in their speech and actions, something which perhaps Dr. Pratt, even in a prior paternalistic medical environment, was not. Additionally, Dr. Pratt's claims regarding truthfulness fall short. Although doctors had once thought that epilepsy and hysteria were linked or that the convulsions associated with one could lead to the other, the "problematic relationship" between the two "had already come under discussion before the nineteenth century," and in 1872 French neurologist Jean-Martin Charcot distinguished hysteria as its own clinical entity.[43] Criteria in Charcot's differential diagnosis included how, during attacks, those with epilepsy but not hysteria experienced an elevated body temperature and "that ovarian compression could relieve symptoms in cases of hysteria, but not for epilepsy . . . while potassium bromide worked for epileptics" but "not for hysterics."[44] It is unclear from the Supreme Court of Illinois' opinion whether Dr. Pratt had attempted the more empirically sound and less invasive treatment of potassium bromide—an anticonvulsive that had been used for epilepsy and "hysterical epilepsy" since the mid-1800s[45]— only that, after each surgery, Mrs. Davis experienced no improvement, grew "gradually worse mentally," and "was adjudged insane and sent to the state asylum."[46] Lastly, the court's ruling against the physician and in favor of Mrs. Davis (who was of sound mind prior to the procedures) also comments on the normative "rightness" of Dr. Pratt's approach:

> Ordinarily, where the patient is in full possession of all his mental faculties and in such physical health as to be able to consult about his condition without the consultation itself being fraught with dangerous consequences to the patient's health, and when no emergency exists making it impracticable to confer with him, it is manifest that his consent should be a prerequisite to a surgical operation.[47]

While the court acknowledged that a physician may follow his own judgment and discretion if "unexpected conditions develop or are discovered in the course of [an] operation" or during emergencies where "action must be taken immediately for the preservation of the life or health of the patient," Mrs. Davis' case did "not fall within either of these two classes."[48]

THE ROOTS OF CONSENT

There is debate among scholars as to how far back the concept of consent can be traced. Some claim that "it is a very old subject which ancient philosophers and physicians have addressed,"[49] while others date it to the twentieth century. According to Dalla-Vorgia and colleagues, for instance, Hippocrates underscored the necessity of coordinating with patients in order to be able to treat their diseases, while Plato's works suggest that patients (at least in relation to "free men") know themselves and what is "good" for them, and thus the role of the doctor "is to help this hidden knowledge emerge from the patient's soul by using the proper arguments."[50] Dalla-Vorgia et al. also highlight how Alexander the Great declared a battle wound "incurable" to provide political and legal cover, and thus encouragement, for a physician hesitant to operate on him and that Emperor Justin II of Byzantium handed his surgeon a scalpel to indicate that it was his decision, and not the clinician's, to undergo a tenuous procedure. Similarly, bioethicist Alexander Capron refers to New York's founding laws of 1665, which required physicians and surgeons to obtain their patients' consent, particularly the riskier the intervention,[51] while historian Mary Fissell describes how, in the crowded medical marketplace of eighteenth-century England, patients' narratives about what was the cause of an illness and how best to treat it were placed on "near-equal hermeneutic footing" with that of the doctor, since any unattended and unhappy patient easily could locate a more willing practitioner elsewhere.[52] All of these examples, however, may speak more to strategic action—in the name of cooperation, limiting liability, or free market competition—rather than a true form of consent.

The modern notion of consent emerged around the same time as the *Pratt* case, where, whether patients won judgments, courts emphasized a right to bodily integrity. For example, the intermediate appellate court in *Pratt* underscored that "the free citizen's first and greatest right, which underlies all the others [is] the right to the inviolability of his person, in other words, his right to himself."[53] Other courts at this time ruled similarly. The Minnesota Supreme Court in *Mohr v. Williams* found that a doctor committed assault and battery when he operated on a patient's left ear after she had provided consent only for an operation on the right. It did not matter, concluded the court, that Dr. Williams performed the procedure skillfully and successfully or that, upon investigation while the patient was anesthetized, the left ear was found to be more diseased and in need of treatment. "If the physician advises his patient to submit to a particular operation," the court stated, "and the patient weighs the dangers and risks incident to its performance, and finally consents, he thereby, in effect, enters into a contract authorizing his physician to operate to the extent of the consent given, but no further."[54] Likewise, the New York Court of Appeals, in an oft-quoted decision written by Benjamin Cardozo, underscored that "[e]very human being of adult years and sound mind has a right to determine what shall be done with his own body; and a surgeon who performs an operation without his patient's consent, commits an assault."[55] In this case, a woman by the name of Mary Schloendorff had consented to a surgical examination to determine the cause of "some disorder of the stomach" but explicitly told the hospital's house physician, the anesthesiologist, and a night nurse that she was "not to be operated on."[56] While she was under ether, the visiting surgeon, in consultation with her physician, discovered a benign fibroid tumor and performed a hysterectomy.[57] (She also subsequently developed gangrene in one arm and had to have some of her fingers amputated.) Schloendorff, however, lost her case due to legal reasons related to the structure of the health care system at the time—despite Cardozo's persuasive language that deemed "the wrong complained of . . . not merely negligence" but "trespass."[58] Regardless, these early twentieth-century decisions highlight that the weighing of risks and benefits of medical treatment and the final determination for what path will be taken belong to the patient.

By mid-century, this was further emphasized by courts, which fleshed out not only what consent should entail but also that it be "informed." The legal introduction of the term "informed consent" appeared in a 1957 California case, *Salgo v. Leland Stanford Jr. University Board of Trustees*, where a patient complaining of leg and back pain underwent a diagnostic procedure. While the test "had been routine and gone well," when Martin Salgo awoke the next day, "his lower extremities were [permanently] paralyzed," and his physicians "admit[ed] that the details of the procedure and the possible dangers therefrom [had not been] explained."[59] The court found this to be unacceptable and stated that a "physician violates his duty . . . if he withholds any facts which are necessary to form the basis of an intelligent consent by the patient to the proposed treatment."[60] Moreover, a physician "may not minimize the known dangers of a procedure or operation in order to induce his patient's consent" and must "explain to the patient every risk attendant upon any surgical procedure or operation, no matter how remote," even if this may prompt a patient's fearful refusal.[61] The court underscored that such consent conversations are not something rote; rather, providers should

> recognize that each patient presents a separate problem, that the patient's mental and emotional condition is important and in certain cases may be crucial, and that in discussing the element of risk a certain amount of discretion must be employed consistent with the full disclosure of facts necessary to an informed consent.[62]

Two other medical malpractice cases, both decided in 1972, reiterated and expanded this idea. The D.C. Circuit in *Canterbury v. Spence* concluded that "[t]rue consent to what happens to one's self is the *informed exercise* of a choice, and that entails an opportunity to evaluate knowledgeably the *options available* and the *risks attendant upon each*,"[63] and the California Supreme

Court in *Cobbs v. Grant* underscored that the "weighing of these risks against the individual subjective fears and hopes of the patient is not an expert skill. Such evaluation and decision is a *nonmedical judgment* reserved to the patient alone."[64] From the perspective of the medical profession, the *Cobbs* case in particular crossed a Rubicon by establishing a "reasonable patient" standard—that what should be disclosed is determined by a *patient's* informational needs, rather than what any "reasonable physician" would discuss in a similar situation. This places an onus on a clinician not only to know for a specific condition the benefits and risks of available therapies, including that of doing nothing, but also to understand (or communicate with) the patient well enough to determine how a treatment and its consequences might affect that individual.[65]

That said, these cases do not simply transfer the responsibility for medical decision-making to patients. The *Salgo* court, for example, acknowledges that "*a certain amount of discretion* must be employed" by a physician in consent conversations,[66] while the D.C. Circuit in *Canterbury* highlights that this discussion occurs between "[p]hysicians and . . . patients of widely divergent socio-economic backgrounds"[67]:

> The average patient has little or no understanding of the medical arts and ordinarily has only his physician to whom he can look for enlightenment with which to reach an intelligent decision. . . . *Duty to disclose is more than a call to speak merely on the patient's request, or merely to answer the patient's questions*; it is a duty to volunteer, if necessary, the information the patient needs for intelligent decision. The patient may be ignorant, confused, overawed by the physician or frightened by the hospital, or even ashamed to inquire.[68]

While this may be courts balancing professional independence and "therapeutic privilege" with patient autonomy, these cases suggest a communicative foundation to informed consent.

A COMMUNICATIVE APPROACH?

Viewed through a Habermasian lens, the dicta in these cases may be an incipient call for a more communicative approach with informed consent, a recognition that it cannot be strategic action but, rather, must allow for dialogue between Fissell's hermeneutically near equals.[69] Beauchamp and Childress' *Principles of Biomedical Ethics* takes this even further, and though it would have been near impossible to acknowledge at the time (since the one book predates the other), their descriptions of consent read compellingly similar to Habermas' *Theory of Communicative Action*.

In critiquing the courts, malpractice law, and medical literature of the time, Beauchamp and Childress emphasize that informed consent is more than just "disclosure" of facts and information by physicians, though disclosure is a part of the consent process. Rather, informed consent consists of multiple elements, including preconditions of competence and voluntariness on the part of the patient, informational aspects involving the discussion of material facts and guidance by the physician, and an understanding of the possible plans that informs a patient's ultimate decision and authorization.[70] Health care providers have both a negative obligation not to impede patients' "autonomous decision-making" regarding medical care and a positive one that fosters their ability to do so. Part of this involves a practitioner actively making a *"recommendation* of one or more actions."[71] In other words, the clinician is not a passive observer who idly awaits a patient's decision but, due to his or her experience and expertise, makes a persuasive argument for what he or she thinks is the best approach in a given situation and opens a dialogue with that individual patient. While two patients may confront a similar diagnosis, what the physician recommends may be different or less valid for one than the other given the unique lifeworlds of each. This is distinct from the medical paternalism of the past. The patient is not ceding control or merely deferring to the physician's authority but, through the offering and challenging of validity claims, striving toward comprehension of medical details, reaching a shared understanding with the provider about proposed therapies in relation to one's own situation, and then engaging in a performative act. The term "consent" in the modern notion of "informed consent" is thus something of a misnomer: "a person must do more than express agreement or comply with a proposal. He or she must *authorize* . . . with substantial understanding and in absence of substantial control by others . . . a professional to do something."[72]

Beauchamp and Childress suggest that physicians should disclose:

> (1) those facts or descriptions that patients or subjects usually consider material in deciding whether to refuse or consent to the proposed intervention or research, (2) information the professional believes to be material, (3) the professional's recommendation, (4) the purpose of seeking consent, and (5) the nature and limits of consent as an act of authorization.[73]

Additionally, the provider ought to make clear any personal conflicts of interest "unrelated to the patient's health, whether research or economic" (otherwise, the consent conversation certainly becomes strategic),[74] and ideally, especially regarding the provision of information that is "material," the provider should take on a "subjective," rather than a "professional practice" or even a "reasonable person," standard. Beauchamp and Childress explain that, similar to the *Cobbs* court, "the professional practice standard subverts the right of autonomous choice," and they take issue with the generalized and hypothetical "reasonable patient" approach as too abstract and thus too difficult to operationalize.[75] Patients vary widely in their personal circumstances and their understanding of medical information (whether due to intellect, education, level of maturity, state of illness, etc.), and some patients do not use the medical information disclosed and may come to the encounter either already having made a decision or wanting to defer to the physician.[76] Thus, the "subjective standard is a preferable *moral* standard of disclosure, because it alone acknowledges persons' specific informational needs."[77] However, in the same breath and contrary to the communicative ideal they seem to be suggesting, Beauchamp and Childress caution that legal and ethical questions arise about "the extent to which a standard should be tailored to the individual patient" because "a doctor cannot reasonably be expected to do an exhaustive background and character analysis of each patient to determine what information would be relevant."[78] Here Beauchamp and Childress may be giving physicians too much of a pass (similar to some of the court decisions they criticize),[79] unintentionally perpetuating a paternalistic *regard* and intentionally acknowledging that such a standard for informed consent, while preferable, is inefficient for medicine and law at a systems level. Habermas, on the other hand, speaks to these concerns by prioritizing intersubjective communication: "communicative action is undermined" when "the functional imperatives of economic or administrative systems are satisfied disproportionally at the expense of lifeworld resources of social solidarity."[80] Beauchamp and Childress thus suggest, without clearly acknowledging, "[t]wo different senses" of the concept of informed consent. The first is similar to a Habermasian communicative action that takes place between provider and patient in the context of a lifeworld that is always already there, while the second is a juridification of this—an excessively monetized or bureaucratized process "that must obtain [and document] legally or institutionally valid consent from patients or subjects before proceeding with diagnostic, therapeutic, or research procedures."[81]

What Beauchamp and Childress are arguing in relation to their first definition of informed consent, and what the *Salgo* and *Cobbs* courts and others intimate (if not always graciously but at least to a certain degree), is that "each patient presents a separate problem"[82] and is therefore unique, revealing that the only way informed consent can be carried out appropriately is through communicative, rather than strategic, action. The goal of the interaction cannot be to "get the patient's consent" in order to tick off an institutionalized step as part of the medical encounter but to "reach consensus with that individual patient" through the examination of validity claims about what is the most fitting medical plan. Like Habermas, Beauchamp and Childress denote that the informed consent conversation needs to be a dialogue between equally respected, if inherently different, individuals, not merely a medical professional providing information from experience and research (such as odds ratios and other statistics) to the patient. They also emphasize that how providers frame details may impact understanding—for example, discussing a treatment in relation to chances of survival versus mortality or using analogies that can convey the probabilities of outcomes nonnumerically and more in line with "ordinary events familiar to the patient or subject ... such as risks involved in driving automobiles or using power tools."[83] Moreover, because physicians are often thought of as more knowledgeable and trustworthy than other professionals, their "[r]ecommendations of treatments or of lifestyle changes ... are likely to be more meaningful than information about the results of empirical studies or surveillance."[84] Thus, being a health care provider comes with a heightened fiduciary duty for what claims are expressed and how and a sincerity about what kinds of persons they hold themselves out to be. A physician should act as an advocate for his or her patient, and the aim of informed consent is to reach a shared understanding about the best medical path situated within, not regardless of, the patient's lifeworld. Because the clinician possesses greater medical knowledge and expertise, this might entail making a reasoned argument, free from conflicts of interest, for one path versus another (although any claim raised must offer an implicit guarantee and be criticizable). For instance, while legal cases and principles in medical ethics underscore that a patient's choice may be valid even if it is not what a "reasonable person" would choose,[85] when a patient's "beliefs are demonstrably false" and "ignorance prevents an informed choice, it may be permissible or possibly even obligatory to promote autonomy by attempting to impose unwelcome information" and "pressure patients or subjects to change their beliefs or to process information differently."[86] Beauchamp and Childress provide the example of a nearly sixty-year-old woman from Appalachia whose doctors, while treating her for a broken hip, discovered she also was suffering from cervical cancer that a hysterectomy would cure. She refused to consent to the procedure because she believed that people with cancer are sickly and she otherwise felt fine. No information the physicians provided, including the results of a biopsy, seemed to sway her, in part because of her limited formal education but also because she (unjustifiably) distrusted her attending physician who was African American. Beauchamp and Childress emphasize that the woman's refusal was not informed but stemmed from a lack of understanding and elements of racism, and only "intense discussions with a white physician and her daughter eventually corrected her belief and led to her consent."[87] Compared with *Pratt v. Davis*, here a communicative approach addressed the patient's lifeworld with the aim of shared understanding (though not necessarily in agreement with all of her views) and reaching a consensus about the hysterectomy-based treatment that, in this case, was efficacious rather than harmful. Beauchamp and Childress echo Habermas' "unforced force" by acknowledging that, in certain instances,

> professionals are morally blameworthy if they do *not* attempt to persuade resistant patients to pursue treatments that are medically essential, and such persuasion need not violate respect for autonomy. Reasoned argument in defense of an option is itself a form of providing information and is often vital to ensuring understanding.[88]

In these ways, Beauchamp and Childress' components of informed consent resemble those of Habermas' communicative action, which requires that: participants are given equal footing and an equal voice in the dialogue; information (in the form of truth, normative, and truthfulness validity claims) is offered sincerely and open to criticism; the aim is a shared or mutual understanding of the situation at hand; and conclusions or decisions are driven by a "compulsionless compulsion" or the "unforced force" of the better argument. Philosopher Jack Simmons also contends that, within Habermas' framework, participants must come to an interaction with a sense of "sportsmanship," meaning that they will engage in a fair manner and respect both each other and the rules of argumentation.[89] In health care, this means: acknowledging the different authorities a clinician and a patient bring to an encounter; applying a more comprehensive, Habermasian form of reasoning (and not the scientistic variety that Max Weber described as an "iron cage"); and seeking mutual understanding rather than "winning."

UNDERMINING CONSENT IN THE TWENTY-FIRST CENTURY

Despite communicative framings of informed consent in foundational books like *Principles of Biomedical Ethics* and in court cases and journal articles that have occurred since, informed consent in practice still tends toward the strategic, and research has repeatedly demonstrated that clinicians struggle with consent conversations due to lack of training, lack of comfort, and/or lack of time. For example, Vossoughi and colleagues surveyed more than 300 medical students, residents, advanced practice nurses, physician assistants, and attending physicians at one academic institution and found that less than two-thirds believed their training in informed consent was adequate; moreover, the "most commonly cited type of training was an informal conversation regardless of the level of practice of the respondent, with lectures or printed materials being the second most frequently selected."[90] One-third of participants also expressed difficulties with "obtaining consent," with medical students primarily reporting knowledge-based barriers and all indicating "insufficient time."[91] At a different institution, Thompson et al. attempted to address the educational component by training surgical residents to "obtain and document informed consent" using a case-based methodology and "standardized patients."[92] Noting that "[v]ery little has been published to guide educators on how to train physicians to obtain informed consent from patients," they found that their low-cost intervention increased the number of consent-related items (based on a checklist developed from professional guidelines) that participants discussed.[93] While research endeavors like these highlight important and ongoing gaps in medical education and the literature, such approaches continue to foster a strategic, rather than a communicative, understanding of informed consent: for example, framing consent as something that is "obtained from patients," employing or suggesting binary (not discussed versus discussed) checklists for the conversation, and focusing training on legal aspects and documentation. To wit: 39 percent of Vossoughi et al.'s respondents "agreed that the primary purpose of informed consent was for medicolegal documentation" (even if 87 percent also stated that it is "to inform the patient"),[94] and Thompson's group—splitting training time between a malpractice attorney and the surgical residency director—allotted fifteen minutes for participant interaction with the standardized patient and ten minutes for "postencounter documentation."[95] Moreover, what they found more concerning was a persistent discrepancy between what residents discussed and what they actually documented in their post-consent notes—concluding that there is a greater need to instruct clinicians in the paperwork-side of things.[96]

Proficiency in the communicative act, however, remains deficient. Hall, Prochazka, and Fink underscore that physicians may "rarely meet even minimal standards of disclosure for the purposes of obtaining informed consent," and they highlight a 1999 investigation by Braddock et al. of primary care physicians and surgeons which found that "[o]nly 9% of the 2553 clinical decisions made during [1057 physician–patient] encounters met the criteria for completely informed decision-making."[97] More recently, Probst and colleagues, examining informed consent education among obstetrics and gynecology residents, concluded that "[n]early 90% of trainees have obtained [informed consent from a patient] for a procedure for which they were unsure of all the risks," and almost two-thirds "expressed a desire for additional training."[98]

In practice, many practitioners also find consent conversations uncomfortable and onerous. Research by Fiona Wood and collaborators revealed that, unless a surgical patient was already considered to be at high risk or was suffering from comorbidities, junior doctors in their study found it difficult "to address the subject [of death as a risk of general anesthesia] adequately or avoid[ed] it completely."[99] A junior vascular surgeon reported: "It's something . . . I don't voluntarily engage in . . . with patients unless they are sort of pointing me down that line."[100] Similarly, in a retrospective analysis of consent practices for six types of surgeries in a hospital in South Wales, Dafydd Loughran concluded that, for one particular operation that carries "a 14% chance of death, a risk of death was only documented in 28% of cases."[101] (While it is possible that a risk might be discussed and just not documented, other possible complications such as bleeding, infection, and the need for a stoma were recorded nearly three-quarters of the time.) Lastly, even among the most adept clinicians, one of the biggest obstacles to carrying out consent is time.[102] This is hardly surprising, especially in the United States, as providers continue to primarily be reimbursed for *doing* things, such as tests and procedures, that excised from their larger contexts have strategic ends, without acknowledging the communicative *acts* that are essential to and part and parcel of the medical relationship and the health of the patient. What gets disclosed and how may correlate to the amount of time a clinician has, not necessarily what is needed, and sometimes consent conversations occur on the day of or just prior to procedures.[103]

While studies in the medical literature do suggest an ideal of informed consent as something communicative—Hall and colleagues, for instance, highlight consent as patient-centered shared decision-making, aimed toward "a mutually acknowledged treatment goal," and "not an event, but a process"[104]—language that is used in health care, medical education, and proposals to improve practice weakens this understanding. For example: Loughran references the need for clinicians to appropriately "*consent a patient* for a procedure or operation,"[105] and Wood et al. discuss junior doctors' "reluctance to *take consent*."[106] Loughran also sent a survey to four UK deaneries that, among other questions, asked surgical trainees whether it would be useful "to have an online resource or mobile app detailing expert consensus recommended mentionable risks for the majority of operations with evidence based incidence rates" (and more than three-quarters said yes),[107] while Wood et al. offer as an "intervention" the suggestion (by several of their participants) that junior doctors "be provided with brief booklets that describe the range of procedures they are expected to consent patients for, and detail procedure-specific information, including how procedures are performed and the perceived benefits and risks associated with such procedures."[108] While checklists, apps, booklets, and standardized forms might be useful as prompts during a communicative dialogue, there is a risk that such tools reinforce or encourage a view that "the consent process [is] a 'perfunctory chore'" and "may make the discussion feel repetitive, reducing doctors' regard for patients' concerns."[109]

And if informed consent weren't challenging enough, issues at higher levels in health care beyond the doctor–patient dyad may undermine communicative action as well. Two examples drawn from U.S. law and medicine illustrate how a system-oriented, rather than a lifeworld-oriented, approach, whether intentionally or inadvertently applied, can result in strategic action and harm patients. While compelled speech laws related to abortion are more readily recognizable as interfering with fundamental concepts of informed consent, less obvious is the financial responsibility form patients often must sign before they even gain access to an exam room, let alone know what treatment options are before them.

Compelled Speech and Abortion

Within U.S. health care, the state has certain duties it must uphold, including what is known as *parens patriae*, or the protection of innocent third parties. In relation to abortion, this has been translated as an interest in protecting a fetus, especially after viability or the point at which it has a greater chance of surviving outside of the womb. While prior to birth a fetus is not legally considered a person and the state's incipient interests must be weighed against clear duties to protect the rights of the mother, as a pregnancy proceeds so does the fetus' potential for personhood. Such balancing based on the concept of viability was at the heart of the U.S. Supreme Court's *Roe v. Wade* in 1973, which made abortion legal in the United States while allowing states some power to regulate or even prohibit abortion at later stages in a pregnancy (save for exceptions to protect the life and health of the mother).[110] The Court's 1992 decision in *Planned Parenthood of Southeastern Pennsylvania v. Casey* reaffirmed *Roe*, though (by ditching the precedent's trimester approach) permitted greater regulation at any stage in a pregnancy as long as a state law does not create an "undue burden," that is, have "the purpose or effect of placing a substantial obstacle in the path of a woman seeking an abortion of a nonviable fetus."[111] *Casey*'s new standard has thus enabled the proliferation of abortion-related laws, such as requiring clinics or abortion providers to meet certain criteria, mandating ultrasounds or waiting periods between consent and the procedure, and compelling physicians to describe ultrasound images or read legislatively prepared scripts that have included medically inaccurate information about the risks of abortion. For example, a law passed in South Dakota (initially blocked by the Eighth Circuit but upheld when reheard *en banc*) requires physicians

> to tell patients, in writing and in person, that an increased risk of depression, suicidal ideation and suicide were "known medical risks of the procedure and statistically significant risk factors to which the pregnant woman would be subjected," despite the lack of credible studies supporting negative post-abortion

psychological outcomes. [Similarly, in] Mississippi and Tennessee, clinicians must orally provide women seeking abortions with false information about an increased risk of breast cancer as a consequence of obtaining an abortion.[112]

Several states also have required physicians to make statements about the (questionable and scientifically unsupported) possibility of "reversing" an abortion[113] and what amount to ideological or moral judgments about when life begins or "whether the fetus is a 'separate' entity" from the woman.[114] While there exist precedents upholding the compelled speech of physicians in certain circumstances,[115] David Orentlicher emphasizes that health care providers have "a duty to speak responsibly" and, in citing the Eighth Circuit's original opinion with regard to South Dakota, that laws violate physicians' First Amendment rights and professional duties when they compel "speech that is untruthful, misleading, or irrelevant."[116] He also notes that, unlike other compelled speech laws, many related to abortion are highly specific about what information must be disclosed and intend to direct women toward continuing a pregnancy based on dubious data, thus subverting the fiduciary relationship and exploiting the trust many patients have in their doctors. Moreover, when ideological statements are included, physicians are forced to become a "mouthpiece" of the state.[117]

Interestingly (though perhaps coincidentally), the Eighth Circuit's original decision against "compelled speech that is *untruthful, misleading,* or *irrelevant*"[118] aligns with Habermas, as the South Dakota law and others like it introduce into the physician–patient relationship indefensible *empirical, expressive,* and *regulative* claims that seek to confuse, rather than clarify.[119] It is not shared understanding and the "unforced force" of the better argument that are supposed to prevail, but a specific goal crafted by certain legislators and their supporters to influence and control women's medical decisions based on shaky and insincere premises (even if the state has a legitimate interest in promoting a certain outcome, birth versus abortion). Those who propose and defend these laws dress them up as ensuring women are provided "material information," and thus these laws superficially wear the costume of "informed consent" while simultaneously undercutting the very purposes of it, converting a process that should be communicative into something intentionally strategic.[120] Or, as Beauchamp and Childress state: "Many forms of informational manipulation are incompatible with autonomous decision-making. For example, deception that involves lying, withholding information, and misleading exaggeration to lead persons to believe what is false are all inconsistent with autonomous choice."[121]

Promises to Pay

In the Pennsylvania law at the heart of *Casey*, the Supreme Court upheld provisions that any woman seeking an abortion be advised that "[m]edical assistance benefits may be available for prenatal care, childbirth and neonatal care" and that the "father is responsible for financial assistance in the support of her child," as financial concerns may constrain a pregnant woman's decision-making autonomy and encourage her to have an abortion when she doesn't want one.[122] (On the other hand, continuing an unwanted pregnancy also can create long-term financial hardships for women and their families, though the *Casey* Court failed to discuss this.[123]) Thus, in Pennsylvania and other states with similar statutes, physicians are required to address possible financial resources for women who opt against abortion (though not the financial risks of being denied one). Oddly, abortion-related compelled speech laws are one of the few places in the U.S. health care system where economics comes into play in informed consent. Legal textbooks that explain informed consent and the American Medical Association's *Code of Medical Ethics* only highlight that disclosure should include (similar to Beauchamp and Childress' list) information relevant to a patient's diagnosis, the "nature and purpose of recommended interventions," and the medical "burdens, risks, and expected benefits of all options, including forgoing treatment."[124] Yet 8.5 percent of Americans (27.5 million) were uninsured in 2018[125] and 29 percent were underinsured,[126] and "about 20% of Americans have substantial medical debt."[127] In the United States, "medical bills account for a majority of unpaid debts sent to collection, and many other studies confirm that illness [whether one's own or that of a family member] often inflicts financial suffering."[128]

Whereas informed consent, or a lack thereof, is governed by tort law, the doctor–patient and hospital–patient relationships are based on contract law. In these contracts, health care providers promise to provide treatment according to an appropriate standard of care, and patients promise to pay, whether directly or through third parties such as insurers.[129] Except in certain circumstances (e.g., emergencies governed by the 1986 EMTALA law), most Americans upon seeking medical care are prompted to complete a patient financial responsibility form. Although the specific language may differ from one practice or specialty to the next, many of these include statements such as, while "this practice will file your claim with your insurance carrier, the patient or responsible party [e.g., a parent or guardian] is ultimately responsible for the charges" (with accounts past due likely assessed late fees and turned over to a collection agency).[130] This form is typically one of several intake documents that are completed in the waiting room before a patient ever sees a clinician or receives a diagnosis or treatment plan. Such an approach makes little logical sense, however, whether under tort or contract law, and only serves the system of health care. Patients cannot reach a shared understanding about the (financial) risks or consequences of care while alone and undiagnosed in the waiting room, nor can one validly sign a contract without a "meeting of the minds" (where both parties agree to identical terms and conditions).[131] Patients end up conceding to an unknowable amount of consideration (the price paid as part of the contract), and one need only read the many recent articles about "surprise billing" to determine how risky this is.[132] For instance, a recent episode of John Oliver's *Last Week Tonight* features the story of Katie Porter, whose appendix burst in 2018 while she was campaigning for the U.S. House seat in California's 45th District. Risking her life, she "didn't call an ambulance because [she] knew it could cost a lot" and had her manager drive her not "to the closest hospital but to the in-network hospital" associated with her insurance; unfortunately, "the surgeon who helped save Porter's life was not [in network], and she got a bill for nearly three thousand dollars."[133] Arguably, someone who became a Congresswoman is in a better position to afford an unplanned medical bill compared to other Americans—most have less than $500 in liquid assets and a third of "families have no savings at all."[134]

Underemphasized in the U.S. health care system is the fact that the informed consent process requires not just discussing the risks of medical procedures but also the consequences: that is, not just what *could* happen but what *will*. These might include bodily changes (e.g., difficulty eating fatty foods following gallbladder removal or not being able to deliver births vaginally after one has had a vertical-incision C-section) or post-operative instructions (e.g., having to irrigate a wound or refrain from driving or lifting heavy weights for a certain period of time). Especially for Americans, a patient's share of the costs of medical care also is a consequence, but one not typically included in informed consent conversations. In part this is because doctors aren't trained to think of cost as related to consent (except, perhaps, for elective procedures) and in part because the U.S. health care system intentionally obscures prices as part of proprietary contractual negotiations between various providers and third-party payers and uses the higher payments of some patients to subsidize those of others. It is a complex system that, even with increasing calls for transparency, makes it impossible to tease out individual charges. In fact, in 2019, the Trump administration issued administrative rules mandating that hospitals post their master price lists, or "chargemasters," online[135] and that health plans "disclose price and cost-sharing information to participants, beneficiaries, and enrollees up front" so that "patients will have accurate estimates of any out-of-pocket costs they must pay to meet their plan's deductible, co-pay, or co-insurance requirements."[136] Unfortunately, the public posting of chargemasters has done little for patients, since they are merely "starting points" for stakeholder negotiations and both inapplicable to an individual's personal situation and incomprehensible for the average person to read;[137] likewise, a co-insurance rate may be meaningless when a patient has no idea what the total cost of a medical bill might be (e.g., complications and further treatment can arise) or when a medical procedure is necessary whether or not a patient can afford his or her share. Several hospitals and the American Hospital Association also immediately sued the Trump administration on the basis that "the requirement to disclose their private negotiations with insurers violates their First Amendment rights."[138] Similarly, while Congress has been making progress on surprise medical billing, no bills have yet been passed, and state laws "cannot fully protect [all] consumers" or for all services.[139]

In *Principles of Biomedical Ethics*, Beauchamp and Childress recognize (though more in relation to medical research) that people might be "constrained by a desperate situation" even if "not controlled by another's intentional manipulation," and thus the "conditions under which an influence is both controlling and morally unjustified . . . are often unclear in concrete situations."[140] Illness itself can be coercive, creating desperate circumstances for those afflicted and their families, and it can be morally deplorable, particularly if understood in relation to social determinants of health.[141] The veil obscuring the strategic action of such "promises to pay" lifts, however, if one examines U.S. health care at the systems level and the "intentional manipulation" by various stakeholders and forces (lobbyists, politicians, capitalist approaches, history). In a system that prioritizes fee-for-service, has allowed for-profit care, and provides universal access only via emergency rooms when illnesses are advanced and expensive (financially and otherwise), promises to pay are cruel and may "render even intentional and well-informed behavior nonautonomous."[142] Thus, like with abortion-related compelled speech laws, patient financial responsibility contracts undermine informed consent even before it begins.

REENVISIONING CONSENT: REALIZING *"ONESELF UNDER CONDITIONS OF COMMUNICATIVELY SHARED INTERSUBJECTIVITY"*[143]

Today, most health care practitioners, lawmakers, and patients should understand informed consent as something more than a checklist of components or a form to be signed, although in practice it often is still seen as difficult, costly, and/or nebulous. This ongoing discomfiture is rooted in the biomedical model in which many modern physicians have been trained and the strategic goals imposed by health care stakeholders, political ideology, and a complicated, inequitable, and expensive system. Though forty years past due, framing informed consent in Habermasian terms would be a clear step to making the concept more understandable and realizable (and might begin to influence other aspects of the system). Although not every consent conversation requires a fully communicative approach (a point to which Habermas would concede),[144] the only way to determine what is a "significant risk" for a particular patient at a given time and to "facilitate coordination" and autonomous decision-making is to engage in an ongoing, two-way interaction where both parties are equal participants and can raise and question validity claims. The excerpt from *House M.D.* at the beginning of this chapter provides an example. Although Dr. Foreman's quote is part of a fictional narrative, it showcases a clinician's poor attempt to discuss a proposed treatment with his underage patient and the patient's parents. Foreman assumes (perhaps rightfully) that the parents' medical knowledge is too lacking in comparison to his, but he also provides no reasons—empirical or expressive—as to why they should trust him. He uses medical jargon to explain "that the problem is this mutated virus" and the treatment "is intraventricular interferon. We implant an Ommaya reservoir under the scalp, which is connected to a ventricular catheter that delivers the antiviral directly to the left hemisphere." It is thus no wonder that the father responds, "You want us to consent to this? I don't even understand what you're talking about."[145] There is no shared understanding or a further effort at such, despite the fact that the father, in saying he doesn't understand, is requesting that Dr. Foreman make explicit the implicit guarantees of his claims. Foreman, on the other hand, thinks that in advocating for his patient he need not understand the boy or the parents, nor they him. All that matters is the strategic aim of a cure. The episode immediately cuts to the operating room where the procedure takes place, and the parents are hardly seen again in the remaining scenes. Viewers are left to presume that the end result equates with a doctor's truthfulness, righteousness, and sincerity—that, even if the interpersonal interactions were dismissive and dehumanizing, the medical encounter was a success. The episode ends as it began, with the teenager playing lacrosse on an outdoor field far from the hospital and no longer a patient. This change in the character's clothing and the scenery also reinforces the idea that the biomedical world is a distinct foreign territory with its own "entrance and exit formalities ... visas ... different languages and etiquettes ... guards and functionaries and hucksters at the border crossing points," where the lives and understandings of doctor and patient seem never to overlap.[146] In a strategic model of informed consent, that is the case.

House M.D., however, also illustrates a more communicative approach. While Foreman's boss, Dr. Gregory House, is characterized throughout the show as an intellectually brilliant but emotionally stunted (and physically disabled) medical professional who "never talks to patients," he actually is repeatedly depicted as engaging in communicative-like interactions. For example, toward the end of the pilot, House has an in-depth conversation with his patient, Rebecca Adler, a kindergarten teacher who has tired of House and his team's experimenting with different but ineffectual treatments for her mysterious and worsening illness. Despite House telling her that he has finally solved the riddle of her disease ("a tapeworm in [her] brain"), she refuses any additional care and states that she just wants to be left "to die with a little dignity."[147] Unlike Foreman, who resorts to an outdated paternalistic style with the teenager's parents, House and Rebecca participate in an authentic, two-way discourse, *sans* medical jargon, not just about the diagnosis and recommended treatment but also in relation to how Rebecca feels about the medical team's prior failed attempts, what caused the injury to House's leg, how he deals with his chronic pain, whether this colors his view of his patients, and the nature of life and death. The conversation travels to all things "human" and is not conducted solely in the language and culture of biomedicine, where Rebecca is recognizable only as a stranded foreigner in need. While House and Rebecca are certainly not equals in navigating medical experience, they are equals in the communicative interaction. When Rebecca demands proof (i.e., a defensible validity claim) that House's latest diagnosis is indeed correct, House abides and finds a noninvasive means of providing compelling evidence: using a "regular, old, no-contrast, hundred-year-old-technology X-ray" on which tapeworms will "light up like shotgun pellets." He explains how he will "X-ray her leg" because "[w]orms love thigh muscle," and if "she's got one in her head . . . there's one in her leg."[148] The episode (and Rebecca's illness) ends after doctor and patient reach a shared understanding of the diagnosis and Rebecca "realize[s] [*herself*] under conditions of *communicatively shared intersubjectivity*"[149] and gladly and autonomously consents to treatment, side effects and all. As she is recovering in her hospital room, Rebecca's kindergarten students visit her, and they climb onto the bed—collapsing these various worlds—so she can hug and kiss them. They give her a card that reads, "We're happy you're not dead, Miss Rebecca," and thanks to the prior communicative engagement, there is evidence that House sincerely thinks so, too.[150] Rebecca is healed, not merely cured.

This interaction in *House M.D.* also highlights what most informed consent training in health care and Beauchamp and Childress' *Principles* do not: it is not just clinicians who must learn new approaches or medical culture that must change. Informed consent is not unidirectional, and it is not (as the *Cobbs* court half-correctly notes) a medical judgment reserved either to the practitioner or patient alone. It is an intersubjective process within the medical relationship in which both practitioner and patient must engage. In fact, as philosopher Erik Nordenhaug suggests, patients likely should come to the medical encounter with a Habermasian intent of realizing "*oneself* under conditions of *communicatively shared intersubjectivity*"—like Rebecca, to say no to and question whatever providers propose, not in an inflexible, knee-jerk way but as a means of creating an opening and space for genuine dialogue and a communicative exchange.[151] Rebecca asks for evidence that House's diagnosis and treatment plan have merit and that he is her advocate, whereas

Foreman's patient and his parents are given the message that it is unreasonable for them to question their doctor's medical conclusions or authenticity. If the latter held true, then patient autonomy and a clinician's fiduciary duty would mean little in health care. "To paraphrase Hegel, there is often more freedom in the no than in the yes," something to which Habermas likely would agree.[152]

Such a cultural shift may seem daunting and thus unlikely, and there may be sufficient remnants in the biomedical system that would resist this change as too time-consuming or corrosive to professional authority. Less likely, however, is the idea that medical educators and practicing clinicians, much like the Belmont commission, would sustain unprompted interest in incorporating more philosophy (and Habermas in particular) into health care training. A surge of inquisitive patients and new social norms are perhaps what is needed (and may be possible; individual autonomy, after all, has fostered and developed alongside informed consent, and many patients already bring questions to a clinical encounter). Once the horse has gained momentum, the Habermasian cart might follow, with the profession calling for better foundations that make sense of and navigate this new territory where providers may now seem more the foreigner.

Whether one watches *House M.D.* or reads Beauchamp and Childress' *Principles*, it becomes clear that in the medical encounter (and elsewhere) we have the capacity as well as a desire to engage in communicative action. By reimagining the concept of reason, Habermas has provided the means to release the Enlightenment's key idea from modern society's increasing hyper-rationalization and emphasis on "teleological efficiency." For while this goal-oriented rationalism has helped to create great wealth and technological innovation in the twentieth and twenty-first centuries, such progress has been a mixed blessing (and one need only reflect on two world wars, looming environmental dystopia, or the unintended consequences of social media as examples). Along for the "retreat [from the] 'dogmatism' and 'superstition'" more associated with the Middle Ages have been "fragmentation, discontinuity and loss of meaning" as well as "anomie and alienation, unstable identities and existential insecurities."[153] Ironically, "the rationalization of administration," the move toward positivism, and the unhitching of the irrational appetites and spirit from Plato's tripartite chariot have "all too often meant the end of freedom and self-determination"[154] and the reemergence of the very dogmatism and superstition we long thought we had escaped.[155] In relation to reason and consent, Habermas offers new paths for old ideas and the key to breaking free from bureaucracy's "steel-hard casing." The concept of informed consent already has in it the seeds of communicative action; they just have yet to be explicitly cultivated and allowed to grow.

NOTES

1. Jürgen Habermas, *Philosophical Introductions: Five Approaches to Communicative Reason*, trans. Ciaran Cronin (Cambridge, UK and Medford, MA: Polity Press, 2018), 80–82, emphasis original.

2. Ibid., 64, emphasis original.

3. *House M.D.*, season 1, episode 2, "Paternity," directed by Peter O'Fallon, written by Lawrence Kaplow, aired November 23, 2004, on Fox Broadcasting.

4. This may not be how informed consent is taught, in medical school or beyond, but the rigors of medical training and the demanding delivery of medical care leave little time for the study of bioethics and philosophy, which continue to be relegated in the modern system as secondary concerns. See, e.g., Govind C. Persad, Linden Elder, Laura Sedig, Leonardo Flores, and Ezekiel J. Emanuel, "The Current State of Medical School Education in Bioethics, Health Law, and Health Economics," *Journal of Law, Medicine & Ethics* 36, no. 1 (Spring 2008): 89–94. While most medical students must complete coursework in bioethics (with some even pursuing master's degrees) and the required number of hours may be increasing, clinicians often still express lack of knowledge or comfort regarding the practice of informed consent. Additionally, regardless of training, the very fact that there is paperwork associated with this communicative act may predispose practitioners, patients, institutions, and culture to misinterpret consent primarily as a strategic, legal event, rather than one whose goal is simply to reach a shared understanding within the medical relationship. Erik Nordenhaug, personal communication, June 13, 2020.

5. Habermas, *Philosophical Introductions*, 88.

6. See Henry K. Beecher, "Ethics and Clinical Research," *The New England Journal of Medicine* 274, no. 24 (June 16, 1966): 1354–60; Maurice H. Pappworth, "Human Guinea Pigs: A Warning," *Twentieth Century* 171 (Autumn 1962): 66–75; and Maurice H. Pappworth, *Human Guinea Pigs: Experimentation on Man* (London: Routledge, 1967).

7. Jean Heller, "Syphilis Victims in U.S. Study Went Untreated for 40 Years," *The New York Times*, July 26, 1972, 1, 8.

8. The National Commission for the Protection of Human Subjects of Biomedical and Behavioral Research, *The Belmont Report: Ethical Principles and Guidelines for the Protection of Human Subjects of Research* (DHEW Publication No. [OS] 78-0012, Washington, DC: United States Government Printing Office, 1978).

9. Beauchamp cited in Bernard A. Schwetz, "Tom Beauchamp: Oral History of the Belmont Report and the National Commission for the Protection of Human Subjects of Biomedical and Behavioral Research," *Office for Human Research Protections*, September 22, 2004, ¶22, https://www.hhs.gov/ohrp/education-and-outreach/luminaries-lecture-series/belmont-report-25th-anniversary-interview-tbeacham/index.html.

10. Ibid., ¶23, ¶166–67.

11. Ibid., ¶168–70.

12. Tom L. Beauchamp and James F. Childress, *Principles of Biomedical Ethics* (New York, NY: Oxford University Press, 1979).

13. Habermas' two-volume treatise takes to task modernity's bastardization of the Enlightenment concept of "reason" and lays out a continuum of sociolinguistic interaction delimited by the poles of "communicative action"—the rationally motivated shared understanding that true informed consent (unknowingly) highlights—and "strategic action," which is instrumental and oriented solely to participants' own individual goals and success. Volume one is subtitled *Reason and the Rationalization of Society*, volume two *Lifeworld and System: A Critique of Functionalist Reason*. Jürgen Habermas, *The Theory of Communicative Action*, trans. Thomas McCarthy (Boston, MA: Beacon Press, 1984).

14. Beauchamp and Childress, *Principles of Biomedical Ethics*.

15. *Pratt v. Davis*, 224 Ill. 300 (1906). See also Paul A. Lombardo, "Phantom Tumors and Hysterical Women: Revising Our View of the *Schloendorff* Case," *The Journal of Law, Medicine & Ethics* 33, no. 4 (Winter 2005): 791–801, doi:10.1111/j.1748-720X.2005.tb00545.x.

16. *Pratt v. Davis*, 304.

17. Cited in Ibid., 305.

18. Lombardo, "Phantom Tumors and Hysterical Women," 798. It is evident from the legal record that Dr. Pratt was both unclear and deceptive in his communication across the course of the two treatments. In a brief, Mrs. Davis stated that "consent was given for the first operation" and that she "erroneously believed" her ovaries had been removed then; by Dr. Pratt's own testimony, however, he intentionally misled her about what was to occur. Neither Mrs. Pratt nor her husband consented to the second operation, when the removal of both ovaries and uterus took place. *Pratt v. Davis*, 308.

19. Dr. Pratt cited in *Pratt v. Davis*, 305 and 309.

20. Cited in Ruth R. Faden and Tom L. Beauchamp, *A History and Theory of Informed Consent* (New York, NY: Oxford University Press, 1986), 122.

21. Habermas, *The Theory of Communicative Action*, vol. 1, 86.

22. Habermas, *Philosophical Introductions*, 88.

23. Dustin B. Garlitz and Hans-Herbert Kögler, "Frankfurt School: Institute for Social Research," in *International Encyclopedia of the Social & Behavioral Sciences*, 2nd edition, ed. James D. Wright (Amsterdam: Elsevier, 2015), 380–86, 383.

24. Habermas, *Philosophical Introductions*, 66, emphasis original.

25. Jürgen Habermas, *On the Pragmatics of Communication*, ed. Maeve Cooke (Cambridge, MA: The MIT Press, 2000), 232–33, emphasis original.

26. Habermas, *Philosophical Introductions*, 68.

27. Max Cherem, "Jürgen Habermas (1929—)," *Internet Encyclopedia of Philosophy*, Last modified no date, https://www.iep.utm.edu/habermas/.

28. Mary E. Fissell, "The Disappearance of the Patient's Narrative and the Invention of Hospital Medicine," in *British Medicine in an Age of Reform*, eds. Roger French and Andrew Wear (New York, NY: Routledge, 1991), 92–109.

29. Habermas, *Philosophical Introductions*, 88.

30. Ibid.

31. Michel Foucault, *The Birth of the Clinic: An Archaeology of Medical Perception*, trans. A. M. Sheridan Smith (New York, NY: Vintage Books, 1994). See also Leigh E. Rich, Jack Simmons, David Adams, Scott Thorp, and Michael Mink, "The Afterbirth of the Clinic: A Foucauldian Perspective on *House M.D.* and American Medicine in the 21st Century," *Perspectives in Biology and Medicine* 51, no. 2 (Spring 2008): 220–37, doi:10.1353/pbm.0.0007.

32. Habermas, *Philosophical Introductions*, 162, emphasis original.

33. Ibid., 73.

34. Cherem, "Jürgen Habermas," ¶7 under "3. The Linguistic Turn into the Theory of Communicative Action."

35. Ibid., ¶6 under "3. The Linguistic Turn into the Theory of Communicative Action," emphasis original.

36. *Pratt v. Davis*, 306.

37. Ibid.

38. American Medical Association, *Code of Ethics of the American Medical Association* (Philadelphia, PA: T. K. and P. G. Collins, 1854), 3–5, https://collections.nlm.nih.gov/ext/mhl/63310430R/PDF/63310430R.pdf. See also Frank A. Riddick, Jr., "The Code of Medical Ethics of the American Medical Association," *The Ochsner Journal* 5, no. 2 (Spring 2003): 6–10. The original AMA *Code*, which did not undergo significant revisions until the turn of the twentieth century, highlights how the speech of a doctor can affect the health of a patient. This continues to be a prevailing idea today, although in an inverse manner—that truth-telling is a physician's duty in lieu of a paternalistic deportment that "unite[s] *tenderness* with *firmness*, and *condescension* with *authority*," 3, emphasis original. As the 1847 *Code* explains on page 5:

> For, the physician should be the minister of hope and comfort to the sick; that, by such cordials to the drooping spirit, he may smooth the bed of death, revive expiring life, and counteract the depressing influence of those maladies which often disturb the tranquillity of the most resigned, in their last moments. The life of a sick person can be shortened not only by the acts, but also by the words or the manner of a physician. It is, therefore, a sacred duty to guard himself carefully in this respect, and to avoid all things which have a tendency to discourage the patient and to depress his spirits.

39. American Medical Association, *Code of Ethics*, 4–5.

40. Janet L. Dolgin, "The Legal Development of the Informed Consent Doctrine: Past and Present," *Cambridge Quarterly of Healthcare Ethics* 19, no. 1 (Winter 2010): 97–109, 97.

41. Translation of the Hippocratic Oath cited in Dolgin, "The Legal Development of the Informed Consent Doctrine," 97.

42. Hippocrates, "The Oath," trans. Francis Adams, *The Internet Classics Archive*, Last modified 1994–2009, http://classics.mit.edu/Hippocrates/hippooath.html.

43. Diana P. Faber, "Jean-Martin Charcot and the Epilepsy/Hysteria Relationship," *Journal of the History of the Neurosciences* 6, no. 3 (December 1997): 275–90, 281 and 283.

44. Ibid., 284.

45. J. M. S. Pearce, "Bromide, the First Effective Antiepileptic Agent," *Journal of Neurology, Neurosurgery & Psychiatry* 72, no. 3 (March 2002): 412. See also Robert A. Gross, "A Brief History of Epilepsy and Its Therapy in the Western Hemisphere," *Epilepsy Research* 12, no. 2 (July 1992): 65–74; and David Noonan, "The Epilepsy Dilemma," *Scientific American* 316, no. 4 (March 2017): 28–29, doi:10.1038/scientificamerican0417-28.

46. *Pratt v. Davis*, 304.

47. Ibid., 305.

48. Ibid., 309–10.

49. P. Dalla-Vorgia, J. Lascaratos, P. Skiadas, and T. Garanis-Papadatos, "Is Consent in Medicine a Concept Only of Modern Times?" *Journal of Medical Ethics* 27, no. 1 (February 2001): 59–61, 59.

50. Ibid., 59.

51. Alexander Morgan Capron, "Where Did Informed Consent for Research Come From?" *The Journal of Law, Medicine & Ethics* 46, no. 1 (March 2018): 12–29.

52. Fissell, "The Disappearance of the Patient's Narrative," 92.

53. Cited in Morgan, "Where Did Informed Consent for Research Come From?" 16. The U.S. Supreme Court in *Union Pacific Railway Company v. Botsford*, 141 U.S. 250 (1891), reached a similar conclusion after the railroad, being sued for negligence, demanded a surgical examination of the plaintiff to determine the extent of the injuries she sustained while a passenger. Though different in circumstance than patients' rights within the medical encounter, the Supreme Court (perhaps echoing the Fourth Amendment) recognized (at 251) that:

> No right is held more sacred, or is more carefully guarded, by the common law, than the right of every individual to the possession and control of his own person, free from restraint or interference of others, unless by clear or unquestionable authority of law. As well said by Judge Cooley, "The right to one's person may be said to be a right of complete immunity: to be let alone."

54. *Mohr v. Williams*, 95 Minn. 261 (1905), 269.

55. *Schloendorff v. The Society of the New York Hospital*, 211 N.Y. 125 (1914), 129–30.

56. Ibid., 133.

57. Ibid. See also Lombardo, "Phantom Tumors and Hysterical Women," and Dolgin, "The Legal Development of the Informed Consent Doctrine."

58. *Schloendorff v. The Society of the New York Hospital*, 129.

59. *Salgo v. Leland Stanford Jr. University Board of Trustees*, 154 Cal.App.2d 560 (1957), 568, 570, and 578.

60. Ibid., 578.

61. Ibid.

62. Ibid.

63. *Canterbury v. Spence*, 464 F.2d 772 (D.C. Cir. 1972), 780, emphasis added.

64. *Cobbs v. Grant*, 8 Cal. 3d 229 (1972), 243, emphasis added.

65. For example: "When there is a common procedure a doctor must, of course, make such inquiries as are required to determine if for the particular patient the treatment under consideration is contraindicated." Here, the court means medical, rather

than personal, contraindications, but there is an intimation that a health care provider should attend to how a specific therapy fits into an individual patient's lifeworld. Moreover, it should be noted that the phrasing used above to describe the "reasonable patient" standard may overemphasize the responsibility as solely on the shoulders of the clinician and, thus, some level of paternalism. In part, this is because the legal question in such cases is framed as what providers should reasonably be expected to disclose in order for patients to make informed, autonomous decisions, rather than the role that patients play during consent conversations. (After all, it is the physician's behavior, or lack thereof, on trial.) However, the *Cobbs* court limits physicians' prior "[u]nlimited discretion" and underscores that "the test for determining whether a potential peril must be divulged is its materiality to the patient's decision." It also offers some description on how clinicians should (and should not) approach informed consent discussions. On the other hand, whether the *Cobbs* court is calling for a full-blown communicative approach may be going too far. *Cobbs v. Grant*, 243–44.

66. *Salgo v. Stanford Board of Trustees*, 578.
67. *Canterbury v. Spence*, 783.
68. Ibid., 780–83, emphasis added.
69. At this time, the individual was becoming ever more pertinent to the medical encounter, despite the fact that medical knowledge was growing increasingly professionalized, scientific, and technocratic and physicians hailed less and less from the same communities and cultural backgrounds as their patients (thus widening the socioeconomic gap). In the midst of civil rights and the rise of bioethics as its own discipline, longstanding paternalism in medicine began to be traded for a new patient autonomy. David J. Rothman, *Strangers at the Bedside: A History of How Law and Bioethics Transformed Medical Decision Making*, 2nd edition (New Brunswick and London: Aldine Transaction, 2003). See also *In re Quinlan*, 70 N.J. 10, 355 A.2d 647 (1976), in which the New Jersey Supreme Court recognized that life-sustaining care could be withdrawn from a patient in a persistent vegetative state. This case was a shift in law and bioethics with regard to treatment refusal or removal.
70. Beauchamp and Childress, *Principles of Biomedical Ethics*, 80.
71. Ibid., 79, emphasis original.
72. Ibid., 78, emphasis original.
73. Ibid., 81. Without the aid of a Habermasian framework, this list and the idea that the provider should make a recommendation trend toward the strategic and against what informed consent should be. In informed consent conversations, any claim made by the clinician (and the patient) should be criticizable, and the recommended path should emerge from the "compulsionless compulsion" of the better argument.
74. Ibid., citing the Supreme Court of California's decision in the case of *Moore v. Regents of the University of California*, 793 P.2d 479 (Cal. 1990) at 483. That said, even if a provider clearly verbalizes, "I am recommending a course of action that will result in greater financial benefit to myself," the consent conversation still seems partially strategic. More needs to be added to Beauchamp and Childress' discussion: for example, that by stating one's conflict of interest, the provider is making an expressive claim about his or her sincerity and perhaps even a regulative claim

about what is socially appropriate, both of which can be challenged communicatively. As Habermas notes, however, the two poles of strategic and communicative action are not "either/or" but, rather, sit on a continuum. Is the "communicative" type of communication ever completely separable from the "strategic," in so far as a speaker arguably always wants something from a listener, even if just attention to the goal of shared understanding? It is important to underscore that these are not binary distinctions but concepts that exist on a spectrum. Nordenhaug, personal communication, June 13, 2020.

75. Beauchamp and Childress, *Principles of Biomedical Ethics*, 82.
76. Ibid., 88.
77. Ibid., 83, emphasis original.
78. Ibid. This, again, has hints of paternalism and an objectifying medical gaze, as if informed consent is a one-way communication where the physician—in an attempt to "safeguard" autonomous decision-making—must investigate the patient as an object to be deciphered. Beauchamp and Childress' perspective may be partially explained by the fact that *Principles of Biomedical Ethics* is directed toward health care providers and not patients. If they had woven a discussion of Habermas into later editions, such implicit biases that informed consent is supposed to combat might be more readily exposed.
79. For example, what if this caution were applied to sexual relations—that a sexual partner could not "reasonably be expected to" understand one's "background and character" as part of the consent process? This seems flimsy in this situation, let alone for a health care professional who might literally hold a patient's life in his or her hands. Jack Simmons, personal communication, February 26, 2020.
80. Habermas, *Philosophical Introductions*, 73.
81. Beauchamp and Childress, *Principles of Biomedical Ethics*, 78.
82. See supra *Salgo v. Stanford Board of Trustees*, 578.
83. Beauchamp and Childress, *Principles of Biomedical Ethics*, 89.
84. Ibid., 80.
85. See, e.g., *Superintendent of Belchertown State School v. Saikewicz*, 373 Mass. 728 (1977). While the court recognized (at 750–51) "the value" of a "reasonable person" inquiry, it noted that "we should make it plain that the primary test is subjective in nature—that is, the goal is to determine with as much accuracy as possible the wants and needs of the individual involved. This may or may not conform to what is thought wise or prudent by most people."
86. Beauchamp and Childress, *Principles of Biomedical Ethics*, 90–91.
87. Ibid., 92.
88. Ibid., 95, emphasis original.
89. Jack R. Simmons, *Habermas' Discourse Ethics: The Attitude Between Modernity and Post Modernity* (PhD diss., Tulane University, 1997), ProQuest Dissertations and Theses.
90. Sarah R. Vossoughi, Robert Macauley, Kathleen Sazama, and Mark K. Fung, "Attitudes, Practices, and Training on Informed Consent for Transfusions and Procedures: A Survey of Medical Students and Physicians," *American Journal of Clinical Pathology* 144, no. 2 (August 2015): 315–21, 317. Additionally, 6 percent of

survey respondents stated that they could not recall whether they had ever received training in informed consent.

91. Ibid., 318.

92. Britta M. Thompson, Rhonda A. Sparks, Jonathan Seavey, Michelle D. Wallace, Jeremy Irvan, Alexander R. Raines, Heather McClure, Mikio A. Nihira, and Jason S. Lees, "Informed Consent Training Improves Surgery Resident Performance in Simulated Encounters With Standardized Patients," *The American Journal of Surgery* 210, no. 3 (September 2015): 578–84, 578.

93. Ibid., 581. In devising the training intervention, they also noted (at 579) that they could find "no existing informed consent cases or checklists" in the literature. With the former, it seems they mean that they could not locate any preexisting scenarios related to the two procedures they selected for their training, laparoscopic cholecystectomy and ventral herniorrhaphy (as many real and educational cases involving surgery and informed consent abound). The latter, however, might suggest that—while checklists can be useful as prompts and reminders in everything from flying planes to performing surgery—such is the antithesis of informed consent.

94. Vossoughi et al., "Attitudes, Practices, and Training on Informed Consent," 318.

95. Thompson et al., "Informed Consent Training Improves Surgical Resident Performance," 579. The researchers also explain that the "didactic training with targeted discussion covered basic tenants of malpractice with emphasis on informed consent."

96. It is not that documentation—for the purposes of the system and to collect data that can inform informed consent discussions—is not important. A UK surgical study, for example, noted that the "process of completing a written consent form was documented in the chronological medical notes in 38% of cases. Complication incidence rates were rarely documented across all operations." Dafydd Loughran, "Surgical Consent: The World's Largest Chinese Whisper? A Review of Current Surgical Consent Practices," *Journal of Medical Ethics* 41, no. 2 (February 2015): 206–10, 207. However, focusing more on what clinicians do after, rather than *during*, conversations with patients fails to attend to the most important and intersubjective aspects of informed consent.

97. Daniel E. Hall, Allan V. Prochazka, and Aaron S. Fink, "Informed Consent for Clinical Treatment," *Canadian Medical Association Journal* 184, no. 5 (March 2012): 533–40, 536.

98. Katie Propst, David M. O'Sullivan, Amanda Ulrich, and Elena Tunitsky-Bitton, "Informed Consent Education in Obstetrics and Gynecology: A Survey Study," *Journal of Surgical Education* 76, no. 4 (August 2019): 1146–52, 1151.

99. Fiona Wood, Sean Michael Martin, Andrew Carson-Stevens, Glyn Elwyn, Elizabeth Precious, and Paul Kinnersley, "Doctors' Perspectives of Informed Consent for Non-Emergency Surgical Procedures: A Qualitative Interview Study," *Health Expectations* 19, no. 3 (June 2016): 751–61, 756.

100. Ibid., 756.

101. Loughran, "Surgical Consent," 206.

102. For example, H. Fukuda, Y. Imanaka, H. Kobuse, K. Hayashida, and G. Murakami, "The Subjective Incremental Cost of Informed Consent and Documentation in Hospital Care: A Multicentre Questionnaire Survey in Japan," *Journal of Evaluation in Clinical Practice* 15, no. 2 (April 2009): 234–41. This study found that not only does informed consent requires clinicians' time but also that there is an increase in economic costs for hospitals.

103. Wood et al., "Doctors' Perspectives of Informed Consent," 751. A majority of participants in the study by Vossoughi et al., "Attitudes, Practices, and Training on Informed Consent," 318–19, "reported spending less than 5 minutes" on consent discussions for nonemergent transfusions and bedside procedures, with only 3 percent spending more than a half hour on those designated as "OR high risk >1 h."

104. Hall et al., "Informed Consent for Clinical Treatment," 533–34; Vossoughi et al., "Attitudes, Practices, and Training on Informed Consent," 316 (footnotes removed), also note that "informed consent should refer to an individualized and ongoing conversation between physician and patient—with the written document merely an attestation that this has taken place."

105. Loughran, "Surgical Consent," 208, emphasis added.

106. Wood et al., "Doctors' Perspectives of Informed Consent," 757, emphasis added.

107. Loughran, "Surgical Consent," 208.

108. Wood et al., "Doctors' Perspectives of Informed Consent," 758.

109. Ibid., 752.

110. *Roe v. Wade*, 410 U.S. 113 (1973).

111. *Planned Parenthood of Southeastern Pennsylvania v. Casey*, 505 U.S. 833 (1992), 877.

112. Sarah Kramer, "Not Your Mouthpiece: Abortion, Ideology, and Compelled Speech in Physician-Patient Relationships," *University of Pennsylvania Journal of Law and Social Change* 21, no. 1 (March 2018): 1–27, 3–4. See also S.D. Codified Laws § 34-23A-10.1(1)(e)(i)–(ii).

113. See, e.g., S.D. Codified Laws § 34-23A-10.1(1)(h) as well as a similar "reversal" law in North Dakota recently blocked by a federal court as violative of a physician's free speech, John Hageman, "Judge Blocks New North Dakota Abortion Law, Finds It Violates Physicians' Constitutional Protections Against 'Compelled Speech'," *Grand Forks Herald*, September 10, 2019, https://www.grandforksherald.com/news/government-and-politics/4654204-Judge-blocks-new-North-Dakota-abortion-law-finds-it-violates-physicians-constitutional-protections-against-compelled-speech.

114. David Orentlicher, "Abortion and Compelled Physician Speech," *The Journal of Law, Medicine & Ethics* 43, no. 1 (Spring 2015): 9–21, 13. For example, S.D. Codified Laws § 34-23A-10.1(1)(b) states that physicians must provide pregnant women with a written statement "[t]hat the abortion will terminate the life of a whole, separate, unique, living human being."

115. See Orentlicher's discussion of breast cancer treatment in the 1970s and 1980s, directed "required request" for organ donation beginning in the 1980s, and the risks of electroconvulsive therapy that are still being debated today.

116. Orentlicher, "Abortion and Compelled Physician Speech," 10.
117. Ibid., 13.
118. Cited in Orentlicher, "Abortion and Compelled Physician Speech," 10, emphasis added.
119. Again, it could be argued that even compelled speech that is truthful and relevant—such as laws that required doctors of breast cancer patients to discuss lumpectomies with radiation as an alternative to radical mastectomies—can become strategic. As Jacques Ellul notes in his *Propaganda: The Formation of Men's Attitudes*, trans. Konrad Kellen and Jean Lerner (New York, NY: Alfred A. Knopf, 1965), truth conveyed by propaganda is a lie. Thus, "it is not just information 'manipulation' but information mediums themselves that are incompatible with autonomous decision-making." Nordenhaug, personal communication, June 13, 2020. Fifty years ago, as Orentlicher, "Abortion and Compelled Physician Speech," explains, such a law was needed to compensate for clinicians failing to properly engage in informed consent, as surgeons tended to recommend—even for patients with small and localized tumors—removing the whole breast and thus causing greater harm than necessary. The state also has a duty to protect the ethical integrity of the medical profession as well as rectify medical standards when they are inadequate as a matter of law. J. Stuart Showalter, *The Law of Healthcare Administration*, 8th edition (Chicago, IL: Health Administration Press, 2017). In such circumstances, strategically compelling physicians what to include in informed consent conversations serves these purposes but likely should be done carefully and sparingly, as doing so may undermine, rather than promote, communicative action.
120. Ironically, according to a recent U.S. Supreme Court case, compelling the speech of crisis pregnancy centers (CPCs) that intentionally deceive women about their aims and what reproductive services they offer seems to be a bridge too far. In *National Institute of Family & Life Advocates v. Becerra*, the Court overturned a California law that required CPCs to post notices that they are not licensed medical facilities and that elsewhere in the state women have access to "free and low-cost family planning services, prenatal care, and abortion." The Court deemed the law an infringement on CPCs' rights to free speech and freedom of religion and suggested that California could instead sponsor a mass media campaign, even though the state provided legislative factfinding data "that public information campaigns had proven to be insufficient" and that many CPCs "employ 'intentionally deceptive advertising and counseling practices [that] often confuse, misinform, and even intimidate women from making fully-formed, time-sensitive decisions about critical health care'." Harvard Law Review, "Leading Case: *National Institute of Family & Life Advocates v. Becerra*, 138 S. Ct. 2361 (2018)," *Harvard Law Review* 132, no. 1 (November 2018): 347–56, 347, 354, and 356.
121. Beauchamp and Childress, *Principles of Biomedical Ethics*, 95.
122. Pa.C.S.A. Title 18 Chap. 32 § 3205(a)(2)(i)–(iii). This is similar to S.D. Codified Laws § 34-23A-10.1(2)(a)–(c).
123. Recent studies by Sarah Miller and Diana Foster and colleagues indicate that women who are unable to access abortion are more likely to live in poverty and endure lasting economic insecurity. Sarah Miller, Laura R. Wherry, and Diana Greene Foster,

"The Economic Consequences of Being Denied an Abortion," *National Bureau of Economic Research, Working Paper No. 26662*, January 2020, 1–52, https://www.nber.org/papers/w26662.pdf. Diana Greene Foster, M. Antonia Biggs, Lauren Ralph, Caitlin Gerdts, Sarah Roberts, and M. Maria Glymour, "Socioeconomic Outcomes of Women Who Receive and Women Who Are Denied Wanted Abortions in the United States," *American Journal of Public Health* 108, no. 3 (March 2018): 407–13. However, the *Casey* Court did acknowledge that Pennsylvania's "spousal notification" requirement might harm women in several ways, including the possible "withdrawal of financial support" by a husband, and that just because a father is legally required to provide financial assistance this "often does not equate with fulfillment." *Planned Parenthood v. Casey*, 893, and in Justice Blackmun's concurrence and dissent at 936.

124. American Medical Association, *Informed Consent: Code of Medical Ethics Opinion 2.1.1*, 1995–2020, ¶5–7, https://www.ama-assn.org/delivering-care/ethics/informed-consent. See also Showalter, *The Law of Healthcare Administration*.

125. Edward R. Berchick, Jessica C. Barnett, and Rachel D. Upton, *Health Insurance Coverage in the United States: 2018* (Washington, DC: U.S. Government Printing Office, 2019), https://www.census.gov/content/dam/Census/library/publications/2019/demo/p60-267.pdf.

126. *The Commonwealth Fund*, "Underinsured Rate Rose From 2014–2018, With Greatest Growth Among People in Employer Health Plans," February 7, 2019, https://www.commonwealthfund.org/press-release/2019/underinsured-rate-rose-2014-2018-greatest-growth-among-people-employer-health.

127. Carlos Dobkin, Amy Finkelstein, Raymond Kluender, and Matthew J. Notowidigdo, "Myth and Measurement—The Case of Medical Bankruptcies," *The New England Journal of Medicine* 378, no. 12 (March 2018): 1076–78, 1076.

128. David U. Himmelstein, Steffie Woolhandler, and Elizabeth Warren, "Myth and Measurement—The Case of Medical Bankruptcies [Letter Response]," *The New England Journal of Medicine* 378, no. 23 (June 2018): 2245–46, 2246.

129. Showalter, *The Law of Healthcare Administration*.

130. Actual "Practice Financial Policy: Patient Responsibility" form the author was required to sign in January 2020 to continue to be seen by a health care provider.

131. Showalter, *The Law of Healthcare Administration*. See also Elizabeth Ann Glass Geltman, "Cost Needs to Be Part of the Medical Informed Consent Process," *HuffPost*, December 8, 2015, https://www.huffpost.com/entry/cost-needs-to-be-part-of-the-medical-informed-consent-process_b_8742926.

132. Hunter Kellett, Alexandra Spratt, and Mark E. Miller, "Surprise Billing: Choose Patients Over Profits," *Health Affairs*, August 12, 2019, https://www.healthaffairs.org/do/10.1377/hblog20190808.585050/full/.

133. *Last Week Tonight With John Oliver*, season 7, episode 1, "Medicare for All," aired February 16, 2020, on HBO.

134. Maggie McGrath, "63% of Americans Don't Have Enough Savings to Cover a $500 Emergency," *Forbes*, January 6, 2016, ¶4, https://www.forbes.com/sites/maggiemcgrath/2016/01/06/63-of-americans-dont-have-enough-savings-to-cover-a-500-emergency/#6721688c4e0d.

135. Elisabeth Rosenthal, "Donald Trump Did Something Right," *The New York Times*, January 21, 2019, https://www.nytimes.com/2019/01/21/opinion/trump-hospital-prices.html.

136. U.S. Department of Health and Human Services, *Trump Administration Announces Historic Price Transparency Requirements to Increase Competition and Lower Healthcare Costs for All Americans*, November 15, 2019, ¶5, https://www.hhs.gov/about/news/2019/11/15/trump-administration-announces-historic-price-transparency-and-lower-healthcare-costs-for-all-americans.html.

137. Nigel Chiwaya and Jeremia Kimelman, "You Can Now Get Your Hospital's Price List. Good Luck Making Sense of It," *NBC News*, January 15, 2019, https://www.nbcnews.com/news/us-news/hospital-price-list-chargemaster-rules-trump-mandate-2019-n959006. For an example of one hospital's chargemaster, see https://www.stjosephshealth.org/images/cdm.csv, which includes 47,609 line items.

138. Reed Abelson, "Hospitals Sue Trump to Keep Negotiated Prices Secret," *The New York Times*, December 4 and 5, 2019, ¶3, https://www.nytimes.com/2019/12/04/health/hospitals-trump-prices-transparency.html. In June 2020, a U.S. district judge ruled against the plaintiffs, who are now appealing the decision. Susan Morse, "American Hospital Association to Appeal Ruling on Price Transparency Lawsuit," *Healthcare Finance*, June 23, 2020, https://www.healthcarefinancenews.com/news/american-hospital-association-appeal-ruling-price-transparency-lawsuit. See also Erik Nordenhaug and Jack Simmons' discussion in "The Outsourcing of Ethical Thinking" in this volume on "the fallacious metaphor that corporations are 'artificial persons'" and, thus, philosophical problems with their "First Amendment rights" trumping individuals' health and welfare (financial and otherwise). Here, an individual's ability to form an informed judgment about the consequences of medical care has been eclipsed to safeguard the negotiations of artificial beings incapable of "distinguishing good and evil." It may be argued that, without such protections, the U.S. health care system would collapse; however, in this system, actual persons often collapse (and even die) due to lack of access to care and/or the means to pay charges unknowable upfront.

139. Jack Hoadley, Beth Fuchs, and Kevin Lucia, "Update on Federal Surprise Billing Legislation: Understanding a Flurry of New Proposals," *To the Point*, December 16, 2019, ¶1, https://www.commonwealthfund.org/blog/2019/update-federal-surprise-billing-legislation-understanding.

140. Beauchamp and Childress, *Principles of Biomedical Ethics*, 96.

141. For example, the fact that African Americans have higher morbidity rates from COVID-19, the disease caused by the novel coronavirus that emerged in late 2019 and became pandemic in 2020, is due to systemic racism in U.S. society and U.S. health care, not any underlying "biological" condition. It is not "race" but racism that is to blame. See, for example, Luke Denne, "In 'Cancer Alley,' a Renewed Focus on Systemic Racism Is Too Late," *NBC News*, June 21, 2020, https://www.nbcnews.com/science/science-news/cancer-alley-renewed-focus-systemic-racism-too-late-n1231602.

142. Beauchamp and Childress, *Principles of Biomedical Ethics*, 94. They advise (at 262) that one should have "unobstructed access to a decent minimum of health

care through some form of universal insurance coverage that operationalizes a right to health care" based on "a fair system of rationing."

143. Habermas, *The Theory of Communicative Action*, vol. 1, xxi, emphasis original.

144. For example, while (ethically and legally) consent is required before a clinician takes a patient's temperature or listens to a patient's heart or lungs via a stethoscope, an in-depth communicative dialogue likely is not needed in most circumstances to reach a shared understanding.

145. *House M.D.*, "Paternity."

146. Arthur Kleinman, *The Illness Narratives: Suffering, Healing, and the Human Condition* (New York, NY: Basic Books, 1988), 181.

147. *House M.D.*, season 1, episode 1, "Pilot," directed by Bryan Singer, written by David Shore, aired November 16, 2004, on Fox Broadcasting.

148. Ibid. Viewers actually see House explain this rationale to his team, not to Rebecca, but it follows his one-on-one conversation with her, and it was that communicative-esque dialogue that prompts House to find an acceptable way to defend his diagnostic claim. Depicting House and Rebecca in a second conversation likely would have undermined the dramatic effect of the first. Instead, viewers are left to assume that House or his subordinates shared this reasoning with Rebecca—the "'unforced force' of the better argument"—as she consents to the X-ray and to the treatment.

149. Habermas, *The Theory of Communicative Action*, vol. 1, xxi, emphasis original.

150. *House M.D.*, "Pilot."

151. Nordenhaug, personal communication, June 13, 2020.

152. Ibid.

153. Thomas McCarthy, "Translator's Introduction," in *The Theory of Communicative Action, Vol. 1: Reason and the Rationalization of Society*, Jürgen Habermas, trans. Thomas McCarthy (Boston, MA: Beacon Press, 1984), v–xxxvii, v.

154. Ibid., v.

155. The two decades of the twenty-first century in the United States alone have been marked by examples such as flimsy rationales for both going to war and declaring victory; vaccination misinformation and refusal; persistent racism, antisemitism, and Holocaust denial; legal and illegal interference with elections; and a president who is estimated to have told 20,000 falsehoods while in office and an unironic public that sees an authenticity in his lack of duplicitousness about his duplicity.

BIBLIOGRAPHY

Abelson, Reed. "Hospitals Sue Trump to Keep Negotiated Prices Secret." *The New York Times*, December 4 and 5, 2019. https://www.nytimes.com/2019/12/04/health/hospitals-trump-prices-transparency.html.

American Medical Association. *Code of Ethics of the American Medical Association*. Philadelphia, PA: T. K. and P. G. Collins, 1854. https://collections.nlm.nih.gov/ext/mhl/63310430R/PDF/63310430R.pdf.

American Medical Association. *Informed Consent: Code of Medical Ethics Opinion 2.1.1*. American Medical Association, 1995–2020. https://www.ama-assn.org/delivering-care/ethics/informed-consent.

Beauchamp, Tom L., and James F. Childress. *Principles of Biomedical Ethics*, 5th ed. New York, NY: Oxford University Press, 2001.

Beecher, Henry K. "Ethics and Clinical Research." *The New England Journal of Medicine* 274, no. 24 (June 16, 1966): 1354–1360.

Berchick, Edward R., Jessica C. Barnett, and Rachel D. Upton. *Health Insurance Coverage in the United States: 2018*. Washington, DC: U.S. Government Printing Office, 2019. https://www.census.gov/content/dam/Census/library/publications/2019/demo/p60-267.pdf.

Capron, Alexander Morgan. "Where Did Informed Consent for Research Come From?" *The Journal of Law, Medicine & Ethics* 46, no. 1 (March 2018): 12–29.

Cherem, Max. "Jürgen Habermas (1929—)." *Internet Encyclopedia of Philosophy*, no date. https://www.iep.utm.edu/habermas/.

Chiwaya, Nigel, and Jeremia Kimelman. "You Can Now Get Your Hospital's Price List. Good Luck Making Sense of It." *NBC News*, January 15, 2019. https://www.nbcnews.com/news/us-news/hospital-price-list-chargemaster-rules-trump-mandate-2019-n959006.

Dalla-Vorgia, P., J. Lascaratos, P. Skiadas, and T. Garanis-Papadatos. "Is Consent in Medicine a Concept Only of Modern Times?" *Journal of Medical Ethics* 27, no. 1 (February 2001): 59–61.

Denne, Luke. "In 'Cancer Alley,' a Renewed Focus on Systemic Racism Is Too Late." *NBC News*, June 21, 2020. https://www.nbcnews.com/science/science-news/cancer-alley-renewed-focus-systemic-racism-too-late-n1231602.

Dobkin, Carlos, Amy Finkelstein, Raymond Kluender, and Matthew J. Notowidigdo. "Myth and Measurement—The Case of Medical Bankruptcies." *The New England Journal of Medicine* 378, no. 12 (March 2018): 1076–1078.

Dolgin, Janet L. "The Legal Development of the Informed Consent Doctrine: Past and Present." *Cambridge Quarterly of Healthcare Ethics* 19, no. 1 (Winter 2010): 97–109.

Ellul, Jacque. *Propaganda: The Formation of Men's Attitudes*. Translated by Konrad Kellen and Jean Lerner. New York, NY: Alfred A. Knopf, 1965.

Faber, Diana P. "Jean-Martin Charcot and the Epilepsy/Hysteria Relationship." *Journal of the History of the Neurosciences* 6, no. 3 (December 1997): 275–290.

Faden, Ruth R., and Tom L. Beauchamp. *A History and Theory of Informed Consent*. New York, NY: Oxford University Press, 1986.

Fissell, Mary E. "The Disappearance of the Patient's Narrative and the Invention of Hospital Medicine." In *British Medicine in an Age of Reform*, edited by Roger French and Andrew Wear, 92–109. New York, NY: Routledge, 1991.

Foster, Diana Greene, M. Antonia Biggs, Lauren Ralph, Caitlin Gerdts, Sarah Roberts, and M. Maria Glymour. "Socioeconomic Outcomes of Women Who Receive and Women Who Are Denied Wanted Abortions in the United States." *American Journal of Public Health* 108, no. 3 (March 2018): 407–413.

Foucault, Michel. *The Birth of the Clinic: An Archaeology of Medical Perception*. Translated by A. M. Sheridan Smith. New York, NY: Vintage Books, 1994.

Fukuda, H., Y. Imanaka, H. Kobuse, K. Hayashida, and G. Murakami. "The Subjective Incremental Cost of Informed Consent and Documentation in Hospital Care: A Multicentre Questionnaire Survey in Japan." *Journal of Evaluation in Clinical Practice* 15, no. 2 (April 2009): 234–241.

Garlitz, Dustin B., and Hans-Herbert Kögler. "Frankfurt School: Institute for Social Research." In *International Encyclopedia of the Social & Behavioral Sciences*, 2nd ed., edited by James D. Wright, 380–386. Amsterdam: Elsevier, 2015.

Geltman, Elizabeth Ann Glass. "Cost Needs to Be Part of the Medical Informed Consent Process." *HuffPost*, December 8, 2015. https://www.huffpost.com/entry/cost-needs-to-be-part-of-the-medical-informed-consent-process_b_8742926.

Gross, Robert A. "A Brief History of Epilepsy and Its Therapy in the Western Hemisphere." *Epilepsy Research* 12, no. 2 (July 1992): 65–74.

Habermas, Jürgen. *On the Pragmatics of Communication*. Edited by Maeve Cooke. Cambridge, MA: The MIT Press, 2000.

Habermas, Jürgen. *Philosophical Introductions: Five Approaches to Communicative Reason*. Translated by Ciaran Cronin. Cambridge, UK and Medford, MA: Polity Press, 2018.

Habermas, Jürgen. *The Theory of Communicative Action, Vol. 1: Reason and the Rationalization of Society*. Translated by Thomas McCarthy. Boston, MA: Beacon Press, 1984.

Habermas, Jürgen. *The Theory of Communicative Action, Vol. 2: Lifeworld and System: A Critique of Functionalist Reason*. Translated by Thomas McCarthy. Boston, MA: Beacon Press, 1984.

Hageman, John. "Judge Blocks New North Dakota Abortion Law, Finds It Violates Physicians' Constitutional Protections Against 'Compelled Speech'." *Grand Forks Herald*, September 10, 2019. https://www.grandforksherald.com/news/government-and-politics/4654204-Judge-blocks-new-North-Dakota-abortion-law-finds-it-violates-physicians-constitutional-protections-against-compelled-speech.

Hall, Daniel E., Allan V. Prochazka, and Aaron S. Fink. "Informed Consent for Clinical Treatment." *Canadian Medical Association Journal* 184, no. 5 (March 2012): 533–540.

Harvard Law Review. "Leading Case: *National Institute of Family & Life Advocates v. Becerra*, 138 S. Ct. 2361 (2018)." *Harvard Law Review* 132, no. 1 (November 2018): 347–356.

Heller, Jean. "Syphilis Victims in U.S. Study Went Untreated for 40 Years." *The New York Times*, July 26, 1972: 1, 8.

Himmelstein, David U., Steffie Woolhandler, and Elizabeth Warren. "Myth and Measurement—The Case of Medical Bankruptcies, Letter Response." *The New England Journal of Medicine* 378, no. 23 (June 2018): 2245–2246.

Hippocrates. "The Oath." Translated by Francis Adams. *The Internet Classics Archive*, Last modified 1994–2009. http://classics.mit.edu/Hippocrates/hippooath.html.

Hoadley, Jack, Beth Fuchs, and Kevin Lucia. "Update on Federal Surprise Billing Legislation: Understanding a Flurry of New Proposals." *To the Point*, December 16, 2019. https://www.commonwealthfund.org/blog/2019/update-federal-surprise-billing-legislation-understanding.

Kaplow, Lawrence, Writer. *House M.D.* Season 1, episode 2, "Paternity." Directed by Peter O'Fallon, featuring Hugh Laurie, Omar Epps, Robert Sean Leonard, Jesse Spencer, Lisa Edelstein, and Jennifer Morrison. Aired November 23, 2004, on Fox. Universal Pictures Home Entertainment, 2012, DVD.

Kellett, Hunter, Alexandra Spratt, and Mark E. Miller. "Surprise Billing: Choose Patients Over Profits." *Health Affairs*, August 12, 2019. https://www.healthaffairs.org/do/10.1377/hblog20190808.585050/full/.

Kleinman, Arthur. *The Illness Narratives: Suffering, Healing, and the Human Condition*. New York, NY: Basic Books, 1988.

Kramer, Sarah. "Not Your Mouthpiece: Abortion, Ideology, and Compelled Speech in Physician-Patient Relationships." *University of Pennsylvania Journal of Law and Social Change* 21, no. 1 (March 2018): 1–27.

Lombardo, Paul A. "Phantom Tumors and Hysterical Women: Revising Our View of the *Schloendorff* Case." *The Journal of Law, Medicine & Ethics* 33, no. 4 (Winter 2005): 791–801.

Loughran, Dafydd. "Surgical Consent: The World's Largest Chinese Whisper? A Review of Current Surgical Consent Practices." *Journal of Medical Ethics* 41, no. 2 (February 2015): 206–210.

McCarthy, Thomas. Translator's Introduction to *The Theory of Communicative Action*, v–xxxvii. Boston, MA: Beacon Press, 1984.

McGrath, Maggie. "63% of Americans Don't Have Enough Savings to Cover a $500 Emergency." *Forbes*, January 6, 2016. https://www.forbes.com/sites/maggiemcgrath/2016/01/06/63-of-americans-dont-have-enough-savings-to-cover-a-500-emergency/#6721688c4e0d.

Miller, Sarah, Laura R. Wherry, and Diana Greene Foster. "The Economic Consequences of Being Denied an Abortion." *National Bureau of Economic Research, Working Paper No. 26662*, January 2020: 1–52. https://www.nber.org/papers/w26662.pdf.

Morse, Susan. "American Hospital Association to Appeal Ruling on Price Transparency Lawsuit." *Healthcare Finance*, June 23, 2020. https://www.healthcarefinancenews.com/news/american-hospital-association-appeal-ruling-price-transparency-lawsuit.

National Commission for the Protection of Human Subjects of Biomedical and Behavioral Research. *The Belmont Report: Ethical Principles and Guidelines for the Protection of Human Subjects of Research*. DHEW Publication No. (OS) 78-0012. Washington, DC: United States Government Printing Office, 1978.

Noonan, David. "The Epilepsy Dilemma." *Scientific American* 316, no. 4 (March 2017): 28–29. doi:10.1038/scientificamerican0417-28.

Nordenhaug, Erik, and Jack Simmons. "The Outsourcing of Ethical Thinking." In *The Twenty-First Century and Its Discontents: How Changing Discourse Norms Are Changing Culture*, edited by Jack Simmons, 15–37. Lanham, MD: Lexington Books, 2020.

O'Brien, Daniel, Charlie Redd, Ben Silva, and Seena Vali, Writers. *Last Week Tonight With John Oliver*. Season 7, episode 1, "Medicare for All." Directed by Paul Pennolino, featuring John Oliver. Aired February 16, 2020, on HBO.

Orentlicher, David. "Abortion and Compelled Physician Speech." *The Journal of Law, Medicine & Ethics* 43, no. 1 (Spring 2015): 9–21.

Pappworth, Maurice H. "Human Guinea Pigs: A Warning." *Twentieth Century* 171 (Autumn 1962): 66–75.

Pappworth, Maurice H. *Human Guinea Pigs: Experimentation on Man*. London: Routledge, 1967.

Pearce, J. M. S. "Bromide, the First Effective Antiepileptic Agent." *Journal of Neurology, Neurosurgery & Psychiatry* 72, no. 3 (March 2002): 412.

Persad, Govind C., Linden Elder, Laura Sedig, Leonardo Flores, and Ezekiel J. Emanuel. "The Current State of Medical School Education in Bioethics, Health Law, and Health Economics." *Journal of Law, Medicine & Ethics* 36, no. 1 (Spring 2008): 89–94.

Propst, Katie, David M. O'Sullivan, Amanda Ulrich, and Elena Tunitsky-Bitton. "Informed Consent Education in Obstetrics and Gynecology: A Survey Study." *Journal of Surgical Education* 76, no. 4 (August 2019): 1146–1152.

Rich, Leigh E., Jack Simmons, David Adams, Scott Thorp, and Michael Mink. "The Afterbirth of the Clinic: A Foucauldian Perspective on *House M.D.* and American Medicine in the 21st Century." *Perspectives in Biology and Medicine* 51, no. 2 (Spring 2008): 220–237.

Riddick, Jr., Frank A. "The Code of Medical Ethics of the American Medical Association." *The Ochsner Journal* 5, no. 2 (Spring 2003): 6–10.

Rosenthal, Elisabeth. "Donald Trump Did Something Right." *The New York Times*, January 21, 2019. https://www.nytimes.com/2019/01/21/opinion/trump-hospital-prices.html.

Rothman, David J. *Strangers at the Bedside: A History of How Law and Bioethics Transformed Medical Decision Making*, 2nd ed. New Brunswick and London: Aldine Transaction, 2003.

Schwetz, Bernard A. "Tom Beauchamp: Oral History of the Belmont Report and the National Commission for the Protection of Human Subjects of Biomedical and Behavioral Research." *Office for Human Research Protections*, September 22, 2004. https://www.hhs.gov/ohrp/education-and-outreach/luminaries-lecture-series/belmont-report-25th-anniversary-interview-tbeacham/index.html.

Shore, David, Writer. *House M.D.* Season 1, episode 1, "Pilot." Directed by Bryan Singer, featuring Hugh Laurie, Omar Epps, Robert Sean Leonard, Jesse Spencer, Lisa Edelstein, and Jennifer Morrison. Aired November 16, 2004, on Fox. Universal Pictures Home Entertainment, 2012, DVD.

Showalter, J. Stuart. *The Law of Healthcare Administration*, 8th ed. Chicago, IL: Health Administration Press, 2017.

Simmons, Jack R. *Habermas' Discourse Ethics: The Attitude Between Modernity and Post Modernity*. PhD diss., Tulane University, 1997. ProQuest Dissertations and Theses.

The Commonwealth Fund. "Underinsured Rate Rose From 2014–2018, With Greatest Growth Among People in Employer Health Plans." *The Commonwealth Fund*, February 7, 2019. https://www.commonwealthfund.org/press-release/2019/und erinsured-rate-rose-2014-2018-greatest-growth-among-people-employer-health.

Thompson, Britta M., Rhonda A. Sparks, Jonathan Seavey, Michelle D. Wallace, Jeremy Irvan, Alexander R. Raines, Heather McClure, Mikio A. Nihira, and Jason S. Lees. "Informed Consent Training Improves Surgery Resident Performance in Simulated Encounters With Standardized Patients." *The American Journal of Surgery* 210, no. 3 (September 2015): 578–584.

U.S. Department of Health and Human Services. *Trump Administration Announces Historic Price Transparency Requirements to Increase Competition and Lower Healthcare Costs for All Americans*, November 15, 2019, https://www.hhs.gov/about/news/2019/11/15/trump-administration-announces-historic-price-transpa rency-and-lower-healthcare-costs-for-all-americans.html.

Vossoughi, Sarah R., Robert Macauley, Kathleen Sazama, and Mark K. Fung. "Attitudes, Practices, and Training on Informed Consent for Transfusions and Procedures: A Survey of Medical Students and Physicians." *American Journal of Clinical Pathology* 144, no. 2 (August 2015): 315–321.

Wood, Fiona, Sean Michael Martin, Andrew Carson-Stevens, Glyn Elwyn, Elizabeth Precious, and Paul Kinnersley. "Doctors' Perspectives of Informed Consent for Non-Emergency Surgical Procedures: A Qualitative Interview Study." *Health Expectations* 19, no. 3 (June 2016): 751–761.

LEGAL CASES

Canterbury v. Spence, 464 F.2d 772 (D.C. Cir. 1972).
Cobbs v. Grant, 8 Cal. 3d 229 (1972).
In re Quinlan, 70 N.J. 10, 355 A.2d 647 (1976).
Mohr v. Williams, 95 Minn. 261 (1905).
Moore v. Regents of the University of California, 793 P.2d 479 (Cal. 1990).
National Institute of Family & Life Advocates v. Becerra, 138 S. Ct. 2361 (2018).
Planned Parenthood of Southeastern Pennsylvania v. Casey, 505 U.S. 833 (1992).
Pratt v. Davis, 224 Ill. 300 (1906).
Roe v. Wade, 410 U.S. 113 (1973).
Salgo v. Leland Stanford Jr. University Board of Trustees, 154 Cal.App.2d 560 (1957).
Schloendorff v. The Society of the New York Hospital, 211 N.Y. 125 (1914).
Superintendent of Belchertown State School v. Saikewicz, 373 Mass. 728 (1977).
Union Pacific Railway Company v. Botsford, 141 U.S. 250 (1891).

Chapter 4

The Rebirth of Canonical Love

Jack Simmons

Following in a tradition that traces its lineage to Europe and arose out of the Middle Ages, twentieth-century attitudes toward love reflected a preference for passion, a private passion that transcends the limits of social mores and reason. Expressions of such love are ubiquitous in art since the Renaissance, and dominate the literature, cinema, music, and behavior of American citizens during the last century, all of which provided support for the sexual revolutions of the 1920s and 1960s. These revolutions rejected classical sexual standards and emphasized individual autonomy in sexual behavior, including free love, sexual liberation for women, and the sex positive movement. New sexual consent standards on college campuses, workplace sexual harassment policies, the #MeToo movement, and the identification of traditional norms with toxic masculinity and rape culture signify a potent reconfiguration of sexual norms in the twenty-first century and a return to norms that predate the romantic love movement: the canonical definition of love that dominated during the Middle Ages.

In 1987, feminist theorist Jane Flax argued that Western culture is transforming, and that the shift is as radical (and gradual) as the shift from medieval to modern culture.[1] This transformation has been fueled by the application of postmodern thinking to questions regarding gender, ethnicity, and sexuality. Given that the earlier postmodern movement in architecture relied heavily upon a medieval aesthetic, as demonstrated in the Piazza d'Italia in New Orleans (1978) and the Guild House in Philadelphia (1963), it should come as no surprise that postmodern morality should involve a return to premodern ideologies (and theologies). In this chapter, I argue that the collision of contemporary discourse theory (e.g., Jürgen Habermas and Lois Pineau) and postmodern feminist theory (e.g., Andrea Dworkin and Catherine McKinnon) recreated medieval sexual norms codified by scholars such as

Gratian and Peter Lombard. These norms emphasize institutional control over sexual behavior for the sake of social order, women's security, and virtuous intimate relationships.

THE AESTHETIC CLUES TO THE RECTIFICATION

In 1982, interviewer John Tibbetts asked actress Sean Young about her love scene with Harrison Ford in the film *Blade Runner*. Tibbetts asked the question in a fashion designed to encourage Young to confirm Ford's status as male icon and sex symbol. Her answer did not support the hoped-for titillation, but Tibbetts too had a more profound concern. Was the scene offensive to feminism because Ford takes the leading role and instructs the woman on how to behave sexually, a seeming violation of the principles of sexual equality and autonomy popular at that time? Like countless Hollywood love scenes, the film depicts a reluctant woman, who gives in to the man's advances only after being physically restrained until she consents. Young was unequivocal in her answer: "No."[2] In the twenty-first century, film and cultural critics have reevaluated the scene and now claim that the love scene should be described as a rape scene.[3] In presenting a sexual assault as a love scene, the film supports a culture of misogyny.

Similarly, Hannah Yasharoff's article "*Animal House* [1978] falls under #MeToo," appearing in *USA Today* asks, "In the era of #MeToo, is it still OK to enjoy *Animal House*?"[4] While Yasharoff acknowledges the film's importance in the history of cinema, and that it is "hilarious," she concludes that its representation of "toxic young male culture" as a joke, and the suggestion "that a guy won't be accepted to a fraternity because he's Middle Eastern," is unacceptable in 2018.[5] She concludes that *Animal House* would have a tough time getting green-lighted by any studio (today) and that although it need not be banned, "we need to become more mindful about the entertainment we consume and be especially cognizant of what it's telling us about acceptable social behaviors."[6] What makes the critiques of *Animal House* and *Blade Runner* so significant is that both are iconic films, classics that left an indelible mark on the end of the twentieth century. The disavowal of these films is more than simply a criticism of directors Ridley Scott and John Landis. This is a call to transform culture and the art and entertainment world is getting the message. Film and TV producers have become significantly more mindful about sex scenes and have begun avoiding such scenes when possible,[7] and museum directors are reassessing whether to display the work of celebrated artists based on the artists' sexual behavior. For example, the *New York Times* reported the reluctance of curators to handle the paintings of Paul Gauguin because of his sexual relations with teenage girls, in this age of "heightened public sensitivity to issues of gender, race and colonialism."[8]

The new sexual norms entered the public consciousness dramatically via the #MeToo movement, when women across the country accused men of sexual misconduct ranging from rape to recounting dirty jokes, often resulting in those men losing positions of power and privilege. Apart from the social transformation playing out in the popular media and reflecting a new sexual morality, institutional policies regulating sexual behavior at colleges and universities signal a profound cultural shift toward a more heteronomous sexuality.

THE NEW NORMAL

In 2014, modifications of Title IX required universities to radically alter their definition of sexual consent and enforcement of sexual assault. The new approach attempts to reduce the frequency of sexual assaults on college campuses by creating model discourse conditions that define valid consent formation and make it objectively clear when consent is given and when it is withheld. These conditions mirror those defined in Jürgen Habermas's ideal speech situation by:

- Acknowledging an unequal power dynamic between men and women in sexual relationships and attempting to neutralize it by a variety of mechanisms, including detailed guidelines for discourse.
- Constructing a rational standard for consensus.
   a All participants have an equal opportunity to participate in the discourse.
   b Any agreement (consent) is arrived at purely based on reason, rather than any external compulsion.
   c Any consent must be universally understandable. There can be no mystery of why the consent was given.
- Establishing rational standards for discourse that produce a "yes" or "no" answer.
- Insisting upon the maintenance of discourse norms throughout the sexual encounter so that agreements may be renegotiated or rescinded at any time.[9]

The effort to reduce sexual assault becomes a matter of discourse and because public and private discourse inherits the virtues and vices of the culture in which it resides. The first step in establishing ideal discourse norms involves a critique of existing social power structures and sources of communicative distortion. This is as true now as it was in the twelfth century.

UNEQUAL POWER AND SEXUALITY

In his book *The Transformation of Title IX*, R. Shep Melnick details how the approach to addressing sexual assault on college campuses shifted from treating sexual assault as a crime, perpetrated by an individual, to understanding sexual assault as, "an omnipresent threat that maintains the economic and physical subordination of women."[10] The shift finds support in the work of second-wave feminists, like Andrea Dworkin and Catharine McKinnon, who advocated for what is sometimes called dominance theory. Dominance theory generally takes a grim view of normal, heterosexual relationships. In her book *Intercourse*, Dworkin attacks the sexual revolution and the sex positive movement and asserts instead that

> The internal landscape [of intercourse] is violent upheaval, a wild and ultimately cruel disregard of human individuality, a brazen, high-strung wanting that is absolute and imperishable, not attached to personality, no respecter of boundaries; ending not in sexual climax but in a human tragedy of failed relationships, vengeful bitterness in an aftermath of sexual heat, personality corroded by too much endurance of undesired, habitual intercourse, conflict, a wearing away of vitality in the numbness finally of habit or compulsion or the loneliness of separation.[11]

Dworkin paints a picture of sexual relations that are not only cruel and oppressive to women but also fundamental to any society conceived in masculine terms, or what she describes as male supremacy. Intentionally evoking the comparison to white supremacy,[12] she argues that male supremacy vitiates women's freedom, including sexual freedom. Under such conditions, individual efforts at sexual liberation and sexual equality become meaningless. Sexual consent becomes absurd and all intercourse is "a means or the means of physiologically making a woman inferior."[13] This is not because a particular man is a rapist. Rather, "intercourse is the pure, sterile, formal expression of men's contempt for women," because of the sexual hierarchy.[14] Under the conditions of male supremacy, sexual consent "is revealed as pallid, weak, stupid, second-class."[15]

In her book *Toward a Feminist Theory of the State*, Catharine McKinnon echoes Dworkin's concern regarding rape culture and concludes that "actual consent or nonconsent . . . is comparatively irrelevant."[16] She describes the conditions of rape culture, such that virtuous women, like young girls, are by definition nonconsenting and hence rapable, while unvirtuous women, like wives and prostitutes, are consenting, whores, and thereby unrapable.[17] In other words, rape culture defines consent and nonconsent independent of the woman's desire. Hence, rape is not the act of an individual, but rather the product of a culture of misogyny. Legal scholar, Janet Halley explains that under U.S. law, force or the threat of force has generally been held to invalidate any consent. If, as dominance feminists maintain, "the force/threat-of-force requirement would be satisfied by the coercive circumstances of everyday life,"[18] then a society of male supremacy means that all heterosexual acts involve force or the threat of force. All sex becomes rape because sexual relationships are defined by social dynamics, rather than the behavior of individuals.

The notion of rape culture had been around since the 1970s, but McKinnon and Dworkin added the caveat that, if the culture tacitly permits rape, by virtue of an ineffective justice system and male-dominated sexual norms, then all women live with the constant fear of rape. Dworkin asks, "Are you afraid now? How can fear and freedom coexist for women in intercourse?"[19] If sexual assault is the primary mechanism for sustaining the oppression of women, how can women be understood to consent to heterosexual sex at all? How can sex be a tool of oppression at one time, and a tool of intimacy another? Under dominance theory, sexual relationships are defined by social dynamics, not individual relationships. Overturning male supremacy and neutralizing the power differential between men and women requires a social solution, and that social solution manifests in contemporary discourse.

The idea of male supremacy has been replaced in the twenty-first-century vernacular with toxic masculinity. The ideas are not identical. Male supremacy references a set of social conditions, including but not limited to, unequal pay, pornography, unenforceable rape laws, sexual harassment, and limitations on reproductive rights. Catharine McKinnon concludes that "Women are raped by guns, age, white supremacy, the state—only derivatively by the penis."[20] In contrast, toxic masculinity describes a set of behaviors common to men that include but are not limited to misogyny, homophobia, violence, greed, and the repression of emotions. Both male supremacy and toxic masculinity express the general principles of rape culture, in which individual efforts to support women's liberation remain ineffective and irrelevant against the backdrop of a culture of misogyny.

The distinction between male supremacy and toxic masculinity may have less to do with the definitions and more to do with changing attitudes around sexual behavior. Though second-wave feminist thinking about rape culture began in the 1970s, it was still viewed as radical and prudish by a culture immersed in the sexual revolution, a revolution that championed women's liberal and sexual freedom. In the twenty-first century, social attitudes surrounding sexuality began to shift, especially around large institutions. Surveys about sexual assault on college campuses supported the idea that universities were havens for sexual misconduct. Sheila McMillen wrote in *The Chronicle of Higher Education* that "I've often wondered if there are more sexual predators in academe than in other environments,"[21] and Senator Kirsten Gillibrand said that "women are at greater risk of sexual assault as soon as they step onto a college campus." Though data suggest that women attending college are less likely to be sexually assaulted, the data may be irrelevant.[22] A national discussion of sexual assault on college campuses helped ideas like rape culture and toxic masculinity gain traction, ideas already present in medieval scholarship.

Medieval thought on sex was, like second-wave feminism, not of a piece. While significant disagreements arose around a wide array of concerns, radical second-wave feminists tend to agree with medieval scholars that sexuality is inherently dangerous, leading to rape, sexual perversion and social injustice. In general, medieval scholars and radical second-wave feminists point to irrationality and the dynamics of masculine power as the source of the problem. In her book *Intercourse*, Dworkin cites Augustine of Hippo to demonstrate the long-standing connection between masculine political power and lust: "In the city of the world both the rulers themselves and the people they dominate are dominated by the lust for domination."[23] This lust is masculine, the woman's body its object. Dworkin explains that Augustine was "keenly aware of the intense carnal pleasures of lust and domination."[24] In her effort to connect political power to the sexual domination of women, Dworkin neatly identifies in Augustine the critical element in Augustine's analysis of lust; it is the loss of reason that corrupts politics and sex.

> Such lust does not merely invade the whole body and outward members; it takes such complete and passionate possession of the whole man, both physically and emotionally, that what results is the keenest of all pleasures on the level of sensation; and, at the crisis of excitement, it practically paralyzes all power of deliberate thought.[25]

Dworkin sees this as a critique of culture, and proof that Augustine believes intercourse (and politics) can take place without the passion of lust, and hence without the violence of domination. Like a good Platonist, Augustine sees the loss of reason as a violation of human nature, and therefore aberrant. The loss of reason is a common philosophical concern and a dominant theme in the medieval critique of sexuality and culture.

Following Augustine's lead, medieval scholars address the problems of sexuality in detail to navigate the troubled waters of lust and domination. In his *Sentences*, Peter Lombard cites Augustine, Gregory, Sextus, and Jerome, to make the case that one of the functions of marriage is to bring order, to avoid the personal and social injury caused by concupiscence and incontinence.[26] Even though he agrees with Augustine that the purpose of marital intercourse is for the sake of children, and with Sextus that anyone who loves his spouse too ardently is an adulterer,[27] he acknowledges that pleasure had in conjugal coitus, unless it is immoderate, is preserved from sin.[28] Thomas Aquinas clarifies that some affection between the parties concerned increases sexual pleasure and that this is an acceptable goal, but it is the hindering of reason, on account of the accompanying bodily change, that represents a moral malice.[29] The loss of reason inherent in sexual passion is critical to the medieval theorist, and the carefully structured institution of marriage offers a mechanism for taming the sexual passions, which even Aquinas notes are natural enough as demonstrated by animals, and directing them toward their proper purpose: procreation.

This did not mean that medieval marriage was immune to politics and lust. Quite the opposite was true. Marriage offered women little protection against the vicissitudes of medieval culture. Medieval marriages often served political or financial purposes, and secular law provided numerous possibilities of escape from fruitless or otherwise inconvenient marriages.[30] C. S. Lewis paints a bleak view of medieval marriage.

> [Medieval] Marriages had nothing to do with love, and no "nonsense" about marriage was tolerated. All matches were matches of interest . . . an interest that was continually changing. When the alliance which had answered would answer no longer, the husband's object was to get rid of the lady as quickly as possible. Marriages were frequently dissolved.[31]

The work of the great twelfth-century jurist Gratian supports Lewis's conclusion. Gratian offers the example of a man who, after he was convicted of adultery and punished, had someone violate his wife by force so that he could dismiss her and marry another.[32]

Gratian recognized the dangerous combination of sex and power and addressed it in detail, dedicating ten chapters in his twelfth-century treatise *Decretum* to a broad array of common sexual hazards, including but not limited to sexual consent, rape, abduction, adultery, sex with slaves, marriage with slaves, sterility, clandestine betrothal, remarriage, and incest.[33] Gratian's treatment of the matter demonstrates a clear recognition that in medieval sexual relations, women occupied a profoundly vulnerable position, that they were regularly subject to socially sanctioned sexual abuse and that marriage could be draconically pragmatic and used as a weapon against their interests. Gratian writes, "A woman has no power, the rule of man takes precedence in all things" (Nulla est mulieris potestas, sed in omnibus uiri dominio subsit), and Gratian attempts to remedy this in canon law.[34]

Against the backdrop of the medieval and contemporary understanding of dominance, heterosexual relationships are defined by social conditions, rather than by the individuals in those relationships, which means that the problem of sexual consent cannot be addressed on an individual basis. Having acknowledged the unequal power dynamic between men and women, both medieval canon law and Title IX guidelines set out to establish a rational standard for discourse and consensus formation.

THE RATIONAL STANDARD

Gratian cites a rational principle to justify equity in sexual relations and create protections for women against misogynist social forces. In *The Treatise on Laws*, Gratian begins with a guiding, rational principle intended to harmonize discordant canons and disagreeable traditions: that natural law and the gospel commands each person to "do to others what he wants done to himself and prohibited from inflicting on others what he does not want done to himself."[35] For example, Gratian rejects the tradition of denying women entry into a church due to menstruation or immediately after child birth, and suggests that the differing restrictions on men and women in the Old Testament on this matter should be understood symbolically.[36] In the *Decretum*, he writes that "Adultery by either sex is to be punished in the same way."[37]

The question of consent was irrelevant outside of marriage because non-marital sex was forbidden, but Gratian applies the rational standard to sexual consent in marriage. Because of the symmetrical relationship of marriage, and its implied equity, Gratian insists that both man and wife have a sexual duty to one another that neither can forgo without permission from the other.[38] James Brundage characterizes Gratian's approach as an effort to create a marital sanctuary for women,

> so far as sexual rights within marriage were concerned, women, he taught, had absolute equality with men. The sex life of the married couple was, or ought to be, an island of comparative privacy where equal rights prevailed, within a larger society where women's rights were severely curtailed.[39]

Gratian is also concerned with consent, as it applies to marriage. Here again, the rational principle applies. In the *Decretum*, he concludes that an agreement must be reasonable, that both people perceive the same thing in the same way, and that consent must be freely given and uncoerced. This means that marital consent maintains an objective quality that may be evaluated by a third party, and that sexual consent may only be given to pursue rational (Church sanctioned) ends: procreation and satisfaction of the marital debt. Personal, private sexual goals are invalid. Gratian, therefore, insists that marriages must be public and that clandestine marriages are unlawful and invalid.[40] Given his commitment to equality, and acknowledgment of the inequities of secular life, Katherine Christensen suggests that legal reformers like Gratian "shared a concern and desire to return to and be guided by the good *mores* of the past" that American medievalist Charles Homer Haskins christened the "renaissance of the twelfth century."[41]

Much like the medieval scholars, the Title IX reform movement acknowledges a culture of irrational sexuality fueled by alcohol, drugs, lust, social pressure and toxic masculinity, and combats that irrationality with discourse norms that require rational decision-making. The University of South Florida's Title IX guidelines equate irrationality with incapacitation: "Incapacitation: a state where someone cannot make rational, reasonable decisions because they lack the capacity to give knowing consent."[42] Coercive forces that limit rationality represent distortions of the discourse norm and invalidate consent. Only consent that is rational and reasonable counts as consent. The rational standard means that consent can be judged externally, by a third party. If a person's consent appears unreasonable, then it is not consent. This has the effect of making sexual consent a public representation, rather than private agreement. If the agreement only makes sense to the people engaged in the agreement, then it is no agreement at all.

The Title IX guidelines also place sexual assault under the preview of sexual harassment: "Sexual harassment is unwelcome conduct of a sexual nature. It includes unwelcome sexual advances, requests for sexual favors, and other verbal, nonverbal, or physical conduct of a sexual nature. Sexual violence is a form of sexual harassment prohibited by Title IX."[43] Linking sexual harassment and sexual violence reveals a more radical form of rationality at play in the new sexual consent standard.

Mane Hajdin argues that on its face, the "unwelcome conduct" creates an irrational standard. Seeking consent for sexual interaction requires a sexual advance, and there is no way of knowing whether the advance is welcome without making it. This creates an infinite regress, such that it would be impossible to comply with the policy (only make welcome sexual advances) except by never engaging in any form of sexual interaction.[44] Hajdin concludes that the standard is flawed because it suggests that sexual advances are intrinsically suspect.[45] But this claim demonstrates Hajdin's blind spot. The Title IX standard attempts to mitigate a culture of irrational sexuality and rape. In such an environment, all sexual advances *are* intrinsically suspect. The solution to the infinite regress is articulated by Lois Pineau in her essay, "Date Rape." Like Gratian, Pineau attempts to undermine the customs surrounding seduction and replace them with a rational standard for consent.[46] She suggests that women pursue sex for some goal (pleasure, procreation, etc.) and that if a woman does not agree that the sex she had with a man was pursuant to a mutually identified goal, then there is no reason to think that she wanted it and it is "rational to presume that the sex was not consensual."[47]

This standard introduces a means–ends rationality to the discursive process for valid sexual behavior. Sexual consent means understanding the sexual goals of your partner and agreeing on how to best achieve those goals. From Pineau's perspective, this creates for the man a "responsibility to know" the woman's sexual goals and an obligation to help her pursue those goals. If a man wants to be sure that he is not forcing himself on a woman, he has an obligation first, to know what she might want out of any sexual encounter and second, to ensure that once the encounter begins, she is enjoying it, or if not enjoying it, to discover if she wishes it to continue. Pineau's standard denies the infinite regress by asserting the "responsibility to know" and shifting the burden of proof so that the woman no longer needs to demonstrate that she did not want the encounter. Instead, the man must prove that it was wanted.

A danger hides in the means–end approach to sexual consent. Because means–end reasoning validates the means based on achieving the end, it necessarily minimizes the role of the people in the process and any personal agreements between them. In other words, the relationship between the individuals becomes irrelevant, and sexual consent becomes tantamount to an exchange of goods and services. In an exchange of goods and services, unsatisfied customers may ask for their money back. In a sexual encounter, an unsatisfied customer may assert that she was raped. Legal scholar and critic of the Title IX standards, Janet Halley summarizes the problem with the new approach to sexual consent: "Under that domination, they [women] may give consent to sex, but that consent is bankrupt from the moment it is given. If they later retract it and declare that the sex was unwanted, they should be believed."[48] The responsibility to know denies the "point of no return" in a sexual encounter and insists that a woman may revoke her consent at any time. Because her partner has an obligation to know what she wants at all times, failure to know is itself evidence of rape.[49] This sort of standard was used in a university case in which a man was found guilty of sexual assault and expelled because he did not end intercourse quickly enough when his partner began to cry.[50]

If Hajdin is right, that knowing whether an advance is wanted requires making the advance, then the new solution is not to make the advances to people protected under Title IX guidelines, and this is the message that the new standards are sending:

> According to a survey conducted earlier this year by LeanIn.Org and SurveyMonkey, 60% of managers who are men are now uncomfortable participating in a common work activity with a woman, such as mentoring, working alone or socializing together . . . and senior-level men are now 12 times more hesitant to have one-on-one meetings with junior women.[51]

By asserting that only reasonable agreements based on shared understanding count as consensual, the new standards mirror Gratian's standard for consent. Under canon law and Title IX, shared understanding implies not only that two or more people perceive the same thing and that they agree to pursue the same goal, but that the goal is objectively clear and socially sanctioned.[52] Canon law generally resolves the ambiguity of consent by insisting on a public marriage ceremony; the woman publicly consents to marriage and the sexual goals inherent to that practice. Similarly, Title IX attempts to address the vagaries of the "responsibility to know" by establishing socially sanctioned norms for sexual consent formation and sexual goals: public representations of consent.

CODIFYING SEXUAL NORMS

Codifying discourse norms that create shared understanding is challenging, as explained in Joan Landes's critique of Habermas's discourse ethics: "a theory of 'public representations' needs to account for the culturally variant ways that humans produce and make use of multiple representations. Pragmatics, the formal use of language in interaction, is best accompanied by a theory and observation of (stylized and informal) bodily gestures and postures."[53] In accord with Title IX and the Dear Colleague letter, colleges and universities across the United States have developed a wide array of discourse guidelines designed to formalize the highly stylized and informal dynamics of sexual intimacy.[54]

Antioch College boasts of being the first institution with a detailed sexual consent standard created by students in 1991 and later adopted as official university policy.[55] The twenty-point Antioch policy may come across as clumsy and mechanical. Point number five reminds us that "each new level of sexual activity requires consent," which can only lead to questions regarding what counts as a new level, and point number seven establishes the universality of the standard by insisting that Antioch's twenty-point procedure "is required regardless of the parties' relationship, prior sexual history or current activity,"[56] which means that the Antioch policy governs all sexual intimacy, inside and outside of marriage. Furthermore, that policy defines sexuality to include, sexual gestures, sexual touching and "sexual penetration of a body opening by any means, including but not limited to vaginal penetration, anal penetration, and oral sex. Penetration, however slight, includes the insertion of objects or body parts."[57] This level of specificity may seem out of place in a university handbook, but it has become the norm. Brown University recommends the "Scarleteen Sexual Inventory List,"[58] which includes a twenty-nine-point checklist, matched with the thirty-one point "Sex Readiness Checklist."[59] The list includes detailed descriptions of model relationships and explicit descriptions of possible sexual encounters.

Virtually all universities and colleges now regulate the sexual behavior of students, administrators and faculty, on and off campus, with streamlined guidelines like those at Elon College:

1. Clear Communication: Words or actions must be used to establish consent. Only a comprehensible, unambiguous, positive and active communication of consent for each sexual act qualifies as consent. The absence of no does not equal yes. Only YES means YES.
2. Freely and Willingly: Effective consent must be established without any coercion, including emotional, psychological, or relational pressure or influence.
3. Unimpaired Decision-Making: Effective consent must be established without impairment by either person. Impairment can include the effects of alcohol or other drugs. In addition, if someone is asleep, passed out, has consumed alcohol or drugs, or is in any other way impaired, she or he may not be able to give legal consent.
4. Step-by-Step: You must establish effective consent for every sex activity. Consenting to one sex act does not mean consenting to any other sex act. Prior sexual activity or an ongoing relationship cannot substitute for effective consent.
5. Subject to Change: At any point during a sexual encounter, both partners should be free to change their mind. If one partner changes his or her mind, then the other partner must respect the decision to limit or end sexual contact.[60]

Following a consumer model, the guidelines seek to ensure that sexual encounters satisfy the participants' expectations and create a liability for undesirable consequences. These guidelines replace the more fluid and nuanced understanding of sexual encounters with a transactional approach that intrudes upon the private rhythms of marriages and long-standing relationships. Furthermore, sexual encounters initiated with the traditional, less formal approach to consent now qualify as rape.

Gratian also sees the law as a tool for refining cultural norms, and he and his contemporaries crafted detailed guidelines to steer the laity clear of the sexual misconduct that they saw as rampant, and construct "a coherent theory of marriage."[61] Much like the contemporary standards, Gratian acknowledges the role of discourse norms and sexual norms in managing relationships, which are largely seen in transactional terms. Gratian freely uses terms and phrases such as debt, negligence and fraud, when describing marital obligations. Like the authors of the "Scarleteen Sexual Inventory List," Gratian offers remarkable detail on questions of valid consent and sexual behavior, attempting to cover all possible cases. Here I have provided a framework that attempts to capture the essence of his effort.

Canon law requires mutual consent, and therefore forbids a man from marrying a woman he has raped (the rape being evidence of nonconsent), giving away a daughter to be married against her consent, or allowing the marriage of children under the age of sexual consent. Gratian stipulates that consent can only arise from shared understanding, "So one who errs does not consent. Thus she was not married, because both did not consent to the same thing, and that is necessary for marriage . . . Error as to person is one thing, error as to fortune another, error as to condition another, and error as to quality yet another."[62] Hence, a woman who marries Steve, thinking that she was marrying Jeff, might rightly assert that she did not consent to the marriage. However, misunderstandings regarding the fortune, condition, or quality of the spouse do not invalidate consent. Hence, canon law forbids:

1. Using a deceitful status change to justify leaving a spouse.
2. Abandoning a wife after discovering that she was not a virgin prior to marriage.
3. Leaving a spouse due to a lack of wealth.
4. Leaving a spouse who turned out to be a slave rather than free.
5. Sending away a sterile wife and taking a new wife for the sake of fecundity.[63]

Finally, marriages must occur in public, to ensure that the discursive norms are met and may be legally represented. Marriage is a legal contract, with legal implications, and the law could not be expected to oversee clandestine or secret agreements.

In addition to the standards for consent, canon law dictated healthy sexual relations within marriage. The only reasonable occasions for intercourse occurred inside of marriage, and then only the missionary position (man on top, face to face) with clothes on was considered acceptable. This limitation was intended to prevent the igniting of dangerous passions. Unlawful sexual behavior included masturbation, fornication, adultery, rape, incest, bestiality, homosexuality, and sodomy. Brundage explains that Gratian's *Decretum* became the standard canon-law textbook and "medieval and modern canonistic treatments of sexual behavior were thus grounded largely on positions and ideas that church leaders found in Gratian's work."[64]

The contemporary and medieval standards consecrate sexual intimacy procedurally. Title IX replaces public marriage vows by appointed representatives of the church with a consent standard designated by appointed university administrators. Sex certainly occurs independent of the Title IX rubric, but it qualifies as rape.

PARALLEL LEGAL SYSTEMS

To enforce the new sexual norms, the medieval Catholic Church set up a system of courts throughout Europe to hear cases on sexual misconduct and marital irregularities, independent of the secular legal system. Brundage writes that "the lawmakers and administrators of the medieval church had to create a law enforcement system that could detect suspected offenders and courts that could try and punish them, in the hope that this would also deter others from imitating their bad example."[65] Evidence, including the detail of canon law and church income based on court fees, suggests that these courts were very busy.[66]

Similarly, Title IX requires universities receiving federal financial assistance to create a parallel legal system for the prompt and equitable resolution of sexual discrimination and sexual violence complaints.[67] This includes the creation of a Title IX coordinator whose sole responsibility is the overseeing of Title IX complaints and the processing of those complaints.[68] And like its medieval counterpart, Title IX policy is intended to transform sexual behavior, not only through the adjudication and punishment of violators, but by "adopting and publishing grievance procedures [that] can serve as preventive measures against harassment and violence."[69] Though the prosecution of the new standards remains uneven, many universities are prosecuting the new discourse norms so aggressively that they are finding themselves at odds with the state legal system. The Chronicle of Higher Education cites Jeannie Suk Gersen who described most of the new standards as, "so broad as to put students engaged in behavior that is overwhelmingly common in the context of romantic relationships to be accused of sexual misconduct," and that federal courts have overturned more than 200 Title IX convictions for violating due process.[70]

In both the medieval and contemporary cases, the parallel legal system was created in response to the perception that the state legal system was incapable or unwilling to handle the nuance of discourse norms around the question of sexuality.

PUBLIC INFORMATION CAMPAIGN

Attempting to change sexual norms and neutralize the power inequities inherent in most sexual encounters requires convincing people that their past sexual behaviors were abusive and wrong. Canonical guidelines for sex in and outside of wedlock may have seemed reasonable enough to scholars and theologians, but to the laity, these regulations seemed contrary to normal human relations. Brundage writes, "sexual relations between unmarried men and women seemed to most people so natural and so inevitable that they could not understand how such conduct could be sinful at all,"[71] and the effort to overcome inequality brought with it the accusation that the common social norms were inherently flawed. To affect social change, the clergy were given instructions to frequently advise and admonish penitents on sexual norms, reminding them that even simple fornication was a serious moral offense.[72]

Gratian's *Decretum* offers a litany of marital and sexual case studies, in the scholastic style of replies and objections. This academic approach warranted the creation of numerous sexual norm manuals and handbooks for clergy who heard confession, and given the exhaustive detail of these manuals, it is difficult to escape the conclusion that sexual sins must have been quite common among medieval people and that the Catholic Church was committed to changing them. [73]

Although the instrument for delivering the information has changed, Title IX includes a robust public information campaign to change sexual norms. This is made evident on the Title IX web pages of most universities. These websites identify a myriad of resources, including voluntary and mandatory sexual harassment trainings for students and employees. They also provide a surprising level of detail in defining discourse and sexual norms, norms that openly contradict the sexual norms of the late twentieth century.

The Violence Prevention and Title IX web page hosted by the University of California at Berkeley offers a link to *EmpowerU*, a violence prevention program sponsored by the university. In one video link, two young women, Jill and Alicia, define what constitutes a positive relationship. The two offer a thorough explanation of consent and the elements of a positive relationship, including visual aids. Jill admits that "no means no" can be a downer, so they advocate, "enthusiastic consent." She explains, "Nothing feels better than asking someone if they want to have sex with you because you want to have sex with them and hearing, yes!"[74] Aware that asking for consent can be awkward, the video hosts Jill and Alicia attempt to demonstrate sexy ways for asking for consent, including a distinction between consent for oral sex and sexual intercourse.[75] Jill demonstrates the following example of a sexy proposition, "You know what would make me feel good, could you, can I . . .?" There is some question as to whether these characterizations of intimate discourse are clear or sexy, but what is perfectly clear is what Jacob Gersen and Jeannie Gersen, professors of law at Harvard University, conclude that university, Title IX guidelines "are how-to's for sexual arousal, proposition, and seduction."[76] The university policies and resources express a whole normative world of assumptions about what makes sex and relationships good, satisfying, worthwhile, meaningful and fulfilling. Under the guise of preventing sexual violence, the universities are providing advice on sex and relationships, and they are not particularly good at it.[77]

TWENTY-FIRST-CENTURY CONSEQUENCES

The similarities between the medieval and contemporary efforts to shift sexual norms are striking, but there are dissimilarities. While both attempt to alleviate the oppression of women in a patriarchal society, the medieval standards emphasize reforming marriage (a remedy ignored by twenty-first-century standards) and the twenty-first-century standards emphasize discourse norms. In both cases, the new norms promoting a rational sexuality (neutralizing power inequities, improving personal safety, and allowing for third-party oversight) reject irrational interpretations of love and sexuality most commonly associated with romantic love, ubiquitous in Western literature and Hollywood cinema.[78]

Though identifying the origins of romantic love remains controversial with historians, Andreas Capellanus's twelfth-century work *The Art of Courtly Love* details the essential elements of a love distinct from the socially sanctioned, rational form of love.[79] Romantic love shows reckless disregard for social convention, personal goals and safety. In romantic love, a person falls in love, and submission to this love demonstrates a virtue that exceeds mundane social expectations. Malory's *The Death of Arthur* offers a clear contrast between canonical love and romantic love. The love between Arthur and Guinevere is a legitimate, pragmatic love, designed to satisfy social convention. When Guinevere's affair with Lancelot leads the realm into civil war, Arthur is sorrier for the loss of his good knights than a queen, because there are plenty of queens he might have had, but such a fellowship of knights shall never be had again.[80] Arthur's response to Guinevere's infidelity can only strike the romantic as harshly utilitarian.

In comparison, Chretien's (de Troyes) *Lancelot* has Guinevere command Lancelot, to fight poorly in the lists as proof of his affection. He humiliates himself, allowing himself to be unhorsed and beaten over and over again, to prove his unwavering devotion.[81] Lancelot's devotion to Guinevere serves no social goals and brings Lancelot short-term pain and the disgrace of being beaten and berated by his fellow knights, and long-term pain and the failure of the realm. Its only purpose is to win Guinevere's affection, and for that he risks Camelot. This is romantic love. This is the sentiment that sells novels, movie tickets, and fills the journals of youthful lovers.

In the Western romantic tradition, it is the mores, morals and laws governing love that threaten and terrorize us. *Romeo and Juliet* represents the essential form of romantic love; the lovers wed without their parents' consent to protect their illicit romance from Juliet's impending, socially sanctioned marriage.[82] This form of romantic love must end in tragedy because their marriage, if allowed to stand, would ultimately threaten their love by making it public and exposing it to social regulation. One of the great challenges of romantic love involves maintaining the romance within socially sanctioned marriage, and there have been more than a few manuscripts dedicated to this elusive goal. Romantic love finds its allure in the transcendental value of profound intersubjectivity, the unique and irrational connection that lovers feel for which there can be no universal formula or recipe, and it was this conception of love that was largely responsible for the sexual revolutions of the 1920s and 1960s, and the gradual demise of canonical love.

Given the popularity of the romantic love movement, the Title IX suggestion that rational, institutionally managed sexual norms will produce better relationships remains controversial. Janet Halley and R. Shep Melnick suggest that the new campus sexual harassment policies arose as a result of a few, overzealous activists: dominance-feminists (Halley mentions Katherine McKinnon by name) in the Department of Education Office for Civil Rights and the Title IX activist movement.[83] Though the connection between Title IX and dominance feminism is clear, Halley and Melnick's criticism does not fully appreciate the shifting norms: the means–end rationality driving them and the broad support the norms receive from students.

Jaclyn Friedman, editor of "Yes Means Yes: Visions of Female Sexual Power and a World without Rape" acknowledges a generational divide on sexual norms.[84] She contends that young people in the twenty-first century struggle setting sexual boundaries, and cites questions she receives from students to illustrate the point: "How do I say 'no' when it makes me feel guilty? How can I have fun hooking up without getting accused of sexual assault? How can I make my friends stop judging me about wanting too much sex, or not enough, or wanting the 'wrong' things?"[85] She explains, students today relish the idea of consent policies that help them realize "what they want (and don't)" want and that it helps them develop the most important sexual relationship a person will ever have, "the one they have with themselves."[86]

Freidman accepts that the new sexual norms contrast with the sexual norms shared by "adults," who generally hate the new policies.[87] She cites fifty-four-year-old Judith Shulevitz, as an example of an adult who views romance as an intimate and private affair. Shulevitz dislikes that new standards define so many normal human interactions as rape. She suggests that the new guidelines invalidate long-standing sexual relationships that might otherwise have been viewed as healthy, normal, and even preferable to the carefully codified relationships described by the new consent standards. Like other advocates of the new sexual norms, Freidman dismisses this old, romantic view of sexuality as conspiring to support rape culture. Friedman's goal, a world without rape, allows no compromise with views of love and sexuality that acknowledge nuance or individuality. In much the same way as the medieval thinkers' view sex outside wedlock as sin, so too do proponents of the contemporary sexual norms see alternative norms as unethical. If the goal is to end rape, then norms designed to achieve that goal are better than norms that may focus on other human goals. Discourse governed by means–end rationality provides little room for pluralist views regarding morality and modes of being in the world.

The same generational tension appears in the *Radiolab* episode "In the No," when thirty-year-old Kaitlin explains that if a woman feels violated after a sexual encounter, then it is rape. She explains that given the imbalance of power between men and women, and what women are taught about pleasure, it might be hard for them to say no, and "how can you [a woman] even know what you want or don't want in those private moments."[88] Kaitlin's standards for consent mirror Pineau's "responsibility to know" criteria: the man is responsible for knowing how the woman feels, and if he is wrong, he is responsible for the consequences, regardless of what the woman said. Kaitlin summarizes the ethos of the Title IX guidelines when discussing the case of a man expelled for not receiving a verbal "yes" even though the woman initiated the sexual interaction by grabbing him and performing oral sex on him, without his requesting it,

> I feel like . . . I'm not seeing [in the men that I know] them understanding the power that they have, that's really easy to—to abuse, you know? Like, how do you fix that? That's what it kind of all comes down to. And, like, there's has to be—there has to be some kind of consequences if we're going to see it change.[89]

Here, Kaitlin echo's dominance feminism's claim that under the conditions of rape culture, consent is meaningless. Only through objective discourse norms can the power dynamic be neutralized.

Forty-two-year-old Hanna Stotland rejects the assertion that feeling violated equals rape, and rejects the belief that a woman can't say no due to social conditioning or power dynamics, "They put her in a pink dress, so now she has to give a blow job."[90] Stotland's response echoes the concerns of a diverse range of feminists, like Camile Paglia (sex positive) and Judith Butler (postmodern), who fear the inevitable reduction of individual autonomy associated with institutionally enforced sexual norms. Wesley Yang explains, "What had begun as an effort to liberate women from the private tyranny of coverture . . . had ended by delivering her into the arms of the state, which had empowered itself to preempt her privacy and annul her autonomy and her will."[91]

Norms designed to prevent sexual assault on college campuses replace the culturally variant forms of interpersonal communication, with objective, transactional discourse norms such as "yes means yes" or "no means no," and detailed criteria to ensure valid agreements. If we replace the variant forms of interpersonal communication with objective, transaction communication, do we not replace the variant forms of interpersonal relationships with transactional relationships? In other words, discourse norms designed to replace subjective encounters with objective encounters may succeed, rendering interpersonal relationships that express their own unique forms and rhythms invalid. Hence, the autonomy Yang and Stotland refer to is not merely the autonomy of consent, it represents the autonomy to express variant forms of life.

Like the canonical standards, that initially ran contrary to common sensibilities but eventually worked themselves into the fabric of Western society, the Title IX regulations too run contrary to the individual autonomy that was the hallmark of the sexual revolution but are imbedding themselves within the cultural consciousness of the twenty-first century. The new norms not only describe the dominant culture of sexuality in terms that reflect medieval sensibilities, but also establish institutional guidelines to correct discourse and behavior that closely model the medieval forms of correction. It is difficult to know how fully the general public will embrace the new norms. Early indicators, such as Secretary of Education, Betsy DeVos's unsuccessful attempts to roll back Title IX regulations and the resignation of Hardball anchor Chris Matthews, support Jane Flax's suggestion that Western culture is experiencing a radical shift, as radical as the shift from medieval to modern culture. It should come as no surprise that the postmodern rejection of the enlightenment would return us to medieval modes of thinking. Flax's only error seems to be her belief that the shift would be gradual.

NOTES

1. Jane Flax, "Postmodernism and Gender Relations in Feminist Theory," *Signs*, Vol. 12, No. 4," *Within and Without: Women, Gender, and Theory* 12, no. 4 (Summer, 1987): 621.

2. John C. Tibbetts, "Blade Runner 1982, Sean Young," *Conversations in the Arts and Humanities*, 1982, https://www.youtube.com/watch?v=vIdlYzbugT8.

3. Casey Cipriani, "Blade Runner 2049 Tries to Make a Love Story Out of the First Blade Runner's Violence," *Browbeat*, Slate, October 12, 2017, http://www.slate.com/blogs/browbeat/2017/10/12/blade_runner_2049_makes_a_love_story_out_of_a_rape_scene.html; Erik Haywood, "There's Something about Blade Runner," *Balder and Dash*, September 2, 2014, https://www.rogerebert.com/balder-and-dash/theres-something-about-blade-runner.

4. Hannah Yasharoff, "*Animal House* falls under #MeToo," *USA Today*, July 30, 2018, D1.

5. Ibid., D3.
6. Ibid.
7. Catherine Shroad, "Cut! Is This the Death of Sex in Cinema?" *The Guardian*, Last modified April 12, 2019, accessed on November 10, 2019, https://www.theguardian.com/film/2019/apr/12/cut-is-this-the-death-of-sex-in-cinema; Ann Hornaday, "Sex Is Disappearing from the Big Screen and Its Making Movies Less Pleasurable," *The Washington Post*, Last modified June 7, 2019, accessed November 10, 2019, https://www.washingtonpost.com/lifestyle/style/sex-is-disappearing-from-the-big-screen-and-its-making-movies-less-pleasurable/2019/06/06/37848090-82ed-11e9-933d-7501070ee669_story.html; Emily Nussbaum, "TV's Reckoning with #MeToo," *The New Yorker*, Last modified May 27, 2019, accessed November 19, 2019, https://www.newyorker.com/magazine/2019/06/03/tvs-reckoning-with-metoo?utm_source=pocket-newtab.
8. Farah Nayeri, "Is it Time the Gauguin Got Canceled?" *New York Times*, Last modified November 18, 2019, accessed November 20, 2019, https://www.nytimes.com/2019/11/18/arts/design/gauguin-national-gallery-london.html.
9. Jürgen Habermas, "Wahrheitstheorien," chap. 1 in *Vorstudien und Ergänzungen zur Theorie des kommunikativen Handelns* (Frankfurt am Main: Suhrkamp, 1984), 177–78: Jürgen Habermas, *Theory of Communicative Action*, Vol. 1, trans. Thomas McCarthy (Boston, MA: Beacon Press, 1984), 25.
10. R. Shep Melnick, *The Transformation of Title XI* (Washington, DC: Brookings Institute Press, 2018), 165.
11. Andrea Dworkin, *Intercourse* (New York, NY: The Free Press, 1987), 21.
12. Ibid., 49, 56, 123, 173–80.
13. Ibid., 137.
14. Ibid., 138.
15. Ibid., 136.
16. Catharine McKinnon, *Toward a Feminist Theory of the State* (Cambridge, MA: Harvard University Press, 1989), 175.
17. Ibid.
18. Janet Halley, "The Move to Affirmative Consent," *Signs: Journal of Women in Culture and Society* (2015), http://signsjournal.org/currents-affirmative-consent/halley/.
19. Dworkin, *Intercourse*, 129.
20. McKinnon, *Toward a Feminist Theory of the State*, 173.
21. Sheila McMillen, "Dirty Old Men on the Faculty," *The Chronicle of Higher Education* LXIV, no. 16 (December 15, 2017): A64.
22. RAINN, "Campus Sexual Violence: Statistics," Last modified February 13, 2020, https://www.rainn.org/statistics/campus-sexual-violence. Data collected by the "Rape, Abuse & Incest National Network" shows that women, aged 18–24, who attend college are less likely to be raped than women of the same age who do not attend college.
23. Dworkin, *Intercourse*, 151.
24. Ibid.
25. Ibid.

26. Peter Lombard, "On the Doctrine of Signs," in *Sentences*, Vol. 4, trans. Guilio Silano (Toronto: Pontifical Institute of Mediaeval Studies, 2010), 185–87.

27. Ibid., 182.

28. Ibid., 185.

29. Thomas Aquinas, *Summa Theologica*, Vol. 1, trans. Fathers of the English Dominican Province (Chicago, IL: Encyclopaedia Britannica, 1952), 768–69.

30. Vern Bullough and James Brundage, "Sex and Canon Law," chap. 2 in *Handbook of Medieval Sexuality* (New York, NY: Garland Publishing Inc., 1996), 39.

31. C. S. Lewis, *The Allegory of Love* (London: Oxford University Press, 1936), 13; Bullough and Brundage, "Sex and Canon Law," 39.

32. Gratian, "Marriage Canons from The Decretum of Gratian, and The Decretals, Sext, Clementines and Extravagantes," trans. John T. Noonan, Jr., *Legal History Sources*, 1967, accessed February 20, 2020, Case 32, http://legalhistorysources.com/Canon%20Law/MARRIAGELAW.htm?fbclid=IwAR3jluvXLMnNPlD-fcLNuLtZ2fpcp5ui_Bp3PdFaWv0XUo-hYtP0AFSk07M#CASE_THIRTY-ONE_.

33. Ibid., Case 31.

34. Gratian, *Decretum Magistri Gratiani*, 2nd edition (New York, NY: Bernhardt Tauchnitz, 1879), accessed November 12, 2020, Case XXXIII, Q V, C XVII, https://geschichte.digitale-sammlungen.de/decretum-gratiani/kapitel/dc_chapter_3_3665.

35. Gratian, *The Treatise on Laws*, trans. Augustine Thompson (Washington, DC: The Catholic University of America Press, 1993), 3.

36. Ibid., 16.

37. Gratian, *Marriage Canons*, Case 32, Q. V, C. 23, http://legalhistorysources.com/Canon%20Law/MARRIAGELAW.htm?fbclid=IwAR3jluvXLMnNPlD-fcLNuLtZ2fpcp5ui_Bp3PdFaWv0XUo-hYtP0AFSk07M#CASE_THIRTY-ONE_.

38. Gratian, *Decretum Magistri Gratiani*, Case XXXIII, Q V, C XI, accessed November 12, 2020, https://geschichte.digitale-sammlungen.de/decretum-gratiani/kapitel/dc_chapter_3_3659.

39. James Brundage, *Law, Sex, and Christian Society in Medieval Europe* (Chicago, IL: The University of Chicago Press, 1987), 255.

40. Gratian, *Marriage Canons*, Case 30, Q. V, C. 2.

41. Gratian, *The Treastise on Laws*, xi.

42. University of San Francisco, *Consent*, Last modified February 10, 2020, https://myusf.usfca.edu/title-ix/consent.

43. Russlynn Ali, "Dear Colleague," *United States Department of Education Office for Civil Rights*, Last modified April 4, 2011 , https://www2.ed.gov/about/offices/list/ocr/letters/colleague-201104.pdf.

44. Mane Hajdin, "Sexual Harassment: The Demarcation Problem," in *The Philosophy of Sex: Contemporary Readings*, ed. Alan Soble (New York, NY: Rowman & Littlefield Publishers, Inc., 1997), 231–32.

45. Ibid., 243.

46. Lois Pineau, "Date Rape: A Feminist Analysis," *Law and Philosophy* 8, no. 2 (1989): 229–33.

47. Ibid., 232.

48. Halley, "The Move to Affirmative Consent."
49. Pineau, "Date Rape," 240.
50. Radio Lab, "In the No, Part 2," *WNYC Studios*, Last modified October 19, 2018, accessed November 20, 2020, https://www.wnycstudios.org/podcasts/radiolab/articles/no-part-2.
51. Connie Loizos, "This Startup is Making Customized Sexual Harassment Training That it Says Employees Won't Hate (or Forget)," *Tech Crunch*, Last modified November 1, 2019, accessed November 8, 2109, https://techcrunch.com/2019/11/01/this-startup-is-making-customized-sexual-harassment-training-that-it-says-employees-wont-hate-or-forget/.
52. Gratian, *Marriage Canon*, Case 29, Q. 1.
53. Joan Landes, "The Public and Private Sphere," in *Feminists Read Habermas: Gendering the Subject of Discourse*, ed. Johanna Meehan (New York, NY: Routledge, 1995), 109.
54. Ali, "Dear Colleague."
55. Jake New, "The 'Yes Means Yes' World," *Inside Higher Ed*, Last modified October 17, 2014, accessed November, 10, 2020, https://www.insidehighered.com/news/2014/10/17/colleges-across-country-adopting-affirmative-consent-sexual-assault-policies.
56. "Sexual Offense Prevention Policy (SOPP) & Title IX," *Campus Life, Antioch College* (2018), Last modified January 12, 2019, https://antiochcollege.edu/campus-life/sexual-offense-prevention-policy-title-ix/.
57. Antioch College, "SOPP."
58. Heather Corinna and C. J. Turett, "Yes, No, Maybe So: A Sexual Inventory Stocklist," *Scarleteen: Sex Ed for the Real World*, 2020, Last modified January 20, 2020, https://www.scarleteen.com/article/advice/yes_no_maybe_so_a_sexual_inventory_stocklist.
59. Ibid.
60. "Consent," *Elon University*, Last modified January 20, 2020, https://www.elon.edu/u/health-wellness/violence-response/get-information/consent/.
61. Brundage, *Law, Sex and Christian Society in Medieval Europe*, 235.
62. Gratian, *Marriage Canon*, Case 29, Q. 1.
63. Ibid., Case 29.
64. Bullough and Brundage, *Handbook of Medieval Sexuality*, 39.
65. Ibid., 45.
66. Ibid., 39.
67. Ali, "Dear Colleagues," 6.
68. Ibid., 7.
69. Ibid., 5.
70. Wesley Yang, "Revolt of the Feminist Law Profs," *The Chronicle Review*, *The Chronical of Higher Education*, Section B, September 6, 2019, B9.
71. Bullough and Brundage, "Sex and Canon Law," 41.
72. Ibid.
73. Ibid.
74. "EmpowerU: Let's Talk About Consent," *University Health Services, University of California Berkeley*, Last modified January 30, 2020, https://uhs.berkeley.edu/file/562.

75. Ibid.

76. Jacob Gersen and Jeannie Gersen, "The College Sex Bureaucracy," *The Chronicle Review, The Chronical of Higher Education*, Section B, January, 13, 2017, B7.

77. Ibid.

78. Lewis, *The Allegory of Love*. Scholars disagree on the origin of romantic love. Some hold that it originated in Arabic and Jewish culture on the Iberian Peninsula and found its way into Provençal courts. Others assert that it has more ancient roots, while C. S. Lewis insists that something unique appeared in southern France in the twelfth century that spawned what we now call romantic love.

79. Andreas Capellanus, *The Art of Courtly Love*, trans. John Jay Parry (New York, NY: Frederick Ungar Publishing Co., 1957).

80. Thomas Malory and John Rhys, *Le Morte D'Arthur* (London: William Caxton, 1906), 173–74.

81. Lewis, *The Allegory of Love*, 28–29.

82. William Shakespeare, "Romeo and Juliet," *The Complete Works of William Shakespeare*, Vol. VI (New York, NY: The University Society, 1901), 1–139. This form of romantic love must end in tragedy because their marriage, if allowed to stand, would ultimately threaten their love by making it public and regulated. One of the great challenges of romantic love involves maintaining the romance with marriage, and there have been more than a few manuscripts dedicated to this elusive goal.

83. Halley, "The Move to Affirmative Consent."

84. Jaclyn Friedman, "Adults Hate 'Yes Means Yes' Laws. The College Students I Meet Love Them," *The Washington Post*, Last modified October 14, 2015, accessed June 28, 2017, https://www.washingtonpost.com/posteverything/wp/2015/10/14/adults-hate-affirmative-consent-laws-the-college-students-i-meet-love-them/?utm_term=.9b114d46b4bb.

85. Ibid.

86. Ibid.

87. Ibid.

88. Radio Lab, "In the No."

89. Ibid.

90. Ibid.

91. Yang, "Revolt of the Feminist Law Profs," B11.

BIBLIOGRAPHY

Ali, Russlynn. "Dear Colleague." *United States Department of Education Office for Civil Rights*, April 4, 2011. https://www2.ed.gov/about/offices/list/ocr/letters/colleague-201104.pdf.

Aquinas, Thomas. *Summa Theologica*, 4 Vols. Translated by Fathers of the English Dominican Province. Chicago, IL: Encyclopaedia Britannica, 1952.

Brundage, James. *Law, Sex, and Christian Society in Medieval Europe*. Chicago, IL: The University of Chicago Press, 1987.

Brundage, James A. "Sex and Canon Law." In *Handbook of Medieval Sexuality*, edited by Vern L. Bullough and James A. Brundate. New York, NY: Garland Publishing Inc., 1996.

Campus Life. "Sexual Offense Prevention Policy (SOPP) & Title IX." *Antioch College*, 2018. Last modified January 12, 2019. https://antiochcollege.edu/campus-life/sexual-offense-prevention-policy-title-ix/.

Capallanus, Andreas. *The Art of Courtly Love*. Translated by John Jay Parry. New York, NY: Frederick Ungar Publishing Co., 1957.

Cipriani, Casey. "Blade Runner 2049 Tries to Make a Love Story Out of the First Blade Runner's Violence." *Browbeat*, October 12, 2017. Accessed December 15, 2017. http://www.slate.com/blogs/browbeat/2017/10/12/blade_runner_2049_makes_a_love_story_out_of_a_rape_scene.html.

Corinna, Heather and Turett, C. J. "Yes, No, Maybe So: A Sexual Inventory Stocklist." *Scarleteen: Sex Ed for the Real World*. Accessed January 20, 2020. https://www.scarleteen.com/article/advice/yes_no_maybe_so_a_sexual_inventory_stocklist.

Dworkin, Andrea. *Intercourse*. New York, NY: The Free Press, 1987.

Elon University. "Consent." *Elon University*. Last modified January 20, 2020. https://www.elon.edu/u/health-wellness/violence-response/get-information/consent/.

Flax, Jane. "Postmodernism and Gender Relations in Feminist Theory." *Signs, Within and Without: Women, Gender, and Theory*, Vol. 12, No. 4. Chicago, IL: University of Chicago Press, Summer, 1987.

Friedman, Jaclyn. "Adults Hate 'Yes Means Yes' Laws. The College Students I Meet Love Them." *The Washington Post*, October 14, 2015. Accessed June 28, 2017. https://www.washingtonpost.com/posteverything/wp/2015/10/14/adults-hate-affirmative-consent-laws-the-college-students-i-meet-love-them/?utm_term=.9b114d46b4bb.

Gersen, Jacob and Gersen, Jeannie Suk. "The College Sex Bureaucracy." *The Chronicle Review*: *The Chronicle of Higher Education*, January 6, 2017.

Gratian. *Decretum Magistri Gratiani*, 2nd ed. New York, NY: Bernhardt Tauchnitz, 1879. https://geschichte.digitale-sammlungen.de/decretum-gratiani/kapitel/dc_chapter_3_3665.

Gratian. "Marriage Canons from The Decretum of Gratian, and The Decretals, Sext, Clementines and Extravagantes." Translated by John T. Noonan, Jr. *Legal History Sources*, 1967. Accessed February 20, 2020. http://legalhistorysources.com/Canon%20Law/MARRIAGELAW.htm?fbclid=IwAR3jluvXLMnNPlD-fcLNuLtZ2fpcp5ui_Bp3PdFaWv0XUo-hYtP0AFSk07M#CASE_THIRTY-ONE_.

Gratian. *The Treatise on Laws*. Translated by Augustine Thompson. Washington, DC: The Catholic University of America Press, 1993.

Habermas, Jürgen. "Wahrheitstheorien." In *Vorstudien und Ergänzungen zur Theorie des kommunikativen Handelns*. Frankfurt am Main: Suhrkamp, 1984.

Habermas, Jürgen. *Theory of Communicative Action*, 2 Vols. Translated by Thomas McCarthy. Boston, MA: Beacon Press, 1984.

Halley, Janet. "The Move to Affirmative Consent." *Signs: Journal of Women in Culture and Society* (2015). http://signsjournal.org/currents-affirmative-consent/halley/.

Hajdin, Mane. "Sexual Harassment: The Demarcation Problem." In *The Philosophy of Sex: Contemporary Readings*, edited by Alan Soble. New York, NY: Rowman & Littlefield Publishers, Inc., 1997.

Haywood, Erik. "There's Something About 'Blade Runner'." *Balder and Dash*, September 2, 2014. Accessed June 15, 2017. https://www.rogerebert.com/balder-and-dash/theres-something-about-blade-runner.

Hornaday, Ann. "Sex is Disappearing from the Big Screen and its Making Movies Less Pleasurable." *The Washington Post*, June 7, 2019. Accessed November 10, 2019. https://www.washingtonpost.com/lifestyle/style/sex-is-disappearing-from-the-big-screen-and-its-making-movies-less-pleasurable/2019/06/06/37848090-82ed-11e9-933d-7501070ee669_story.html.

Lombard, Peter. "On the Doctrine of Signs." In *Sentences*, 4 Vols. Translated by Guilio Silano. Toronto: Pontifical Institute of Mediaeval Studies, 2010.

Landes, Joan. "The Public and Private Sphere." In *Feminists Read Habermas: Gendering the Subject of Discourse*. Edited by Johanna Meehan. New York, NY: Routledge, 1995.

Lewis, C. S. *The Allegory of Love*. London: Oxford University Press, 1936.

Loizos, Connie. "This Startup is Making Customized Sexual Harassment Training That it Says Employees Won't Hate (or Forget)." *Tech Crunch*, November 1, 2019. Accessed November 8, 2109. https://techcrunch.com/2019/11/01/this-startup-is-making-customized-sexual-harassment-training-that-it-says-employees-wont-hate-or-forget/.

Malory, Thomas and Rhys, John. *Le Morte D'Arthur*. London: William Caxton, 1906.

Melnick, R. Shep. *The Transformation of Title XI*. Washington, DC: Brookings Institute Press, 2018.

McKinnon, Catharine. *Toward a Feminist Theory of the State*. Cambridge, MA: Harvard University Press, 1989.

McMillen, Sheila. "Dirty Old Men on the Faculty." *The Chronicle of Higher Education* LXIV, no. 16 (December 15, 2017): A64.

MyUSF. "Consent." *University of San Francisco*. Accessed February 10, 2020. https://myusf.usfca.edu/title-ix/consent.

Nayeri, Farah. "Is it Time Gauguin Got Canceled?" *New York Times*, November 18, 2019. Accessed November 20, 2019. https://www.nytimes.com/2019/11/18/arts/design/gauguin-national-gallery-london.html.

New, Jake. "The 'Yes Means Yes' World." *Inside Higher Ed*, October 17, 2014. Accessed November 10, 2020. https://www.insidehighered.com/news/2014/10/17/colleges-across-country-adopting-affirmative-consent-sexual-assault-policies.

Nussbaum, Emily. "TV's Reckoning with #MeToo." *The New Yorker*, May 27, 2019. Accessed November 19, 2019. https://www.newyorker.com/magazine/2019/06/03/tvs-reckoning-with-metoo?utm_source=pocket-newtab.

Pineau, Lois. "Date Rape: A Feminist Analysis." *Law and Philosophy* 8, no. 2 (1989): 217–243.

Radio Lab. "In the No, Part 2." *WNYC Studios*, October 19, 2018. Accessed November 20, 2020. https://www.wnycstudios.org/podcasts/radiolab/articles/no-part-2.

RAINN. "Campus Sexual Violence: Statistics." *RAINN*. Last Modified February 13, 2020. https://www.rainn.org/statistics/campus-sexual-violence.

Shakespeare, William. "Romeo and Juliet." In *The Complete Works of William Shakespeare*, 4 Vols. New York, NY: The University Society, 1901.

Shoard, Catherine. "Cut! Is This the Death of Sex in Cinema?" *The Guardian*, April 12, 2019. Accessed November 10, 2019. https://www.theguardian.com/film/2019/apr/12/cut-is-this-the-death-of-sex-in-cinema.

Tibbetts, John C. "Blade Runner 1982, Sean Young." *Conversations in the Arts and Humanities*, 1982. Accessed October 20, 2017. https://www.youtube.com/watch?v=vIdlYzbugT8.

University Health Services. "EmpowerU: Let's Talk About Consent." *University of California Berkeley*. Last modified January 30, 2020. https://uhs.berkeley.edu/file/562.

Yasharoff, Hannah. "*Animal House* Falls under #MeToo." *USA Today*, July 30, 2018.

Yang, Wesley. "Revolt of the Feminist Law Profs." *The Chronicle Review*, September 6, 2019.

Part 2

TRIBAL DISCOURSE

Chapter 5

The Social Justice Discourse Ethic

Contours and Causes

Robert Gressis

Imagine you're a politically aware progressive Democrat in 2011. What would you have talked about? Probably Occupy Wall Street, the killing of Osama bin Laden, the financial crisis of 2008, Obamacare, and perhaps President Obama or the Tea Party Movement. How would you talk about it? Well, someone who was politically aware in 1981 probably would have been able to recognize and understand most of your terminology, save for the proper names. But now, imagine that, while you're discussing Occupy Wall Street with a friend, you fall into a coma, only to wake up eight years later. Besides some dispiriting bodily changes, what differences would you notice?

When it comes to politics, I think the things that would most stand out to you would be changes in vocabulary and outlook. "Intersectionality," "microaggressions," "white privilege," and many other new or differently used terms and phrases would perplex you. Moreover, the concepts that new language conveyed—for example, that America is fundamentally a patriarchal, white supremacist country, that individuals define their own gender identity, and that words can be a form of violence—would strike you as radically left-wing, if not preposterous. You would probably wonder: what happened?

I also wonder what happened.

In this chapter, I wonder in particular about two things. I wonder a little about what caused the sudden emergence of this new way of talking.[1] And I wonder a lot about how this new way of talking could have won so much assent, given how radical it is. I join these two wonderings together in this chapter's main motivating question: how did the preferred way of talking of such a radical outlook become so widespread so quickly?

The structure of the chapter is as follows. In §2, I describe how this new way of talking, which I call "social justice discourse," feels from the outside—to conservatives, moderates, or even to progressives from 2011.

In §3, I articulate the presuppositions that animate it, and show how they render it coherent, at least to its adherents (I call the set of these presuppositions the "social justice outlook"). In §4, I go on a brief tangent on ideological oppression, as belief in ideological oppression is one of two basic philosophical positions that justify the social justice outlook. In §5, I then present what I call the "social justice discourse ethic" (SJDE), which are three rules that adherents of social justice discourse abide by when they judge their own and others' talking. Then, in §6, I finally address the question that motivates this chapter: how did such a radical outlook convince so many people to adopt its terminology and ethic so quickly? In §6, I give an answer to that question from the perspective of the social justice left. This involves accepting that, not only are there right answers to moral questions, but that one of the things that explains social progress over the centuries is that the right answers just have better arguments for them, or are more intuitively obvious, than the wrong answers. This progressive moral realism is, besides belief in ideological oppression, the other basic philosophical position that justifies the social justice worldview. In §7, I offer an internal critique of the social justice outlook: that is, I argue that there are tensions between various elements of the social justice worldview. Finally, in §8, I give an alternative answer to this chapter's motivating question. According to this alternative answer, though social justice discourse's adoption has been widespread and sudden, its prevalence is best explained by widespread dishonesty on the part of most people who engage in it. I also argue that, even though social justice leftists accept the social justice outlook, the movement isn't *shaped* by concern for the oppressed, but is instead shaped by a desire for power for the verbally sophisticated. In other words, to the question, "what explains why such a radical worldview has won such widespread acceptance so quickly?" I answer: it hasn't won widespread acceptance. Something else is going on.

1. Social Justice Discourse, Seen from the Outside

To conservatives, moderates, and many liberals, the way the social justice left engages in discourse seems like a series of "heads-I-win, tails-you-lose" interactions. Let me give some examples.

A. Righteous indignation from me, hatred from you: if a person of color, a woman, a gay person, a trans-person, or some intersection thereof says something apparently hateful about whites, men, straights, cis-people, or some intersection thereof, social justice leftists will defend this as non-bigoted. But if a white person, a man, a straight person, or a cis-person says something similarly derogatory about people of color, women, gays, or trans-people, then social justice leftists will condemn this as bigoted, even if the remarks are exactly parallel, but for the switched targets.[2]

B. Emotional labor for me, white fragility from you: if a white person asks a person of color to explain something about race to him that he doesn't understand, the person of color has the right to be offended, and to not comply, on the grounds that he is imposing extra "emotional labor" on her.[3] By contrast, if a white person doesn't want to talk about race with a person of color, social justice leftists will decry his recalcitrance as "white fragility."[4]

C. My testimony is revelatory, yours is distorted: social justice leftists take the testimony of members of oppressed groups to be important to alerting them to wrongs; the thought is, a member of an oppressed group, by virtue of her first-personal experience of suffering, is better positioned to identify certain kinds of wrongs than even sympathetic members of dominant groups (aka "allies").[5] However, when other members of oppressed groups testify to personal experiences that go against the social justice narrative, their testimony is dismissed as being improperly motivated.[6]

There are no doubt other such win–win (or lose–lose, depending on who you are) interactions that people critical of social justice leftism could invoke. Now, a reader sympathetic to social justice leftism may object to the way I described A-C. However, my point in listing them was not to offer a neutral description of the phenomena, but rather to make clear how the interactions *feel* for people unsympathetic to the social justice left. To such people, it feels like the rules of discourse are rigged: people on the social justice left can say whatever they want and be praised for it, but when people not on the social justice left use (seemingly) the same approach, they're told, in one way or another, that they may not—the rules are different for them.

Up until 2012, the typical American would find a rule like, "don't make hateful generalizations about a particular race" commonsensical, and she would have thought that moral condemnation of someone who flouted such a rule appropriate. But now, the rule seems to be, "don't make hateful generalizations about a particular race, unless it's white people," and condemnation, moral or otherwise, is doled out by social justice leftists (and those who accept their discourse) to people who criticize such rules as unfair.[7] It is this appearance that makes social justice discourse feel like something radical.

2. The Outlook Underlying Social Justice Discourse

Despite its apparent, radical feel, social justice discourse has an underlying outlook that makes it principled, and perhaps even reasonable. I articulate four presuppositions of this outlook below. I do not claim that they exhaust the social justice way of thinking, but I do think they are important ones, in that they make clear why social justice activists view discourse in the particular way they do. I call the set of all four of them "the social justice outlook":

1. *The Power Claim*: social justice leftists believe that there are dominant groups in society that hold significant power, in that they create social norms (including norms of discourse) that benefit them (the dominant groups), that harm subordinate (i.e., marginalized or oppressed) groups, and that the rest of society is expected to follow. The groups whose dominance is most remarked upon are: whites, men, straights, and cis people.
2. *The Value Claim*: social justice leftists believe that this arrangement—some groups being dominant while others are subordinate—is an immensely bad thing, and want to change it. The groups that are dominant don't deserve to be dominant, and the groups that are marginal don't deserve to be marginal. Indeed, as much as possible, no group should be undeservedly dominant, but instead, every group should be as deservedly liberated as possible. The way to do this is to make sure that, as much as possible, social norms give neither advantage nor disadvantage to any group, unless they deserve such advantage or disadvantage.[8]
3. *The Difficulty Claim*: ceteris paribus, it's harder to be a member of a marginal group than it is to be a member of a dominant group. Consequently, norms that expect the same conduct or output from the marginal and the dominant are unfair, just as it would be unfair to expect one runner to tie the racing time of another runner with a forty-yard head start.[9]
4. *The Fairness Claim*: the norms dominant groups create often lurk under the guise of rules that appear to be neutral among all groups. But despite appearances, these norms benefit dominant groups and disadvantage subordinate groups. Moreover, dominant groups do not consciously create these norms; instead, mechanisms exist in the way institutions and culture are structured. This is what it means for a society to be *systemically* heteronormative, racist, or sexist: owing to the very structure of its culture and institutions, seemingly neutral rules and expectations will advantage straight, white, cis males while disadvantaging queer, non-white, trans, and female people.[10]

To summarize: (1) groups in society have unequal power; (2) this inequality is unjust and should change so that they have equal power; (3) because of this inequality, it's unfair to treat dominant and subordinate groups equally; (4) apparently neutral norms are unfair, because they treat dominant and subordinate groups equally.

Once you appreciate (1)–(4), social justice discourse makes a lot more sense. To take just the three cases I raised above:

A. Righteous indignation from me, hatred from you: imagine dominant group, D oppresses marginal group M. Given that D is oppressing M, it's appropriate for members of M to be upset about D's mistreatment of them. By contrast, if members of D are upset that members of M are chafing at their oppression, this is inappropriate. For example, if Dom wrongs Marge and Marge gets upset about it, Marge's being upset doesn't wrong Dom; by contrast, if Dom wrongs Marge and then condemns Marge for getting upset, this is a further wrong by Dom, and demonstrates a character flaw.
B. Emotional labor from me, white fragility from you: as (3), the Difficulty Claim, notes, it is, *ceteris paribus*, harder to be a part of a marginalized group than it is to be a member of a dominant group. Because society is arranged to benefit dominant groups and disadvantage marginal groups, the average member of a marginal group will suffer more—having such things as greater stress, worse educational preparation, more anxiety, less wealth, and so on—than the average member of a dominant group. Consequently, a dominant person's asking a marginal person to explain and justify her outrage in a manner that the dominant person wants is to privilege the dominant person's ease over the marginal person's emotional labor. That's unfair, so the marginal person's complaining about it is appropriate. By contrast, a marginal person's asking a dominant person to explain and justify his privilege in a manner comfortable for the marginal person is to privilege the marginal person's ease over the dominant person's emotional labor. That's fair, so the dominant person's complaining about it is inappropriate.
C. My testimony is revelatory, yours is distorted: Since many institutions are systemically biased against people of color, women, gays, and transpeople, testimony from such minorities that asserts bias is likely to be true. By contrast, because mainstream institutions are not systemically biased against conservatives (or in favor of, e.g., people of color), testimony to the contrary is likely distorted (in that, at best, it's probably reporting loss of unfair advantages rather than actual disadvantages).

3. Ideological Oppression and Identity

So far, I have presented only the social justice outlook, but I have not yet discussed a social justice discourse ethic (SJDE). I will get to that in the next section. Before that, though, I want to answer a question: why do social justice leftists focus so much on language and representation?

There is a common, potted history of leftism that explains how we got from Marxism, with its focus on economic issues and its consequent dismissal of normative theorizing as a product of bourgeois class consciousness[11] to social justice leftism, with its ubiquitous (or rampant, if you prefer) moralizing[12] and focus on language and representation.[13] That history goes like this: classical Marxism predicted that the condition of workers would deteriorate to the point that they would have to incite a revolution, which would usher in a communistic state. However, this didn't happen.[14] Why not? The answer given by thinkers in the Frankfurt School is that culture is a powerful force that can affect how economic forces manifest, and one that capital has taken advantage of for its own ends. Consequently, to bring about a communistic society wherein workers have freedom, intellectuals cannot simply help laborers organize or, worse, lie back and wait for the revolution to happen on its own: no, they have to contribute to cultural discourse and shape it so that it articulates and supports proletarian interests.

Now, culture is a big, amorphous thing, admitting of many possible definitions, but useful for the story I'll tell is William Sewell's conceptualization of it as "a system of symbols and meanings" (Sewell 2005: 44). So, not only does it include intellectual and artistic products, but also what people take to be of value, what kinds of means they consider as being available to achieve their ends, and the stereotypes people use to think about each other.[15] So, one way capital could use culture to deflect proletarian liberation was, for example, through racism: by stigmatizing blacks, not only could their commodification (through slavery) come more easily, but the labor movement could be set against itself, with white laborers reviling, excluding, and terrorizing black laborers, which not only allowed white laborers to prop up their own self-esteem (thereby making their socioeconomic inferiority to capitalists more bearable), but which also made it harder for the labor movement to achieve its interests. In other words, racism was a force capital could use against labor.

So, here is another potted history, this time about racism in the United States.[16] First, progressives thought that using legal and political means, such as ending segregation and criminalizing workplace discrimination, would be enough to end racism. Though they mostly succeeded in achieving their legal aims, they didn't eliminate racism. This encouraged a second phase, using sites of norm-dissemination—schools, television, businesses—to eliminate *explicit* displays of racism. Though they mostly succeeded in eliminating explicit racism, racism persisted. So, they have now moved on to a third phase: trying to eliminate oppressive ideology, the ideology that makes people unwitting accomplices in their own oppression or in their oppression of others.

This leads to ideology critique. As Sally Haslanger presents it, there are two kinds of oppression: repressive (this includes coercive measures such as the state use of force) and ideological (this covers oppression that is "enacted unthinkingly or even willingly by the subordinated or privileged" [Haslanger 2017: 149]). Thus, when someone is oppressed by ideology, she is oppressed because it narrows the range of options that appear to her to be acceptable. As mentioned above, if culture is a shared system of symbols and meanings, then oppressive ideology is when a culture structures thought so that various alternative ways of thinking and acting—ways that would benefit an oppressed group—are foreclosed while others—namely, those that benefit an oppressing group—are salient. It is in this way that people can participate in their own oppression, and it is also how members of dominant groups might unthinkingly contribute to oppression.[17]

Moreover, because humans are social animals, we find it necessary to learn and internalize our cultural schemas, not only because we need to learn them in order to function in society, but also so that we can develop a sense of self. However, since our identities are formed by our cultures, and since cultures can include oppressive ideological components, it follows that we can incorporate oppressive ideologies as deep parts of our identities, making challenges to them feel threatening to our sense of self.[18]

For example, imagine a girl, Peggy, who grows up in a culture whose most celebrated female exemplars are women who are warm, compassionate, and accepting while the most celebrated male exemplars are competitive, assertive, and inspiring. Peggy could easily come to think that she should behave in ways she associates with female exemplars and not with male ones. Should she come to think in this way, then she may feel guilt on occasions where she behaves in a more typically masculine fashion and pride when she behaved in a more feminine way. Moreover, certain kinds of career paths, such as joining the police, will not even occur to her to pursue. So, the line of thought, "I should consider becoming a policeman" will be closed off to her. In addition, if someone were to tell her that she should be more assertive, say, with her husband, then this would strike her as offensive: what women *should* do is be more caring, not more assertive. To say that she should be more assertive will appear to her like a moral inversion, and so even if she tried it, she may find it to be "not her," and consequently, pressure to act more assertive will feel to her like pressure to go against her integrity, or even her nature. By the same token, the more that some women are portrayed as doing stereotypically masculine labor, or having stereotypically masculine traits, the more that women like Peggy will consider doing such things herself, and the less unnatural they will feel to her.

We're now positioned to understand why social justice leftists emphasize language and representation. The history of civil rights movements shows that oppressive structures are not eliminable just through state action. Consequently, progressives must also focus on changing oppressive ideology. However, because oppressive ideology can co-opt people even when they are not explicitly aware of it (indeed, even when they are trying to escape it), it is not enough to focus just on explicit demonstrations of racist, sexist, and heteronormative, attitudes but also on the cultural signs and symbols that corral people's ways of thinking into cooperation with unjust structures. That's why social justice leftists focus on language and representation.

Because this view of ideology is a fundamental claim that undergirds the social justice outlook (i.e., claims 1–4 in §3), it's worth reducing these remarks about ideological oppression into a single phrase. So, I abbreviate what I have said about ideological oppression as, simply, (I) *ideological oppression*.

4. The Social Justice Discourse Ethic

I believe that the foregoing story is not salient to the average American social justice leftist or, more broadly, to the average American who feels internal pressure to use social justice discourse. While many social justice leftists—especially those who teach in universities, write for influential outlets, and are prominent in activism—can justify themselves in the terms I gave in §§3–4, I suspect (based simply on face-to-face interactions) that this is not true of the rank-and-file. And for the purposes of this chapter, I assume (without argument) an elite theory[19] according to which cultural influence is mostly top-down: intellectuals come up with the theories animating social justice discourse, educators, artists, and journalists propound those theories, activists bring up and inspire the legal changes needed to help the process, and the rank-and-file (people who aren't activists or members of a professional political class, but who sympathize with, or are susceptible to sympathizing with, the theory in question) provide the heft, electoral and social, to change politics and culture.[20] I should note, though, that despite my acceptance of elite theory, I don't think that intellectuals can get the rank-and-file to believe just anything; if what they ask of their devotees is simply too demanding, then it won't take.

Given that the SJDE governs the average social justice leftist, many of whom are not as intellectually sophisticated as the theorists, it follows that its rules, when put into practice, are going to be less nuanced than they would be if everyone were a theorist. So here, as I see them, are the rules of social justice discourse.

I. *Reverence for the oppressed*: Members of oppressed groups ought to be treated with greater reverence than members of dominant groups. The more oppressed groups a person is part of, the greater the reverence she ought to be given. Some oppressed groups are more oppressed than others (e.g., transgender people are more oppressed than cisgender people) and so should, correspondingly, be treated with more reverence.[21]

II. *Dogmatism about oppression*: certain claims (e.g., the harmfulness of racism and the existence of patriarchy) are either so obviously true or so important that they should be presupposed. Indeed, some people go so far as to hold that certain kinds of claims that deny or diminish the significance of oppressive structures count as structural or systemic violence.[22] Because the reality of oppression and oppressive structures should be presupposed, and because denial of them is a kind of violence, arguments that and interlocutors who deny or diminish these moral or empirical claims should (usually) be dismissed as "problematic" or as "gaslighters."[23]

III. *Effects over intent*: the effects of one's language matter significantly more than what one intended. Because oppressive ideology often structures thought in ways that are extremely difficult to discover, one need not harbor, for example, racial animus to speak, think, or act in racist ways. Moreover, because members of oppressed groups are better situated to detect harm, negative effects on them—in the form of felt offense—are much better indicators of racist speech than the intent behind it.[24]

Those three rules significantly structure social justice discourse and amount to the SJDE. It's worth pausing to say more about each of them.

First, take *reverence for the oppressed*. We should revere the oppressed because of the truths of the *difficulty claim* (that, ceteris paribus, it's harder to be a member of a marginalized group than it is to be a member of a dominant group) and the *fairness claim* (fairness means treating people who have greater burdens differently from those with lighter burdens). In practice, reverence means being more credulous about reports of suffering made by members of oppressed groups than about similar reports made by members of dominant groups, listening especially closely to those who are more marginalized than yourself, and making a conscious effort to learn about the situations of the oppressed.[25]

Second, take *dogmatism about oppression*.[26] This part of the SJDE receives its motivation from the *value claim* (that oppression is an immensely bad thing, and upending it is of immense moral importance) in combination with *ideological oppression*. Given the importance of liberating the oppressed, and given how ideological oppression works, it is both urgent to make social progress and just as important to keep the social progress that has been made. There are two elements to this claim. First, seeing forms of oppression can be extremely difficult. Often, we don't even have the vocabulary to describe a form of oppression some people suffer, but once we develop it, we can see it, and so become better positioned to stop it.[27] Second, once a kind of oppression has been conceptualized and confirmed, it's important to stop having debates about it (if possible),[28] as such debate makes people treat illegitimate views as legitimate,[29] which could either prolong the time it takes to make moral progress, or even allow for its reversal. (It's also worth noting that *dogmatism about oppression* and the *value claim* also seem to presume some kind of moral realism,[30] as this will come up when I offer my social-justice-friendly explanation for the swift prevalence of the SJDE.)

Finally, take *effects over intent*. The *power claim* (society consists of some relatively dominant and some relatively marginalized groups), in combination with *ideological oppression* motivates *effects over intent*. The justification for *effects over intent* goes like this: the most powerful groups in society have the most control over ideology, and they tend to use ideology (either by design, by accident, or merely habitually) to keep themselves in power. In addition, people's personalities are formed by a culture that incorporates oppressive ideology into its symbols and meanings. Consequently, people's personalities, especially those in dominant groups, develop within oppressive categories. This means that, even if they intend no harm, they are predisposed to think and act in ways that maintain their dominance. Consequently, if we want to liberate oppressed groups, we should focus on harmful effects of speech rather than the intent behind it.[31]

5. A Social Justice Explanation for the Prevalence of Social Justice Discourse

I can now attempt to answer the motivating question of this chapter: What explains the sudden, widespread adoption of social justice discourse, given how radical it is? I take it for granted that social justice language—previously unusual terms and phrases such as "cis," "intersectionality," "microaggressions," and "white privilege"—is not only widespread but also has become so only very recently.[32] What explains this?

Although there are a variety of explanations, I want to focus on three, because I think their insights, differences, and limitations are most instructive for understanding the emergence of the social justice movement: Adolph Reed Jr.'s Marxian explanation,[33] Angelo Codevilla's Nietzschean explanation,[34] and Bradley Campbell and Jason Manning's explanation based on cultural transition.[35]

On Reed's view, a noteworthy feature of contemporary anti-racist politics is that its social scientific analyses are, generally, explanatorily vacuous. They point to a disparity between, say, white and black Americans, and then conclude that white racism is the cause, without undertaking a more nuanced analysis. Reed claims that the reason anti-racist politics uses such coarse approaches is that "its fundamental goal is propagation of the view that inequalities or injustices suffered by black Americans should be understood as resulting from generic white racism. Its objective, that is, is rhetorical and ideological, not political and programmatic" (Reed 2018: 107).

Why does anti-racist politics have a rhetorical and ideological goal rather than a political and programmatic one? On Reed's view, this is because "anti-racist politics is a professional-managerial class politics. Its adherents are . . . committed fundamentally to pursuit of racial parity within neoliberalism, not social transformation" (Reed 2018: 110).

Reed offers two pieces of evidence for this contention. The first is that anti-racist activists were sharply critical of Bernie Sanders's 2016 socialist proposals, while being supportive of Hillary Clinton's less socialist ones. If they were interested in a more left-wing politics, then the reverse would have been the case. The second reason to think that anti-racist politics is a part of "neoliberalism" rather than left-wing is that it self-consciously descends from the black power politics of the 1960s. But advocates of this politics ("black powerites," Reed calls them) "generally depended on ruling class largess for realization of their programmatic objectives. That was their alternative to trying to form broad, popular coalitions and to navigate the compromises and constraints that sort of politics requires" (Reed 2018: 110–11). The tactics that "black powerites" used required a functioning capitalistic system to work; so too does contemporary anti-racist politics; and presumably Reed would think the same of the social justice left overall.

Whereas Reed traces the roots of the contemporary anti-racist movement to the black power movements of the 1960s, Codevilla finds the inspiration for "political correctness" (which I take to be more or less equivalent with what I am calling "social justice discourse") in the work of Antonio Gramsci.

Gramsci (as Codevilla presents him) agreed with Marx in two ways. First, he agreed that the ultimate goal should be a worker's paradise. Second, he agreed that people usually arrived at their fundamental political beliefs as a result of social factors, rather than from argumentation. However, he contradicted Marx in that he thought that moral and ideological factors, rather than economic ones, explained most of why people took the political positions they did. Consequently, he thought the key to reforming society was to take control of cultural institutions.

Though Gramsci recommended subverting traditional, liberal ways of talking and giving them progressive meaning, Codevilla sees the social justice movement as having followed Lenin's approach, and therefore as trying to eliminate nonprogressive discourse through force or coercion. Codevilla thinks this of the social justice movement for two reasons. First, he thinks that its concerns are the same as the concerns of its leaders, and its leaders are academics and intellectuals.[36] Second, he sees contemporary academics and intellectuals on the social justice left as having, as their main concern, the demonization of bourgeois culture: "[t]hey see the culture of what Marxists call 'bourgeois morality' as the negation of their identity and authority. That identity, their identity, is to be promoted, endlessly, by endless warfare against that culture" (Codevilla 2016: 38).

Reed and Codevilla agree that the social justice left has its shape because of who leads it, and both agree that academics, primarily, are the ones who lead it. Consequently, despite the fact that social justice discourse emphasizes justice for oppressed groups, Reed and Codevilla see it as really being about advancing the interests of an academic class. Where Reed and Codevilla disagree is on how to characterize that class: Reed sees it as conservative, because it accepts a capitalist framework. Codevilla sees it as leftist, because it is anti-bourgeois.

Whereas Reed and Codevilla see the social justice movement as more of the same—either more capitalism or more leftism, respectively—for Bradley Campbell and Jason Manning, the social justice outlook marks something new, a transition to a new moral culture.

Campbell and Manning describe a moral culture as "a prevailing pattern of morality" (Campbell and Manning 2018: 12). They see the West as having transitioned from an honor culture to a dignity culture, and now as transitioning from a dignity culture to a victimhood culture.[37]

In an honor culture, what determines your moral status is how honored you are by other members of your culture, and what tends to determine how honored you are is your physical ability. Because your moral status depends on others' opinions of you, it's in your interest to be sensitive to slights (failure to do so will lead to your gradual moral diminution and corresponding loss of privileges), and also to take violent action against whomever slighted you. In short, in an honor culture you should be sensitive to offense, and when you notice it, you must deal with it yourself (turning to other people to help you would be an admission of weakness).

In a dignity culture, what determines your moral status is your intrinsic moral worth, your dignity. Because your moral status is not dependent on others' opinions, it follows that the best way to exemplify dignity is to act in a self-controlled way that shows that you can live up to your moral worth. Members of dignity cultures have incentives to ignore slights, for their doing so shows their self-control, and hence their ability to act in a dignified manner. However, when it comes to greater offenses—say, violent assaults—then members of a dignity culture will turn to neutral third parties to deal with those harms. Doing so is not a sign of weakness, but rather everyone's duty to respect their own and others' intrinsic moral worth.

Finally, in a victimhood culture, what determines your moral status is your victimization. The more hardship you suffer, the more lauded you get. This makes sense, in that social plaudits are one way of compensating someone for the harms he suffers as a result of his social characteristics. However, because victimization elevates you, you have incentive to be sensitive to slights (similar to an honor culture). On the other hand, because physical prowess is not valued as in honor culture, and because someone who is victimized is generally not thought to have power, members of victimhood cultures deal with slights by turning to third parties to settle them.

Campbell and Manning think that, since the 1960s, four features of American society have become increasingly prominent, and have led to the emergence of a victimhood culture:[38] (1) increasing social equality; (2) increasing administrative growth; (3) increasing racial, sexual, and gender diversity; and (4) increasing access to partisan supporters.[39]

Because of increasing social equality (among racial groups, between men and women, for LGBTQ people, etc.), the United States has become a more socially equitable society, and the more socially equitable a society is, the more that "overstratification"—departures from equality—becomes socially unacceptable. Similarly, the more diverse a society becomes, the more that "underdiversity"—expressions of hostility to diversity—becomes socially condemned.[40] Increasing administrative growth not only allows people to turn to administrative third parties to settle conflict, but it actually encourages this, for the growth of available administrative solutions to conflict tends to discourage people from trying to settle conflict privately.[41] Finally, because media allow increasing access to partisan supporters, there is incentive to publicize your grievances in cases of social conflict.[42]

These four features are most pronounced in university settings, which is why the microaggression program finds its greatest support there. That said, although higher education has all kinds of diversity, one kind it does not have, at least among professors and administrators, is ideological diversity.[43] And in homogeneous societies, it is precisely departures from homogeneity (i.e., some kind of diversity) that is punished. This is why there is increasing support in academia for sanctioning those who disagree with the microaggression program.[44] (Similarly, although America has become more socially equitable since the 1960s, it has also become more economically inequitable over that time. On Campbell and Manning's analysis, that would suggest, ceteris paribus, less concern over departures from economic equality than over departures from social equality.[45])

The two biggest advantages of Campbell and Manning's explanation over Reed's or Codevilla's explanations are, first, that whereas Reed and Codevilla characterize the social justice movement merely as another manifestation of a decades- or centuries-long phenomenon, Campbell and Manning explain why it has its particular features. Second, Campbell and Manning's theory explains why the social justice movement emerged roughly when it did, whereas Reed's and Codevilla's theories don't. Consequently, I prefer Campbell and Manning's theory.

There is one limitation and one worry about Campbell and Manning's changing-moral-culture theory. The limitation is that Campbell and Manning take a deterministic approach to moral cultural change. In other words, they don't investigate whether there are good, normative reasons for changing from a dignity to a victimhood culture. The worry is that they don't give strong evidence that we are actually undergoing a cultural change; indeed, there are reasons to think that the sudden and widespread change, which is presupposed by this chapter's motivating question, hasn't happened at all.

In the remainder of this section, I supplement Campbell and Manning's theory with Michael Huemer's argument for moral realism based on moral progress. In the next section (§7), I bring up tensions within the social justice worldview. And in the final section (section §8), I explain why there is reason to think that we are not transitioning to a victimhood culture.

According to Huemer, one good argument for accepting moral realism is moral progress.[46] Over the entirety of human history until about 400 years ago, illiberalism was regnant. But, starting around 400 years ago, and then happening rapidly around 50–100 years ago, liberalism became dominant across the globe (Huemer defines liberalism as follows: "liberalism (1) recognizes the moral equality of persons, (2) promotes respect for the dignity of the individual, and (3) opposes gratuitous coercion and violence" [Huemer 2016: 1987]). Huemer thinks the best explanation for the more-or-less worldwide consensus on liberalism is that it is objectively morally correct.

Why does the fact that so many societies have recently adopted liberalism support moral realism? Because alternative explanations for the emergence of this relatively recent consensus—namely, evolutionary and cultural explanations—don't work. It's unlikely to be an evolutionary explanation, because liberalism emerged too recently on the scene to result from evolutionary adaptation.[47] And cultural explanations don't work because they don't account for all the data; while there may be a good cultural explanation for why liberalism developed in, say, the United States, the facts that it became accepted in so many different cultures, and in so many of them at around the same time, make a cultural explanation unlikely to be the whole story.[48] In other words, at least part of the best explanation for why so many societies converged on liberalism is that liberalism is correct.[49]

Huemer also offers a story about how moral progress occurs. The basic idea is this: in every society, there are some people who are slightly less affected by evolutionary and cultural biases than others; because these people are, on average, better at reasoning, the more that a society carves out a place for people with such reasoning talents to use them, the more that they converge closer to the truth of liberalism. And because they are generally of higher status than most people, other high status people pay attention to them. As time goes on, the culture progresses ever closer to the truth of liberalism.[50]

The same kind of reasoning can apply to the acceptance of social justice discourse. The people likeliest to accept the social justice outlook and to promote social justice discourse are academics (as both Reed and Codevilla admit). The fact that so many people who are so situated do accept the social justice outlook is reason to think that the social justice outlook is true. In other words, convergence, especially convergence among intellectuals in different cultural settings (Campbell and Manning note that the microaggressions program has expanded from America to other countries[51]) is best explained by the truth of the social justice outlook.

Call Huemer's story *progressive moral realism*. It and *ideological oppression* are the main philosophical supports of the social justice outlook.

6. Tension within the SJDE

Above, I claimed that the SJDE has three elements: (I) *reverence for the oppressed*, (II) *dogmatism about oppression*, and (III) *effects over intent*. In addition, I claimed that the SJDE rests on the social justice outlook, which consists of four presuppositions: (1) the *power claim* (dominant groups have the most power in society), (2) the *value claim* (dominant groups having power is a bad thing), (3) the *difficulty claim* (*ceteris paribus*, it's more difficult being a member of an oppressed group than it is being a member of a dominant group), and (4) the *fairness claim* (rules that don't take the difficulty claim into account are unfair). Finally, I believe that two other claims, (i) *ideological oppression* and (ii) *progressive moral realism*, justify the social justice outlook. Call (i) and (ii) together "the basics." So, the basics support the outlook, and the outlook supports the discourse ethic.

I now want to argue that problems arise when you accept all of the basics, the outlook, and the discourse ethic. Some of these problems come with trying to combine some of these with each other. Other problems are simply problems about the plausibility of one of the tenets, presuppositions, or claims taken in isolation.

The first criticism comes from Campbell and Manning. Recall that, on Campbell and Manning's view, what grants someone in a victimhood culture moral status is how much she has suffered. Their point is not that people who accept the social justice outlook explicitly think this, but that patterns in their behavior, or at least in what they say they care about, show that they accord higher status to people who have suffered than to people who have not (this is what I called "reverence for the oppressed"). On Campbell and Manning's view social justice advocates revere the oppressed because that is a way of compensating for their victimization. But therein lies the tension: the more you elevate a victim, the less victimized she becomes, which in turn means that at some point you should either stop elevating her or even positively denigrate her.[52]

Because of this diluting effect, believers in the social justice worldview (and *a fortiori*, those who accept victimhood culture) face an incentive not to acknowledge that victimization brings with it this benefit—doing so would make the program unstable. In addition, other members of oppressed groups have an incentive to accentuate or even fabricate their oppression, so as to receive aid and comfort. That at least some people think that victimization brings benefits is supported by the increasing incidence of so-called hate crime hoaxes—that is, when people fabricate a hate crime against themselves in the hopes that it will generate support.[53]

A second criticism is that *reverence for the oppressed* is *prima facie* quite crude. Even if it's true, on average, that it's more difficult being a member of an oppressed group than it is being a member of a dominant group (and this isn't obviously true for, say, Asians of Japanese descent,[54] or blacks of Nigerian descent[55]—facts that themselves need explanation), operating on this basis in face-to-face interactions oversimplifies. Not only can individual differences often overwhelm group differences—a gay, black, female who is the child of working-class, loving parents may have a less difficult life than a straight, white, male child of rich but unloving parents—but empirical work has confirmed certain states of affairs that thwart what one would predict, given the *power claim* and the *difficulty claim* (which are two presuppositions that undergird *reverence for the oppressed*).[56]

In response, an adherent of the SJDE can admit this, but point out that people can be quite nuanced in how they use an ethic. As Haslanger has said, learning how to treat people is like learning how to navigate the rules of the road: people not only know the rules of the road but also when to follow them.[57]

However, it's plausible that greater complexity in the rules of social discourse disadvantages some people while advantaging others. In particular, people who aren't particularly perceptive or able to process complex rules will be more disadvantaged than people who are perceptive and able to process complex rules. In other words, increasing the nuance of social rules advantages the neurotypical and what one might call the "cognitively privileged" (i.e., those who are, for whatever reason, more able to deal with complicated information than others). So, relying on the nuance of common folk to salvage the plausibility of *reverence for the oppressed* may actually disadvantage certain kinds of oppressed people. To paraphrase Jonah Goldberg, complexity is a tax.[58]

In addition, it seems that, in actual practice, adherents to the social justice outlook are selective about their belief in the ability of people to handle nuance. For example, Rebecca C. Hetey and Jennifer L. Eberhardt point out that exposing white Americans to racial disparities in incarceration tends to make whites more punitive rather than less. Consequently, they recommend that any presentation of statistics showing racial disparities in crime be accompanied by contextualization, that is, pointing to the institutional racism that (they presume) is responsible for the black-white disparity in incarceration rates.[59] Thus, it seems that, from a social justice left perspective, there is reason to worry about the ability of common people, at least when they are white, to handle nuance, at least when it comes to issues about which they are dominant. But if there is reason to worry about their nuance when it comes to issues having to do with their dominance, it seems like there is reason to think they won't be able to handle the nuance needed to properly employ the SJDE.

This leads to a second criticism, this time of combining *reverence for the oppressed* with *effects over intent*: this combination makes it difficult for members of a dominant group to relate to members of an oppressed group. The more you revere (or pander to) someone, the less equitable a relationship you can have. And the less equitable a relationship you can have, the less you can relate to her. This suggests that members of dominant groups won't want to have relationships with members of minority groups (insofar, at least, as the member of the dominant group thinks that she will be expected to abide by *reverence for the oppressed* and *effects over intent*). Members of minority groups might also not want to have relationships with members of dominant groups who accepted *reverence for the oppressed* and *effects over intent*, on the grounds that a relationship with such a person would feel inauthentic and unsatisfying.

A third criticism of the social justice outlook focuses on combining *progressive moral realism* with *ideological oppression*. If the social justice outlook is right, then its truth, in combination with the truth of *progressive moral realism*, partly explains why the SJDE has spread so quickly, as it also supports the *value claim*, the *fairness claim*, and *dogmatism about oppression*, which themselves support the SJDE. However, the more obvious the truth of the SJDE is, the less worrisome *ideological oppression* is: after all, the more clear-cut the case for the SJDE, the less able ideological oppression will be at keeping people from seeing the plausibility of the SJDE.

On the other hand, the more distorting ideological oppression is, the more we have to worry that the SJDE is itself a result of ideological oppression, as Marxists like Reed Jr. think. That is, if social justice leftists are right that ideological oppression is a way that the powerful manage to convince others to abide by norms that support the powerful, then the fact that the SJDE has spread so widely means that those who are most able to propound the SJDE become powerful themselves; consequently, social justice leftists have reason to worry (as the *power claim* in combination with *ideological oppression* would have it) that, because social justice leftists have so much influence over the culture (and are, in this way, powerful), the SJDE is itself a set of norms that advance the interests of the powerful.

7. What's Really Going on? A Nietzschean Explanation

As a matter of fact, I think that the social justice movement has the shape it has, and is advocated for in the way it is, in large part because it serves the interests of certain culturally powerful elites, namely academics. That's a bold claim, and it's a mean one, so in this section I try to justify it while also softening its nastiness.

Here's a basic presupposition of *my* outlook: if a social movement is authentic, then its members should behave in a way consistent with that social movement's expressed goals. For example, if a temperance movement claims that alcoholism is a terrible thing, but its members don't usually try to help alcoholics, and in fact get regularly drunk, that's reason to think that the movement is not *actually* about what it *claims* it's about.

Here's a real-life example, which comes from Kate Manne. After describing Donald Trump's remark that not just doctors, but also women, should be punished for having abortions, Manne quotes Hillary Clinton's remark that Trump was "saying what all [Republicans] believe." Clinton's claim was this: although pro-life activists and politicians regularly *claim* that their main motivation is to protect unborn babies, in reality, they want to control and punish women. Manne agrees: "Clinton was right. And though such claims may be impolitic, they are also important to make, as opposed to maintaining the pretense that this is a purely ethical and religious question . . . I believe it is too late in the day to keep up the charade" (Manne 2016: 92).

On Manne's view, we should not see the pro-life movement as being motivated by protecting fetuses, because if that's what it was about, then pro-lifers would behave differently from how they behave: "if [the pro-life movement] was about preventing abortions as such . . . then why not do everything in one's power to make available those many—and often cheap—forms of contraception that demonstrably do not allow fertilization to occur? But this is manifestly not happening, as we see in the Supreme Court's decision in *Burwell v. Hobby Lobby* (2014)" (Manne 2016: 99). Similarly, we should not see the pro-life movement as being motivated by a desire to police women's sexuality, because if it were, then pro-lifers would permit abortions in cases of rape and incest, and yet a lot don't.[60]

Instead, we should see the pro-life movement as being motivated by the desire to reinforce a view of what women *should* be like. Women who have abortions strike pro-lifers as "[w]ithholding and failing to give . . . being cold, callous, and heartless; neglecting their natural duty to provide safe haven and nurture, by evicting a vulnerable being from their rightful home, their birthright" (Manne 2016: 99). Manne goes further, psychoanalyzing the pro-life movement as ultimately being motivated by men, particularly men whose egos were wounded by some women rejecting their standards of feminine behavior: "[t]he fetus . . . serves as a powerful cultural symbol or surrogate for certain men's sense of being neglected or deprived by women. And their sense of vulnerability can be projected onto the fetus, thus allowing them to feel outrage on behalf of another supposed person . . . it is often easier to take the moral high ground than admit to feeling rejected and wounded" (Manne 2016: 100).

This is the kind of analysis that bears kinship to my own. I submit that if the social justice movement were authentic, then it would behave differently. In particular, it would operate differently in two main ways.

First, there would be much more emphasis on practices that require their advocates to give of themselves rather than to castigate others. As Musa al-Gharbi documents,[61] the wealthiest cities in the United States have the highest concentration of institutions and people who claim to adhere to the social justice outlook, and yet those cities have extremely high wealth inequality and don't employ policies designed to redistribute that wealth to the minorities they claim to regard as oppressed. Not only do such places not employ redistributive policies, but the charitable causes that upper-class and upper-middle-class leftists donate to are rarely ones that help racial minorities in particular.[62] This suggests that one of the reasons to adopt social justice discourse is to show to others (and even yourself) that you are "doing something" about injustice without having to pay a high personal price.

Second, there would be more attention paid to what I above called "cognitive privilege." If you have "cognitive privilege," you have greater than average verbal acuity, sensitivity to context, ability to educate yourself about an issue, and access to knowledge about the concerns of the social justice left. Most members of the social justice movement are cognitively privileged, and are unduly harsh toward people who are cognitively disadvantaged. This is seen from the facts that they use cumbersome language, they expect people to have familiarity with their terms and chastise them when they don't, they seem fairly unconcerned about working-class white people, and they're overly laudatory about the importance of education.

People who accept the social justice outlook often see education as the key to the good life, and naturally so. If you think that oppressive ideology is the main barrier currently preventing us from having a just society, it makes sense that you would valorize education, for education is the most obvious means by which people could free themselves from oppressive ideology.

Let me give an example. In the preface to his book, *How Propaganda Works*, Jason Stanley movingly writes of the work of his late father, the sociologist Manfred Stanley, and how it inspired him. It's worth quoting at length:

My father's view of autonomy was richer than mere non-domination by others. His worldview *required every citizen to be provided with a liberal education, the goal of which would be to foster the capacity for autonomous decision making about one's life plans,* where this involved the kind of reflection that, for him, allowed for *genuine* autonomy. . . . The target of my father's book [*The Technological Conscience*] is what he often called "technicism," the view that scientific expertise and technological advancements are the solution to the problems of the human condition. My father saw two chief dangers in the technicist worldview. First, it seeks to replace a liberal education with vocational technical skills. *The technicist educational system therefore seeks to rob us of the capacity for autonomy.* Secondly, *a technicist culture encourages a tendency to defer one's practical decisions to the epistemic authority of experts.* (Stanley 2015: xi, italics mine)

Both Stanleys seem to think that without a liberal education—of the sort that, well, people like them (and me) have and provide—a person cannot have "genuine" autonomy. Without a liberal education, people do not have "the capacity for autonomous decision making about one's lifeplans." And so, such people would have to "defer [their] practical decisions to the epistemic authority of experts." The message seems to be: people need professors to be autonomous.[63]

This is a very flattering to professors. And it's certainly in our interests for people to believe it. But what's funny about it is that, though the thinking is that a liberal education allows you to make decisions without having to defer to experts, when it comes to issues of social justice, the SJDE teaches people *precisely* to defer their practical decisions to the epistemic authority of experts (recall *dogmatism about oppression, reverence for the oppressed,* and *effects over intent*). So, on the one hand, it's important for people to be educated, so that they can think for themselves, but on the other hand, there are certain substantive, nonobvious, and controversial claims that must be believed on pain of moral turpitude.

Now, for all I have written, a social justice leftist can believe most of it. After all, it could be that the reason that we're changing from a dignity to a victimhood culture is that the claims of victimhood culture are correct and, in Huemerian fashion, we're collectively coming to see that. And, even if it's true that intellectuals steer the social justice movement into directions that benefit them, it could be that this is often how morally progressive movements happen. The measure of the social justice movement must be taken on the good it does when the transition to victimhood culture is more complete. (That's me softening the meanness of my inauthenticity claim. To put it in other terms: yes, the social justice movement is inauthentic, but most social movements are, and since the social justice outlook is correct, the good the movement does outweigh its inauthenticity.)

But this all assumes that we *are* transitioning to a victimhood culture. There is good reason to think, contrary to the presupposition of this chapter's motivating question, that, though social justice *discourse* has won widespread acceptance, the social justice *outlook* has not.

According to the Hidden Tribes project, the U.S. population consists of seven "tribes," each of which has their own attitude and approach to politics: Progressive Activists, Traditional Liberals, Passive Liberals, the Politically Disengaged, Moderates, Traditional Conservatives, and Devoted Conservatives. Here is how Hidden Tribes describes Progressive Activists:

> Progressive Activists have strong ideological views, high levels of engagement with political issues, and the highest levels of education and socioeconomic status. Their own circumstances are secure (they feel safer than any group), which perhaps frees them to devote more attention to larger issues of justice in society around them. They have an outsized role in political discourse, even though they comprise a small portion of the total population (about 1 in 12 Americans). They are highly sensitive to issues of fairness and equity in society, particularly with regards to race, gender, and other minority group identities. Their emphasis on existing power structures leads them to be very pessimistic about fairness in America. (Dawkins et al. 2018: 30)

Of the seven tribes, Progressive Activists best covers what I have been calling "social justice leftists." And they make up only 8 percent of the population.

Now, it could be that some of the other tribes—say, the 11 percent who are traditional liberals, the 15 percent who are passive liberals, or much of the 26 percent who are politically disengaged—share the social justice outlook, but simply differ on how important to rank its concerns compared to, say, economic concerns. However, according to the same study that divided America into seven tribes, "80 percent [of Americans] . . . believe that political correctness has gone too far. By contrast, only 30 percent of Progressive Activists believe political correctness has gone too far" (Hawkins et al. 2018: 98). This suggests that, if there is a change from a dignity to a victimhood culture, it is incipient rather than developed. More strongly than that, it suggests we are *not* transitioning to a victimhood culture. And that would mean that Campbell and Manning's analysis works only for college campuses.

If this is right, then why have most other Americans adopted social justice discourse? The answer, I think, has to do with an idea that Nicholas Nassim Taleb calls "minority rule."

Minority rule is when a small minority manages to get a large majority to act like the small minority wants.[64] An example is kosher eating. As it happens, a large majority of American food products are kosher, despite the fact that very few Americans keep kosher. There are two reasons for this. First, people who keep kosher can only eat kosher food, but people who don't keep kosher can eat both kosher and non-kosher food. Second, it's not particularly expensive to make food kosher. So, because it's not expensive to make your food kosher, and because otherwise you won't get the business of that small minority who does keep kosher, just about all food becomes kosher.

The same phenomenon may have taken place with social justice discourse. Of roughly 8 percent of the population, the following is true: not only will they only use social justice discourse, but they will chastise those who don't. By contrast, 67 percent or so of the population is happy to use either social justice discourse or the discourse that prevailed before 2012. (The remaining 25 percent—the 19 percent who are Traditional Conservatives and the 6 percent who are Devoted Conservatives—will chafe or rebel, respectively, against using the terminology but since they don't have nearly the power to affect the culture that Progressive Activists have, their resistance hasn't achieved much success. Yet.)

If this explains the prevalence of social justice discourse, then it suggests that what social justice leftists have mainly achieved is changing the way people talk.[65] And even this much they have done more through obstreperousness than by getting people to see the light. Far from "foster[ing] the capacity for autonomous decision making about one's life plans," social justice leftists have been encouraging people to "defer [their] practical decisions to the epistemic authority of experts."

And so here's what I think the social justice movement is really about: though most social justice leftists care about the issues they raise, the movement is shaped by the fact that fairly well-off, intelligent academics are trying to get higher status. This is why they're not as concerned about issues of class (they're fairly well-off, remember) and why discourse is emphasized (it's what they're good at). It's also why so many of their programs for social improvement involve more education (diversity training, sensitivity training, and college in general) with comparatively little attention to whether more education actually works.[66] Whether this is *all* it amounts to depends on whether we are *really* turning into a victimhood culture, or whether this moment is, ultimately, evanescent enthusiasm.

NOTES

1. For evidence of its sudden and widespread emergence, see Tabarrok (2019).
2. The Sarah Jeong affair is a good example of this. See Sullivan (2018) and Beauchamp (2018).

3. In Jess Zimmerman's words, "the constant labor of placating men and navigating patriarchal expectations is exhausting because it's *work* (italics hers)." See Zimmerman (2015).

4. See DiAngelo (2018).

5. "A crucial part of the project of critical theory is to listen to first-person (especially first-person plural) knowledge claims . . . I take this commitment to be grounded, at least in part, in epistemic humility: we should listen to those directly affected by the practices in question because they are likely to have better access to morally relevant facts" (Haslanger 2017: 166).

6. See, for example, Bouie (2016).

7. I hasten to add: the social justice left receives *lots* of criticism, from the right and the left.

8. I include these caveats about desert so as to forestall objections such as "so, do social justice leftists think that mass murderers should have the same status as saints?"

9. In John Scalzi's memorable phrase, "In the role playing game known as The Real World, 'Straight White Male' is the lowest difficulty setting there is" (Scalzi 2012).

10. Joe Feagin, who first canonized the phrase, "systemic racism", defines it as follows: "Systemic racism includes the complex array of antiblack practices, the unjustly gained political-economic power of whites, the continuing economic and other resource inequalities along racial lines, and the white racist ideologies and attitudes created to maintain and rationalize white privilege and power. *Systemic* here means that the core racist realities are manifested in each of society's major parts . . . each major part of U.S. society—the economy, politics, education, religion, the family—reflects the fundamental reality of systemic racism" (Feagin 2010: xiv).

11. See, for example, Leiter (2015).

12. See Kaufman (2017).

13. For a conservative telling of this history, see Codevilla (2016). For a progressive version, see Rorty (1998).

14. At least, not in western, industrialized states. And many communists will declare that the places where it did happen weren't "real" communism.

15. Haslanger (2017) uses Sewell's conceptualization of culture to make this point.

16. I take this story from Haslanger (2017).

17. See Haslanger (2017: 159–160 and 162–163).

18. See Haslanger (2017: 158).

19. Pareto (1983) and Mills (2000) contain canonical formulations of elite theory.

20. The political scientist Stacy Ulbig informs me that my approach is in keeping with mainstream research in political science on "opinion leaders."

21. This idea of using the degrees of oppression people suffer as a way of determining the order in which they should speak is sometimes known as the "progressive stack" (see Jacobson 2017). It is associated with intersectionality—the theory that people with multiply oppressed identities face distinct forms of oppression—but doesn't necessarily follow from it (see Coaston 2019). For evidence, besides the progressive stack, that anyone actually accepts *reverence for the oppressed*, see

Kelly and Roedder (2008). For evidence that *reverence for the oppressed* is at least somewhat widespread, see Uhlmann, Pizarro, and Tannenbaum and Ditto (2009) (this study shows that liberals are more likely to sacrifice a white person to save black people than they are to sacrifice a black person to save white people. I suspect that this result would be more pronounced if done today).

22. See Galtung (1969) for the canonical discussion of structural violence.

23. Some personal testimonies support *dogmatism about oppression*; see, for example, Weinstein (2017) and Maroja (2019). In addition, there is some evidence that *dogmatism about oppression* is widespread, at least in university settings. According to a survey of "1,078 currently enrolled college students in the United States,"

> 53% of students surveyed reported that they do not think their college or university frequently encourages students to consider a wide variety of viewpoints and perspectives . . . 32% of conservatives (vs. 8% of liberals) were very reluctant to discuss politics in the classroom . . . 29% of conservatives (vs. 8% of liberals) were very reluctant to discuss gender in the classroom . . . 30% of conservatives (vs. 15% of liberals) were very reluctant to discuss race in the classroom. (Stevens 2017)

I also take the incidence of speaker-disinvitations to be support *dogmatism about oppression*. As of October 19, 2019, the organization FIRE (Foundation for Individual Rights in Education) had a database of 437 attempted disinvitations. Of those 437, approximately 56% occurred between 2012 and 2019. Moreover, of the total disinvitations, about 60% came from groups that were politically left of the speaker (by FIRE's reckoning), but between 2012 and 2019, approximately 68% of the disinvitation attempts came from left-wing groups. These two figures suggest that since 2012, disinvitation-attempts are becoming more numerous, and are becoming more left-wing (see Foundation for Individual Rights in Education 2019). Finally, I would also count "cancel culture," assuming it's a real phenomenon (see Herzog 2019 for an overview), as evidence supporting *dogmatism about oppression*.

24. See, for example, Utt (2013). Evidence that *effects over intent* is widespread can be found in Campbell and Manning (2018), in which they document the microaggressions movement. According to Derald Wing Sue, whom Campbell and Manning describe as "probably more responsible for the success of the microaggression program than anyone else" (Campbell and Manning 2018: 3), microaggressions are "the brief and commonplace daily verbal, behavioral, and environmental indignities, *whether intentional or unintentional*, that communicate hostile, derogatory, or negative racial, gender, and sexual orientation, and religious slights and insults to the target person or group" (Sue 2010: 5, emphasis mine, cited in Campbell and Manning 2018: 3). I am not aware of any evidence documenting how widespread concern about microaggressions is, though Campbell and Manning list a number of universities and corporations that implement programs meant to combat them (see Campbell and Manning 2018: 16–17).

25. An especially striking example of *reverence for the oppressed* can be found in Kelly and Roedder (2008), where they argue that professors should give higher grades

to black students than to white ones for qualitatively identical work, to compensate for the (alleged) fact that professors harbor implicit bias against blacks, and so are apt to grade them lower than white students for qualitatively identical work. See Kelly and Roedder (2008: 532–535).

26. What I am calling "dogmatism about oppression" receives forceful defense in Fantl (2018). In a nutshell, Fantl's argument is that when it comes to "flawless" arguments that have conclusions we know to be false (and hence are misleading flawless arguments), we should not engage those arguments open-mindedly, lest we end up believing false conclusions. We should also not engage those arguments close-mindedly, lest we act in bad faith. Consequently, we should not engage with those arguments at all. I take it this advice is directed especially to those who may not be philosophically sophisticated enough to see the allegedly illicit assumptions or inferences in those arguments.

27. The classic example is sexual harassment. See Fricker (2007: 149–50).

28. I write "if possible" because some social justice adherents will admit that if a position they think refuted still commands widespread support, they have to continue debating it. See, for example, Sosis (2019).

29. Plausibly, this motivates some of the support for no-platforming movements. See, for example, Holley (2017).

30. "[T]he presupposition that there are *some* moral truths cannot be avoided by those engaged in justified political resistance" (Haslanger 2017: 165).

31. Some evidence that *effects over intent* is part of the SJDE comes from the facts that college campuses have become increasingly concerned about microaggressions (see Campbell and Manning 2018 and Lukianoff and Haidt 2018), and many conservative students report self-censorship (see Kabbany 2019). Microaggressions can be remarks or behaviors that, despite often being unintentional, offend or discomfort members of oppressed groups; the fact that they can be unintentional doesn't matter when it comes to determining sanction against those who use them, thus making concern about them evidence for *effects over intent*. Similarly, conservative self-censorship may support *effects over intent*, in that conservatives don't express themselves for fear that doing so may offend people; this suggests that conservative students, at least, think that a fair number of people in their academic environments accept *effects over intent*.

32. My main evidence that social justice discourse is both widespread and recent comes from Georgia State University political science graduate student Zach Goldberg's graphs, three of which (he has at least eighteen) are mentioned in Tabarrok (2019). There are also supporting anecdotes, as least for social justice discourse's prevalence, such as the Gillette advertisement making use of the phrase "toxic masculinity" (see Gillette 2019), and an article written by George Packer for the *Atlantic* documenting what he saw as excesses of political correctness in primary and secondary education in New York City (see Packer 2019).

33. See Reed Jr. (2018).

34. See Codevilla (2016).

35. See Campbell and Manning (2018), as well as Lukianoff and Haidt (2018), which sounds some of the same themes.

36. Note that Codevilla, following Pareto, thinks that organizations *in general* have the concerns of their leaders, so the social justice movement is not unusual in this regard. See Codevilla (2016: 38).

37. See Campbell and Manning (2018: 12–16).

38. The main evidence Campbell and Manning offer to support their claim that we are transitioning into a victimhood culture is what they call the "microaggression program" (Campbell and Manning 2018: 3). This includes not only an increasing sensitivity in universities and business to microaggressions, but also greater employment of safe spaces and trigger warnings, and increasing incidence of hate crime hoaxes.

39. See Campbell and Manning (2018: 62–63).

40. "Attempts to increase stratification . . . are more deviant where stratification is at a minimum; likewise, attempts to decrease diversity are more deviant where diversity is at a maximum" (Campbell and Manning 2018: 59).

41. See Campbell and Manning (2018: 44–46).

42. See Campbell and Manning (2018: 63). For rank-and-file members of the social justice left, this is true of social media in particular.

43. For evidence that college and university faculty and administrators are ideologically homogeneous, see Brennan and Magness (2019: 302–306).

44. See Campbell and Manning (2018: 64–65).

45. See al-Gharbi (2019) for some evidence that this has happened.

46. See Huemer (2016).

47. See Huemer (2016: 1994–1998).

48. See Huemer (2016: 1998–1999).

49. See Huemer (2016: 2000–2001).

50. See Huemer (2016: 2001–2002 and 2003–2006).

51. See Campbell and Manning (2018: 17).

52. See Campbell and Manning (2018: 24 and 167–68). They cite Rosen (2011), wherein Rosen writes, "I am a white, cisgender gay guy . . . the queer equivalent of 'The Man' . . . parties become less diverse when I walk in." In other words, by 2011 Rosen had gone from someone who was oppressed, and so, deserved plaudits, to someone who was not oppressed, perhaps even an oppressor, and so either deserved no plaudits or out-and-out sanction.

53. For discussion of hate crime hoaxes, see chapter 4 of Campbell and Manning (2018) and Reilly (2019).

54. "[T]he Japanese [in Brazil and the United States] are advantaged over the local white populations in terms of educational attainment. The latter engenders higher wages in both Brazil and the United States despite the notable differences between those two countries in regard to history and economic development. In Brazil, the bivariate wage differential between Japanese and whites is exceedingly large. In the United States, the Japanese have a significant positive advantage in obtaining higher wages net of the exogenous independent variables" (Maia, Sakamoto, and Wang 2015: 562).

55. Coleman Hughes writes, "nearly all black immigrant groups out-earn American blacks, and many—including Ghanaians, Nigerians, Barbadians, and Trinidadians & Tobagonians—out-earn the national average. Moreover, black immigrants are

overrepresented in the Ivy Leagues. Though they comprised only 8 percent of the U.S. black population in the 2010 census, 41 percent of African Americans attending Ivy League schools were of immigrant origin in 1999. Five years later, the *New York Times* reported a finding by two Harvard professors that as many as two-thirds of Harvard's black students "were West Indian and African immigrants or their children, or to a lesser extent, children of biracial couples" (Hughes 2018).

56. The most surprising claim relevant to this comes from the work of Raj Chetty, which shows that, while "black men grow up to earn substantially less than . . . white men [among those who grow up in families with comparable incomes] . . . black women earn slightly *more* than white women *conditional on parent income*" (Chetty et al. 2018: 3, emphasis theirs). In other words, though white women earn more on average than black women, black women actually earn more on average than white women when you control for parental income.

57. See Teichman and Dupree (2019).

58. Goldberg's phrase is "Complexity is a subsidy" for the rich. See Goldberg (2018: 206).

59. See Hetey and Eberhardt (2018). See also Munton (2019) for a possible explanation for why making accurate statistical claims about disparities between demographic groups may be unwise, especially if those disparities result from unjust social structures.

60. See Manne (2016: 98–99).

61. See Al-Gharbi (2019: 3–4).

62. See Al-Gharbi (2019: 4–5). Note that al-Gharbi's evidence predates the massive influx of money from corporations and individuals to the organization, Black Lives Matter.

63. See, for example, Keillor (2016).

64. See Taleb (2016).

65. In their defense, Campbell and Manning would point out that what determines whether people are part of a moral culture is not what they believe but how they behave (see Campbell and Manning 2018: 145). So, if social justice discourse is widespread, then that's enough for our discourse to count as being part of victimhood culture, even if few people believe the words they speak. But if we're really transitioning to victimhood culture, there must be reason to believe that these changes in discourse will stick; and if I'm right that there is widespread disbelief in the social justice outlook, then I think this increases the likelihood that these changes won't stick, and that victimhood culture is not a culture at all, but a bubble.

66. See Bregman (2012), Caplan (2016), and Dobbin and Kalev (2016).

WORKS CITED

Al-Gharbi, Musa 2019. "Resistance as Sacrifice: Toward an Ascetic Antiracism," *Sociological Forum*, vol. 34, pp. 1197–1216. The page numbers I use are from the preprint available at https://osf.io/preprints/socarxiv/wd54z/, accessed July 13, 2020.

Beauchamp, Zack 2018. "In defense of Sarah Jeong," *Vox*, August 3. https://www.vox.com/policy-and-politics/2018/8/3/17648566/sarah-jeong-new-york-times-twitter-andrew-sullivan, accessed October 7, 2018.

Bouie, Jamelle 2016. "There's No Such Thing as a Good Trump Voter," *Slate*, November 15. https://slate.com/news-and-politics/2016/11/there-is-no-such-thing-as-a-good-trump-voter.html, accessed October 9, 2019.

Bregman, Peter 2012. "Diversity Training Doesn't Work," *Harvard Business Review*, March 12. https://hbr.org/2012/03/diversity-training-doesnt-work, accessed October 18, 2019.

Brennan, Jason and Magness, Philip 2019. *Cracks in the Ivory Tower: The Moral Mess of Higher Education*. Oxford: Oxford University Press.

Campbell, Bradley and Manning, Jason 2018. *The Rise of Victimhood Culture: Microaggressions, Safe Spaces, and the New Culture Wars*. London: Palgrave Macmillan.

Caplan, Bryan 2018. *The Case Against Education: Why the Education System Is a Waste of Time and Money*. Princeton, NJ: Princeton University Press.

Chetty, Raj, Hendren, Nathaniel, Jones, Maggie, and Porter, Sonya R. 2018. "Race and Economic Opportunity in the United States: Executive Summary," *The Equality of Opportunity Project*. https://opportunityinsights.org/wpcontent/uploads/2018/04/race_summary.pdf, accessed October 23, 2019.

Coaston, Jane 2019. "The intersectionality wars," *Vox*, May 28. https://www.vox.com/the-highlight/2019/5/20/18542843/intersectionality-conservatism-law-race-gender-discrimination, accessed October 18, 2019.

Codevilla, Angelo M. 2016. "The Rise of Political Correctness," *Claremont Review of Books*, vol. 16, pp. 37–43.

DiAngelo, Robin 2018. *White Fragility: Why It's So Hard for White People to Talk about Racism*. Boston, MA: Beacon Press.

Dobbin, Frank and Kalev, Alexandra 2016. "Why Diversity Programs Fail: And What Works Better," *Harvard Business Review*, vol. 94, pp. 52–60.

Fantl, Jeremy 2018. *The Limitations of the Open Mind*. Oxford: Oxford University Press.

Feagin, Joe R. 2010. *Racist America: Roots, Current Realities, and Future Reparations*, 2nd Edition. New York, NY: Routledge.

Foundation for Individual Rights in Education 2019. *Disinvitation Database*. https://www.thefire.org/research/disinvitation-database/, accessed October 19, 2019.

Fricker, Miranda 2007. *Epistemic Injustice: Power and the Ethics of Knowing*. Oxford: Oxford University Press.

Gallup 2019. "Abortion." https://news.gallup.com/poll/1576/abortion.aspx, accessed October 18, 2019.

Galtung, Johan 2019. "Violence, Peace, and Peace Research," *Journal of Peace Research*, vol. 6, pp. 167–191.

Gillette 2019. "We Believe: The Best Men Can Be," *YouTube*, January 13. https://www.youtube.com/watch?v=koPmuEyP3a0, accessed November 5, 2019.

Goldberg, Jonah 2018. *Suicide of the West: How the Rebirth of Tribalism, Populism, Nationalism, and Identity Politics is Destroying American Democracy*. New York, NY: Crown Forum.

Gross, Neil 2013. *Why Are Professors Liberal and Why Do Conservatives Care?* Cambridge, MA: Harvard University Press.

Haslanger, Sally 2017. "Culture and Critique," *Aristotelian Society Supplementary Volume*, vol. 91, pp. 149–173.

Hawkins, Stephen, Yudkin, Daniel, Juan-Torres, Miriam, and Dixon, Tim 2018. Hidden Tribes: A Study of America's Polarized Landscape," *More in Common*. https://static1.squarespace.com/static/5a70a7c3010027736a22740f/t/5bbcea6b7817f7bf7342b718/1539107467397/hidden_tribes_report-2.pdf, accessed October 24, 2019.

Heatey, Rebecca C. and Eberhardt, Jennifer L. 2018. "The Numbers Don't Speak for Themselves: Racial Disparities and the Persistence of Inequality in the Criminal Justice System," *Current Directions in Psychological Science*, vol. 27, pp. 183–187.

Herzog, Katie 2019. "Cancel Culture: What Exactly Is This Thing?," *The Stranger*, September 17. https://www.thestranger.com/slog/2019/09/17/41416013/cancel-culture-what-exactly-is-this-thing, accessed November 5, 2019.

Holley, Peter 2017. "A Conservative Author Tried to Speak at a Liberal Arts College. He Left Fleeing an Angry Mob," *The Washington Post*, March 4. https://www.washingtonpost.com/news/grade-point/wp/2017/03/04/a-conservative-author-tried-to-speak-at-a-liberal-college-he-left-fleeing-an-angry-mob/, accessed October 18, 2019.

Huemer, Michael 2016. "A Liberal Realist Answer to Debunking Skeptics: The Empirical Case for Realism," *Philosophical Studies*, vol. 173, pp. 1983–2010.

Hughes, Coleman 2018. "The Racism Treadmill," *Quillette*, May 14. https://quillette.com/2018/05/14/the-racism-treadmill/, accessed October 12, 2019.

Jacobson, William A. 2017. "'Progressive Stack' Racial/Gender Speaker Hierarchy an Occupy Wall Street Legacy," *Legal Insurrection*, October 22. https://legalinsurrection.com/2017/10/progressive-stack-racialgender-speaker-hierarchy-an-occupy-wall-street-legacy/, accessed October 18, 2019.

Kabbany, Jennifer 2019. "Poll: 73 Percent of Republican Students have Withheld Political Views in Class for Fear Their Grades Would Suffer," *The College Fix*, September 4. https://www.thecollegefix.com/poll-73-percent-of-republican-students-have-withheld-political-views-in-class-for-fear-their-grades-would-suffer/, accessed October 10, 2019.

Kaufman, Daniel A. 2017. "Morality Everywhere?," *The Electric Agora*, September 2. https://theelectricagora.com/2017/09/02/morality-everywhere/, accessed October 8, 2019.

Keillor, Garrison 2016. "Donald Trump Won. Let the Uneducated have Their Day," *Chicago Tribune*, November 9. https://www.chicagotribune.com/opinion/commentary/ct-donald-trump-wins-uneducated-voters-20161109-story.html, accessed October 24, 2019.

Kelly, Daniel and Roedder, Erica 2008. "Racial Cognition and the Ethics of Implicit Bias," *Philosophy Compass*, vol. 3, pp. 522–540.

Leiter, Brian 2015. "Why Marxism Still Does Not Need Normative Theory," *Analyse und Kritik*, vol. 37, pp. 23–50.

Lukianoff, Greg and Haidt, Jonathan 2018. *The Coddling of the American Mind: How Good Intentions and Bad Ideas Are Setting up a Generation for Failure*. London: Penguin Books.

Maia, Alexandre Gori, Sakamoto, Arthur, and Wang, Sharron Xuanren 2015. "Socioeconomic Attainments of Japanese Brazilians and Japanese Americans," *Sociology of Race and Ethnicity*, vol. 1, pp. 467–474.

Manne, Kate 2016. *Down Girl: The Logic of Misogyny*. Oxford: Oxford University Press.

Maroja, Luana 2019. "Self-Censorship on Campus Is Bad for Science," *The Atlantic*, May 28. https://www.theatlantic.com/ideas/archive/2019/05/self-censorship-campus-bad-science/589969/, accessed October 19, 2019.

Mills, C. Wright 2000. *The Power Elite*. Oxford: Oxford University Press.

Munton, Jessie 2019. "Beyond Accuracy: Epistemic Flaws with Statistical Generalizations," *Philosophical Issues: A Supplement to Noûs*, vol. 29, pp. 228–240.

Packer, George 2019. "When the Culture War Comes for the Kids," *The Atlantic*, October. https://www.theatlantic.com/magazine/archive/2019/10/when-the-culture-war-comes-for-the-kids/596668/, accessed November 5, 2019.

Pareto, Vilfredo 1983. *The Mind and Society*, ed. Arthur Livingston, trans. Andrew Bongiorno and Arthur Livingston. New York, NY: AMS Press.

Reed, Jr., Adolph 2018. "Antiracism: A Neoliberal Alternative to a Left," *Dialectical Anthropology*, vol. 42, pp. 105–115.

Reilly, Wilfred 2019. *Hate Crime Hoax: How the Left is Selling a Fake Race War*. Washington, DC: Regnery.

Rorty, Richard 1998. *Achieving Our Country: Leftist Thought in Twentieth-Century America*. Cambridge, MA: Harvard University Press.

Rosen, Zack 2011. "In Defense of the Gay, White Male," *Jezebel*, January 27. https://jezebel.com/in-defense-of-the-gay-white-male-5745172, accessed November 5, 2019.

Scalzi, John 2012. "Straight White Male: The Lowest Difficulty Setting There Is," *Whatever: This Machine Mocks Fascists*, May 15. https://whatever.scalzi.com/2012/05/15/straight-white-male-the-lowest-difficulty-setting-there-is/, accessed October 17, 2019.

Sewell, William H. J. 2005. "The Concept(s) of Culture," in *Practicing History: New Directions in Historical Writing after the Linguistic Turn*, ed. Gabrielle M. Spiegel. New York, NY: Routledge, pp. 35–61.

Sosis, Cliff 2019. "Robin Dembroff," *What Is It Like to Be a Philosopher?*, August 22. http://www.whatisitliketobeaphilosopher.com/#/robin-dembroff/, accessed October 17, 2019.

Stanley, Jason 2015. *How Propaganda Works*. Princeton, NJ: Princeton University Press.

Stevens, Sean 2017. "The Campus Expression Survey: Summary of New Data," *Heterodox Academy*, December 20. https://heterodoxacademy.org/the-campus-expression-survey-summary-of-new-data/, accessed October 19, 2019.

Sue, Derald Wing 2010. *Microaggressions in Everyday Life: Race, Gender, and Sexual Orientation*. Hoboken, NJ: Wiley and Sons.

Sullivan, Andrew 2018. "When Racism Is Fit to Print," *New York Magazine*, August 3. http://nymag.com/intelligencer/2018/08/sarah-jeong-new-york-times-anti-white-racism.html?utm_source=tw&utm_medium=s3&utm_campaign=sharebutton-t, accessed October 7, 2019.

Tabarrok, Alex 2019. "The NYTimes is Woke," *Marginal Revolution*. https://marginalrevolution.com/marginalrevolution/2019/06/the-nytimes-is-woke.html, accessed October 10, 2019.

Taleb, Nicholas Nassim 2016. "The Most Intolerant Wins: The Dictatorship of the Small Minority," *Medium*. https://medium.com/incerto/the-most-intolerant-wins-the-dictatorship-of-the-small-minority-3f1f83ce4e15, accessed October 18, 2019.

Teichman, Matt and Dupree, Emily 2019. "Sally Haslanger Discusses Ideology," *Elucidations*, ep. 114, May 15. https://lucian.uchicago.edu/blogs/elucidations/2019/05/15/episode-114-sally-haslanger-discusses-ideology/, accessed October 11, 2019.

Uhlmann, Eric Luis, Pizarro, David A., Tannenbauam, David, and Ditto, Peter H. 2009. "The Motivated Use of Moral Principles," *Judgment and Decision Making*, vol. 4, pp. 476–491.

Utt, Jamie 2013. "Intent vs. Impact: Why Your Intentions Don't Really Matter," *everyday feminism*, July 30. https://everydayfeminism.com/2013/07/intentions-dont-really-matter/, accessed October 18, 2019.

Weinstein, Bret 2017. "The Campus Mob Came for Me—and You, Professor, Could Be Next," *The Wall Street Journal*, May 30. https://www.wsj.com/articles/the-campus-mob-came-for-meand-you-professor-could-be-next-1496187482?shareToken=std70d4e33eeda4319bebe684e6fed2fd4&reflink=article_email_share, accessed October 19, 2019.

Zimmerman, Jess 2015. "'Where's My Cut?': On Unpaid Emotional Labor," *The Toast*, July 13. https://web.archive.org/web/20180107060717/http://the-toast.net/2015/07/13/emotional-labor/, accessed October 7, 2019.

Chapter 6

Dealing with the Devil

Objectification of Counter-Partisans and Political Compromise

Stacy G. Ulbig

In the shadow of one of the coarsest and most rancorous presidential elections in American history, an armed sexagenarian Illinois man who had volunteered for the Bernie Sanders 2016 primary campaign opened fire on a group of Republican congress members practicing for a charity baseball game in Virginia. Many were not especially surprised to learn of the attack, seeing it as "a natural, if sick, extension of the virulence that surrounds the country's increasingly tribal politics."[1] The symptoms and manifestations of such rage have become ever more prevalent in the past decade. The Senate's 2009 party-line vote on proposed health care legislation marked what one observer called, "the culmination of more than a generation of partisan polarization of the American political system, and a precipitous decline in collegiality and collaboration in governing."[2] Many of those occupying the halls of Congress seem to agree. In the wake of the 2009 health care vote, Senator John D. Rockefeller IV observed, "It has gotten so much more partisan. This was so wicked. This was so venal." Citing "campaigns of destruction" that revolved "around destroying the other side" and increased incivility among her fellow senators, Olympia Snowe retired in 2012.[3] Two years earlier, Arlen Specter expressed similar dismay when he delivered his final speech from the Senate floor. In his "closing argument" to his Senate colleagues and the American people, he explained that the collegial debate and bipartisan compromise of three decades earlier had gone by the wayside.[4] Instead, he said, as more and more senators insisted on ideological purity among party members, "compromise" had "become a dirty word."

Scholars, too, have noted such tendencies which they often refer to as political teamsmanship. Some argue, for instance, that polarization trends reflect not only ideologically based policy decisions, but "Congress members' increasing efforts to favorably differentiate their own party from the opposition."[5] "When this happens, partisans can become driven by a growing team spirit that is disconnected from policy considerations."[6] Some contend that such conditions represent well the idea of strategic disagreement.[7] As researchers Michael Barber and Nolan McCarty explain, actors refuse to compromise (even when compromise was feasible or even desirable) in order to transfer blame for a stalemate to the other side and gain electoral advantage.[8] The result, they argue, is to create battles over issues for which little ideological difference exists. Retiring senator Arlen Specter saw this mindset as a leading cause in the polarization of the political parties and the resulting gridlock in the policymaking process. As he put it, "[p]olitics is no longer the art of the possible when senators are intransigent in their positions."[9] An unwillingness to compromise in order to come to policy decisions also appears among academic observers' top concerns.[10] In the American setting, some point to the polarization of the mass public as the source of governmental gridlock that destroys the cooperation needed to find solutions to today's most pressing problems, and recent studies reveal a polarized electorate that appears to be less willing to seek equitable compromises on the important political issues of the day.[11]

It is precisely this sort of recalcitrance, and its connections to political incivility and partisan polarization that I scrutinize in the pages that follow. In this chapter, I will explore the ways in which objectification across partisan lines works to degrade political compromise. I first argue that political partisanship operates as a social identity that leads to the objectification, and frequent vilification, of individuals across party lines. Next, I seek to empirically verify such an effect by showing that those who more strongly self-identify as either Democrats or Republicans tend to portray their partisan opponents as being motivated by iniquitous personal character. Subsequently, I investigate the way in which objectifying counter-partisans as fundamentally bad people relates to a reluctance to engage in meaningful compromise, and find that those attributing their political opponents' behavior to poor personal character are less likely to offer equitable compromises across party lines. I conclude by discussing the implications of these findings for effective governance.

COMPROMISE AND EFFECTIVE GOVERNANCE

Otto van Bismarck is credited with saying that "politics is the art of the possible, the attainable—the art of the next best," and Habermas argued that "compromises make up the bulk of political process."[12] The American nation was forged in compromise between large and small states, northern and southern interests, and proponents of state versus national control. In the twenty-first century, however, compromise has become what some call a lost art.[13] The rhetoric and behavior and congressional officeholders lend support to such a diagnosis. Party line voting occurred about 60 percent of the time in the early 1970s, but by 2017 nearly nine in ten congressional votes split along party lines.[14] Even compared with a comparable period from four decades ago party loyalty has increased.[15] The mid-1980s also saw an incumbent Republican president up for reelection and a Congress split between Republicans, with a close majority of the Senate, and Democrats steering the House. Yet, four decades ago, compromises were made on key pieces of legislation related to race relations, crime, and budget issues.[16] In contrast, the 112th Congress, which met from 2011 to 2013, and today's 116th Congress, have exhibited far less cross-partisan cooperation. In fact, the Brookings Institute reported that the 112th Congress, which saw party unity on more than 95 percent of all votes, passed the fewest laws since the 82nd Congress in the early 1950s despite more than 7,000 introductions. It is no wonder then, that so many have sounded the alarm about the resulting gridlock that prevents pressing social issues from being addressed.[17]

Despite widespread alarm about the dearth of compromise in twenty-first-century American politics, our understanding of the dynamics underlying such intense partisan obduracy remains somewhat limited. Causes ranging from partisanly gerrymandered districting practices to the institutional design of the U.S. Congress to the nature of the policy solutions under consideration have been subjected to much investigation.[18] Others have argued that changes in the "social fabric of Capitol Hill" have impeded the development of cross-partisan personal friendships that support bipartisan trust and civility[19]—a perspective reinforced by former senator Evan Bayh upon his retirement from public office. "When I was a boy, members of Congress from both parties, along with their families, would routinely visit our home for dinner or the holidays. This type of social interaction hardly ever happens today and we are the poorer for it. It is much harder to demonize someone when you know his family or have visited his home." Rising incivility, he argued, impeded bipartisan cooperation when it came to negotiation. After all, as he said, "[i]t's difficult to work with members actively plotting your demise." Bayh also directed his dismay at the American public, saying that elected officials reflect the sentiments of those who continue to elect them to office. From rank-and-file voters to the president, he argued, the "most ideologically devoted elements in both parties must accept that not every compromise is a sign of betrayal or an indication of moral lassitude."[20]

US, THEM, AND THE OBJECTIFICATION OF PARTISAN OPPONENTS

Like an increasing number of scholars before me, I argue that the polarization seen in contemporary American politics is driven more by ingrained emotional reactions to counter-partisans than by cross-party disagreements about the proper scope of governmental authority.[21] I contend that much of the polarization across partisan lines in contemporary American politics results from the strong social affiliations individuals feel with their own party in contrast to that they feel toward the opposite party. As others have argued, I believe that such "affective polarization" derives from partisan and ideological social identities (more powerfully than issue positions).[22] Social identities have repeatedly been found to generate favorable attitudes and behaviors toward other members of the in-group, while out-group members become targets of derogation and derision.[23] Researchers have long recognized that strong identification with a particular ethnic/racial group frequently leads to showing privilege toward others sharing the same racial/ethnic identity and intolerance and disrespect for, as well as violence toward, other demographic groups.[24] Partisan identification can operate similarly, leading to denigration of partisan opponents and an unwillingness to engage the other side in a meaningful way.[25]

Social identity theorists argue that deeply held intergroup prejudices spring from the human instinct to define both ourselves and others in terms of the social groups with which we most closely identify. Four decades ago, Tajfel and Turner provided a succinct elucidation of social identity theory, offering a three-staged process by which social identities form and operate.[26] According to their theory, we first process the world we encounter by placing both ourselves and others into social categories based on recognizable characteristics such as race, gender, or socioeconomic status. In doing so, we then create social identities for ourselves and others.[27] Finally, in much the same way groups might fight over tangible resources such as food or water, rival social group members contend with one another in order to maintain self-esteem. Individuals compete by using their social identities to compare themselves to others, focusing on the positive aspects of the in-group to which they belong and the negative aspects of the out-group to which they compare themselves.[28]

Experimental research has long established the strength of in-group/out-group classifications, even with regard to distinctions made along arbitrary lines and in situations where the participants have no preexisting common interests.[29] When assembled as a nominal group, people rather quickly start saying they think of themselves in terms of the group and believing that their own group members are superior to those identified with other groups.[30]

Outside the laboratory setting the social identity process can be expected to have even more influence over perceptions and attitudes. For, as some have argued, the development of social identities serves as a primary means of childhood and cultural socialization.[31] Hence, social identities are likely to form early in the lifespan and endure over a lifetime, gaining reinforcement from repeated favorable comparisons to out-groups, and frequently leading to prejudice and discrimination against out-group members.[32]

The development and persistence of partisan identification in both the United States and abroad has been described in much the same manner.[33] An emotional attachment, partisan identification develops through early childhood socialization and tends to persist over a lifetime.[34] In the same way comparisons of social identity frequently lead to negative feelings toward an out-group, comparisons based on partisan identities result in negative affect toward the opposing party. Even those who identify as nonpartisan (purely Independent) express negativity toward the competing partisan groups of Democrats and Republicans.[35] Just as repeated, biased comparisons to out-groups work to strengthen social identities, partisan identities have been argued to become more stable over the lifespan as a result of continued social reinforcement.[36] Further, the very issues that animate much of the American political scene—fights over relative partisan power, economic issues, and moral/cultural battles—have been argued to underlie and accentuate many social identity group conflicts.[37] Thus, there are good reasons to believe that partisan identification operates in much the same manner as social identification to create the sort of affective mass polarization and cross-partisan disrespect that has been highlighted in twenty-first-century politics. In fact, there is even some evidence that partisan biases may influence decision-making more than racial and gender biases.[38] It is little wonder then that when partisan identities come under threat, civility toward counter-partisans falls by the wayside.

Such an argument does not necessarily exclude the possibility that Democrats and Republicans disagree about prominent political issues of the day based on differing ideological viewpoints. Rather, a social identity perspective can help to explain why such divisions have become increasingly prevalent in the mass electorate. As Bertrand Russell noted, "Every man, wherever he goes, is encompassed by a cloud of comforting convictions, which move with him like flies on a summer day."[39] Reassuring partisan convictions have been shown to affect the perceptions many have of counter-partisans, with motivated reasoning leading to perceptual biases favoring the in-group.[40] Recent research further suggests that such "automatic association is very much related to the ways in which voters evaluate and interpret the political world."[41] For instance, partisans greatly exaggerate (by about 300 percent on average) the degree to which stereotypical groups support both major U.S. parties—reporting, for example, that there are far more LGBT supporters in Democratic Party and more wealthy people in Republican Party than is the case.[42] Such tendencies can lead to similar distortions of the typical ideological positions of both parties, and, interestingly, these effects have been observed for perceptions of both one's own party as well as the opposite party.[43]

Researchers have long pointed to the increased alignment of partisan and ideological identities among both officeholders and the mass electorate as an important catalyst of such sentiments.[44] With slim partisan majorities in Congress, contemporary policy debates frequently take on tones of intense zero-sum, intergroup battles rather than bipartisan negotiations to arrive at a policy solutions that address the nation's interests. Coupled with ideological sorting along party lines over the past five decades, such socially based inclinations have resulted in a stronger connection between issue stances and partisan identities.[45] At the same time, and perhaps more importantly, preexisting partisan identities have led to exaggerated perceptions of the ideological distance between parties and misperceptions about the ideological diversity that actually exists within parties.

The rhetoric surrounding today's high-profile political happenings readily reflects the ways in which contemporary politics has become a game of one-upmanship in which partisan social identities stand paramount above almost everything else. As candidates vied for the 2020 Democratic presidential nomination in Iowa, less than half were focused on the issue positions of those in the field. About six in ten caucus-goers in that state reported that "beating Trump was more important than agreeing with a candidate's positions."[46] It is no wonder then that, high-profile Democratic candidates focus their campaign messages more on beating the incumbent president than on working to bridge the partisan divide to build the cooperation necessary to tackle the nation's pressing problems. Elizabeth Warren, for instance, roused audiences by saying, "Our number one job is to beat Donald Trump,"[47] and Michael Bloomberg actively curated his "image as . . . a guy who wants to beat Trump."[48] Democratic voters, blinded by the emotion attached to their partisan identities, cheered loudly as Bloomberg told his supporters at a rally, "Let me . . . tell you why I'm in this race . . . I'm running to beat Donald Trump."[49]

Things in the Republican Party looked much the same. Following the impeachment trial of President Trump, in which a single vote by Senator Mitt Romney broke against party lines, the rogue Republican senator was targeted as "a member of the resistance [who] should be expelled from" the party.[50] Romney's vote was viewed as a betrayal to the in-group of Republicans, and he was painted as a traitor who acted as an agent of the out-group Democrats. Even the president took to social media with a video "claiming that Romney was a 'Democrat secret asset.' "[51]

POLITICAL COMPROMISE IN A TIME OF PARTISAN POLARIZATION

Taken together, the arguments and evidence in favor of viewing partisanship as socially based identities rather than issue based calculations go a long way toward explaining the dismal state of political compromise in contemporary politics. Since ideological perceptions of both oneself and others likely have some of their origins in partisan social identities, it is perhaps not surprising that many voters, despite reporting stronger ideological commitments, continue to hold relatively unconstrained issue positions in many ways similar to those observed more than a half a century ago.[52] Additionally, the growing bitterness targeted at political opponents by ideologues from both the left and the right can be better explained. Like partisan identities, ideological self-perceptions can work to increase "affective polarizations against outgroup ideologues, even at low levels of policy attitude extremity or constraint."[53] Instead of acknowledging the issue positions they realistically have in common, members from both sides of the aisle tend to employ partisan and ideological labels to denigrate and vilify their political adversaries.

A social identity perspective on partisan polarization would suggest that such behaviors spring "from threatened group status and interparty competition."[54] As outlined by many early social identity theorists, social group identities serve to maintain self-esteem by distinguishing in-group members as separate from and superior to out-group rivals. Threats from out-group members coupled with assurances of superiority from in-group members have been shown to generate intense emotional responses.[55] These tendencies can be so strong that group identities are sometimes experienced "as an extended part of the self" such that brain activity responses to pain and suffering of fellow group members resembles that of personal physical pain.[56] Though some argue that feelings relying on socially based partisan identities tend to result in increasingly negative perceptions of political rivals, others contend that a social identity operates to satisfy psychological needs for inclusion in the favored group as well as exclusion from rival groups.[57] Self-categorization theorists (SCT), believe that social identities help account for intra-group, as well as intergroup dynamics—helping to explain both the cohesion within parties and the polarization between them that others have pointed out.[58] This is argued to occur because salient social identities cause individual group members to strive to become the "prototypical" in-group member.[59] That is, in-group members will overtly shift their attitudes and behaviors away from those held by an out-group in order to receive validation from the in-group.[60] Conversely, even suggesting that in-group members might share beliefs or actions with outgroups, especially intensely despised ones, can lead to negative in-group social treatment (i.e., derogation or shaming).[61] It would seem that as Tocqueville observed, when one contravenes group opinion "[y]ou are free not to think as I do . . .. but from this day on, you are a stranger among us."[62]

Importantly, there is also evidence that the most strongly identified group members will be influenced to a greater degree, and thus have stronger emotional reactions to out-group threat.[63] Thus, "strongly identified group members are more inclined to feel angry when threatened by an out-group because they believe they can prevail in an intergroup competition."[64] Further, as both those in office and in the electorate increasingly sorted themselves along ideological lines, the overlap between partisan identity and ideological identity strengthened. And the partisan realignment of the mass electorate led to long-standing sociodemographic group cleavages along class, race, and gender lines aligning more directly with partisan identity as well. In short, "America has gone from being a nation of cross-cutting political identities to a nation of highly aligned political identities." That congruence has been shown to strengthen preexisting identities.[65] Consequently, as partisan identities came to align with other politically relevant identities, cross-partisan animosities rose. As researchers have been observing for more than a decade, intolerance, biased group assessments, and anger tend to accompany the alignment of social identities.[66] After all, in such a political cosmos, an invective hurled across party lines is an insult not only to one's partisan social identity, but to one's ideological, racial, sexual, and class identities as well. And, according to social identity theory, the reaction to an out-group threat is typically to identify with the in-group more strongly. As a result, even minor out-group insults become magnified into serious threats that justify more immediate and virulent counter-attacks.[67]

Group threat has also been linked to increases in anxiety levels, "which incline partisans towards heightened . . . anger which promotes action," perhaps explaining why incivility has been making more frequent appearances on the political landscape in recent years.[68] As partisan emotions have spiraled ever higher, some have noted an increase in "oversimplified, inaccurate and derogatory beliefs concerning the other [partisan] group that are identified as the enemies."[69] Even less engaged and committed partisan identifiers can more easily distinguish themselves from their perceived political enemies and have their passions enflamed by insults hurled across the partisan divide. Thus, partisan elites find themselves leading increasingly committed masses into conflict on the electoral and policymaking battlefields of contemporary politics.

"The Abyss of Total Devaluation"

Many would question the ability of emotional attachments to a political party, even intense ones, to drive individuals to physically assault members of the opposing party. To understand how this could feasibly be the case, we might begin with a perspective offered by German philosopher Carl Schmitt when he wrote of the "inevitability of a moral compulsion."[70] Like social identity theorists, he focused on in-group bias and out-group denigration, arguing that combatants in intergroup rivalries must "consider the other side as entirely criminal and inhuman, as totally worthless. Otherwise, they are themselves criminal and inhuman." Such group dynamics, he contended, "compell[ed] ever new, ever deeper discriminations, criminalizations, and devaluations to the point of annihilating all unworthy life." American political discourse in recent years provides ample evidence of such inter-partisan attitudes as well as the "absolute enmity" that Schmitt sees as a predecessor to physical annihilation of the out-group.

The words of modern scholars echo eerily of Schmitt's, with some claiming that identity with social groups "represents a process of depersonalization," in which partisan opponents are "defamed, delegitimized and dehumanized."[71] According to recent research from the field of social psychology, decreased social engagement and acceptance of violence against groups viewed as less than fully human accompany the dehumanization of out-groups.[72] And such processes appear to be at work in contemporary American politics with partisans on both sides of the aisle view the opposing party as significantly less human and more mechanistic than their own party.[73] Correspondingly, those who more strongly rated the opposition party as less human also expressed a desire to socially and morally distance themselves from out-party members. The latter, moral distancing, suggests that political identities have become "a marker for basic decency," and partisan opponents "are deemed to lack basic compassion, or basic loyalty to the country."[74] The very motives and integrity of counter-partisans are questioned, and a "primal sense of 'us against them' makes partisans fixate on the goal of defeating and even humiliating the opposition at all costs."[75] Thus, as some have argued dehumanization and moral judgment are intricately linked and may lead to a heightened sense of threat and lowered sense of empathy toward partisan opponents.[76] This seems to especially be the case when groups are actively engaged in conflict.[77] In fact, researches have documented a connection between blatant dehumanization and aggression in the context of a political campaign, finding that between 5 and 15 percent of the partisans they surveyed endorse violence against their political opponents.[78]

In such a political climate, even positions overtly defended as sincere and rational, issue-based decisions have been argued to instead be motivated by an "automatic, basic need to defend our social group" and maintain individual self-esteem.[79] While partisans may believe they take policy stands based on more objective reasoning, they are to a large degree driven by a desire to protect their party, and in doing so they defend themselves.[80] Strong partisan attachments and the biases which accompany them diminish the capacity for objectively assessing information related to public policy.[81] A Democrat who defends her party's stand on immigration and a Republican who defends his party's stance on gun rights are, in effect, defending their own identities as members of their parties (and of the ideological and sociodemographic groups that comprise that party). Even those with little substantive political knowledge can be expected to respond in this manner. After all, party labels and all the group identities they entail represent perhaps the archetypal easy, symbolic issue—operating on an emotional, gut-level that requires little cognitive effort.[82] Since many issues that animate contemporary political debates activate the ideological and socio-demographic group allegiances encompassed by partisan identities, policy battles frequently focus less on actual policy outcomes than on defeating the partisan enemy. In such a political climate both sides come to embrace the view that "[t]here are two sides to every issue: one side is right and the other is wrong, but the middle is always evil,"[83] and opportunities for compromise erode.

PARTISAN OBJECTIFICATION IN AMERICAN POLITICS

To test the proposition that those who objectify their partisan opponents express less willingness to engage in meaningful compromise, I rely on data from a 2015 survey of a random sample of eligible young voters.[84] Respondents to this survey reported political attitudes from across the political spectrum. Reflective of the American population in general, about one-third of the study participants claimed at first to be Independents when it came to partisan identity. And just as with the general population, when pushed they split fairly evenly between leaning more toward the Democratic Party, leaning more toward the Republican Party, and being truly independent of both parties. The remaining respondents split between the two major parties, with almost 42 percent reporting a Republican identity and fewer (about 28 percent) claiming an allegiance to the Democratic Party. Similarly, more than half (53 percent) report ideological leanings that do not strongly align with one party or the other, but only about half of those claim to be completely moderate. The remainder say they are either slightly liberal (15 percent) or slightly conservative (15 percent). And while relatively small shares of the participants report extremely liberal or conservative positions, a substantial proportion (about 39 percent) claim moderate ideological outlooks and slightly more report conservative than liberal perspectives.

To assess intergroup attitudes, I asked respondents a series of questions targeting their partisan opponents. Self-identified Republicans were asked a series of questions tapping their feelings about Democrats; those calling themselves Democrats were asked about their sentiments regarding Republicans; and self-professed Independents were asked about members of either of the two major American political parties.[85] Respondents were asked to react to three statements about their partisan opponents by expressing their level of agreement (strongly agree, agree, disagree, or strongly disagree) with each of the following statements:

(a) "Some of the actions of the [opposing party] and [its] leaders are a result of a 'bad' internal character."
(b) "Some of the actions of the [opposing party] and [its] leaders are a result of an intentional desire to harm me and members of my party."
(c) "[Members of the opposing party] are a threat to the nation's well-being."

Responses to these questions are summarized in figure 6.1. As shown, more than 40 percent of those asked reported that the members and leaders of the opposing party were motivated by "bad" internal character. That is, they viewed their partisan opponents as moral inferiors. Responses to the second and third statements suggest the degree to which respondents tended to personalize their perceptions of their political enemies. While nearly two-thirds (65 percent) contended that opposition party members were *intentionally* attempting to harm them and members of their partisan group, only about

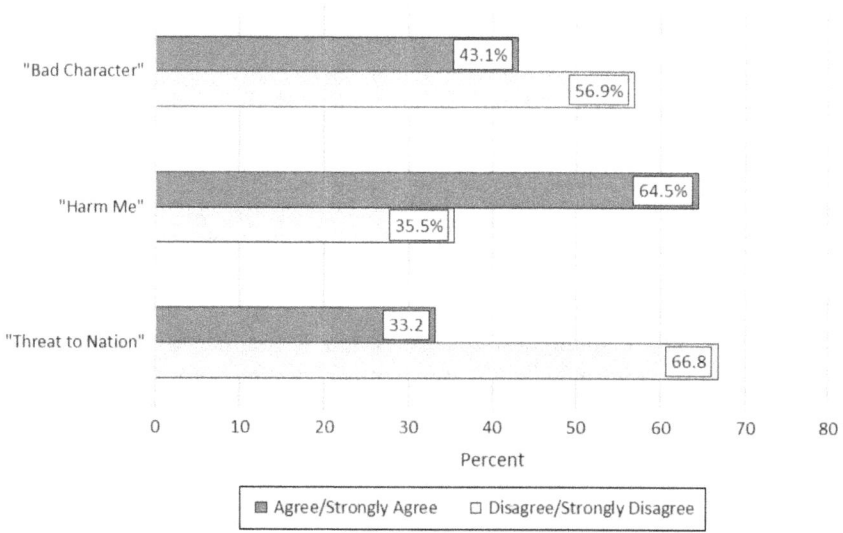

Figure 6.1 View of Opposite Party.

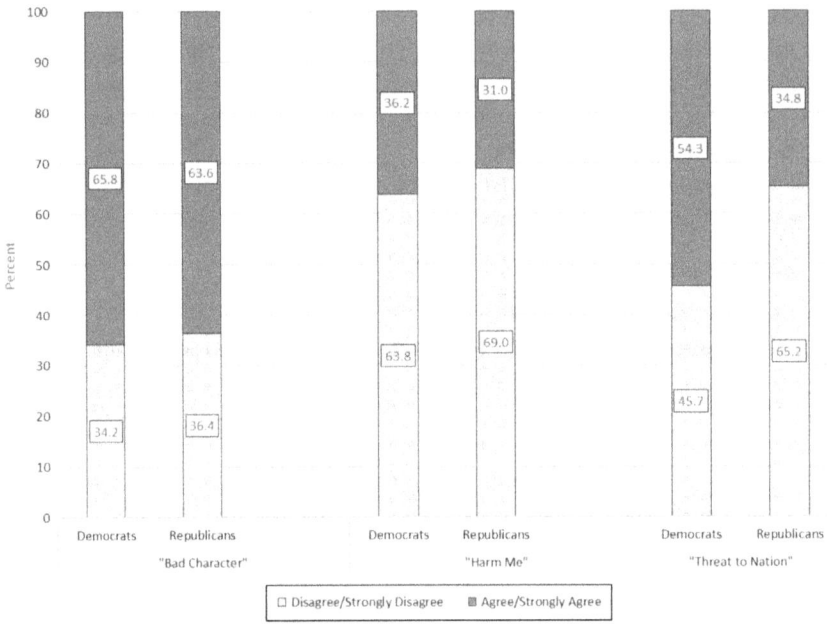

Figure 6.2 Democratic and Republican Views of One Another.

one-third (33 percent) felt that out-partisans were a threat to the nation as a whole.

Further analysis revealed that the contours of these sentiments were remarkably similar across party lines (see figure 6.2). Though Democrats showed a slight tendency to be more eager to accuse Republicans of having bad character and being intent on harming them, the sentiments are largely shared in the reverse by Republicans.[86] Interestingly, however, a higher proportion of Democratic identifiers expressed the opinion that Republicans were not merely a threat to them and their fellow partisans but to the nation as a whole.[87] More than half (54 percent) of self-identified Democrats claimed they agreed or strongly agreed that Republicans threatened the nation as a whole. In contrast, less than a third (31 percent) of Republicans agreed or strongly agreed that Democrats posed the same sociotropic threat. The partisan difference on the national threat measure may be indicative of the ways in which Democratic self-identification tends to activate other highly salient, politically relevant social cleavages such as race, ethnicity, gender, and income more than Republican self-identification does. That is, those identifying with the Democratic Party are more likely to also identify as lower income and/or as racial, ethnic, and gender minorities than Republican identifiers are to identify with their income, racial, ethnic, or gender identities.

Such overlapping identities can serve to exacerbate cognitive and affective reactions triggered by references to party symbols.[88]

I assessed respondents' compromise points by asking them to identify the point (on a 0 to 100 point scale) at which Democrats and Republicans should meet when attempting to address the most important issues facing the country. A score of zero on the compromise scale indicated that Democrats would get everything they wanted, whereas a score of 100 meant that Republicans would get everything they desired. In addition to the raw numeric compromise points reported I also created a measure of the extremity of the proposed compromise point by "folding" the 100-point compromise scale.[89] This measure thus ranges from 0 to 50, with higher values indicating more extreme compromise positions. Reported compromise points are summarized in figure 6.3.

On the whole, my study participants reported a mean raw compromise point of nearly an even split, though, as expected, the mean compromise points reported by partisan identifiers benefited their own side. For their part, nonpartisan respondents reported an almost neutral ideal compromise point, averaging only about a single point Democratic advantage. Partisan identifiers, on the other hand, recorded compromise points more favorable to their own party, with Republicans showing a slightly stronger overall tendency to do so than Democrats. While Democrats, on average, felt that slightly advantageous compromises favoring their side (at about a 55–45) split were ideal, Republicans preferred, on average, compromising closer to a 65–35

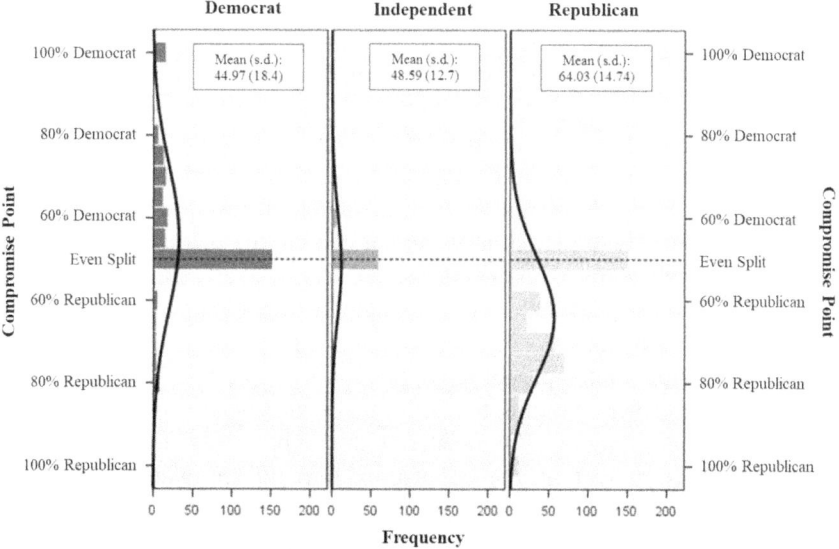

Figure 6.3   Willingness to Compromise.

split that favored their side. Interestingly, the partisan compromise points somewhat mirrored the partisan makeup the chambers of the U.S. Congress at the time—Senate seats were very evenly split along partisan lines and the Republicans held about a 14 percent advantage in House seats.

DEALING WITH THE DEVIL

I next assessed the relationships between cross-partisan attitudes and a willingness to make political compromises using a multivariate regression approach.[90] The first of these models, presented on table 6.1, reflects the relationships among all respondents regardless of their partisanship. Looking first to the effects of partisanship, those who self-identified as either Democrat or Republican tended to report less equitable compromises than those who identified with neither party.[91] The magnitude of these tendencies was similar across party lines, with Democrats reporting compromise positions that were about five points in their own party's favor and Republicans reporting points that were five and half points in their favor.[92] Further, those who express stronger partisan identities suggested even more extreme, and thus less equal, compromises. Those who reported feeling strongly attached to their political party reported compromise points that were, on average, about six points higher than those reported by nonpartisan Independents.

Turning next to the attitudinal measures of out-party objectification, those who viewed their partisan opponents as driven by malign character offered compromise points that were more uneven, by almost three points, on average.[93] This effect appears to be compounded by the 2.6 point increase in compromise position reported by those who felt the opposite party was intentionally attempting to harm them. Interestingly, though, perceiving one's partisan enemies as a threat to the nation showed no overall relationship with willingness to compromise among the full sample of respondents.

The remaining columns on table, which display the results separately for each partisan subsample, shed a more nuanced look at all three relationships, however. Separate analyses of self-proclaimed Republicans and Democrats corroborate the previous findings with regard to perceptions of bad character and harmful intent on the part of the opposite party. For both Democratic and Republican identifiers, holding the belief that counter-partisans are driven to intentionally harm them was associated with compromise offers that favored their own party more than the opposition. Republicans were estimated to give their party almost a 2.4 point advantage and Democrats deal their party about a 2.6 point edge when they saw those on the other side as out to harm them. When assessing the personal character of their partisan adversaries, Republicans dealt an almost two point disadvantage to their opponents if they

Table 6.1 Views of the Opposition Party and Willingness to Compromise

	All Respondents		Republicans		Democrats	
"Bad People"	2.715	***	1.898	*	3.250	**
	(0.743)		(1.019)		(1.257)	
"Harm Me"	2.637	***	2.369	**	2.580	**
	(0.784)		(1.042)		(1.207)	
"National Threat"	−0.479		2.229	**	−4.076	***
	(0.654)		(0.918)		(1.186)	
Democrat	4.906	**	----		----	
	(1.888)					
Republican	5.486	***	----		----	
	(1.876)					
Strong Partisan	6.336	***	7.113	***	2.374	
	(1.199)		(1.378)		(2.338)	
Liberal	−0.121		1.146		−0.967	
	(1.397)		(2.240)		(2.092)	
Conservative	2.790	*	2.934		2.655	
	(1.440)		(1.844)		(2.959)	
Strong Ideology	3.317	*	3.179		0.037	
	(1.972)		(2.449)		(3.714)	
Constant	−7.719	***	−6.285	**	6.287	*
	(2.701)		(3.132)		(5.495)	
Number of Cases	764		401		291	
Adjusted R-squared	0.1632		0.2165		0.1115	

Notes: Response variable is extremity of reported compromise point, ranging from 0 to 50 with higher values indicating less equal compromise. Cell entries are OLS regression coefficients and standard errors (in parentheses). ***p < 0.01; **p < 0.05; *p < 0.10 (two-tailed).

believed Democrats were basically bad people, and Democrats returned the favor by offering slightly more than three point disadvantage to Republicans when they ascribed the same character flaw to the other side.

Interestingly, the non-relationship between perceptions of national threat and willingness to compromise are better explained by the separate party analyses. The results suggest that beliefs that the opposite party poses a threat to the entire nation, rather than to just one's own party, show countervailing effects across party lines. Among Republican identifiers, the belief that

Democrats were a threat to the nation was associated with a tendency to benefit the Republicans by, on average, about two points in cross-partisan compromises. In contrast, those who associated themselves with the Democratic Party reported compromise positions that were about four points, on average, closer to even when they asserted that the Republican Party was a threat to the nation.

This unanticipated relationship among Democratic identifiers may be an artifact of the context in which this survey was conducted. At the time this survey was fielded, Republicans held firm control of both chambers of the U.S. Congress. Perhaps Democratic identifiers, despite their personal assessments about the character and intent of their partisan opponents, recognized the practical realities of negotiating political compromises when the opposing party held the power to effectively ignore any offer they felt was too extreme. This argument, of course, contradicts a good deal of what social identity theorists have argued, but does fit well with arguments that the personalization of out-party sentiment can have behavioral implications. The results presented here suggest that when Democrats were primed with questions about whether Republicans are people with malign character or harmful personal intent, they expressed an unwillingness to engage in meaningful compromise, but when their views about less personal (i.e., more national) concerns were activated their recalcitrance to negotiation subsided.

OBJECTIFICATION AND THE POTENTIAL FOR EFFECTIVE GOVERNANCE

Stepping back from the particular relationships illustrated by these analyses, I next offer a view of what the results, taken as a whole, suggest about the potential for the type of bipartisan compromise that many believe is essential to effective democratic governance.[94] The estimates presented in figure reflect the compound effects of partisanship and objectification of the opposing party as people of "bad internal character."[95] The values enclosed by dashed ovals represent the share of the final policy outcome that partisan believe their party should receive. The values indicated on the brackets indicate the estimated gap between suggested compromise points.

Reflecting the findings from the regression model, stronger partisans tend to report more extreme compromise points. The small squares and circles respectively represent the estimated compromise positions of those identifying as Republicans and Democrats. The larger squares and circles represent those who report strongly (as opposed to weakly or only leaning toward) identifying with the parties. Among those who did not believe that the opposing party is comprised of people with bad internal character, typical Democrats

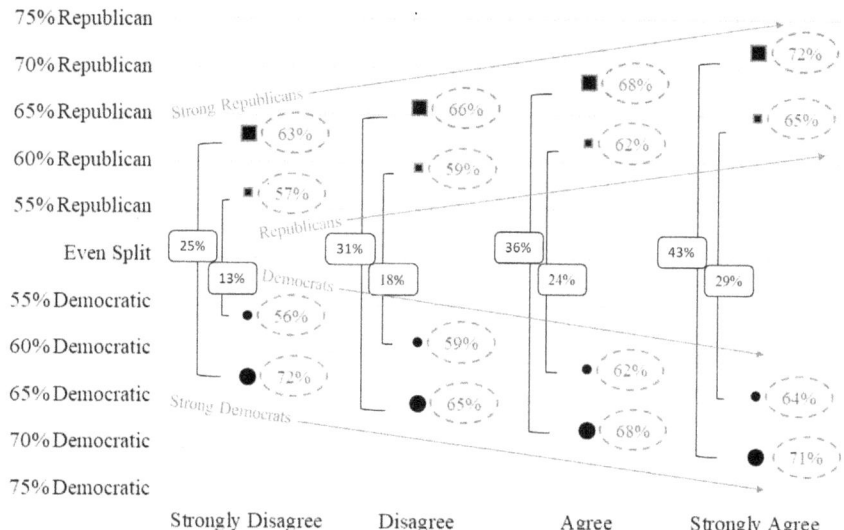

Figure 6.4 Estimated Compromise Points.

are estimated to offer compromise points that show about a seven percentage point advantage to their side and typical Republicans are estimated to do about the same, offering a compromise that is estimated to benefit their own party by about six percentage points. Together, these tendencies result in about a thirteen point gap between the initial positions of the two sides. While hardly inconsequential, disagreements of this sort represent much more surmountable divides than the twenty-nine point gulf between similar partisan who strongly believed that those on the other side of the bargaining table represent people of bad character (see the estimates on the far right-hand side of this figure). When strong partisan identifications are introduced, these chasms expand even more. Strong partisans who harbor little perception of opponents with bad internal character are estimated to begin negotiations about twenty-five points apart, while their counterparts who ascribe deficient character to their opponents are estimated to begin bargaining from forty-three points apart. The latter separation represents nearly half of the entire hypothetical space for negotiation.[96]

Many contemporary Americans bemoan the lack of political compromise evident among those in Congress, as well as among those with whom they have everyday conversations. Increasingly, politics at both the elite and mass level have become the battleground for a zero-sum game in which both sides feels that conceding any ground to their opponents represents not just practical political horse-trading, but an unthinkable act of negotiation with immoral, and somehow less human, "others." As Senator Evan Bayh lamented at the time of his retirement, the most "devoted elements in both parties [view] every compromise [as] a sign of betrayal or an indication of moral lassitude."[97] For their part, academic researchers have argued that a context of partisan polarization and objectification can have a deleterious effect on political compromise. After all, the perception of a group's humanity brings with it a moral obligation to treat out-group members as equals, but when out-group derogation erodes perceptions of the oppositions' morality and humanness the chances of equitable compromises decrease.[98] Though "compromises make up the bulk of political processes,"[99] my results suggest they are likely to remain rare occurrences. These findings fit well with recent research suggesting that citizens may express support for compromise and politicians who make them in principle but not in practice.[100]

Though the picture painted by the arguments and analyses presented in this chapter may be grim, all may not be lost. Seeking to better understand the psychological roots of such habits and norms in an effort to address their behavioral consequences, a number of scholars have been working to develop strategies for countering ingrained ways of responding to contrary viewpoints. For instance, some researchers focus on developing the habit of actively open-minded thinking (AOT) as a remedy, or least a salve, for incivility in politics. AOT involves teaching students (and others) to seek out reasons why their initial conclusions about a topic might be incorrect, which is argued to help people "to think on their own . . . [and] understand the nature of expert knowledge, and, more generally, the nature of academic" inquiry.[101] This type of thinking requires that an individual exhibit several characteristics. First, a person needs to develop an affinity for engaging in and enjoying cognitive tasks that require effort.[102] People who develop this propensity have been shown to be less likely to assert conclusions unsupported by evidence.[103] Second, an individual needs to exhibit "perseverance and passion for long-term goals," what some have called "grit."[104] Third, a person needs to become a maximizer, not a satisficer. That is, he should seek out more information before deciding he is informed enough to make a decision.[105] Instead of seeking enough information for a conclusion that is "good enough," he needs to aim at achieving the highest expected utility (the most accurate conclusion) from his decision and therefore needs to seek all possibly relevant information. Though implementing such strategies on a broad scale may seem unrealistic, many contend that the polarization and vitriol so prevalent today was fed, at least in large part, by the opinion leadership of elected officials and mass media outlets. Should such strategies take root among the political elite and opinion leaders who serve as important information sources for the mass public widespread change would likely follow.

NOTES

1. Mark Z. Barabek, "Reaction to Shooting at Congressional Baseball Practice Reveals a Nation That Doesn't Just Disagree. It Hates," *Los Angeles Times*, Last modified June 24, 2017, https://www.latimes.com/politics/la-na-pol-shooting-politics-20170614-story.html.

2. David M. Herszenhorn, "In Senate Health Care Vote, New Partisan Vitriol," *The New York Times*, Last modified December 24, 2009, https://www.nytimes.com/2009/12/24/us/politics/24assess.html.

3. David Sharp, "Snowe Won't Miss Partisanship: Retiring Senator Plans to Nurture Centrists with Books, Speeches, PAC," *The Washington Times*, Last modified, December 31, 2012, https://www.washingtontimes.com/news/2012/dec/31/snowe-wont-miss-partisanship-plans-to-nurture-cent/.

4. Carl Hulse, "Arlen Specter's Closing Argument," *The New York Times*, Last modified, December 21, 2010, https://thecaucus.blogs.nytimes.com/2010/12/21/arlen-specters-closing-argument/?searchResultPosition=4.

5. Michael Barber and Nolan McCarty, "Causes and Consequences of Polarization," in *Political Negotiation: A Handbook* (Cambridge, MA: Brookings Institution Press, 2015), 37. See also Frances E. Lee, *Beyond Ideology: Politics, Principles, and Partisanship in the U.S. Senate* (Chicago, IL: University of Chicago Press, 2009).

6. Lilliana Mason, "Party Polarization Is Making Us More Prejudiced," in *Political Polarization in American Politics*, eds. Daniel J. Hopkins and John Sides (New York, NY: Bloomsbury Academic, 2015), 55.

7. John B. Gilmour, *Strategic Disagreement: Stalemate in American Politics* (Pittsburgh, PA: University of Pittsburgh Press, 1995); Timothy Groseclose and Nolan McCarty, "The Politics of Blame: Bargaining before an Audience," *American Journal of Political Science* 45, no. 1 (2001): 100–19.

8. Barber and McCarty, "Causes and Consequences of Polarization."

9. Hulse, "Arlen Specter's Closing Argument."

10. E. Halperin and J. J. Gross, "Intergroup Anger in Intractable Conflict: Long-Term Sentiments Predict Anger Responses During the Gaza War," *Group Processes and Intergroup Relations* 14 (2011): 477–88; I. Maoz and C. McCauley, "Psychological Correlates of Support for Compromise: A Polling Study of Jewish-Israeli Attitudes Toward Solutions to the Israeli-Palestinian Conflict," *Political Psychology* 26 (2005): 791–808.

11. Marc Hetherington and Thomas J. Rudolph, *The Emergence of Polarized Trust*, Last modified August 21, 2014, doi:10.2139/ssrn.2484755; Pew Research Center for People and the Press, "Political Polarization in the American Public," *Pew Research Center Report*, Last modified, June 12, 2014, https://www.people-press.org/2014/06/12/political-polarization-in-the-american-public/.

12. Jürgen Habermas, "Three Normative Models of Democracy," *Constellations* 1, no. 1 (1994): 1–10.

13. David Davenport, "Congress and the Lost Art of Compromise," *Forbes*, Last modified January 24, 2020, https://www.forbes.com/sites/daviddavenport/2018/01/24/congress-and-the-lost-art-of-compromise/#1540069ed597.

14. Logan Dancy and Geoffrey Sheagley, "Partisanship and Perceptions of Party-Line Voting in Congress," *Political Research Quarterly* 71, no. 1 (2018): 32–45. Lower party-line voting suggests that partisans were able to come to compromises more readily in the earlier period. This tendency was likely the results of cross-cutting identities of the era. For instance, even into the 1970s, a sizable number of southern Democrats still held conservative views on the social issues of the time.

15. Jeffrey D. Grynaviski, "Congress Used to Pass Bipartisan Legislation – Will It Ever Again?" *The Conversation*, Last modified January 24, 2019, https://theconversation.com/congress-used-to-pass-bipartisan-legislation-will-it-ever-again-107134.

16. For details on the 98th Congress, see David R. Mayhew, *Divided We Govern: Party Control, Lawmaking, and Investigations, 1946–2002*, 2nd edition (New Haven, CT: Yale University Press, 2005).

17. While gridlock has often been characterized as problematic, there are some who believe stalemate to be preferable to government action. If government action, on average, produces worse outcomes than not governmentally addressing problems then gridlock becomes the better choice. Additionally, an argument can be made that when there is no working majority for a particular policy, no agreement is better than an agreement reached through compromise. E.g., Jonathan Rauch, "How American Politics Went Insane," *The Atlantic Monthly*, July/August, 2016.

18. For a concise overview of much of this literature, see Jane Manbridge and Cathi Jo Martin, *Political Negotiation: A Handbook* (Cambridge, MA: Brookings Institution Press, 2015).

19. For discussions of the erosion bipartisan friendliness, see Barber and McCarty, "Causes and Consequences of Polarization," 38 and Juliet Eilperin, *Fight Club Politics: How Partisanship Is Poisoning the House of Representatives* (Lanham, MD: Rowman and Littlefield, 2007).

20. Evan Bayh, "Why I'm Leaving the Senate," *The New York Times*, Last modified February 20, 2010, https://www.nytimes.com/2010/02/21/opinion/21bayh.html.

21. For such arguments see: Hetherington and Rudolph, *The Emergence of Polarized Trust*; Leonie Huddy, Lilliana Mason, and Lene Arøe, "Expressive Partisanship: Campaign Involvement, Political Emotion, and Partisan Identity," *American Political Science Review* 109, no. 1 (2015): 1–17; Shanto Iyengar, Gaurav Sood, and Yphtach Lelkes, "Affect, Not Ideology A Social Identity Perspective on Polarization," *Public Opinion Quarterly* 76, no. 3 (January 1, 2012): 405–31; Shanto Iyengar and Sean J. Westwood, "Fear and Loathing across Party Lines: New Evidence on Group Polarization: Fear and Loathing Across Party Lines," *American Journal of Political Science* 59, no. 3 (July 2015): 690–707; Diane M. Mackie, Thierry Devos, and Eliot R. Smith, "Intergroup Emotions: Explaining Offensive Action Tendencies in an Intergroup Context," *Journal of Personality and Social Psychology* 79, no. 4 (2000): 602–16; Lilliana Mason, "'I Disrespectfully Agree': The Differential Effects of Partisan Sorting on Social and Issue Polarization," *American Journal of Political Science* 59, no. 1 (2015): 128–45; H. Tajfel, "Social Categorization, Social Identity, and Social Comparisons," in *Differentiation Between Social Groups*, ed. H. Tajfel (London, UK: Academic Press, 1978), 27–60.

22. Lilliana Mason, "Ideologues without Issues: The Polarizing Consequences of Ideological Identities," *Public Opinion Quarterly* 82, no. S1 (April 11, 2018): 866–87.

23. M. B. Brewer, "The Many Faces of Social Identity: Implications for Political Psychology," *Political Psychology* 22, no. 1 (2001): 115–25; J. L. Gibson, "Do Strong Group Identities Fuel Intolerance?: Evidence from the South African Case," *Political Psychology* 27, no. 5 (2006): 665–705; F. Wilmer, *The Social Construction of Man, the State, and War: Identity, Conflict, and Violence in the Former Yugoslavia* (New York, NY: Routledge, 2002).

24. J. Haidt, E. Rosenberg, and H. Hom, "Differentiating Diversities: Moral Diversity Is Not Like Other Kinds," *Journal of Applied Social Psychology* 33 (2003): 1–36; E. Mullen and L. J. Skitka, "Exploring the Psychological Underpinnings of the Moral Mandate Effect: Motivated Reasoning, Group Differentiation, or Anger?" *Journal of Personality and Social Psychology* 90 (2006): 629–43; M. T. Parker and R. Janoff-Bulman, "Lessons from Morality-Based Social Identity: The Power of Outgroup 'Hate,' Not Just Ingroup 'Love'," *Social Justice Research* 26 (2013): 81–96; L. J. Skitka, C. W. Bauman, and E. G. Sargis, "Moral Conviction: Another Contributor to Attitude Strength or Something More?" *Journal of Personality and Social Psychology* 88 (2005): 895–917.

25. See previous note for more on how racial and ethnic social identities operate.

26. H. Tajfel and J. C. Turner, *An Integrative Theory of Intergroup Conflict*, eds. W. G. Austin and S. Worchel (Monterey, CA: Brooks/Cole, 1979).

27. Brewer, "The Many Faces of Social Identity," 115–25; Tajfel, "Social Categorization," 27–60; Tajfel and Turner, *An Integrative Theory of Intergroup Conflict*; H. Tajfel and J. C. Turner, "The Social Identity Theory of Intergroup Behavior," in *The Psychology of Intergroup Relations*, eds. S. Worcheland and W. G. Austin (Chicago, IL: Nelson-Hall, 1986), 349.

28. Brewer, "The Many Faces of Social Identity," 115–25; Gibson, "Do Strong Group Identities Fuel Intolerance?" 665–705; Wilmer, *The Social Construction of Man*.

29. Michael Billig and Henri Tajfel, "Social Categorization and Similarity in Intergroup Behaviour," *European Journal of Social Psychology* 3, no. 1 (1973): 27–52; Henri Tajfel, *Human Groups and Social Society: Studies in Social Psychology* (Cambridge, UK: Cambridge University Press, 1981). See also: Vernon L. Allen and David A. Wilder, "Categorization, Belief Similarity, and Intergroup Discrimination," *Journal of Personality and Social Psychology* 32, no. 6 (1975): 971–77; Marilynn B. Brewer and Madelyn Silver, "Ingroup Bias as a Function of Task Characteristics," *European Journal of Social Psychology* 8, no. 3 (1978): 393–400; Willem Doise and Anne Sinclair, "The Categorisation Process in Intergroup Relations," *European Journal of Social Psychology* 3, no. 2 (1973): 145–57.

30. Christopher J. Devine, "Ideological Social Identity: Psychological Attachment to Ideological In-Groups as a Political Phenomenon and a Behavioral Influence," *Political Behavior* 37 (2014): 1–27.

31. S. A. Weldon, "The Institutional Context of Tolerance for Ethnic Minorities: A Comparative, Multilevel Analysis of Western Europe," *American Journal of Political Science* 50, no. 2 (2006): 331–59.

32. Tajfel and Turner, *An Integrative Theory of Intergroup Conflict*.

33. American studies: A. Gerber and D. Green, "Rational Learning and Partisan Attitudes," *The American Political Science Review* 42, no. 3 (1998): 794–818; S. Greene, "Understanding Party Identification: A Social Identify Approach," *Political Psychology* 20, no. 2 (1999): 393–403; D. Green, B. Palmquist, and E. Schickler, *Partisan Hearts and Minds* (New Haven, CT: Yale University Press, 2002). Comparative perspectives: Dominic Abrams, "Political Distinctiveness: An Identity Optimising Approach," *European Journal of Social Psychology* 24, no. 3 (1994): 357–65; D. Abrams and N. Elmer, "Self-Denial as a Paradox of Political and Regional Social Identity: Findings from a Study of 16- and 18 Year-Olds," *European Journal of Social Psychology* 22 (1992): 279–95; J. Duck, M. Hogg, and D. Terry, "Me, Us and Them: Political Identification and the Third-Person Effect in the 1993," *Australian Federal Election. European Journal of Social Psychology* 25 (1995): 195–215; C. Kelly, "Identity and Intergroup Perceptions in Minority-Majority Contexts," *Human Relations* 43 (1990): 583–99; C. Kelly, "Identity and Levels of Influence: When a Political Minority Fails," *British Journal of Social Psychology* 29 (1990): 289–301; C. Kelly, "Intergroup Differentiation in a Political Context," *British Journal of Social Psychology* 27 (1988): 319–32; C. Kelly, "Political Identity and Perceived Intragroup Homogeneity," *British Journal of Social Psychology* 28 (1989): 239–50.

34. A. Campbell, P. E. Converse, W. E. Miller, and D. E. Stokes, *The American Voter* (New York, NY: Wiley, 1960).

35. Greene, "Understanding Party Identification," 393–403.

36. D. F. Alwin, R. L. Cohen, and T. M. Newcomb, *Political Attitudes Over the Life Span: The Bennington Women After Fifty Years* (Madison, WI: University of Madison Press, 1991); J. A. Krosnick and D. F. Alwin, "Aging and Susceptibility to Attitude Change," *Journal of Personality and Social Psychology* 57, no. 3 (1989): 416–25; D. O. Sears and C. L. Funk, "Evidence of Long-Term Persistence of Adults' Political Predispositions," *The Journal of Politics* 61, no. 1 (1999): 1–28.

37. M. J. Esman, *An Introduction to Ethnic Conflict* (Cambridge: Polity, 2004); N. G. Jesse and K. P. Williams, *Ethnic Conflict: A Systematic Approach to Cases of Conflict* (Washington, DC: CQ Press, 2011).

38. Iyengar and Westwood, "Fear and Loathing across Party Lines," 690–707.

39. Bertrand Russell, "Dreams and Facts," *The Athenaeum Nos 4,642, 4,623*, April 18, 25, 1919: 198–99, 232–33.

40. Larry Bartels, "Partisanship and Voting Behavior 1952–1996," *American Journal of Political Science* 44, no. 1 (2008): 35–50; Jennifer Jerit and Jason Barabas, "Partisan Perceptual Bias and the Information Environment," *Journal of Politics* 74, no. July (2012): 672–84; Stephen P. Nicholson, "The Jeffords Switch and Public Support for Divided Government," *British Journal of Political Science* 35 (2005): 343–56; Thomas F. Pettigrew, "The Ultimate Attribution Error: Extending Allport's Cognitive Analysis of Prejudice," *Personality and Social Psychology Bulletin* 5, no. 4 (1979): 461–76; David P. Redlawsk, "Hot Cognition or Cool Consideration? Testing the Effects of Motivated Reasoning on Political Decision Making," *Journal of Politics* 64, no. 4 (2002): 1021–44.

41. Alexander G. Theodoridis, "Me, Myself, and (I), (D), or (R)? Partisanship and Political Cognition through the Lens of Implicit Identity," *The Journal of Politics* 79, no. 4 (2017): 1264.

42. Douglas J. Ahler and Gaurav Sood, "The Parties in Our Heads: Misperceptions about Party Composition and Their Consequences," *The Journal of Politics* 80, no. 3 (July 1, 2018): 964–81.

43. D. J. Ahler, "Self-Fulfilling Misperceptions of Public Polarization," *The Journal of Politics* 76, no. 3 (2014): 607–20; Andrew Gelman, "How Better Educated Whites Are Driving Polarization," in *Political Polarization in American Politics*, eds. Daniel J. Hopkins and John Sides (New York, NY: Bloomsbury Academic, 2015).

44. For an overview of this line of thinking, see Susan Davis, "This Congress Could Be Least Productive since 1947," *USA Today*, Last modified, August 14, 2012, https://abcnews.go.com/Politics/congress-productive-1947/story?id=17007199.

45. The concept of ideological sorting refers to the major realignment of both officeholders and the mass electorate over the latter half of the twentieth century. As the two major parties realigned over civil rights related issues during the latter part of the twentieth century, partisan elites, the media, and the electorate began linking more conservative stances with the Republican label and more liberal stances with the Democratic label. As demographic groups moved their support from one party to the other in response to the changes in the party platforms, rank-and-file Republicans and Democrats increasingly perceived the ideological difference between their own party and the opposing party as much more significant. For more on the concept and dynamics of ideological sorting see: Steven E. Schier and Todd E. Eblery, *Polarized: The Rise of Ideology in American Politics* (Lanham, MD: Rowman & Littlefield, 2016); A. Gerber, G. Huber, D. Doherty, and C. Dowling, "Personality and the Strength and Direction of Partisan Identification," *Political Behavior* 34 (2012): 653–88; Hans Noel, *Political Ideologies and Political Parties in America* (New York, NY: Cambridge University Press, 2013); Laura Stoker and M. Kent Jennings, "Of Time and the Development of Partisan Polarization," *American Journal of Political Science* 52, no. 3 (2008): 619–35; P. DiMaggio, J. Evans, and B. Bryson, "Have Americans' Social Attitudes Become More Polarized?" *American Journal of Sociology* 102 (1996): 690–755; Ariel Malka and Yphtach Lelkes, "More than Ideology: Conservative–Liberal Identity and Receptivity to Political Cues," *Social Justice Research* 23, no. 2–3 (2010): 156–88; Christopher Ellis and James A. Stimson, *Ideology in America*, 1 edition (New York: Cambridge University Press, 2012); Devine, "Ideological Social Identity," 509–35; S. E. Asch, "Effects of Group Pressure Upon the Modification and Distortion of Judgment," in *Groups, Leadership and Men*, ed. H. Guetzkow (Pittsburgh, PA: Carnegie Press, 1951); B. R. Berelson, P. F. Lazarsfeld, and W. N. McPhee, *Voting: A Study of Opinion Formation in a Presidential Campaign* (Chicago, IL: University of Chicago Press, 1954); Muzafer Sherif, *The Psychology of Social Norms* (Oxford, England: Harper Torchbooks, 1966); John C. Turner, *Social Influence* (Belmont, CA, US: Thomson Brooks/Cole Publishing Co, 1991).

46. Matt Viser and Toluse Olorunnipa, "Iowa Caucuses Descend into Chaos as Delay Leaves Outcome Uncertain," *The Washington Post*, Last modified February 3,

2020, https://www.washingtonpost.com/politics/iowa-caucuses-descend-into-chaos-as-delay-leaves-outcome-uncertain/2020/02/04/27b3d128-45f4-11ea-8124-0ca81eff cdfb_story.html.

47. Ibid.

48. Jandos Rothstein, "Michael Bloomberg and the Dangers of 'Any Blue Will Do' Politics," *The American Prospect*, Last modified February 17, 2020, https://prospect.org/politics/michael-bloomberg-candidacy-mirror-image-trump/.

49. Paul Garber and WFDD, "Bloomberg Makes Pitch To NC Voters," *WUNC, North Carolina Public Radio*, Last modified February 13, 2020, https://www.wunc.org/post/bloomberg-makes-pitch-nc-voters.

50. Burgess Everett, "Romney Denies Trump Unanimous Republican Support," *Politico*, Last modified February 5, 2020, https://www.politico.com/news/2020/02/05/sen-mitt-romney-will-vote-to-convict-trump-breaking-with-fellow-republicans-110848.

51. Lauren Egan, "Romney, Vilified by Trump and his Allies for Voting to Convict, Finds Respect Back Home," *NBC News*, Last modified February 9, 2020, https://www.nbcnews.com/politics/trump-impeachment-inquiry/romney-vilified-d-c-vote-convict-trump-finds-respect-support-n1133106.

52. That is, even though an individual may express a strong commitment to either a "conservative" or "liberal" ideology, his issue expressed stances on particular issues do not cohere well to such a framework. For more on the concept and empirical reality of ideological constraint see: Philip E. Converse, "The Nature of Belief Systems in Mass Publics (1964)," *Critical Review* 18, no. 1–3 (2006): 1–74; Christopher Achen and Larry Bartels, "Democracy for Realists: Holding up a Mirror to the Electorate," *Juncture* 22, no. 4 (2016): 269–75; Donald R. Kinder and Nathan P. Kalmoe, *Neither Liberal nor Conservative: Ideological Innocence in the American Public*, 1st edition (Chicago, IL University of Chicago Press, n.d.); Mason, "Ideologues without Issues," 866–87.

53. Mason, "Ideologues without Issues," 280.

54. Leonie Huddy and Lilliana Mason, "Measuring Partisanship as a Social Identity, Predicting Political Activism," *Paper presented at the Annual Meeting of the International Society for Political Psychology*, July 7–10, 2010, 5.

55. Huddy, Mason, and Aarøe, "Expressive Partisanship," 1–17; Lewis A. Coser, *The Functions of Social Conflict* (New York, NY, US: Free Press, 1956); J. S. Lerner and D. Keltner, "Fear, Anger, and Risk," *Journal of Personality and Social Psychology* 81, no. 1 (July 2001): 146–59; Jennifer S. Lerner and Dacher Keltner, "Beyond Valence: Toward a Model of Emotion-Specific Influences on Judgement and Choice," *Cognition and Emotion* 14, no. 4 (2000): 473–93; Robert A. LeVine and Donald T. Campbell, *Ethnocentrism: Theories of Conflict, Ethnic Attitudes, and Group Behavior* (Oxford, England: John Wiley & Sons, 1972); George, W. Marcus, Russell Neuman, and Michael MacKuen, *Affective Intelligence and Political Judgment* (Chicago, IL: University of Chicago Press, 2000).

56. Naomi Ellemers and Kees van den Bos, "Morality in Groups: On the Social-Regulatory Functions of Right and Wrong," *Social and Personality Psychology Compass* 6, no. 12 (2012): 878–89.

57. On negative perceptions of rivals, see: Hetherington and Rudolph, *The Emergence of Polarized Trust*; Tajfel, "Social Categorization," 27–60; Tajfel and Turner, *An Integrative Theory of Intergroup Conflict*; Tajfel and Turner, "The Social Identity Theory of Intergroup Behavior," 349. For arguments about inclusion in favored groups: Brewer, "The Many Faces of Social Identity," 115–25; Elizabeth Suhay, "Explaining Group Influence: The Role of Identity and Emotion in Political Conformity and Polarization," *Political Behavior* 37, no. 1 (2015): 221–51.

58. For an overview of the self-categorization theory see Suhay, "Explaining Group Influence."

59. Dominic Abrams, Margaret Wetherell, Sandra Cochrane, Michael A. Hogg, and John C. Turner, "Knowing What to Think by Knowing Who You Are: Self-Categorization and the Nature of Norm Formation, Conformity and Group Polarization*," *British Journal of Social Psychology* 29, no. 2 (1990): 97–119; J. C. Turner, "Social Categorization and Self-Concept: A Social Cognitive Theory of Group Behavior," in *Advances in Group Process: Theory and Research*, ed. E. J. Lawler (Greenwich, CT: JAI Press, 1985); J. C. Turner, M. A. Hogg, P. J. Oakes, S. D. Reicher, and M. S. Wetherell, *Rediscovering the Social Group: A Self-Categorisation Theory* (Oxford, UK: Blackwell, 1987); Turner, *Social Influence*.

60. On overt signaling and its motivations: Russell D. Clark and Anne Maass, "Social Categorization in Minority Influence: The Case of Homosexuality," *European Journal of Social Psychology* 18, no. 4 (1988): 347–64; Wendy Wood, Gregory J. Pool, Kira Leck, and Daniel Purvis, "Self-Definition, Defensive Processing, and Influence: The Normative Impact of Majority and Minority Groups," *Journal of Personality and Social Psychology* 71, no. 6 (1996): 1181–93; Suhay, "Explaining Group Influence," 221–51; Elizabeth Theiss-Morse, *Who Counts as an American? The Boundaries of National Identity* (Cambridge: Cambridge University Press, 2009); Turner, "Social Categorization and Self-Concept," 77–121; Turner et al., *Rediscovering the Social Group*.

61. José Per Marques, Dominic Abrams, and Rui G. Serôdio, "Being Better by Being Right: Subjective Group Dynamics and Derogation of in-Group Deviants When Generic Norms Are Undermined," *Journal of Personality and Social Psychology* 81, no. 3 (2001): 436–47.

62. *Democracy in America*, Vol. I, Part II, Chapter 7.

63. Erin C. Cassese and Mirya R. Holman, "Playing the Woman Card: Ambivalent Sexism in the 2016 U.S. Presidential Race," *Political Psychology* 40, no. 1 (2019): 55–74; Deborah J. Terry and Michael A. Hogg, "Group Norms and the Attitude–Behavior Relationship: A Role for Group Identification," *Personality and Social Psychology Bulletin* 22, no. 8 (1996): 776–93; Deborah J. Terry, Michael A. Hogg, and Katherine M. White, "The Theory of Planned Behaviour: Self-Identity, Social Identity and Group Norms," *British Journal of Social Psychology* 38, no. 3 (1999): 225–44; Maria Rosaria Cadinu and Marcella Cerchioni, "Compensatory Biases after Ingroup Threat: 'Yeah, but We Have a Good Personality'," *European Journal of Social Psychology* 31, no. 4 (2001): 353–67; Mackie, Devos, and Smith, "Intergroup Emotions," 602–16.

64. Huddy and Mason, "Measuring Partisanship as a Social Identity," 5.

65. Mason, "'I Disrespectfully Agree'," 128–45.

66. Brewer, "The Many Faces of Social Identity," 115–25; Iyengar, Sood, and Lelkes, "Affect, Not Ideology A Social Identity," 405–31; Elmar Schlueter, Peter Schmidt, and Ulrich Wagner, "Disentangling the Causal Relations of Perceived Group Threat and Outgroup Derogation: Cross-National Evidence from German and Russian Panel Surveys," *European Sociological Review* 24, no. 5 (December 1, 2008): 567–81; M. Sherif, O. J. Harvey, B. J. White, W. R. Hood, and C. W. Sherif, *Intergroup Conflict and Cooperation: The Robbers Cave Experiment*, Vol. 10 (Norman, OK: University Book Exchange, 1961).

67. Mason, "'I Disrespectfully Agree'," 128–45; Thomas Sowell, *A Conflict of Visions: Ideological Origins of Political Struggles*, Revised (New York, NY: Basic Books, 2007).

68. Huddy and Mason, "Measuring Partisanship as a Social Identity," 5.

69. Thomas B. Edsall, "No Hate Left Behind: Lethal Partisanship Is Taking Us into Dangerous Territory," *The New York Times*, Last modified March 13, 2019, https://www.nytimes.com/2019/03/13/opinion/hate-politics.html.

70. Carl Schmitt, *The Theory of the Partisan: A Commentary/Remark on the Concept of the Political* (Berlin: Duncker & Humblot, 1963).

71. Devine, "Ideological Social Identity," 509–35; Edsall, "No Hate Left Behind."

72. Luca Andrighetto, Cristina Baldissarri, Sara Lattanzio, Steve Loughnan, and Chiara Volpato, "Human-Itarian Aid? Two Forms of Dehumanization and Willingness to Help after Natural Disasters," *The British Journal of Social Psychology/The British Psychological Society* 53 (2014): 573–84; N. Ellemers, *Morality and the Regulation of Social Behavior: Groups as Moral Anchors* (New York, NY: Psychology Press, 2017); G. T. Viki, D. Osgood, and S. Phillips, "Dehumanization and Self-Reported Proclivity to Torture Prisoners of War," *Journal of Experimental Psychology* 49, no. 3 (2013): 325–28.

73. Erin C. Cassese, "Partisan Dehumanization in American Politics," *Political Behavior*, Last updated April, 2019, doi:10.1007/s11109-019-09545-w.

74. David M. Brooks, "Why Partyism Is Wrong – The New York Times," *The New York Times*, Last modified October 28, 2014, https://www.nytimes.com/2014/10/28/opinion/david-brooks-why-partyism-is-wrong.html; Nathan Kalmoe and Lilliana Mason, "Lethal Mass Partisanship: Prevalence, Correlates, & Electoral Contingencies," *Paper Presented at the Annual Meeting of the American Political Science Association*, 2018.

75. Shanto Iyengar and Masha Krupenkin, "The Strengthening of Partisan Affect," *Political Psychology* 39, no. S1 (2018): 201–18; see also Sean Theriault, "Partisan Warfare Is the Problem," in *Political Polarization in American Politics*, eds. Daniel J. Hopkins and John Sides (New York, NY: Bloomsbury Academic, 2015), 12–13.

76. For the link between dehumanization and moral judgment see Cassese, "Partisan Dehumanization in American Politics"; Ellemers, *Morality and the Regulation of Social Behavior*. On the implications of dehumanization and moral

judgment: L. Andrighetto, C. Baldissarri, S. Lattanzio, S. Loughnan, and C. Volpato, "Humanitraian Aid? Two Forms of Dehumanization and Willingness to Help After Natural Disasters," *British Journal of Social Psychology* 53, no. 3 (2014): 573–84; N. Haslam and S. Loughnan, "How Dehumanization Promotes Harm," in *The Social Psychology of Good and Evil*, ed. A. G. Miller (New York, NY: The Guilford Press, 2016), 140–58; C. W. Leach, N. Ellemers, and M. Barreto, "Group Virtue: The Importance of Morality (vs. Competence and Sociability) in the Positive Evaluation of In-Groups," *Journal of Personality and Social Psychology* 93, no. 2 (2007): 234–49; R. Nagar and I. Maoz, "Predicting Jewish-Israeli Recognition of Palestinian Pain and Suffering," *Journal of Conflict Resolution* 61, no. 2 (2017): 372–97.

77. A. Bandura, *Moral Disengagement: How People Do Harm and Live with Themselves* (New York, NY: Worth Publishers, 2016).

78. N. Kteily and E. Bruneau, "The Politics and Real-World Consequences of Minority Group Dehumanization," *Personality and Social Psychology Bulletin* 43, no. 1 (2017): 87–104; Kalmoe and Mason, "Lethal Mass Partisanship."

79. Mason, "'I Disrespectfully Agree'," 128–45. See also, Robert Gressis' arguments in this volume about the anti-war movement of the George W. Bush era and the contemporary pro-life movement.

80. Brooks, "Why Partyism Is Wrong."

81. Larry M. Bartels, "Beyond the Running Tally: Partisan Bias in Political Perceptions," *Political Behavior* 24 (2002): 117–50; James N. Druckman, Erik Peterson, and Rune Slothuus, "How Elite Partisan Polarization Affects Public Opinion Formation," *American Political Science Review* 107, no. 1 (2013): 57–79; Laurel Harbridge, Neil Malhotra, and Brian F. Harrison, "Public Preferences for Bipartisanship in the Policy Making Process," *Legislative Studies Quarterly* 39, no. 3 (2014): 327–55; Iyengar and Westwood, "Fear and Loathing across Party Lines," 690–707; Thomas J. Leeper and Rune Slothuus, "Political Parties, Motivated Reasoning, and Public Opinion Formation," *Advances in Political Psychology* 35 (2014): 129–56.

82. For more on "easy issues" see Edward G. Carmines and James A. Stimson, *Issue Evolution: Race and the Transformation of American Politics* (Princeton, NJ: Princeton University Press, 1989).

83. Ayn Rand, *Capitalism: The Unknown Ideal* (New York, NY: New American Library, 1966), 255.

84. The survey sample included 827 undergraduate students from a representative public university. The survey had a completion rate of 59.1 percent, and respondents ranged in age from 18 and 25 years old, with an average age of about 22. White (Anglo) subjects comprised about half (48.8 percent) of the sample, while about 18 percent of the study participants were black (African-American), slightly more than 20 percent were Hispanic (Latino), less than to 2 percent were Asian-American, and almost 5 percent identified themselves as some other race or ethnicity.

85. I considered those who reported a leaning, weak, or strong preference for a major party as partisans. Only those who reported complete independence from both parties were considered Independents.

86. Independent samples difference of means tests confirmed no statistically significant differences between the self-identified Democratic and Republican subsamples on these two measures (two-tailed tests, $p > 0.05$).

87. An Independent samples difference of mean test confirmed that this difference was statistically significant at the $p < 0.05$, two-tailed level.

88. For more on the reinforcing nature of overlapping social identities and their connections to partisanship, see the ideological sorting literature referenced earlier.

89. I did so by calculating the absolute value of the difference between an even split (of 50) and the raw numeric point offered by each respondent (i.e., |compromise point − 50|), creating measure of the distance from an equal compromise point that each reported point represented.

90. Multivariate regression is a statistical technique that enables estimation of the effects that key causal factors (attitudes toward the opposition party) have on the response factor (reported compromise points). Though regression estimates cannot offer deterministic predictions, they can offer some probabilistic insight into the correlative relationships between causal and response variables.

91. The positive and significant coefficients for the "Democrat," "Republican," and "Strong Partisan" indicators document positive relationships between identification as either a Democrat or Republican and a higher compromise point.

92. The slightly higher compromise positions of Republicans may be reflective of the fact that the Republican Party held a majority in the both chambers of the U.S. Congress at the time of the survey. Respondents from that party may have been expressing their belief that the majority party should benefit more from policy decisions than the minority party.

93. The positive and significant coefficients for the "bad people" and "harm me" attitudes suggests a direct relationship between holding views that counter-partisans are fundamentally bad people who are out to harm one (or one's group members) and support for less equitable compromises.

94. E. Halperin, "Emotional Barriers to Peace: Negative Emotions and Public Opinion About the Peace Process in the Middle East," *Peace and Conflict: Journal of Peace Psychology* 17 (2011): 22–45; E. Halperin, A. Russell, C. S. Dweck, and J. J. Gross, "Anger, Hatred, and the Quest for Peace: Anger Can Be Constructive in the Absence of Hatred," *Journal of Conflict Resolution* 55 (2011): 274–91; Hetherington and Rudolph, *The Emergence of Polarized Trust*; Maoz and McCauley, "Psychological Correlates of Support for Compromise," 791–808.

95. Compromise point estimates derived from the "All Respondents" model on Table 1. Partisanship and attitude toward opposite party set to appropriate values, ideology variables held neutral.

96. That is, a 43-point divide equates to about 43 percent of the 100-point policy space 0 to +100) proposed in the question asked of respondents.

97. Bayh, "Why I'm Leaving the Senate."

98. On the connection between out-group derogation and compromise, see Cassese, "Partisan Dehumanization in American Politics." Also see Ellemers and van den Bos, "Morality in Groups," 878–89, who present evidence that even when groups are in moral agreement, group members may still believe that the in-group is better at acting on those moral values and resist compromise with the out-group.

99. Habermas, "Three Normative Models of Democracy," 1–10.

100. D. J. Ahler and D. E. Broockman, "The Delegate Paradox: Why Polarized Politicians can Represent Citizens Best," *The Journal of Politics* 80, no. 4 (2018): 1117–33; Matt Grossman and David A. Hopkins, *Asymmetric Politics: Ideological Republicans and Group Interest Democrats* (Oxford, UK: Oxford University Press, 2016); Harbridge, Malhotra, and Harrison, "Public Preferences for Bipartisanship," 327–55; Timothy J. Ryan, "No Compromise: Political Consequences of Moralized Attitudes," *American Journal of Political Science* 61, no. 2 (2017): 409–23.

101. Jonathan Baron, "Why Teach Thinking? An Essay," *Applied Psychology: An International Review* 42, no. 3 (1993): 191–214.

102. John T. Cacioppo, Richard E. Petty, and Chuan F. Kao, "The Efficient Assessment of Need for Cognition," *Journal of Personality Assessment* 48, no. 3 (1984): 306–7.

103. Carol Anne M. Kardash and Roberta J. Scholes, "Effects of Preexisiting Beliefs, Epistemological Beliefs, and Need for Cognition on Interpretation of Controversial Issues," *Journal of Educational Psychology* 88, no. 2 (1996): 260–71.

104. Uriel Haran, Ilana Ritov, and Barbara A. Mellers, "The Role of Actively Open-Minded Thinking in Information Acquisition, Accuracy, and Calibration," *Judgment and Decision Making* 8, no. 3 (2013): 188–201; Angela L. Duckworth, Christopher Peterson, Michael D. Matthews, and Dennis R. Kelly, "Grit: Perseverance and Passion for Long-Term Goals," *Journal of Personality and Social Psychology* 92, no. 6 (2007): 1087–101.

105. Haran, Ritov, and Mellers, "The Role of Actively Open-Minded Thinking," 188–201.

REFERENCES

Abrams, D., and N. Elmer. "Self-Denial as a Paradox of Political and Regional Social Identity: Findings from a Study of 16- and 18 Year-Olds." *European Journal of Social Psychology* 22 (1992): 279–295.

Abrams, Dominic. "Political Distinctiveness: An Identity Optimising Approach." *European Journal of Social Psychology* 24, no. 3 (1994): 357–365.

Abrams, Dominic, Margaret Wetherell, Sandra Cochrane, Michael A. Hogg, and John C. Turner. "Knowing What to Think by Knowing Who You Are: Self-Categorization and the Nature of Norm Formation, Conformity and Group Polarization." *British Journal of Social Psychology* 29, no. 2 (1990): 97–119.

Achen, Christopher, and Larry Bartels. "Democracy for Realists: Holding up a Mirror to the Electorate." *Juncture* 22, no. 4 (2016): 269–275.

Ahler, D. J. "Self-Fulfilling Misperceptions of Public Polarization." *The Journal of Politics* 76, no. 3 (2014): 607–620.

Ahler, D. J., and D. E. Broockman. "The Delegate Paradox: Why Polarized Politicians Can Represent Citizens Best." *The Journal of Politics* 80, no. 4 (2018): 1117–1133.

Ahler, Douglas J., and Gaurav Sood. "The Parties in Our Heads: Misperceptions about Party Composition and Their Consequences." *The Journal of Politics* 80, no. 3 (July 1, 2018): 964–981.

Allen, Vernon L., and David A. Wilder. "Categorization, Belief Similarity, and Intergroup Discrimination." *Journal of Personality and Social Psychology* 32, no. 6 (1975): 971–977.

Alwin, D. F., R. L. Cohen, and T. M. Newcomb. *Political Attitudes Over the Life Span: The Bennington Women After Fifty Years*. Madison, WI: University of Madison Press, 1991.

Andrighetto, L., C. Baldissarri, S. Lattanzio, S. Loughnan, and C. Volpato. "Humanitraian Aid? Two Forms of Dehumanization and Willingness to Help After Natural Disasters." *British Journal of Social Psychology* 53, no. 3 (2014): 573–584.

Andrighetto, Luca, Cristina Baldissarri, Sara Lattanzio, Steve Loughnan, and Chiara Volpato. "Human-Itarian Aid? Two Forms of Dehumanization and Willingness to Help after Natural Disasters." *The British Journal of Social Psychology/The British Psychological Society* 53 (2014): 573–584.

Asch, S. E. "Effects of Group Pressure upon the Modification and Distortion of Judgment." In *Groups, Leadership and Men*, edited by H. Guetzkow. Pittsburgh, PA: Carnegie Press, 1951.

Bandura, A. *Moral Disengagement: How People Do Harm and Live with Themselves*. New York, NY: Worth Publishers, 2016.

Barabek, Mark Z. "Reaction to Shooting at Congressional Baseball Practice Reveals a Nation That Doesn't Just Disagree. It Hates." *Los Angeles Times*, n.d. https://www.latimes.com/politics/la-na-pol-shooting-politics-20170614-story.html.

Barber, Michael, and Nolan McCarty. "Causes and Consequences of Polarization." In *Political Negotiation: A Handbook*. Cambridge, MA: Brookings Institution Press, 2015.

Baron, Jonathan. "Why Teach Thinking? An Essay." *Applied Psychology: An International Review* 42, no. 3 (1993): 191–214.

Bartels, Larry. "Partisanship and Voting Behavior 1952-1996." *American Journal of Political Science* 44, no. 1 (2008): 35–50.

Bartels, Larry M. "Beyond the Running Tally: Partisan Bias in Political Perceptions." *Political Behavior* 24 (2002): 117–150.

Bayh, Evan. "Why I'm Leaving the Senate." *The New York Times*. Last Modified February 20, 2010. https://www.nytimes.com/2010/02/21/opinion/21bayh.html.

Berelson, B. R., P. F. Lazarsfeld, and W. N. McPhee. *Voting: A Study of Opinion Formation in a Presidential Campaign*. Chicago, IL: University of Chicago Press, 1954.

Billig, Michael, and Henri Tajfel. "Social Categorization and Similarity in Intergroup Behaviour." *European Journal of Social Psychology* 3, no. 1 (1973): 27–52.

Brewer, Marilynn B., and Madelyn Silver. "Ingroup Bias as a Function of Task Characteristics." *European Journal of Social Psychology* 8, no. 3 (1978): 393–400.

Brewer, M. B. "The Many Faces of Social Identity: Implications for Political Psychology." *Political Psychology* 22, no. 1 (2001): 115–125.

Brooks, David M. "Why Partyism Is Wrong —The New York Times." *The New York Times*. Last Modified October 28, 2014. https://www.nytimes.com/2014/10/28/opinion/david-brooks-why-partyism-is-wrong.html.

Cacioppo, John T., Richard E. Petty, and Chuan F. Kao. "The Efficient Assessment of Need for Cognition." *Journal of Personality Assessment* 48, no. 3 (1984): 306–307.

Cadinu, Maria Rosaria, and Marcella Cerchioni. "Compensatory Biases after Ingroup Threat: 'Yeah, but We Have a Good Personality'." *European Journal of Social Psychology* 31, no. 4 (2001): 353–367.

Campbell, A., P. E. Converse, W. E. Miller, and D. E. Stokes. *The American Voter*. New York, NY: Wiley, 1960.

Carmines, Edward G., and James A. Stimson. *Issue Evolution: Race and the Transformation of American Politics*. Princeton, NJ: Princeton University Press, 1989.

Cassese, Erin C. "Partisan Dehumanization in American Politics." *Political Behavior*, n.d. doi:10.1007/s11109-019-09545-w.

Cassese, Erin C., and Mirya R. Holman. "Playing the Woman Card: Ambivalent Sexism in the 2016 U.S. Presidential Race." *Political Psychology* 40, no. 1 (2019): 55–74.

Clark, Russell D., and Anne Maass. "Social Categorization in Minority Influence: The Case of Homosexuality." *European Journal of Social Psychology* 18, no. 4 (1988): 347–364.

Converse, Philip E. "The Nature of Belief Systems in Mass Publics (1964)." *Critical Review* 18, no. 1–3 (2006): 1–74.

Coser, Lewis A. *The Functions of Social Conflict*. New York, NY, US: Free Press, 1956.

Dancy, Logan, and Geoffrey Sheagley. "Partisanship and Perceptions of Party-Line Voting in Congress." *Political Research Quarterly* 71, no. 1 (2018): 32–45.

Davenport, David. "Congress and the Lost Art of Compromise." *Forbes*, n.d. https://www.forbes.com/sites/daviddavenport/2018/01/24/congress-and-the-lost-art-of-compromise/#1540069ed597.

Davis, Susan. "This Congress Could Be Least Productive since 1947." *USA Today*. Last Modified, August 14, 2012. https://abcnews.go.com/Politics/congress-productive-1947/story?id=17007199.

Devine, Christopher J. "Ideological Social Identity: Psychological Attachment to Ideological In-Groups as a Political Phenomenon and a Behavioral Influence." *Political Behavior* 37, no. 3 (September 1, 2015): 509–535.

DiMaggio, P., J. Evans, and B. Bryson. "Have Americans' Social Attitudes Become More Polarized?" *American Journal of Sociology* 102 (1996): 690–755.

Doise, Willem, and Anne Sinclair. "The Categorisation Process in Intergroup Relations." *European Journal of Social Psychology* 3, no. 2 (1973): 145–157.

Druckman, James N., Erik Peterson, and Rune Slothuus. "How Elite Partisan Polarization Affects Public Opinion Formation." *American Political Science Review* 107, no. 1 (2013): 57–79.

Duck, J., M. Hogg, and D. Terry. "Me, Us and Them: Political Identification and the Third-Person Effect in the 1993." *Australian Federal Election. European Journal of Social Psychology* 25 (1995): 195–215.

Duckworth, Angela L., Christopher Peterson, Michael D. Matthews, and Dennis R. Kelly. "Grit: Perseverance and Passion for Long-Term Goals." *Journal of Personality and Social Psychology* 92, no. 6 (2007): 1087–1101.

Edsall, Thomas B. "No Hate Left Behind: Lethal Partisanship Is Taking Us into Dangerous Territory." *The New York Times*, n.d. https://www.nytimes.com/2019/03/13/opinion/hate-politics.html.

Egan, Lauren. "Romney, Vilified by Trump and His Allies for Voting to Convict, Finds Respect Back Home." *NBC News*. Last Modified February 9, 2020. https://www.nbcnews.com/politics/trump-impeachment-inquiry/romney-vilified-d-c-vote-convict-trump-finds-respect-support-n1133106.

Eilperin, Juliet. *Fight Club Politics: How Partisanship Is Poisoning the House of Representatives*. Lanham, MD: Rowman and Littlefield, 2007.

Ellemers, N. *Morality and the Regulation of Social Behavior: Groups as Moral Anchors*. New York, NY: Psychology Press, 2017.

Ellemers, Naomi, and Kees Bos. "Morality in Groups: On the Social-Regulatory Functions of Right and Wrong." *Social and Personality Psychology Compass* 6, no. 12 (2012): 878–889.

Ellis, Christopher, and James A. Stimson. *Ideology in America*, 1st ed. New York, NY: Cambridge University Press, 2012.

Esman, M. J. *An Introduction to Ethnic Conflict*. Cambridge: Polity, 2004.

Everett, Burgess. "Romney Denies Trump Unanimous Republican Support." *Politico*, n.d. https://www.politico.com/news/2020/02/05/sen-mitt-romney-will-vote-to-convict-trump-breaking-with-fellow-republicans-110848.

Garber, Paul, and WFDD. "Bloomberg Makes Pitch To NC Voters." *WUNC, North Carolina Public Radio*, n.d. https://www.wunc.org/post/bloomberg-makes-pitch-nc-voters.

Gelman, Andrew. "How Better Educated Whites Are Driving Polarization." In *Political Polarization in American Politics*, edited by Daniel J. Hopkins and John Sides. New York, NY: Bloomsbury Academic, 2015.

Gerber, A., and D. Green. "Rational Learning and Partisan Attitudes." *The American Political Science Review* 42, no. 3 (1998): 794–818.

Gerber, A., G. Huber, D. Doherty, and C. Dowling. "Personality and the Strength and Direction of Partisan Identification." *Political Behavior* 34 (2012): 653–688.

Gibson, J. L. "Do Strong Group Identities Fuel Intolerance?: Evidence from the South African Case." *Political Psychology* 27, no. 5 (2006): 665–705.

Gilmour, John B. *Strategic Disagreement: Stalemate in American Politics*. Pittsburgh, PA: University of Pittsburgh Press, 1995.

Green, D., B. Palmquist, and E. Schickler. *Partisan Hearts and Minds*. New Haven, CT: Yale University Press, 2002.

Greene, S. "Understanding Party Identification: A Social Identify Approach." *Political Psychology* 20, no. 2 (1999): 393–403.

Groseclose, Timothy, and Nolan McCarty. "The Politics of Blame: Bargaining before an Audience." *American Journal of Political Science* 45, no. 1 (2001): 100–119.

Grossman, Matt, and David A. Hopkins. *Asymmetric Politics: Ideological Republicans and Group Interest Democrats*. Oxford, UK: Oxford University Press, 2016.

Grynaviski, Jeffrey D. "Congress Used to Pass Bipartisan Legislation—Will It Ever Again?" *The Conversation*, n.d. https://theconversation.com/congress-used-to-pass-bipartisan-legislation-will-it-ever-again-107134.

Habermas, Jürgen. "Three Normative Models of Democracy." *Constellations* 1, no. 1 (1994): 1–10.

Haidt, J., E. Rosenberg, and H. Hom. "Differentiating Diversities: Moral Diversity Is Not Like Other Kinds." *Journal of Applied Social Psychology* 33 (2003): 1–36.

Halperin, E. "Emotional Barriers to Peace: Negative Emotions and Public Opinion About the Peace Process in the Middle East." *Peace and Conflict: Journal of Peace Psychology* 17 (2011): 22–45.

Halperin, E., and J. J. Gross. "Intergroup Anger in Intractable Conflict: Long-Term Sentiments Predict Anger Responses During the Gaza War." *Group Processes and Intergroup Relations* 14 (2011): 477–488.

Halperin, E., A. Russell, C. S. Dweck, and J. J. Gross. "Anger, Hatred, and the Quest for Peace: Anger Can Be Constructive in the Absence of Hatred." *Journal of Conflict Resolution* 55 (2011): 274–291.

Haran, Uriel, Ilana Ritov, and Barbara A. Mellers. "The Role of Actively Open-Minded Thinking in Information Acquisition, Accuracy, and Calibration." *Judgment and Decision Making* 8, no. 3 (2013): 188–201.

Harbridge, Laurel, Neil Malhotra, and Brian F. Harrison. "Public Preferences for Bipartisanship in the Policy Making Process." *Legislative Studies Quarterly* 39, no. 3 (2014): 327–355.

Haslam, N., and S. Loughnan. "How Dehumanization Promotes Harm." In *The Social Psychology of Good and Evil*, edited by A. G. Miller, 140–158. New York, NY: The Guilford Press, 2016.

Herszenhorn, David M. "In Senate Health Care Vote, New Partisan Vitriol." *The New York Times*. Last Modified December 24, 2009. https://www.nytimes.com/2009/12/24/us/politics/24assess.html.

Hetherington, Marc, and Thomas J. Rudolph. *The Emergence of Polarized Trust*. Last Modified August 21, 2014. doi:10.2139/ssrn.24847554.

Huddy, Leonie, and Lilliana Mason. "Measuring Partisanship as a Social Identity, Predicting Political Activism." *Annual Meeting of the International Society for Political Psychology*, 5, 2010.

Huddy, Leonie, Lilliana Mason, and Lene Aarøe. "Expressive Partisanship: Campaign Involvement, Political Emotion, and Partisan Identity." *American Political Science Review* 109, no. 1 (2015): 1–17.

Hulse, Carl. "Arlen Specter's Closing Argument." *The New York Times*. Last Modified, December 21, 2010. https://thecaucus.blogs.nytimes.com/2010/12/21/arlen-specters-closing-argument/?searchResultPosition=4.

Iyengar, Shanto, and Masha Krupenkin. "The Strengthening of Partisan Affect." *Political Psychology* 39, no. S1 (2018): 201–218.

Iyengar, Shanto, Gaurav Sood, and Yphtach Lelkes. "Affect, Not Ideology: A Social Identity Perspective on Polarization." *Public Opinion Quarterly* 76, no. 3 (January 1, 2012): 405–431.

Iyengar, Shanto, and Sean J. Westwood. "Fear and Loathing across Party Lines: New Evidence on Group Polarization: Fear and Loathing Across Party Lines." *American Journal of Political Science* 59, no. 3 (July 2015): 690–707.

Jerit, Jennifer, and Jason Barabas. "Partisan Perceptual Bias and the Information Environment." *Journal of Politics* 74, no. July (2012): 672–684.

Jesse, N. G., and K. P. Williams. *Ethnic Conflict: A Systematic Approach to Cases of Conflict*. Washington, DC: CQ Press, 2011.

Kalmoe, Nathan, and Lilliana Mason. "Lethal Mass Partisanship: Prevalence, Correlates, & Electoral Contingencies." *Annual Meeting of the American Political Science Association*, 2018.

Kardash, Carol Anne M., and Roberta J. Scholes. "Effects of Preexisiting Beliefs, Epistemological Beliefs, and Need for Cognition on Interpretation of Controversial Issues." *Journal of Educational Psychology* 88, no. 2 (1996): 260–271.

Kelly, C. "Identity and Intergroup Perceptions in Minority-Majority Contexts." *Human Relations* 43 (1990): 583–599.

———. "Identity and Levels of Influence: When a Political Minority Fails." *British Journal of Social Psychology* 29 (1990): 289–301.

———. "Intergroup Differentiation in a Political Context." *British Journal of Social Psychology* 27 (1988): 319–332.

———. "Political Identity and Perceived Intragroup Homogeneity." *British Journal of Social Psychology* 28 (1989): 239–250.

Kinder, Donald R., and Nathan P. Kalmoe. *Neither Liberal nor Conservative: Ideological Innocence in the American Public*, 1st ed. Chicago, IL: University of Chicago Press, n.d.

Krosnick, J. A., and D. F. Alwin. "Aging and Susceptibility to Attitude Change." *Journal of Personality and Social Psychology* 57, no. 3 (1989): 416–425.

Kteily, N., and E. Bruneau. "The Politics and Real-World Consequences of Minority Group Dehumanization." *Personality and Social Psychology Bulletin* 43, no. 1 (2017): 87–104.

Leach, C. W., N. Ellemers, and M. Barreto. "Group Virtue: The Importance of Morality (vs. Competence and Sociability) in the Positive Evaluation of In-Groups." *Journal of Personality and Social Psychology* 93, no. 2 (2007): 234–249.

Lee, Frances E. *Beyond Ideology: Politics, Principles, and Partisanship in the U.S. Senate*. Chicago, IL: University of Chicago Press, 2009.

Leeper, Thomas J., and Rune Slothuus. "Political Parties, Motivated Reasonong, and Public Opinion Formation." *Advances in Political Psychology* 35 (2014): 129–156.

Lerner, Jennifer S., and Dacher Keltner. "Beyond Valence: Toward a Model of Emotion-Specific Influences on Judgement and Choice." *Cognition and Emotion* 14, no. 4 (2000): 473–493.

Lerner, J. S., and D. Keltner. "Fear, Anger, and Risk." *Journal of Personality and Social Psychology* 81, no. 1 (July 2001): 146–159.

LeVine, Robert A., and Donald T. Campbell. *Ethnocentrism: Theories of Conflict, Ethnic Attitudes, and Group Behavior*. Oxford, England: John Wiley & Sons, 1972.

Mackie, Diane M., Thierry Devos, and Eliot R. Smith. "Intergroup Emotions: Explaining Offensive Action Tendencies in an Intergroup Context." *Journal of Personality and Social Psychology* 79, no. 4 (2000): 602–616.

Malka, Ariel, and Yphtach Lelkes. "More than Ideology: Conservative–Liberal Identity and Receptivity to Political Cues." *Social Justice Research* 23, no. 2–3 (2010): 156–188.

Mansbridge, Jane, and Cathi Jo Martin. *Political Negotiation: A Handbook*. Cambridge, MA: Brookings Institution Press, 2015.

Maoz, I., and C. McCauley. "Psychological Correlates of Support for Compromise: A Polling Study of Jewish-Israeli Attitudes Toward Solutions to the Israeli-Palestinian Conflict." *Political Psychology* 26 (2005): 791–808.

Marcus, George, W. Russell Neuman, and Michael MacKuen. *Affective Intelligence and Political Judgment*. Chicago, IL: University of Chicago Press, 2000.

Marques, José, Dominic Abrams, and Rui G. Serôdio. "Being Better by Being Right: Subjective Group Dynamics and Derogation of in-Group Deviants When Generic Norms Are Undermined." *Journal of Personality and Social Psychology* 81, no. 3 (2001): 436–447.

Mason, Lilliana. "'I Disrespectfully Agree': The Differential Effects of Partisan Sorting on Social and Issue Polarization." *American Journal of Political Science* 59, no. 1 (2015): 128–145.

———. "Ideologues without Issues: The Polarizing Consequences of Ideological Identities." *Public Opinion Quarterly* 82, no. S1 (April 11, 2018): 866–887.

———. "Party Polarization Is Making Us More Prejudiced." In *Political Polarization in American Politics*, edited by Daniel J. Hopkins and John Sides, 55. New York, NY: Bloomsbury Academic, 2015.

Mayhew, David R. *Divided We Govern: Party Control, Lawmaking, and Investigations, 1946–2002*, 2nd ed. New Haven, CT: Yale University Press, 2005.

Mullen, E., and L. J. Skitka. "Exploring the Psychological Underpinnings of the Moral Mandate Effect: Motivated Reasoning, Group Differentiation, or Anger?" *Journal of Personality and Social Psychology* 90 (2006): 629–643.

Nagar, R., and I. Maoz. "Predicting Jewish-Israeli Recognition of Palestinian Pain and Suffering." *Journal of Conflict Resolution* 61, no. 2 (2017): 372–397.

Nicholson, Stephen P. "The Jeffords Switch and Public Support for Divided Government." *British Journal of Political Science* 35 (2005): 343–356.

Noel, Hans. *Political Ideologies and Political Parties in America*. New York, NY: Cambridge University Press, 2013.

Parker, M. T., and R. Janoff-Bulman. "Lessons from Morality-Based Social Identity: The Power of Outgroup 'Hate,' Not Just Ingroup 'Love'." *Social Justice Research* 26 (2013): 81–96.

Pettigrew, Thomas F. "The Ultimate Attribution Error: Extending Allport's Cognitive Analysis of Prejudice." *Personality and Social Psychology Bulletin* 5, no. 4 (1979): 461–476.

Pew Research Center for People and the Press. "Political Polarization in the American Public." *Pew Research Center Report*. Last modified, June 12, 2014. https://www.people-press.org/2014/06/12/political-polarization-in-the-american-public/.

Rand, Ayn. *Capitalism: The Unknown Ideal*. New York, NY: New American Library, 1966.

Rauch, Jonathan. "How American Politics Went Insane." *The Atlantic Monthly*, July/August, 2016.

Redlawsk, David P. "Hot Cognition or Cool Consideration? Testing the Effects of Motivated Reasoning on Political Decision Making." *Journal of Politics* 64, no. 4 (2002): 1021–1044.

Rothstein, Jandos. "Michael Bloomberg and the Dangers of 'Any Blue Will Do' Politics." *The American Prospect*. Last Modified February 17, 2020. https://prospect.org/politics/michael-bloomberg-candidacy-mirror-image-trump/.

Russell, Bertrand. "Dreams and Facts." *The Athenaeum Nos 4,642, 4,623*, April 18, 1919: 25.

Ryan, Timothy J. "No Compromise: Political Consequences of Moralized Attitudes." *American Journal of Political Science* 61, no. 2 (2017): 409–423.

Schier, Steven E., and Todd E. Eblery. *Polarized: The Rise of Ideology in American Politics*. Lanham, MD: Rowman & Littlefield, 2016.

Schlueter, Elmar, Peter Schmidt, and Ulrich Wagner. "Disentangling the Causal Relations of Perceived Group Threat and Outgroup Derogation: Cross-National Evidence from German and Russian Panel Surveys." *European Sociological Review* 24, no. 5 (December 1, 2008): 567–581.

Schmitt, Carl. *The Theory of the Partisan: A Commentary/Remark on the Concept of the Political*. Berlin: Duncker & Humblot, 1963.

Sears, D. O., and C. L. Funk. "Evidence of Long-Term Persistence of Adults' Political Predispositions." *The Journal of Politics* 61, no. 1 (1999): 1–28.

Sharp, David. "Snowe Won't Miss Partisanship: Retiring Senator Plans to Nurture Centrists with Books, Speeches, PAC." *The Washington Times*. Last Modified, December 31, 2012. https://www.washingtontimes.com/news/2012/dec/31/snowe-wont-miss-partisanship-plans-to-nurture-cent/.

Sherif, M., O. J. Harvey, B. J. White, W. R. Hood, and C. W. Sherif. *Intergroup Conflict and Cooperation: The Robbers Cave Experiment*, Vol. 10. Norman, OK: University Book Exchange, 1961.

Sherif, Muzafer. *The Psychology of Social Norms*. Oxford, England: Harper Torchbooks, 1966.

Skitka, L. J., C. W. Bauman, and E. G. Sargis. "Moral Conviction: Another Contributor to Attitude Strength or Something More?" *Journal of Personality and Social Psychology* 88 (2005): 895–917.

Sowell, Thomas. *A Conflict of Visions: Ideological Origins of Political Struggles*. Revised. New York, NY: Basic Books, 2007.

Stoker, Laura, and M. Kent Jennings. "Of Time and the Development of Partisan Polarization." *American Journal of Political Science* 52, no. 3 (2008): 619–635.

Suhay, Elizabeth. "Explaining Group Influence: The Role of Identity and Emotion in Political Conformity and Polarization." *Political Behavior* 37, no. 1 (2015): 221–251.

Tajfel, H. "Social Categorization, Social Identity, and Social Comparisons." In *Differentiation Between Social Groups*, edited by H. Tajfel, 27–60. London, UK: Academic Press, 1978.

Tajfel, H., and J. C. Turner. *An Integrative Theory of Intergroup Conflict*. Edited by W. G. Austin and S. Worchel. Monterey, CA: Brooks/Cole, 1979.

———. "The Social Identity Theory of Intergroup Behavior." In *The Psychology of Intergroup Relations*, edited by S. Worchel and W. G. Austin, 349. Chicago, IL: Nelson-Hall, 1986.

Tajfel, Henri. *Human Groups and Social Society: Studies in Social Psychology.* Cambridge, UK: Cambridge University Press, 1981.

Terry, Deborah J., and Michael A. Hogg. "Group Norms and the Attitude–Behavior Relationship: A Role for Group Identification." *Personality and Social Psychology Bulletin* 22, no. 8 (1996): 776–793.

Terry, Deborah J., Michael A. Hogg, and Katherine M. White. "The Theory of Planned Behaviour: Self-Identity, Social Identity and Group Norms." *British Journal of Social Psychology* 38, no. 3 (1999): 225–244.

Theiss-Morse, Elizabeth. *Who Counts as an American? The Boundaries of National Identity.* Cambridge: Cambridge University Press, 2009.

Theodoridis, Alexander G., ed. "Me, Myself, and (I), (D), or (R)? Partisanship and Political Cognition through the Lens of Implicit Identity." *The Journal of Politics* 79, no. 4 (2017): 1264.

Theriault, Sean. "Partisan Warfare Is the Problem." In *Political Polarization in American Politics*, edited by Daniel J. Hopkins and John Sides, 12–13. New York, NY: Bloomsbury Academic, 2015.

Tocqueville, Alexis de. *Democracy in America.* Edited by Harvey C. Mansfield and Delba Winthrop. Chicago, IL: The University of Chicago Press, 2002.

Turner, J. C. "Social Categorization and Self-Concept: A Social Cognitive Theory of Group Behavior." In *Advances in Group Process: Theory and Research*, edited by E. J. Lawler, 77–121. Greenwich, CT: JAI Press, 1985.

Turner, J. C., M. A. Hogg, P. J. Oakes, S. D. Reicher, and M. S. Wetheral. *Rediscovering the Social Group: A Self-Categorisation Theory.* Oxford, UK: Blackwell, 1987.

Turner, John C. *Social Influence.* Belmont, CA, US: Thomson Brooks/Cole Publishing Co, 1991.

Viki, G. T., D. Osgood, and S. Phillips. "Dehumanization and Self-Reported Proclivity to Torture Prisoners of War." *Journal of Experimental Psychology* 49, no. 3 (2013): 325–328.

Viser, Matt, and Toluse Olorunnipa. "Iowa Caucuses Descend into Chaos as Delay Leaves Outcome Uncertain." *The Washington Post*, n.d. https://www.washingtonpost.com/politics/iowa-caucuses-descend-into-chaos-as-delay-leaves-outcome-uncertain/2020/02/04/27b3d128-45f4-11ea-8124-0ca81effcdfb_story.html.

Weldon, S. A. "The Institutional Context of Tolerance for Ethnic Minorities: A Comparative, Multilevel Analysis of Western Europe." *American Journal of Political Science* 50, no. 2 (2006): 331–359.

Wilmer, F. *The Social Construction of Man, the State, and War: Identity, Conflict, and Violence in the Former Yugoslavia.* New York, NY: Routledge, 2002.

Wood, Wendy, Gregory J. Pool, Kira Leck, and Daniel Purvis. "Self-Definition, Defensive Processing, and Influence: The Normative Impact of Majority and Minority Groups." *Journal of Personality and Social Psychology* 71, no. 6 (1996): 1181–1193.

Chapter 7

From "Post-Racial America" to #BlackLivesMatter

Rethinking Race for the Twenty-First Century

Elizabeth Butterfield

In 2008, when Barack Obama was elected the first African American president of the United States of America, many people naively saw this as a sign that America had left behind its tragic racist history. Finally, many argued, we can say that we live in a time and place in which people are just *people*, in which racist barriers and injustices no longer exist. More and more, people began to refer to twenty-first-century America as a "post-racial" society.[1]

The belief that the problems of racism that had plagued our society for generations had now been *fixed* was a very comforting one for some Americans, as it confirmed our own American ideology and sense of self-image. The story that we have come to tell ourselves is that America is a genuine meritocracy in which any hardworking and motivated individual can achieve the American Dream, no matter their background. From this perspective, the election of America's first black president was the ultimate proof that the American Dream really is possible.

Interestingly, this claim that we have overcome racism—that it is a relic of our past and we can now move on—can be a comfortable conclusion for people at opposite ends of the political spectrum. For those who care deeply about righting the wrongs of racism and racial injustice, it was incredibly meaningful to see this country freely elect its first black president. Surely this was a sign of progress, a step forward. While to those who were either unconcerned with racial injustice or who actively objected to policies aimed at righting past racist wrongs, Obama's election was taken as a proof that we are no longer justified in complaining about racism, because clearly, racially based barriers to success in American society no longer exist. Any obstacles, they argued, must be traced to an individual's own personal failings.

Even at the time of Obama's election, however, not everyone agreed that America had become a post-racial society. Polls continued to show that when Americans were asked whether racism still exists, responses differed sharply depending on one's racial identity (as well as one's political affiliation). For example, when a 2014 *Washington Post* poll asked whether all races are treated equally in the criminal justice system, only 10 percent of African Americans responded with yes, in contrast with about 50 percent of white Americans.[2]

As I write this in 2020, however, in the fourth year of the presidency of Donald Trump, and in the wake of global anti-racist protests in the wake of the death of George Floyd, we find ourselves in a very different historical moment. So much has happened in recent years to draw our attention anew to the role that racial identity plays in everyday experience. It is hard to imagine that anyone could seriously argue today that American society is post-racial. I see four major shifts that are coming to define our current discourse surrounding racial identity in the twenty-first century.

First, from 2013 onward, the #BlackLivesMatter movement and the ensuing public demonstrations led to a growing awareness in mainstream American culture of what racial minorities have always known—that African Americans face a heightened risk of violence relative to white Americans. With the public outcry surrounding the deaths of Trayvon Martin, Michael Brown, Eric Garner, Breonna Taylor, and George Floyd, to name only five of the multitude, the nation was irrevocably shaken out of its comforting belief that we had reached a post-racial age. Mainstream culture once again has been forced to grapple with the fact that racial injustices continue to exist, and that racial identity has concrete consequences in the world in terms of the risk of violence we face, our treatment by law enforcement, and our experiences in the criminal justice system. Attention to the mass incarceration of black men in America finally entered the mainstream media and political discourse, helped along by Michelle Alexander's 2010 book *The New Jim Crow: Mass Incarceration in the Age of Colorblindness*, and Ava DuVernay's 2016 award-winning documentary, *13th*.[3]

Second, since the election of Trump in 2016, we have seen white nationalist and white supremacist groups "go mainstream."[4] In 2019, *Time Magazine* reported that white supremacist violence has been on the rise,[5] and the *Washington Post* reported that "According to the most recent annual report by the Anti-Defamation League (ADL), which has long tracked extremist activity, 39 of the 50 extremist-related murders tallied by the group in 2018 were committed by white supremacists, up from 2017, when white supremacists were responsible for 18 of 34 such crimes."[6] And, in 2020, during the widespread anti-racist protests in the wake of the death of George Floyd, white supremacists were found to be posing online as Antifa with the goal of calling for violence and inflaming racial tensions.[7] This growth in the mainstream visibility of white nationalism, as well as the increase in white nationalist violence, may be part of a larger wave of racist backlash to the election of Barack Obama, simply coming a little later than expected. It is also clearly tied to the increasing racial and ethnic diversity in the United States, as white nationalist groups voice concerns over the loss of a white majority.

But many observers claim that another causal factor we cannot ignore is President Trump's own rhetoric, which has led these groups to feel more emboldened. For example, after the 2017 white nationalist rally in Charlottesville, Virginia, at which a counter-protester was killed, Trump responded by saying that there were "very fine people on both sides."[8] As reported in *The Guardian* in 2019, "Experts in white supremacist thought largely agree that Trump is actively spreading the ideas that underpin this ideology . . . using nearly identical language. . . . President Trump has really set up a baseline for bigotry in political discourse in the United States that has helped create the terrain where this is more possible."[9]

Third, in recent years we have seen a growing number of conversations and confrontations in the public sphere on the topic of white privilege, addressed so powerfully in Robin DiAngelo's 2018 book *White Fragility: Why It's So Hard for White People to Talk about Racism*.[10] By the end of the twentieth century, American mainstream culture was already very familiar with the idea that one's racial identity shapes how others out in the world perceive you and treat you. But in 2020, we have moved from that externalized understanding of the experience of race to a more internalized introspection, beginning to explore how our personal experiences shape our own individual perspectives. The positions each of us holds in society's web of the distribution of power and privilege provide us with unique insights, but conversely, they can also blind us to certain realities.

This "standpoint epistemology," first introduced by black feminists like Patricia Hill Collins in the 1990s,[11] has finally entered the mainstream discourse in a powerful way. We can see this in the current discussions of white privilege, and the claim that white people often simply don't even see the realities of racial injustice that exist right in front of them, because their privilege enables them to ignore it, and they rarely directly experience it themselves.

Finally, all of these shifts are occurring at a time when the very notion of racial identity itself appears as more fluid and complex than ever before. Historically, the discourse of race in America has fixated on the binary of "black" and "white," as if these two races were real, self-evident, and the only two options. This binary was *always* an oversimplified fiction; the history of who counts legally and culturally as "white" and "nonwhite" in this country has always been shifting and dynamic. Consider, for example, the history of the changing understanding of the racial identity, and consequently social status, of Irish and Italian immigrants in America, and the shifting status of Asian and Latinx Americans today.[12] In 2020, the complexities of racial identity are more visible in mainstream culture than ever before.

Add to this the fact that we are also living in a time of competing identity politics. On the one hand, mainstream culture is finally paying attention to the fact that we can't talk about any one element of identity purely in isolation from others. For example, if the "Women's March" claims to speak for "women's interests," exactly *which* women do we mean? And who is included and excluded under that label? Are we talking about white, black, Asian, Latinx, or mixed women? Straight or LGBTQ? Cis-gender or trans women? Working-class or wealthy women? Christian, Jewish, Muslim, Hindu, Pagan, or atheist women? And so on. On the other hand, we find ourselves in arguments among competing identity groups over which type of oppression is primary or deserves the most immediate attention. There is an emphasis on the particularity of our identities, and an overall lack of unity, in the context of an America that is deeply individualistic in its culture and ideology.

Given all of the factors that set the stage for our encounter with race in the twenty-first century, the questions this chapter aims to address are: How ought we to understand racial identity today? And what can and should we hope for, regarding the role that race will come to play in the future? Should our goal be a future that is colorblind and post-racial, in which races no longer exist, or no longer play any meaningful role in society? Or is another future desirable? This is of course an issue with a long history, notably found in W. E. B. DuBois's writings in the late nineteenth century regarding the "conservation of race."[13] Now we ask again, what approach to racial identity will serve us best as we move forward into the twenty-first century?

To answer these questions, first I will briefly deconstruct and historicize the category of race itself. I will then argue that, rather than abandoning racial identities altogether, we should seek to create—or *re*construct—a new understanding of race that will serve us better in the future. Finally, I will propose that in response to the dominant trends of twenty-first-century American culture, we would be well served to cultivate the virtue of patience. I do not mean patience with injustice—justice and social chance cannot wait. But I will recommend an attitude of intellectual patience, and in particular, patience with ambiguity, in order to allow ourselves to more fully and clearly understand ourselves, others, and the world we live in and wish to create.

BEYOND THE DREAM OF A COLORBLIND FUTURE

Recently I found myself helping to organize a community workshop with the goal of raising awareness of ongoing contemporary racism, racist injustice, and white privilege. The group who had requested this workshop was composed of mostly white, well-educated, middle- to upper-middle class, willing participants who were actively committed to fighting racism. On the day of the workshop, when we opened up the floor for discussion, one statement was repeated by several of the white participants: "I don't see color. When I meet someone new, I don't even notice their race."

I will admit, I was surprised to hear that. I wondered, what could this possibly mean? Did they intend for this statement to be taken literally? I had a hard time accepting that anyone living in America today could honestly say that they simply did not *see* racial identity at all. Life in twenty-first-century America is so replete with racial markers that it seems impossible to ignore, unless perhaps we think of this in terms of the metaphor of a fish swimming in water: perhaps, just as the water is so ever-present in the fish's experience that the fish never comes to an awareness of it, race is so much a part of our culture, so taken for granted, that some people no longer even notice it? Or perhaps the white privilege of the speakers enabled them to ignore race? I think it is fair to say that a nonwhite person living in America would *not* claim that they "don't even see color," simply because their daily experiences moving through American society would force them to pay attention to it whether they wanted to or not.

Could it be that the statement, "I don't see color," is actually a lie, one that they were telling to others, or to themselves? To call it a "lie" implies that there was an intentional choice on the part of the speaker to deceive, and that does not necessarily seem plausible in this case. What I have come to believe is that this was intended as neither a literal statement nor a lie, but rather, as an imprecise way of expressing what is really a very meaningful anti-racist moral claim: "I value all human lives as equally important, and I have the intention of respecting all human beings as equal. So I choose to not assign value or meaning to racial difference."

Many of these same participants went on to claim that we should all strive to be colorblind, and to aim for a future where racial difference simply no longer exists. They argued that we are all really just the same underneath—we are all human. And the next step in this argument is usually to claim that race is not and never was *real*, so there is no reason to continue to pay attention to racial difference. We would be better off if we could simply move beyond racial identity altogether.

And yes, it is true, race is not real in any meaningful biological sense, and the idea that racial identities entail the possession of sets of characteristic traits has been clearly demonstrated to be false. There is no objectively fixed, absolute, or self-evident category of "race."[14] Our very concept of race has a history and grew out of a specific time and place. Race is not universal or ahistorical. Not all peoples in all time periods have had a concept of race as it appears in modern Western history, and the understanding of racial categories is not fixed or consistent around the world or across cultures. We are the products of a history that happened to take skin color and regional origin, and to assign them meanings in the distribution of power and privilege, but things did not have to be this way. The development of the concept of race, and the role it has played in our history, was the product of contingent human choices and the exercise of power.

Many authors have skillfully deconstructed the notion of race, showing that race is not self-evident or obvious or objectively true, but rather "a product of numerous histories, institutions, and processes of inscription."[15] I will not repeat these arguments here, but will only offer a list of helpful starting places. Charles Mills, in *The Racial Contract*, traces the development of the concept of race in early modern European social contract theory.[16] Omi and Winant show in their classic *Racial Formation in the United States* how race in America was defined by social, political, and economic forces, and used as a tool to justify the power of those with European ancestry.[17] And Steve Martinot in *The Rule of Racialization* traces the shifting definitions of whiteness, and its corresponding privileges, through the history of American law.[18]

So yes, when these participants argued that race is not real, they were completely right. But I believe that the next step—to conclude from this observation that our best way forward would be to abandon the concept of race altogether, to aim for a colorblind future—is a mistake. It is easy to look back on our tragically racist past and present, bearing witness to so much racially based suffering, violence, oppression, discrimination, and injustice, and to conclude from this that the source of the problem must have been the very act of identifying people in terms of race itself. It is as if to say that to notice race at all must be an inherently racist act. From this perspective, it appears that the concept of racial identity itself is the problem, and that recognizing differences among us, or particularities of our identities, must necessarily lead to a sense of separation and to injustice. The conclusion is that we need a more unified future in which race simply no longer exists, in which people are seen as "just people."

This dream of a colorblind future fits well with American political ideology and its roots in the humanism of the eighteenth-century European Enlightenment. According to Lucius Outlaw, in this context which emphasizes human equality, to pay attention to difference "runs counter to some of the most basic social and political philosophies and practices that became the foundations [of our modern nation states.] The emphasis on *particularity* over universality (that is, emphasis on difference rather than sameness) threatens the always tenuous historic achievements of modern social, political, economic, and cultural life."[19] From this perspective, the ideal future would seem to be one in which we no longer pay any attention to the differences that separate us, and instead, in the name of equality, emphasize our common humanity.

However, I do not believe that this dream of a colorblind future is possible, or desirable. While it is true that race is not *real*, we continue to need to preserve the concept of race and racial identity for at least three reasons.

First of all, if we lived in a genuinely colorblind future in which racial identity no longer existed, how would we learn about, and learn from, our history? We need a working concept of race, and of our own family and cultural histories, in order to be able to understand ourselves and our world. We have family lineages, cultural and linguistic contexts, material circumstances, and experiences of privilege or disenfranchisement that have shaped us, and in the context of American society, these are tied in multiple and diverse ways to the roles racial identities have played in our history. What we need is not to abandon the concept of race altogether, but rather, to find a way to talk about our experiences of race in the past and present—especially with our children—that does not replicate past mistakes, and that does not lead to future injustices.

Second, practically speaking, we need to retain a concept of race because, unfortunately, racially based injustices continue to structure the world we inhabit. If we cannot speak of racial difference, we cannot name and address racism when it occurs.[20]

Third, what if race could be understood as a *positive* aspect of someone's sense of identity? Those who argue that we should strive for a colorblind or post-racial future seem to assume that racial difference is itself a problem, and they approach race solely as a source of oppression. But must this be the case?

Lucius Outlaw has argued that "even if, in the very next instant, racism and perverted, invidious ethnocentrism in every form and manifestation would disappear forever" (which, he acknowledges, is not likely to happen), races and racial identity must be "conserved."[21] Following W. E. B. DuBois, who, in his 1897 *The Conservation of Races* "sought to rethink 'race' in support of a project that would 'conserve' races in the context of democratic pluralism."[22] Outlaw argues that we ought to conserve race and ethnicity "as vital components of a philosophical anthropology, and of a social and political philosophy."[23] Outlaw explains that group identities are fundamental to human flourishing, and that we can therefore benefit from race as one type of group identity. As Outlaw explains,

> Individuals are necessary, but they are neither sufficient not self-sufficing . . . Whether or not an individual can enjoy a relatively . . . flourishing life is tied to

the well-being of the group . . . The well-being of the group requires concerted action predicated on self-valorization *within the context of a shared identity* without succumbing to chauvinism. Further, *the racial and/or ethnic life-world provides the resources and nurturing required for the development, even, of individual talent and accomplishment.*[24]

Having a sense of shared history and identity with others can be useful for community development as well as for individual flourishing. In this sense, understanding the role of racial identity in our past and present can honor the experiences of those who came before us, value the importance of each unique perspective,[25] and help us come to see how these histories and contexts have shaped who we have become. The solution, therefore, is not the rejection of racial identity altogether, but rather a rethinking of race in a way that is, as Outlaw writes, "more adequate in the present and near future to the exigencies of life in racially and ethnically complex societies, [and] both socially useful and consistent with democratic justice."[26]

RECONCEPTUALIZING RACE FOR THE TWENTY-FIRST CENTURY—PATIENCE WITH AMBIGUITY

There are multiple reasons to conserve a concept of racial identity. But given that race is a human construction, and not a self-evident or fixed absolute, how ought we to understand it? And how can we reconceive racial identity in a way that will serve us well today, and that will help us to create a better future? In what follows, I will argue that as we undertake this project, one of the things we need most is the virtue of *patience*—and, in particular, a patience with *ambiguity*.

This does not come easily for us. It may be the case, as Simone de Beauvoir remarked, that it is simply part of the human condition to be uncomfortable with ambiguities.[27] As free human beings, we regularly find ourselves in situations where we have options before us and choices to make, but the answers are not clear, and there is no guarantee that we are going to get it "right." This encounter with ambiguity leads us to feel anxiety, and we are constantly tempted to flee this anxiety by looking outside of ourselves for easy, simple answers. We look for well-defined, simplistic positions to align ourselves with, and we then grant them the authority of objective truth, so that we can abdicate our responsibility for our own choices.

It may have always been this way to a certain extent, but I would argue that the discomfort with ambiguity is particularly heightened in our own time. This is the age of the tweet, where ideas must be expressed in 140 characters.

In a fast-moving media environment with dwindling attention spans, we want quick answers, easy labels, and simple resolutions. We live in a time that celebrates busy-ness, lack of sleep, constant distraction and overwhelm. We are in a constant state of feeling rushed, with so many forces competing for our attention. In this context, we have less and less time, energy, and tolerance for complexity.

But the topics of race, racial identity, and racism are not simple or straightforward—they are complex, and they can also feel emotionally threatening. To enter into a conversation about race risks a potential for conflict, hurt, anger, confrontation, misunderstanding and feeling misunderstood. The topic can raise our adrenaline and anxiety, making it even more tempting to flee. Rather than taking the time or energy required to explore the complexities and ambiguities, we are tempted to run toward easy sound-bites. We can see this in the prevalence of oversimplification, quick accusations, and defensiveness in discussions of race today. We may also find this in Americans' growing tendency to isolate ourselves into what may be called intellectual echo chambers, surrounding ourselves with others who share our same views, and avoiding real engagement with others who may disagree or challenge our assumptions.

However, in order to come to a new understanding of race that is not only more accurate, but also better suited to the future, we require a totally different approach. We must run counter to the rushed impatience of our time. What we need is to slow things down, to be willing to simply sit for a while with the ambiguities, and to take the time to think through complexities. Instead of rushing to quick conclusions, we must take time to listen attentively to others, to explore ourselves, and to try to be okay *without* a quick or easy answer. We should strive to tolerate uncertainties and ambiguities, and to have patience with ideas that make us uncomfortable. If we are to have the strength and stamina to sit patiently with ambiguity, we will also need to carve out some relatively quiet personal space in our lives, apart from the frenetic distractions of media.[28]

In what follows, I will argue that there are five areas in which we would be well served by the virtue of patience as we reconceptualize racial identity: (1) in coming to understand race as both *real* and *unreal,* beyond the extremes of essentialism and anti-essentialism; (2) as we consider race in relation to other social identities, and embrace a model of intersectionality; (3) as we attempt to understand the role race plays in our personal experiences, reconciling what may seem like opposite claims: that we are both free individuals and socially determined at the same time; (4) as we come to understand that we are all the same, and we are all different; and (5) as we strive to be open to learning about the experiences of others, to understand that empathy is both required and also ultimately impossible.

1. Conceptualizing Race beyond Essentialism and Anti-Essentialism.

Race is real. And race is unreal. Both are true, and both are untrue.

At the essentialist extreme, we find the historical claim that race is real in the sense of being an essence, a biological category that predetermines someone to possess a set of characteristic traits that are particular to that racial group. This is demonstrably false. But at the opposite anti-essentialist extreme, for example, in some varieties of postmodernism, we find the claim that race is a pure fiction. As the contingent product of human discourse, race is nothing but a social construct, and as some have argued, can and should therefore be easily dismissed.

As I have argued above, while race is not a biological reality, and racial identities are not fixed, universal, or self-evident, race continues to play a very real role in our experience. It structures the world that we encounter in material and cultural ways. It is a part of the set of conceptual and linguistic tools that we use to form our sense of self, and it can also be the basis of meaningful group identities. What we need, then, is the patience to sit with this ambiguity and to explore the complexity of ways that race is both real and unreal at the same time. We will need to understand race as both a contingent human construct, putting it into cultural and historical context, and as something real that is built into our material and cultural reality. (In my book, *Sartre and Posthumanist Humanism*,[29] I have used the tools of Sartre's later Marxist-Existentialism in engagement with the paradigm of intersectionality, drawing upon critical race theory, feminist theory, and Frankfurt School critical theory, to build a framework for understanding human identity in a way that can move beyond essentialism and anti-essentialism, taking a dialectical approach to reconceptualizing race.)

2. Race and Other Social Identities: The Model of Intersectionality

In the twenty-first century, we continue to talk about race as if it is a distinct category, as a social identity that can be studied or discussed on its own. We generalize about racialized experiences, and we break down statistics and polls by racial groups. Sometimes we even find ourselves in a sort of competitive identity politics, arguing over which form of oppression is primary or deserves the most attention in the immediate present: racism, sexism, homophobia, and so on.

But at the same time, there is a growing awareness that we can *never* really speak accurately about one type of social identity in isolation from others. For example, we may generalize about a person's racial experience as a white American by saying that they benefit from white privilege. But this does not tell the whole story. We are always also more than this one social identity. Are we talking about a white man or a white woman? And if a woman, cis-gender woman or a trans woman? Straight or queer? Wealthy or working class? All of these other identities carry with them particular experiences stemming from our society's structuring of the distribution of power and privilege. I may experience privilege in some areas of my life while simultaneously experiencing disadvantage in others. For example, as a white woman in a straight marriage, I benefit from the white privilege and heteronormativity that are built into the structures of American society, while also experiencing disadvantages from sexist structures that continue to exist.

It is more accurate, then, to think of each of these social identities as an axis, and to understand the complexity of human identity as a collection of multiple intersecting axes of identity. This model of "intersectionality" emerged in the early 1990s in the writings of black feminists like Kimberlé Crenshaw, who drew attention to intersecting experiences of racism and sexism.[30] As I have argued elsewhere, we can then use this model of intersectionality to move from an understanding of oppression to an understanding of human identity more generally.[31] Race, class, and gender still matter in America today because they operate *together*, as intersecting categories, simultaneously structuring the experiences of everyone in our society. They affect group access to power and privilege. But rather than thinking of elements of identity as separate entities, or even as competing forms of oppression, Patricia Hill Collins has argued that it is much more helpful to think about these different aspects of identity "relationally," and to look for connections between them.[32]

It appears, then, that it will always be inaccurate to talk about race as a stand-alone entity, as if it could be understood separately from other axes of identity. And yet, it is also crucially important to be able to generalize about the role race plays in our society. On a personal level, it continues to be meaningful to identify shared experiences with others along those axes. And on a political level, while we recognize that any generalization about racialized experience must be incomplete, we must also be able to concretely measure the role race plays in things like the criminal justice system, access to educational resources, or the quality of health care, if we hope to identify and address racial injustices. As we take up the model of intersectionality and engage with these complexities and ambiguities, the virtue of patience will serve us well.

3. We Are Both Free and Determined

We have seen that from the perspective of intersectionality, while it is important to be able to generalize about someone's experience of racial identity, this will always also be an abstraction, since race is only one among many intersecting identities. You could say that this means that a person is always also *more than* their racial identity. The same can be said at a deeper level, as we come to fundamental questions about the human condition: who am I, and what makes me who I am? What are the roles of nature and nurture? How can I be both individual *and* social, both free *and* determined?

When we talk about race and the role it plays in American society, we tend to emphasize determinism, focusing on how race shapes the world we encounter. Racist injustices concretely influence our material environments and the options we are presented in the world. When someone perceives us as "white" or "black," for example, this affects the assumptions they will make about us, what they expect from us, and how we are treated. Cultural assumptions about racial identities are also built into the linguistic and cultural tools we have for understanding ourselves and our world. All of this is true—and yet, we are always also *more than* our racial identities. We are also free individuals with our own choices to make, and to a very great extent we are responsible for how we create our lives.

Jean-Paul Sartre provides a helpful model for understanding this experience of freedom and determinism in his early work, *Being and Nothingness*,[33] which he then develops into a much richer account of human experience in his later Marxist-Existentialist work, *The Critique of Dialectical Reason*.[34] Sartre explains that I am always both "facticity" and "transcendence." Facticity refers to the facts of my life that are outside of my control—things like where and when I was born, the language(s) I was raised in (which subsequently provided me with the cultural and linguistic tools for forming an understanding of myself and of the world), the fact that I have a body and material needs, and the fact that I encounter a world in which others perceive me in ways that are ultimately outside of my control. Transcendence refers to my ability to transcend or rise above these facts. Transcendence is my freedom, and in particular, my noetic freedom of consciousness to choose how I will interpret my experiences and how I will react to them. Dialectically speaking, then, I am never fully free and never fully determined. I am always both. I am *free in situation*. According to Sartre, I can always make something out of what I have been made into.[35]

Consider Sartre's claim that "I am what I am not, and I am not what I am." Or alternatively, "I am what I am in the mode of not being it."[36] To apply this to racial identity, we could say that whiteness plays a central role in my facticity, but it does not fully define who I am as a person. At any moment, whiteness structures my experiences in the world I encounter. It has concrete consequences for how I am perceived by others, and it affords me certain privileges that nonwhite people do not experience. For example, I am able to walk through an expensive store in a mall in a primarily white part of town without being followed by a security guard, because my whiteness enables me to "belong." But at any moment, I am also more than this experience of whiteness. I am also a free consciousness, and to a certain extent I can choose what racial identity will mean to me, how I will interpret it, and how I will react to the world and meanings I encounter. While how I am perceived by others is ultimately outside of my control, I am also free to create my own sense of identity, and to choose the attitudes I will take up in response. My whiteness shapes my experiences and the world I encounter, but I can also choose what attitude I want to take up in response to my whiteness. For example, I may choose to take up an attitude of openness and curiosity in order to learn more, and when confronted with the realities of unjust white privilege, I may choose to actively pursue becoming an anti-racist ally.

In twenty-first-century America, we find a great deal of impatience with this ambiguity of freedom and determinism in discussions of race. In a rush to find quick answers and uncomplicated positions, many oversimplify what is actually a complex human experience by emphasizing one extreme or the other, claiming that we are either *fully* free or *fully* determined. Sartre described this tendency to want to oversimplify the ambiguity of human experience as "bad faith," and he outlined two common forms.[37]

In the first form of bad faith, someone attempts to reduce transcendence to facticity, arguing that we are *fully- or over-determined* by the situation. This would be to go to the extreme of ignoring freedom. For example, we could point to twentieth-century sociological writings that claimed that to live as a nonwhite person in a racist society was to experience "social death,"[38] preventing the nonwhite person from developing any sense of self or agency whatsoever. But clearly this is going too far. As Howard McGary[39] has argued in response, while living in an oppressed position obviously has concrete negative consequences for human flourishing, humans are also creative beings who can find ways to survive. For example, McGary discusses the situation of someone living in conditions of slavery, who experiences social alienation and a lack of recognition in society at large, but who can also find creative ways to get those social needs met in other relationships, for example, in family or in community. The point is that human beings are not *completely* socially determined. Even in the most horrifying and dehumanizing conditions, humans are always also free, at least in the sense of the noetic freedom of consciousness, and can still find ways to develop agency. This strength is the source of resistance! Without this freedom within situation, we'd have no hope for social change.

In the second form of bad faith, someone attempts to reduce facticity to transcendence, arguing that we are *fully free*. This is to deny the reality of determinism in our situation. We can see this in the claims that racism no longer exists, that the American Dream is entirely possible, and that we live in a true meritocracy. We also see this in the claim that the election of Obama proves that social identities like race no longer pose a problem in our society; a motivated, talented, and hardworking individual can achieve anything, and if someone does not succeed, this must be due to their own individual failings. From a Sartrean perspective, these claims are in bad faith because they deny the reality of the current situation, in which racial injustices continue to structure our society.

According to Sartre, to live in "good faith"[40] is a matter of taking up an attitude of honesty with oneself, recognizing that I am always both free *and* determined, and being willing to take responsibility for that. In terms of racial identity, this means recognizing that at one and the same time, I am a free individual, and I am also shaped by multiple social identities. The various positions I hold in society's web of the distribution of power and privilege can determine my experience in obvious ways, as they structure the world I encounter. But sometimes they may also determine my experience in ways that are less easy to perceive, for example, as they influence my worldview, my values, and what I do and do not notice. For example, my experience of white privilege allows me to move through the world in a way that may make me blind to the racist obstacles that nonwhite people experience, simply because I am never forced to pay attention to them. But Sartre would remind us that while we are determined, we are also always free and responsible. It is up to me to choose my attitude and how I will respond to my situation. When uncomfortable truths are brought to my attention, I can choose how I will react. And the honesty of good faith requires that I have the patience to sit with—rather than attempt to flee—the many ambiguities of my freedom, and responsibility, in situation.

4. We Are All the Same, and We Are All Different: Anti-Racism and Humanism

"I don't see color." In this statement, we hear the claim that we are all the same—we are all *human*. We hear the moral call to treat everyone as possessing inherent worth and dignity. And at a certain level, yes, of course, we are all human, and we should be striving for a future of equality and justice for all.

But there are also at least two problems with an *overemphasis* on human commonality. First, the notion of human equality that emerged from Enlightenment humanism and that forms the foundation of American democracy offered a vision of the universally human that actually applied, not to all humans, but only to a very specific segment of the population. In this case, "normal" or "universal" actually defaulted to white, male, propertied, Protestant humans. Lucius Outlaw, therefore, refers to Enlightenment humanism as a "fraudulent universalism," since it excluded certain racial groups and "masked" and "rationalized" forms of domination.[41] This means that when we appeal to a common or universal humanity today, it must be within the context of recognizing this history, and being attentive to not repeating these same mistakes of exclusion.

Second, to overemphasize our sameness runs the risk of ignoring or discounting real differences in our experiences. Blacks and whites really do experience American society differently according to how these identities structure the world we encounter. It is important for so many reasons that we stay open to acknowledging these differences, and to learning about the experiences of others.

Would it be better, then, to go to the opposite extreme of emphasizing difference? Might it be the case that we are so divided by social identities like race that we cannot appeal to *anything* whites and nonwhites have in common?

Once again, what is required is the patience to sit with the ambiguity of the situation, recognizing that both are true: we are all the same, and we are all different. To respect one another entails recognizing our commonalities, while also acknowledging and being open to learning about the particularities of our unique experiences. This is powerfully expressed in the first two lines of a poem by Pat Parker titled, "For the White Person Who Wants to Know How to Be My Friend."

The first thing you do is to forget that I'm Black.
Second, you must never forget that I'm Black.[42]

Politically, we must also have patience with this ambiguity, given the model of intersectionality. On the one hand, it is sometimes important for us to be able to generalize about social identities, and to focus on just one type of injustice at a time. Gayatri Spivak refers to this as "strategic essentialism."[43] Sometimes, we clearly need to be able to identify and address racism on its own. But given our intersectionality as well as our common humanity, we must be careful to not become so entrenched in fighting one form of injustice that it prevents us from recognizing the importance of others as well. In this spirit, Patricia Hill Collins has argued that one of the defining features of black feminist thought is its "recurring humanist vision," and a concern for "the solidarity of humanity." She writes, "Black women's struggles are part of a wider struggle for human dignity and empowerment."[44] Quoting Shirley Chisholm, she continues, "In the end, antiBlack, antifemale, and all forms of discrimination are equivalent to the same thing—antihumanism."[45]

5. Empathy Is Required, and Empathy Is Impossible

In order to heal our racist past, and to reconceive the role racial identity should play in our future, what we absolutely require is *empathy*. We are called to listen to the experiences of others, to try to see the world from another's perspective, and in our own minds and feelings, to try to imaginatively recreate what someone else has lived through. And at the same time, we must also recognize that this is ultimately impossible. My attempts to listen and to truly understand, to see and feel what another has seen or felt, will always be incomplete. And yet I am called to try anyway. Once again, this requires a patience with ambiguity.

First, as we attempt to empathize with others—especially across wide divides of difference—it is helpful to take up an attitude of patient Socratic wisdom. As Socrates taught, true wisdom lies in knowing that I will never have complete knowledge, and that I will always have more to learn. As we open to listening attentively to others, we should do so knowing that we will never have complete understanding, and that whatever we learn will always be only a partial view. The other person is always also more than what I perceive, as are we all. Iris Marion Young offers the advice that, as we practice respectful listening, we should also keep in mind that no one is *required* to answer our questions—any information that the other shares is given to us as a gift.[46]

Second, the practice of empathy will require a patience of sitting with things that make us uncomfortable. For example, consider a situation in which I, as a white woman, am attempting to practice open listening in a discussion of racism with a black man. I may go into this situation with the best of intentions, hoping to learn something about someone else's experiences that are different from mine. But as I listen, I may hear claims about inequality or discrimination that I find hard to understand, because they don't match my own experiences. I may have trouble imagining that they are real, especially if they contradict the assumptions I have absorbed from the dominant narrative that tell me America is a land of freedom and justice for all. I may come to see that my whiteness has given me the ability to move through American society with relative ease, oblivious to real racist injustices. In response, I may feel defensive. I may feel embarrassed for not seeing these things before. I may feel ashamed of the unfair advantages I have benefited from. I may feel guilt about ways I have contributed to the problem. I may feel sadness and pain as I learn about the suffering of others. And in response to this discomfort, I may be tempted to flee from engagement with the topic altogether.

One common stumbling block in discussions of race in twenty-first-century America is the common practice of shaming. This could take the form of the public shaming of others, often in social media. Or it could be more personal, when in response to learning some uncomfortable truths about ourselves, we begin to shame ourselves. Let me be clear—I am not arguing that we should not call out injustice whenever and wherever it occurs! If we are to have any hope of building a better future, of course we have to call out racism and bigotry loud and clear! It is crucial that both personally and culturally we take responsibility for the roles we play in creating the world we live in.

But in shaming, we move beyond simply holding someone responsible for their actions. Shaming takes it a step further, to a deeper dishonoring of someone's very being, as if the "crime" is a permanent mark upon their identity. The problem is that this implies that change, learning, and making amends are all impossible. Shaming treats a person as wholly corrupt, and forgets that we are always also more than or other than this action. We may be determined by our past, but we are also always free to make new and different choices in the future.

If we are really going to engage in difficult conversations around race, and do our own ongoing inner work, we are going to have to be willing to risk making mistakes. The real danger in an atmosphere of shaming is that it tends to shut down openness to communication or to learning. Rather than shaming, it would be helpful to cultivate an attitude of *curiosity*.[47] To practice the open listening required for empathy, it is helpful to take an attitude of compassion with both self and others, as we sit patiently with discomfort and ambiguity, take responsibility, ask for and give forgiveness, and move on—taking more risks, making more mistakes, and trying again, trusting that change and growth are possible.

"JUSTICE CAN'T WAIT"

To reconceptualize racial identity in a way that is more accurate today, and to create a future that can recognize race without recreating racism, we will need to embrace a dialectical understanding of many opposing truths: race is both real and unreal, a fictional historical construct and a meaningful part of our lives; it is important to be able to talk about race as a category on its own, and we can never fully understand race without also acknowledging its intersections with other social identities; we are all free, and at the same time we are all determined; we are our social identities, and we are always also individuals who are more than or other than these labels; we are all the same, and we are all different; and we are called to empathize while also acknowledging that full empathetic understanding is impossible.

I have argued that as we reconceptualize race for the twenty-first century, we will be well served to nurture the virtue of *patience*. But I anticipate a powerful objection. As Dr. King wrote from the Birmingham jail, "Justice too long delayed is justice denied."[48] It has happened far too often that those seeking social change have been told, "just slow down, be patient." In this historical context, for a white scholar like me to advocate patience must sound suspect. So let me be clear: I am *not* arguing that we should slow down the pace of change or the work for political progress! Justice can't and shouldn't have to wait. We need change *now*. Actually, we need change yesterday. I am not arguing that anyone should patiently tolerate injustice—just the opposite.

The type of patience I am advocating has to do, instead, with how we react to what I see as dominant trends in twenty-first-century American culture. Already in 1964, Herbert Marcuse was concerned that the American cultural environment of ever-present media, entertainment, and advertisement was putting us as individuals into a situation of constant distraction. In this state, he feared, we were losing the private mental space and independence of thought required in order to have any clear understanding of our own situation, and of the sources of our suffering. He saw the constant distraction of the media environment and consumer culture as a danger that could stifle real social change.[49]

I would argue that what Marcuse identified has only become more extreme today. In 2020, we are bombarded from all sides by media in its myriad forms, in a culture that glorifies overwork, lack of sleep, and an overwhelming fast-paced news cycle. With the constant pinging of notifications in the background, it can be hard to even catch our breath. But as Marcuse observed, if we are going to change the world for the better, we need to be able to slow down, step away, and see the world clearly for what it is. We need to be able to come to an awareness of our own experience, and we need to be able to truly listen to others. In this way, it would serve us well to carve out some quiet, empty, personal space *apart* from media distractions, in order to have the time, energy and strength to sit patiently with the ambiguities and complexities of our situation. This will help us on our way to meaningful social change.

NOTES

1. See for example: Daniel Schorr, "A New, 'Post-Racial' Political Era in America," *NPR*, January 28, 2008, https://www.npr.org/templates/story/story.php?storyId=18489466; Michael C. Dawson and Lawrence D. Bobo, "One Year Later and the Myth of a Post-Racial Society," *Du Bois Review: Social Science Research on Race* 6, no. 2 (2009): 247–49, https://dash.harvard.edu/handle/1/10347165.

2. Dan Balz and Scott Clement, "On Racial Issues, America Is Divided Both Black and White and Red and Blue," *Washington Post*, December 27, 2014, https://www.washingtonpost.com/politics/on-racial-issues-america-is-divided-both-Blac

k-and-white-and-red-and-blue/2014/12/26/3d2964c8-8d12-11e4-a085-34e9b9f09a58_story.html.

3. Ava DuVernay, Dir, *13th*, Kandoo Films, 2016. *13th* was nominated for an Academy Award for Best Documentary Feature, and was awarded the Primetime Emmy Award for Outstanding Documentary. Michelle Alexander, *The New Jim Crow: Mass Incarceration in the Age of Colorblindness* (New York, NY: New Press, 2010).

4. Luke Darby, "How White Supremacy Went Mainstream in the US: 8chan, Trump, Voter Suppression," *Guardian*, August 11, 2019, https://www.theguardian.com/us-news/2019/aug/11/el-paso-shooting-white-supremacy-8chan-voter-suppression.

5. Brian Levin, "Why White Supremacist Attacks Are on the Rise Everywhere," *Time*, March 21, 2019, https://time.com/5555396/white-supremacist-attacks-rise-new-zealand/.

6. Felicia Sonmez and Ashley Parker, "As Trump Stands by Charlottesville Remarks, Rise of White-Nationalist Violence Becomes an Issue in 2020 Presidential Race," *Washington Post*, April 28, 2019, https://www.washingtonpost.com/politics/as-trump-stands-by-charlottesville-remarks-rise-of-white-nationalist-violence-becomes-an-issue-in-2020-presidential-race/2019/04/28/83aaf1ca-69c0-11e9-a66d-a82d3f3d96d5_story.html.

7. Donie O'Sullivan, "White Supremacists Pose as Antifa Online, Call for Violence," *CNN Business*, June 2, 2020, https://www.cnn.com/2020/06/02/tech/antifa-fake-twitter-account/index.html.

8. Sonmez and Parker, "As Trump Stands by Charlottesville Remarks."

9. Darby, "How White Supremacy Went Mainstream."

10. Robin DiAngelo, *White Fragility: Why It's So Hard for White People to Talk About Racism* (Boston, MA: Beacon Press, 2018).

11. Patricia Hill Collins, "Defining Black Feminist Thought," in *The Second Wave*, ed. Linda Nicholson (New York, NY: Routledge, 1997).

12. For a historical account of how the legal and cultural categories of "white" and "nonwhite" in America have developed and changed through the years, see Steve Martinot, *The Rule of Racialization: Class, Identity, Governance* (Philadelphia, PA: Temple University Press, 2003). See also Michael Omi and Howard Winant, *Racial Formation in the United States* (New York, NY: Routledge, 1986). For a discussion of the shifting status of Asian Americans today, see Min Zhou, "Are Asian Americans Becoming 'White'?" in *Race, Class, and Gender: Intersections and Inequalities*, 10th Edition, eds. Margaret Andersen and Patricia Hill Collins (Boston, MA: Cengage Learning, 2020). For a discussion of Latinx identity and the categories of race and ethnicity, see Eduardo Bonilla-Silva, "We Are All Americans! The Latin Americanization of Racial Stratification in the USA," in *Race, Class, and Gender: Intersections and Inequalities*, 10th Edition, eds. Margaret Andersen and Patricia Hill Collins (Boston, MA: Cengage Learning, 2020).

13. W. E. B. Du Bois, "The Conservation of Races," in *African-American Social and Political Thought, 1850–1920*, ed. Howard Brotz (New Brunswick, NJ: Transaction Publishers, 1992).

14. See Lucius Outlaw, *On Race and Philosophy* (New York, NY: Routledge, 1996), 53.

15. Michael Ryan, *Marxism and Deconstruction: A Critical Articulation* (Baltimore, MD: John Hopkins University Press, 1982), 24.

16. Charles Mills, *The Racial Contract* (Ithaca, NY: Cornell University Press, 1997).

17. Omi and Winant, *Racial Formation in the United States*.

18. Martinot, *The Rule of Racialization*.

19. Outlaw, *On Race and Philosophy*, 145 and 149.

20. Patricia Huntington, "Fragmentation, Race, and Gender: Building Solidarity in the Postmodern Era," in *Existence in Black*, ed. Lewis Gordon (New York, NY: Routledge, 1997).

21. Outlaw, *On Race and Philosophy*, 157.

22. Ibid., 151.

23. Ibid., 136.

24. Ibid., 157. Emphasis added.

25. For a more detailed discussion of this, see the notion of "standpoint epistemology" in Collins, "Defining Black Feminist Thought."

26. Outlaw, *On Race and Philosophy*, 136 and 157.

27. Simone de Beauvoir, *Pour une morale de l'ambiguïté* (Paris: Gallimard, 1947).

28. Herbert Marcuse, *One-Dimensional Man* (Boston, MA: Beacon Press, 1964), 10.

29. Elizabeth Butterfield, *Sartre and Posthumanist Humanism* (Frankfurt: Peter Lang, 2012).

30. Kimberlé Crenshaw, "Demarginalizing the Intersection of Race and Sex: A Black Feminist Critique of Antidiscrimination Doctrine, Feminist Theory, and Antiracist Politics," in *Feminist Legal Theory: Foundations*, ed. D. Kelly Weisberg (Philadelphia, PA: Temple University Press, 1993).

31. Butterfield, *Sartre and Posthumanist Humanism*.

32. Margaret Andersen and Patricia Hill Collins, "Why Race, Class, and Gender Still Matter," in *Race, Class, and Gender: Intersections and Inequalities*, 10th Edition, eds. Margaret Andersen and Patricia Hill Collins (Boston, MA: Cengage Learning, 2020).

33. Jean-Paul Sartre, *L'être et le néant* (Paris: Gallimard, 1943).

34. Jean-Paul Sartre, *Critique de la raison dialectique* (Paris: Gallimard, 1960).

35. See Thomas Flynn, *Existentialism: A Very Short Introduction* (Oxford: Oxford University Press, 2006), 49: "The mantra of Sartrean humanism […] is that you can always make something out of what you've been made into."

36. Sartre, *L'être et le néant*.

37. Ibid.

38. See for example Orlando Patterson's *Slavery and Social Death: A Comparative Study* (Cambridge, MA: Harvard University Press, 1982).

39. Howard McGary, "Alienation and the African-American Experience," in *Theorizing Multiculturalism: A Guide to the Current Debate*, ed. Cynthia Willett (Maiden, MA: Blackwell, 1998).

40. Sartre, *L'être et le néant*.
41. Outlaw, *On Race and Philosophy*, 150.
42. Pat Parker, "For the White Person Who Wants to Know How to Be My Friend," *Callaloo* 23, no. 1 (2000): 73.
43. Gayatri Chakravorty Spivak, "Subaltern Studies: Deconstructing Historiography," in *The Spivak Reader: Selected Works of Gayatri Chakravorty Spivak*, eds. Donna Landry and Gerald MacLean (New York, NY: Routledge, 1996), 203–35. See page 204 for "strategic essentialism."
44. Collins, "Defining Black Feminist Thought," 256.
45. Ibid., 257.
46. Iris Marion Young, *Intersecting Voices: Dilemmas of Gender, Political Philosophy, and Policy* (Princeton, NJ: Princeton University Press, 1997).
47. Thanks to Everett Considine for the phrase, "Don't shame. Get curious."
48. Martin Luther King, *Letter from the Birmingham Jail* (San Francisco, CA: Harper San Francisco, 1994).
49. Marcuse, *One-Dimensional Man*.

BIBLIOGRAPHY

Alexander, Michelle. *The New Jim Crow: Mass Incarceration in the Age of Colorblindness*. New York, NY: New Press, 2010.

Andersen, Margaret, and Patricia Hill Collins. "Why Race, Class, and Gender Still Matter." In *Race, Class, and Gender: Intersections and Inequalities*, 10th Edition, edited by Margaret Andersen and Patricia Hill Collins. Boston, MA: Cengage Learning, 2020.

Balz, Dan, and Scott Clement. "On Racial Issues, America Is Divided Both Black and White and Red and Blue." *Washington Post*, December 27, 2014. https://www.washingtonpost.com/politics/on-racial-issues-america-is-divided-both-Black-and-white-and-red-and-blue/2014/12/26/3d2964c8-8d12-11e4-a085-34e9b9f09a58_story.html.

Beauvoir, Simone de. *Pour une morale de l'ambiguïté*. Paris: Gallimard, 1947.

Bonilla-Silva, Eduardo. "We Are All Americans! The Latin Americanization of Racial Stratification in the USA." In *Race, Class, and Gender: Intersections and Inequalities*, 10th Edition, edited by Margaret Andersen and Patricia Hill Collins. Boston, MA: Cengage Learning, 2020.

Butterfield, Elizabeth. *Sartre and Posthumanist Humanism*. Frankfurt: Peter Lang, 2012.

Collins, Patricia Hill. "Defining Black Feminist Thought." In *The Second Wave*, edited by Linda Nicholson. New York, NY: Routledge, 1997.

Crenshaw, Kimberlé. "Demarginalizing the Intersection of Race and Sex: A Black Feminist Critique of Antidiscrimination Doctrine, Feminist Theory, and Antiracist Politics." In *Feminist Legal Theory: Foundations*, edited by D. Kelly Weisberg. Philadelphia, PA: Temple University Press, 1993.

Darby, Luke. "How White Supremacy Went Mainstream in the US: 8chan, Trump, Voter Suppression." *Guardian*, August 11, 2019. https://www.theguardian.com/us-news/2019/aug/11/el-paso-shooting-white-supremacy-8chan-voter-suppression.

Dawson, Michael C., and Lawrence D. Bobo. "One Year Later and the Myth of a Post-Racial Society." *Du Bois Review: Social Science Research on Race* 6, no. 2 (2009): 247–249. https://dash.harvard.edu/handle/1/10347165.

DiAngelo, Robin. *White Fragility: Why It's So Hard for White People to Talk About Racism*. Boston, MA: Beacon Press, 2018.

Du Bois, W. E. B. "The Conservation of Races." In *African-American Social and Political Thought, 1850–1920*, edited by Howard Brotz. New Brunswick, NJ: Transaction Publishers, 1992.

DuVernay, Ava, Dir. *13th*. Kandoo Films, 2016.

Flynn, Thomas. *Existentialism: A Very Short Introduction*. Oxford: Oxford University Press, 2006.

Huntington, Patricia. "Fragmentation, Race, and Gender: Building Solidarity in the Postmodern Era." In *Existence in Black*, edited by Lewis Gordon. New York, NY: Routledge, 1997.

King, Martin Luther. *Letter from the Birmingham Jail*. San Francisco, CA: Harper San Francisco, 1994.

Levin, Brian. "Why White Supremacist Attacks Are on the Rise Everywhere." *Time*, March 21, 2019. https://time.com/5555396/white-supremacist-attacks-rise-new-zealand/.

Marcuse, Herbert. *One-Dimensional Man*. Boston, MA: Beacon Press, 1964.

Martinot, Steve. *The Rule of Racialization: Class, Identity, Governance*. Philadelphia, PA: Temple University Press, 2003.

McGary, Howard. "Alienation and the African-American Experience." In *Theorizing Multiculturalism: A Guide to the Current Debate*, edited by Cynthia Willett. Maiden, MA: Blackwell, 1998.

Mills, Charles. *The Racial Contract*. Ithaca, NY: Cornell University Press, 1997.

Omi, Michael, and Howard Winant. *Racial Formation in the United States*. New York, NY: Routledge, 1986.

O'Sullivan, Donie. "White Supremacists Pose as Antifa Online, Call for Violence." *CNN Business*, June 2, 2020. https://www.cnn.com/2020/06/02/tech/antifa-fake-twitter-account/index.html.

Outlaw, Lucius. *On Race and Philosophy*. New York, NY: Routledge, 1996.

Parker, Pat. "For the White Person Who Wants to Know How to Be My Friend." *Callaloo* 23, no. 1 (2000): 73.

Patterson, Orlando. *Slavery and Social Death: A Comparative Study*. Cambridge, MA: Harvard University Press, 1982.

Ryan, Michael. *Marxism and Deconstruction: A Critical Articulation*. Baltimore, MD: John Hopkins University Press, 1982.

Sartre, Jean-Paul. *L'être et le néant*. Paris: Gallimard, 1943.

Sartre, Jean-Paul. *Critique de la raison dialectique*. Paris: Gallimard, 1960.

Schorr, Daniel. "A New, 'Post-Racial' Political Era in America." *NPR*, January 28, 2008. https://www.npr.org/templates/story/story.php?storyId=18489466.

Sonmez, Felicia, and Ashley Parker. "As Trump Stands by Charlottesville Remarks, Rise of White-Nationalist Violence Becomes an Issue in 2020 Presidential Race." *Washington Post*, April 28, 2019. https://www.washingtonpost.com/politics/as-trump-stands-by-charlottesville-remarks-rise-of-white-nationalist-violence-becomes-an-issue-in-2020-presidential-race/2019/04/28/83aaf1ca-69c0-11e9-a66d-a82d3f3d96d5_story.html.

Spivak, Gayatri Chakravorty. "Subaltern Studies: Deconstructing Historiography." In *The Spivak Reader: Selected Works of Gayatri Chakravorty Spivak*, edited by Donna Landry and Gerald MacLean, 203–235. New York, NY: Routledge, 1996.

Young, Iris Marion. *Intersecting Voices: Dilemmas of Gender, Political Philosophy, and Policy*. Princeton, NJ: Princeton University Press, 1997.

Zhou, Min. "Are Asian Americans Becoming 'White'?" In *Race, Class, and Gender: Intersections and Inequalities*, 10th Edition, edited by Margaret Andersen and Patricia Hill Collins. Boston, MA: Cengage Learning, 2020.

Part 3

THE PANDEMIC

Chapter 8

Lessons from the Death Zone

What Jon Krakauer's Into Thin Air *Can Teach Us about the COVID-19 Pandemic and Why We May Be Doomed to Repeat It*

Leigh E. Rich

It seems like a scene from a sci-fi story: Unbeknownst to humans mindlessly embroiled in their everyday lives, an alien life-form crash-lands on Earth. The few in this proverbial faraway city who may have noticed something amiss in their midst do not register the true impact of an otherwise quiet event. Whether this ignorance is by accident or intent is not readily clear and, over time, will spawn condemnations and conspiracy theories about who knew what and when. As details emerge and coalesce in the collective consciousness, prognosticators—those both preposterous and prudent—will raise rationales (the ease of the illogical outpacing the labored empirical) to explain what is happening along with "I told you so's" about being better prepared. The alien will remain elusive as long as it can, proliferating in one locale then the next, until it reaches through replication every corner of the globe. Its wily maneuvers and bewildering tactics will thwart humankind's efforts, at least for the present, creating confusion and chaos. And, so, it advances in its relentless and singular mission: to survive.

Like many science-fiction narratives that center around "first contact," we find ourselves in a singular time. The novel coronavirus has been dubbed so for a reason. While not extraterrestrial, it is new—new to us—a viral entity not previously identified. As such, we are only now beginning to study its stratagems and vulnerabilities, and we lack vaccines, treatments, and, above all, immunity. SARS-CoV-2, as all of its names imply, is indeed alien.

And, yet, all at once, it is not.

Governmental entities, whether the World Health Organization or the National Security Council's Pandemic Response Team, and academicians like Laurie Garrett[1] and the Johns Hopkins Center for Health Security (complete with terrifying "table top" exercises and widely read tomes) have long been promising "not if, but when." As we ask—"Could the pandemic have been predicted?" and "Could our responses have been better planned?"—the answers, to a great degree, are yes. Epidemics and pandemics are nothing new (see the once-recurring waves of smallpox and the plague, the flus of 1957 and 1968, or the novel 2003 SARS-CoV-1 and 2009's H_1N_1), even if this particular virus is.

So why are we (still) scrambling with our trousers 'round our ankles? Is it (willful) ignorance? Hubris? Our human inability truly to understand or assess risk? Is it lack of political will and our continued construction of societies on a wobbly, Shavian infrastructure that attempts to sort the "deserving" poor from the "undeserving"?[2] Is it our systems, born in colonialism and slavery, that prioritize unbridled growth over human rights and sustainability?[3] Here, too, per our sci-fi and scholarly soothsayers, signs point to yes.

Unlike fictional leaders caught unaware of alien infiltration, our very real ones knew of this very real risk, even if the COVID-19 moment is, in its details, unique. To be sure, as philosophers and writers have cautioned, we "cannot step into the same river twice."[4] Georg Hegel in his *Lectures on the Philosophy of History* preached that

> what experience and history teach is . . . that peoples and governments never have learned anything from history, or acted on principles deduced from it. Each period is involved in such peculiar circumstances, exhibits a condition of things so strictly idiosyncratic, that its conduct must be regulated by considerations connected with itself, and itself alone. Amid the pressure of great events, a general principle gives no help.[5]

A century and a half later, journalist Jon Krakauer, recovering from a "murderous" trek on Mount Everest that killed twelve people, concluded something of the same:

> to believe that dissecting the tragic events of 1996 in minute detail will actually reduce the future death rate in any meaningful way is wishful thinking. The urge to catalog the myriad blunders in order to "learn from the mistakes" is for the most part an exercise in denial and self-deception. . . . In the midst of postmortem ratiocination, it is easy to lose sight of the fact that climbing mountains will never be a safe, predictable, rule-bound enterprise.[6]

Regardless—and with the caveat that one should tread carefully when making analogies in the course of crises[7]—past experience, despite an exceptional present, must offer *some* helpful lessons to combat the all-too-Earthly alien among us. Krakauer's time on Everest and, more importantly, the teachings he took from it provide a heuristic of what we have done wrong in twenty-first-century America. (One might rightly surmise in what pandemic pastimes I've recently partaken and, hence, the switch from *Men in Black* scenarios to armchair adventure climbing.) Like scaling the mountain, "conquering" SARS-CoV-2 is not a "safe, predictable, rule-bound enterprise," and we shouldn't expect our leaders never to misstep. But some "general principle[s]" could—and should—have given us help.

Three, in particular, come to mind: (1) parsing prior paths can lead to better prescience and presents; (2) rights do not exist in a vacuum but as a correlative of duties; and (3) true leadership mitigates moral distress. To disregard these and focus instead on the strategic goal of "reaching one's summit" (sometimes by any means necessary) amounts to little more than pompous photo ops at the cost of livelihoods and lives.

"I SEE IN THE NEAR FUTURE A CRISIS THAT UNNERVES ME"[8]

Like the novel coronavirus, Everest simultaneously is and is not a known quantity. It straddles human-made boundaries and stretches where airplanes fly. Its weather at various elevations ranges from mild to inconceivably cold.[9] Its glacial valley is unpredictable and unstable.[10] Every day and every climb on Everest is different, and, yet, the treks, both commercial and otherwise, could not occur (no less succeed) without knowledge of those who have gone before. Expeditions, particularly guided ones, are not completely developed anew, and certain tactics and strategies, based on prior experiences, have been prefigured.[11]

Something similar could be said of COVID-19. One need only read Boccaccio's *Decameron* or Daniel Defoe's *A Journal of the Plague Year* to find parallels from Europe's plagued past.[12] At play were methods of social distancing, restricted travel, quarantines, and confinement at home (though far more stringent than today), along with worries about what this all meant with regard to trade and individual liberties. Defoe, for instance, discusses how "the country people who brought provisions" would stay just outside of town "with their goods, where they sold what they brought, and went immediately away," while bakers and butchers were deemed essential workers.[13] "[P]eople used all possible precaution," he notes in his pseudo-historical chronicle (except for the struggling classes already wanting for resources):

> When any one bought a joint of meat in the market they would not take it off the butcher's hand, but took it off the hooks themselves. On the other hand, the

butcher would not touch the money, but have it put into a pot full of vinegar, which he kept for that purpose. The buyer carried always small money to make up any odd sum, that they might take no change. They carried bottles of scents and perfumes in their hands, and all the means that could be used were used; but then the poor could not do even these things, and they went at all hazards.[14]

Likewise, scapegoats were named and unjustly punished (shouldering the burden both as "cause" and "effect"), and charlatans abounded with inert-to-dangerous miracle medicines and misinformation,[15] alongside debates about the faithfulness or foolishness of religious congregation.[16] Little was known about true causes or cures; the asymptomatic were as dangerous as those clearly "marked";[17] and some leaders acted with more diligence and dignity than others.

While epidemic plague may seem remote and dated, recent scourges also offer comparable tutorials about public health preparedness. Although many today allude to the 1918–1919 influenza pandemic, which killed approximately 675,000 Americans and 50 million globally,[18] the flus of the mid-twentieth century may be more apt.[19] The 1957–1958 outbreak of the new H_2N_2 "caused between one and two million deaths worldwide" and, though "comparatively mild," resulted in a small economic impact and "some societal disruption due to school and workplace absenteeism . . . mostly concentrated among children, school teachers, and healthcare workers."[20] Thanks to a new international surveillance system and network of laboratories, this also "was the first time that comprehensive surveillance was used to track the spread and burden of the disease," alongside an expedited experiment in the development, distribution, and uptake of a new vaccine.[21]

Times were similar even if also a-changin' (with today's doubled U.S. population, factory farming, increased air travel, and various forms of 24-7 media), but, surely, people realized what could happen when factoring in a more virulent virus and shifting variables. Such forward planning, however, failed to materialize (at least in any appropriately resourced way), as changes in U.S. morbidity and mortality, economic and military priorities, and overall culture steered attention away from infectious diseases to those noncommunicable.[22] Making matters worse, this new route was laid atop one carved a century or so ago that detoured biomedicine (read: "real" health care) away from public health, ensuring those trained in the former would have little knowledge of the vastly underfunded latter and those of the latter would lack the power to influence the path ahead.[23] The Patient Protection and Affordable Care Act of 2010 tried to chart a united course up this particular mountain but (especially under recent Republican leadership) with minimal success. Even amid the pandemic, limited and contradictory federal actions have resulted in muddled preventive measures, deficient testing, and anemic attempts at contact tracing—effective public health tactics that are far less expensive (in all senses) than hospital-based heroism, with or without ventilators.[24] As journalist Nick Heil concluded, following his analysis of Everest's 2006 season (nearly as lethal as ten years prior), "[t]oo much has been written, said, filmed, and photographed for anyone going to Mount Everest not to be fully aware of the risks of climbing to 29,035 feet."[25]

THE FATAL FLAW IN "EVERY MAN FOR HIMSELF"

Unlike tertiary care, built into (even the name of) public health is the understanding that we are "all in this together," that individual well-being relies on community health and the physical, social, and structural environments in which we live. On Everest, however, this cooperative element often is absent. In *Into Thin Air*, Jon Krakauer notes that, in comparison to his many years of climbing other peaks, he didn't know his Everest companions or their skills, and "[e]ach client was in it for himself or herself, pretty much":

> In this godforsaken place, I felt disconnected from the climbers around me—emotionally, spiritually, physically—to a degree I hadn't experienced on any previous expedition. We were a team in name only, I'd sadly come to realize. Although in a few hours we would leave camp as a group, we would ascend as individuals, linked to one another by neither rope nor any deep sense of loyalty.[26]

This self-centered approach has been common to most modern Everest experiences, in part because of the limitations of assisting others in such a remote and dangerous environment. For example, those climbing to reclaim bodies often end up leaving them there, and individuals coming to another's aid may be barely riding the line of supporting themselves.[27] Rescue attempts can place clients, guides, and Sherpas at risk for a favorable outcome that is "slim at best. . . . No nonambulatory climber has ever been brought down from above 8,000 meters."[28] While such egoism may appear prudent, in some instances, climbers in the "Death Zone" (above 8,000 meters or approximately 26,000 feet) have trekked past others when assistance might actually have helped.[29] In the 1996 season, a Japanese team approaching the summit from the north side allegedly ignored three Indian climbers in distress. Defending their actions, a member of the Japanese group said they "were too tired to help. Above 8,000 meters is not a place where people can afford morality,"[30] and they later publicly released a report emphasizing that on Everest "'it is common sense' that every climber should be held accountable for their actions, 'even on the brink of death'."[31] This ethic, which places personal glory over the lives of others, demonstrates a narcissism peculiar to the Everest sport. (International maritime principles, for example, require helping vessels in distress or sailors fallen overboard, even during competitive races.[32]) If this Darwinian ethos may be unappealing in mountaineering, it is disgraceful in public health.

Stepping past neighbors in need has occurred (although not exclusively) during the SARS-CoV-2 pandemic. Perhaps the best illustration—though, like many Everest stories, with conflicting reports—is the Trump administration's purported offer of "large sums of money" to lure a German biotech firm "to move its research wing to the United States and develop [its coronavirus] vaccine 'for the U.S. only'."[33] Or Trump and Senate Majority Leader Mitch McConnell suggesting that states be left to go bankrupt.[34] Or the Federal Emergency Management Agency commandeering state-secured shipments of supplies,[35] even while states have been forced to compete with each other in the purchasing of personal protective equipment, tests, and ventilators. In this "every jurisdiction for itself," costs of medical resources (when available) have skyrocketed and individualized paths have had to be carved. Republican Governor Larry Hogan of Maryland, for example, conducted secret talks with a South Korean manufacturer (and translated through Hogan's Korean-American wife) to ensure that 500,000 test kits made it to his state.[36] For his efforts, Trump condemned Hogan's "brink-of-death" deal-making and, in so many words, dubbed him dumb.[37] Meanwhile, Project Airbridge, an effort by Trump's son-in-law adviser Jared Kushner to subsidize cargo flights for major medical companies, "cost taxpayers at least $91 million" but underdelivered on promised supplies (especially N95 masks) and enabled administration allies to profit from no-bid contracts.[38] The companies, for which the Department of Justice authorized antitrust waivers, were not required to pass on savings to states or hospitals and were allowed to sell half of the inventory on the private market.[39] With no coherent and coordinated federal response, states have had to act as independent expeditions all clamoring for the top—no matter how many climbers gasping for air they pass along the way.[40]

Trump and Kushner also have claimed dominion over the Strategic National Stockpile and have changed the language on its website to reflect a lessened sense of federal duty.[41] During a White House Coronavirus Task Force briefing, Kushner emphasized that "the federal stockpile was ... supposed to be our stockpile; it's not supposed to be state stockpiles that they then use."[42] This statement echoes that of the Japanese Everest team—that it is "common sense" whose resources these are and individual states are accountable for their own actions and reserves. The "our" in Kushner's claim, however, is a fiction, which, through the performance of his utterance, becomes an artificial being endowed with property rights and against which states must compete.[43] When asked to explain who or what "our" referred to, President Trump provided a tautological response: "You know what 'our' means? United States of America. . . . That's what it means. . . . Our. Our.

It means the United States of America. And then we take that 'our' and we distribute it to the states. Not that we have to."[44] Unlike the above examples, which reflect a basic social Darwinist model that merely leaves the "least fit" behind, here human life becomes a tradable commodity. To reach the summit (or keep "our" equipment for "ourselves"), "your" climbers might have to die. The stockpile is no longer the "nation's largest supply of life-saving pharmaceuticals and medical supplies for use in a public health emergency" and from which "state, local, tribal, and territorial responders [can] request federal assistance," but that of an artificial entity that owns these resources and has sole discretion over whether and when to dole them out.[45] It is not a function of the *capacity* to help but the *will*. After all, the federal government (at least according to the Trump administration) is "not an ordering clerk": It is not here to serve the interests of citizens but, like single-minded Everest enthusiasts, itself.[46] And through the fiction—that a United States exists without its people or summiting Everest is worth more than saving a life—profits may be made. Executive branch efforts like Project Airbridge have "taken advantage of the pandemic to boost some of the country's biggest companies while doing little . . . to ameliorate national shortages of PPE" and possibly creating "a lasting impact on everything from health care costs to the consolidation of corporate power."[47] Moreover, a false "our" that possesses a national stockpile resembles a shell company that can evade liability and make decisions based more on politics than the public's health.[48]

This Everest "Death Zone" mentality similarly has spread (like another lethal virus) among those protesting orders to shelter at home or wear masks. Granted, certain means of protecting one another are more difficult and have greater consequences than others, and it is understandable that some citizens, especially those out of work, find such mandates a true "life-or-death" financial burden. But claiming only one's "right to" misses the embedded duty, as well as risks, that a right places on others.[49] A mother with her daughter at a rally in Texas, for example, stated that she is "not worried about catching the virus. If we did catch the virus, I feel that we're healthy enough to fight it,"[50] while a protester in Indiana argued, "If I get sick, then I am going to bear the consequences of my getting sick. . . . If anybody else gets sick, they bear the consequences of their free choice without government coercion to do so."[51] Missing from this discourse, however, just as it is atop Everest, is a recognition that risk of infectious disease (and, really, all illness) is not something one bears alone. Perhaps, indeed, the woman and her seven-year-old are "healthy enough to fight" infection (despite the fact that such prognoses are currently beyond even the most experienced physician) or the Indianapolis gent possesses the resources to withstand a (sometimes) lengthy, pricy, and deadly disease. Others may not be as lucky, nor will our patchwork health care system, which fails to cover all and leaves families (and society) financially injured even when patients manage to make it off the mountain. The "right" to risk exposure places others in harm's way and begs legal and ethical questions of state and individual responsibility. Members of a community also have a right to be free from infection or, at least, a reasonable opportunity to be.[52] Yet, especially in the United States, we have a tendency to proclaim individual rights without acknowledging that this is only one part of the equation and that rights must be balanced and may be difficult to define. Even in an individualist society, we rationally exchange some of our "perfect freedom" to avoid a life that is "solitary, poore, nasty, brutish, and short."[53] To be sure, most citizens wish to guard against a slippery slide into authoritarianism, but there is a danger in assuming that well-being exists outside of a legal system (which is meant to limit authority, not enable it) or in treating a "specific problem" (such as certain rights during the current pandemic) "as if it were far less complex than it really is."[54]

The state has obligations to preserve life and protect innocent third parties (of others' behaviors and decisions), and balancing individual and communal freedom is no easy task. Yet there has been pushback even over the wearing of masks to protect others and prevent spread, an act that fits the definition of a least restrictive alternative[55] (though neither the only nor a panacea). One man's tweet, after retailer Costco required customers and employees to don face masks, exemplifies the misinterpretation of constitutional rights (and contract law): "You have hit a new low . . . you are an American corporation with an obligation to support our American values, dictating face mask [*sic*] for your workers is one thing but forcing this on your loyal members who paid for a membership is a complete abuse of power."[56] It is difficult to know where to begin—whether how to define "our American values" or unpacking the idea that there is a right to climb the mountain in any given way, even at great danger to others, simply because one has paid. The loyalty this man claims for Costco, so easily undone by having to wear a mask while shopping, reflects the shallow egoism Krakauer noted in Everest climbers. Rather than safeguarding individual rights while buying in bulk, what this tweet performs is an act of "zero-sum" virtue signaling[57] that aligns non-wearers of masks with "our American values" and those who cover their faces (and the corporations that support it) with something sinister and anti-American.[58] Protesting masks has become an adventure game of its own, where one side wins only if the other loses. After all, no one remembers the individuals who attempted to summit Everest, only those who do.[59] Ironically, there are laws on the books that make mask-wearing in public illegal and thus raise similar constitutional questions these protesters contest. In our partisan, strategic times, many have ignored this legal contradiction or linked the wearing of masks to "the Muslim veil" (a discriminatory assertion with clear First Amendment implications)[60] or emasculation (because protecting oneself with a mask, but not a gun, shows "weakness").[61] President Trump has refused to wear a mask, even at enclosed rallies and while visiting businesses and cities with mandates,[62] and he himself and others in his administration and larger orbit (e.g., Chris Christie and the late Herman Cain) have (not unsurprisingly) contracted the virus. The president has "even suggested that he views masks as a political statement against him personally."[63]

MORAL COURAGE IN THE FACE OF DISTRESS

Even with the best of leaders, systemic issues can engender problems. For instance, although Krakauer respected and trusted his Everest guides, he learned in hindsight the bias built into the power dynamics of the climb. The inherent dangers of the trek and its transactional foundation meant that Krakauer and members of his group "had been specifically indoctrinated not to question [their] guides' judgment" and, thus, were unconsciously primed not to see them as anything other than "invincible."[64] At the heights on Everest, however, anyone can experience distress, including the guides and Sherpas who often carry heavier loads and make many trips between camps to prepare the route or help clients in need. For Krakauer, beyond the given hypoxia, his "inability to discern the obvious" when his companions were in trouble "was exacerbated to some degree by the guide–client protocol," which restricted decision-making to the highest echelons of the team: Rob Hall, the expedition leader, and guides Mike Groom and Andy Harris.[65] Such a "chain of command" is a rational safety protocol to prevent chaos and foolish mistakes, given that climbers vary in experience and skill. This arrangement, however, where subordinates have no voice, can amplify the consequences of errors that might be caught earlier. For example, when Krakauer arrived on the "Balcony" (above 27,400 feet) with one of the Sherpas about an hour ahead of their climbing mates, he and Ang Dorje realized that no ropes had been fixed in advance as the guides from multiple companies had earlier agreed.[66] Krakauer had the skill, experience, and time to help rectify the situation and avoid what would turn into "a time-consuming bottleneck" for everyone summiting, but "Rob had explicitly forbidden [him] to go ahead" (and there was no other non-client nearby to assist Ang Dorje with the task).[67] Instead, the two sat in the snow and waited until another Sherpa arrived, a delay that contributed to the season's loss of life.

While Krakauer, like all climbers on Everest, suffered during his trek from oxygen deprivation and exhaustion that impeded his discernment (especially after summiting and on his way back to Camp IV), the expedition's organizational structure exacerbated the tragedy. In the 1970s and 1980s, a similar situation was identified among nurses, who often spend far more time at the bedside with patients yet have far less power over care-related decisions.[68]

Scholars such as Andrew Jameton have examined the moral distress these health care providers experience when caught between speaking up about inappropriate medical orders and repercussions in one's job. Unlike moral uncertainty or moral dilemmas, moral distress poses a unique ethical position. With uncertainty, one "does not know the ethically correct course, but feels a nagging uncertainty, a sense that something is not quite right"; with a dilemma, "two or more opposing actions can be equally ethically justified and the agent, unable to carry out both actions, faces" a predicament in determining which path to follow.[69] Moral distress, however, occurs when one "knows, or believes she knows, the ethically appropriate action, but feels constrained from acting because of some obstacle inherent in the situation, such as lack of time or supervisory support, institutional or legal constraints, or physician power over nursing and nursing practice."[70]

Such distress has occurred during the pandemic as well, particularly among essential workers on the front lines and even experts at higher levels. From those in health care and government to grocery clerks and food processors, many have been forced to choose between professional duty and personal welfare (financial and physical), while stifling real concerns about a lack of protective equipment, safety nets, and strategic plans. In an era focused more on image management than facts and feedback, no insubordination seems safe, even if it is for the greater good.[71] It has not mattered whether individuals are, like Krakauer, skilled in needed areas or eyewitnesses to events. Hospitals have implemented policies that limit what health care providers can post on social media (restrictions such as "positive and uplifting messages that support your colleagues and our organization") and prohibit them from speaking to the press.[72] Some have been warned, suspended, or fired—and also publicly shamed via "wanted" posters that alert hospital security and other employees that a once-trusted teammate is now *persona non grata*.[73] Within government, those who have failed to "tiptoe" the line have been reassigned or replaced. To wit: Navy Captain Brett Crozier was relieved as command of the *Theodore Roosevelt* "after he pleaded for more help fighting a novel coronavirus outbreak aboard his ship,"[74] and vaccine scientist Rick Bright was removed as director of the Biomedical Advanced Research and Development Authority when he "raised health concerns over [the anti-malarial] drug repeatedly pushed by President Trump as a possible cure."[75] When asked about Bright's repositioning to a smaller role at the National Institutes of Health, the president denied all knowledge: "I never heard of him. . . . The guy says he was pushed out of a job, maybe he was, maybe he wasn't. You'd have to hear the other side."[76] Even top members of the Coronavirus Task Force have hesitated to speak frankly, whether for fear of reprisal or losing the spotlight they have to disseminate truthful information to confused Americans. Physician and "world-renowned global health official" Deborah Birx,[77] serving as the coronavirus response coordinator, not only minimized her reply to Trump's suggested treatments of "hit[ting] the body with a tremendous . . . light" or injecting disinfectant,[78] but also later provided cover for his unproven and dangerous remedies: "When he gets new information, he likes to talk that through out loud and really have that dialogue—and so that's what dialogue he was having. I think he just saw the information at the time immediately before the press conference and he was still digesting that information."[79]

Addressing moral distress after the fact is as important as doing so in the moment, with candid "after-action" conversations essential to prevention. Unlike Birx, chairman of the Joint Chiefs of Staff Mark Milley set a positive example when he apologized for accompanying the president on his walk through Lafayette Square—cleared of peaceful protesters in the wake of George Floyd's death—for a White House photo op. "I should not have been there," General Milley has stated, indicating that he "agonized" for days over his appearance. "My presence in that moment and in that environment created a perception of the military involved in domestic politics. . . . The protests that have ensued not only speak to [Floyd's] killing [at the hands of police], but also to the centuries of injustice toward African-Americans. . . . We all need to do better."[80] Such truthful dialogue is a minimum for change. While similar Everest photo ops abound and, like Trump, climbers continue to pursue their personal goals and mountainous "dream,"[81] others advocate for policies and procedures that can be put into place. In *Dark Summit*, Heil takes to task the perspective that on Everest "no one can be held accountable for the others" and that "[e]ach step higher is a personal choice and a personal responsibility."[82] Instead, he ends his evaluation of the 2006 season by applauding the "intensified discussions" that occurred among expedition operators and Chinese officials (both of whom, of course, have capitalistic interests in the perpetuation of climbs). On the table were possible "regulations and rescue programs" that could prevent deaths and "better cope with emergencies."[83] Though some proposals may be more feasible in terms of costs and physics than others, simply determining that there is nothing to learn from history and thus nothing to be done is a failure of both duty and imagination.

Whether regarding Everest or SARS-CoV-2, we also must look "beyond the mountain." The poverty at its base, inequitable access to rudimentary resources, and human rights violations create as much, if not more, risk to individual and social welfare,[84] and time and energy spent debating "magic bullet" routes (like hydroxychloroquine and remdesivir) and waiting for a medivac vaccine capable of flying at 30,000 feet wastes political will that could change systems and prevent not just one disease but many.[85] Following the COVID-19 pandemic, critical and transparent assessments that care little for partisanship will be crucial if there is to be hope for avoiding or mitigating the consequences when the next "alien" entity arrives.

"WE'RE IN GREAT SHAPE THOUGH"[86]

Whatever lessons from our present climb we might apply to future ones, two difficulties remain: Like the coronavirus itself, prevention is nearly invisible, and particularly in our "Goaded Age," strategic goals reign king.

How can we begin to address each?

As public health professionals know, primary prevention—which thwarts injury or illness before it occurs—lacks the panache of tertiary medical heroics and shoulders the burden of negatively proving resources were well spent (i.e., an investment was successful because nothing happened). The contemporary anti-vaccine movement, for example, argues that inoculation is not needed for diseases that (virtually) no longer exist, highlighting how leaders of any effective public health policy "may never be rewarded for their effort because the outcome will be a calamity that never occurred, a disaster we never felt. We punish only the most undeniable of failures and routinely miss the most profound successes."[87] Yet, a public health approach is used in national defense allocations, where mountains of money support preventive efforts, including a standing army (and navy and air force, now also a space force) just in case. Scientists and health care professionals have tried tying public health to national security, but, as is currently evident, that expedition is still stuck at base camp. Our present predicament, though, should prove that public health is key to economic health. How we apply this very painfully acquired truth, only time—and health policy—will tell.[88]

Unfortunately, when collective goals and the communal good are less important than simply reaching the top, instead of approaching potential problems from the perspective of national welfare, we get arbitrary presidential edicts, stacked courts taking precedence over rational legislation,[89] bigoted protesters playing victim,[90] and state governments undermining public health measures and exploiting a pandemic to prohibit abortion[91]—claiming "there are more important things than living"[92] (except for the unborn) and that prioritizing "the economy over Americans' health 'is the lesser of two evils'."[93] If the American population, like the competing factions on Everest, are encouraged to engage "in a place where brute strength and ruthlessness overrule compassion, civility, and fair play,"[94] how can we conquer this pandemic or prepare for future ones? On the "grand stage" of Everest, if climbers (amateur or professional, ascending for personal or public reasons) only count the achievement ("in the first case because of its cathartic potency . . . in the latter because of its undiminished power to impress"), what does "this imply when it [comes] to the welfare of others?"[95] Undertaking any monumental task should entail careful preparation and serious reflection that aligns investment with values and recognizes that "achievement" doesn't always mean getting to the top.[96] In 2006, several Sherpas, climbing outfitters, and clients reached much greater heights when they stopped their own summits to assist another in need, a coordinated "rescue on a scale never before seen on the north side."[97] Despite near perfect conditions that day, the rescuers in the "Death Zone" chose to sit with climber-in-need Lincoln Hall "for nearly four hours, [while] casting disappointed gazes toward the [peak]."[98]

Even when we all are looking out for each other, however, another risk remains: escalating commitment of futile plans.[99] Everest clients, who may spend upwards of $65,000 to join a team, are not wont to turn around,[100] and despite signed agreements, differences can arise about who is in charge.[101] For guides and Sherpas, reputations are made on the number of customers they convey to the top, and Sherpas can earn more in two months than "in a full year of herding yaks." Guiding people up Everest thus turns the physical ascent into "a path of socioeconomic and social advancement" for them and their families.[102] Escalation is built into every aspect of a climb, both before one steps foot on the mountain and after: Teams with sponsorships (from businesses, media outlets, or schoolchildren) may feel the die has been cast, and those who succeed can "descend transformed"—changed from their prior ordinary lives "into motivational speakers, authors, television personalities, sponsored athletes, mountain guides, or 'life coaches'."[103] In this regard, Everest provides a microcosm for the coronavirus pandemic, a summit vastly larger and immensely more perilous in light of our hyper-strategic focus in the twenty-first century. Today, politicians, media, and activists often create new types of "Death Zones," with irrational commitments that fly in the face of prevention and interfere with truth. To name but a few: President Trump has stubbornly stuck to downplaying scripts;[104] the CDC doubled down on dodgy homegrown tests;[105] and Fox News flippantly mocked effective measures such as contact tracing, knowing full well the influence it and its hosts carry with conservative citizens.[106] Instead of a coordinated rescue, we have been left stranded and hypoxic, because every individual is after his own summit. If disease is always political, then perhaps the political egoism of the neoliberal subject is the ultimate pestilence.[107]

So what will we learn, not just today but also tomorrow, as we look back and the present becomes past? It certainly is not "useless to revert to [the] similar circumstances" of prior times, as Hegel suggests, but he is likely correct that our "pallid shades of memory [will] struggle in vain with the life and freedom of the Present."[108]

NOTES

1. Laurie Garrett, *The Coming Plague: Newly Emerging Diseases in a World Out of Balance* (New York, NY: Farrar, Straus and Giroux, 1994).

2. See, for example, George Bernard Shaw, *Major Barbara* (Auckland: The Floating Press, 2009), originally published in 1907, and Fintan O'Toole, "The Lie That Poverty Is a Moral Failing Was Buried a Century Ago. Now It's Back," *The Guardian*, October 18, 2017, https://www.theguardian.com/commentisfree/2017/oct/18/george-bernard-shaw-poverty-moral-myth.

3. See, for example, Edward Abbey, *Desert Solitaire: A Season in the Wilderness* (New York, NY: McGraw-Hill, 1968).

4. Heraclitus, paraphrased in Plato's *Cratylus* at 402a. Plato, *Cratylus*, trans. C. D. C. Reeve (Indianapolis, IN and Cambridge: Hackett Publishing Company, Inc., 1998), 33.

5. Georg W. F. Hegel, *Lectures on the Philosophy of History*, 3rd edition, trans. J. Sibree (London: Henry G. Bohn, 1861), 6.

6. Jon Krakauer, *Into Thin Air: A Personal Account of the Mount Everest Disaster* (New York, NY: Anchor Books, 1998), 356–58.

7. Barbara Reynolds, in collaboration with Julia Hunter Galdo and Lynn Sokler, *Crisis and Emergency Risk Communication* (Atlanta, GA: Centers for Disease Control and Prevention, 2002).

8. Often misattributed to Abraham Lincoln. Thomas F. Schwartz, "Lincoln Never Said That," *For the People* 1, no. 1 (Spring 1999): 4–6, http://www.abrahamlincolnassociation.org/Newsletters/1-1.pdf. Regardless of the quote's real source, it offers an apt comparison here, including in full.

9. Master Kungga Dundruk, "Everest Base Camp Weather: A Detailed Guide to Climate and Weather of Everest Base Camp in Tibet," *Tibet Vista*, November 18, 2019, https://www.tibettravel.org/tibet-travel-advice/climate-and-temperature-of-ebc.html.

10. For example, en route to the summit from the Nepal side, the Khumbu Icefall is "a half mile or so of constantly shifting glacier" that "can move 6 feet in just one day," with crevasses appearing or vanishing in even less time. The Associated Press, "Khumbu Icefall: Unsteady & Deadly," *The Denver Post*, April 22, 2014, updated April 27, 2016, https://www.denverpost.com/2014/04/22/khumbu-icefall-unsteady-deadly/, ¶2. Moreover, climate change has brought increased changes. Bennett Slavsky, "How Climate Change is Making Mount Everest More Dangerous: Though Overcrowding Was a Deadly Factor on Mount Everest This Year, Climate Change Might Prove More Devastating in the Long Run," *Climbing*, May 29, 2019, https://www.climbing.com/news/climate-change-on-mount-everest-old-bodies-and-new/.

11. This is evident in most of the books written about Everest as well as television programs such as the Discovery Channel's *Ultimate Survival: Everest* (2004) and *Everest: Beyond the Limit* (2006–2009). In most cases, especially for individuals climbing with expedition companies, a "tried-and-true recipe" is in place. This does not always guarantee success or safety, nor does it necessarily make for a stirring narrative. Shows and books thus tend to focus on personal dramas and instances where climbers have defied team leader orders or proven techniques.

12. While these are works of fiction and Defoe's eighteenth-century novel speaks to the 1665 plague of London, both were written during outbreaks. Boccaccio birthed the *Decameron* in the midst of the 1348 epidemic, which he richly (even if briefly)

describes in the first day's introduction. Defoe, though safely ensconced by time and geography, remembers England's last major plague epidemic while one raged in Marseilles in the early 1720s. His *Journal* draws on multiple sources, including bills of mortality from London's Great Plague and works published shortly thereafter. Frank Bastian, "Defoe's *Journal of the Plague Year* Reconsidered," *The Review of English Studies* 16, no. 62 (May 1965): 151–73. Many other resources could be used here to illustrate how societies and individuals have responded to past epidemics and what we currently might learn from them, including those from Samuel Pepys, John Bell, Thomas Sydenham, Nathaniel Hodges, Walter George Bell, Richard Bradley, François Chicoyneau, etc. Defoe's *Journal*, however, "embodie[s] in a picturesque form the substance of various writings that preceded it." Charles Creighton, *A History of Epidemics in Britain*, Vol. 1 (London: Cambridge University Press, 1891), 646.

13. Daniel Defoe, *A Journal of the Plague Year* (London: Cassell and Company, 1909), 101. Originally published in 1722.

14. Ibid., 99.

15. The "common people," Defoe writes in *A Journal of the Plague Year* on page 42 (emphasis added),

> ran to conjurers and witches, and all sorts of deceivers, to know what should become of them (who fed their fears, and kept them always alarmed and awake on purpose to delude them and pick their pockets), so they were as mad upon their running after quacks and mountebanks, and every practising old woman, for medicines and remedies; storing themselves with such multitudes of pills, potions, and preservatives, as they were called, that they not only spent their money, but *even poisoned themselves beforehand, for fear of the poison of the infection*, and prepared their bodies for the plague, instead of preserving them against it.

One need only compare this description with Jim Bakker's peddling of Silver Solution or President Donald J. Trump's promotion of hydroxychloroquine and "internal treatments" of sunlight and disinfectants. U.S. Food and Drug Administration, "Coronavirus Update: FDA and FTC Warn Seven Companies Selling Fraudulent Products that Claim to Treat or Prevent COVID-19," *FDA*, March 9, 2020, https://www.fda.gov/news-events/press-announcements/coronavirus-update-fda-and-ftc-warn-seven-companies-selling-fraudulent-products-claim-treat-or. White House, "Remarks by President Trump, Vice President Pence, and Members of the Coronavirus Task Force in Press Briefing," *White House*, April 23, 2020, https://www.whitehouse.gov/briefings-statements/remarks-president-trump-vice-president-pence-members-coronavirus-task-force-press-briefing-31/.

16. Defoe, *A Journal of the Plague Year*, 129 and 212–13, censures both the ministers of religion (and medicine) who fled their duties and the parishioners who defied the risks of gathering together:

> there were some people who, notwithstanding the danger, did not omit publicly to attend the worship of God, even in the most dangerous times; and though it is true that a great many clergyman did shut up their churches, and fled, as other people did, for the safety of their lives, yet all did not do so. Some ventured to officiate and to keep up the assemblies of the people by constant prayers, and sometimes sermons or brief exhortations to repentance and reformation, and this as long as any would come to hear them.

And:

> the people were brought into a condition to despair of life and abandon themselves, so this very thing had a strange effect among us for three or four weeks; that is, it made them bold and venturous, they were no more shy of one another, or restrained within doors, but went anywhere and everywhere, and began to converse. . . . As it brought the people into public company, so it was surprising how it brought them to crowd into the churches. They inquired no more into whom they sat near to or far from, what offensive smells they met with, or what condition the people seemed to be in, but looking upon themselves all as so many dead corpses, they come to the churches without the least caution, and crowded together, as if their lives were of no consequence compared to the work which they came about there.

17. "[M]en went about apparently well many days after they had the taint of the disease in their vitals, and after their spirits were so seized as that they could never escape it, and that all the while they did so they were dangerous to others." Defoe, *A Journal of the Plague Year*, 241.

18. National Center for Immunization and Respiratory Diseases (NCIRD), "1918 Pandemic (H1N1 Virus)," *Centers for Disease Control and Prevention*, March 20, 2019, https://www.cdc.gov/flu/pandemic-resources/1918-pandemic-h1n1.html, ¶1.

19. Likewise, we (should) have learned from our social and political responses to HIV in the 1980s, which included stigmatizing the gay community, delaying experimental treatments, and undermining comprehensive sex education that teaches behavioral changes to mitigate the spread of the disease.

20. Patrick R. Saunders-Hastings and Daniel Krewski, "Reviewing the History of Pandemic Influenza: Understanding Patterns of Emergence and Transmission," *Pathogens* 5, no. 4 (December 2016): 66, doi:10.3390/pathogens5040066, ¶2–3 under "6. 1957–1958: Asian Flu."

21. Although the disease was being tracked on a global scale, "expertise and methodological rigour were still lacking in this area." Saunders-Hastings and Krewski, "Reviewing the History of Pandemic Influenza," ¶4 under "6. 1957–1958: Asian Flu."

22. Laurie Garrett and others have incorrectly stated that, in 1969, Surgeon General William H. Stewart told Congress, "It is time to close the book on infectious diseases, and declare the war against pestilence won." However, "the primary source for the quote has never been identified," and "Dr. Stewart unequivocally recognized that infections would always remain an important problem, and that 'maintenance of a vigilant effort . . . will always be required'." Brad Spellberg and Bonnie Taylor-Blake, "On the Exoneration of Dr. William H. Stewart: Debunking an Urban Legend," *Infectious Diseases of Poverty* 2, no. 1 (February 2013): 3, doi:10.1186/2049-9957-2-3, ¶1 under "Background" and ¶9 under "The Seeds of an Urban Legend." That said, a general shift in cultural ideas about U.S. disease burdens occurred in the latter half of the twentieth century, with a greater focus on chronic illnesses such as heart disease and diabetes.

23. Paul Starr, *The Social Transformation of American Medicine: The Rise of a Sovereign Profession and the Making of a Vast Industry* (New York, NY: Basic Books, 1982).

24. That said, prevention, testing, and tracing do require a well-funded workforce. One estimate calls for "approximately 100,000 (paid or volunteer) contact tracers" and "$3.6 billion in emergency funding to state and territorial health departments." Crystal Watson, Anita Cicero, James Blumenstock, and Michael Fraser, "A National Plan to Enable Comprehensive COVID-19 Case Finding and Contact Tracing in the US," *Johns Hopkins Center for Health Security*, April 10, 2020, https://www.centerforhealthsecurity.org/our-work/pubs_archive/pubs-pdfs/2020/200410-national-plan-to-contact-tracing.pdf, 3.

25. Nick Heil, *Dark Summit: The True Story of Everest's Most Controversial Season* (New York, NY: Holt Paperbacks, 2008), 250.

26. Krakauer, *Into Thin Air*, 213.

27. See *Everest: Beyond the Limit*, season 1, episode 6, "The Final Cost," produced by Dick Colthurst and Tomi Landis, aired December 19, 2006, on the Discovery Channel, for a discussion of how difficult it is to save climbers (alive or dead) and endnote 65 for an example of how Krakauer was unable to help his companions in need.

28. Heil, *Dark Summit*, 239. Whether this remains the case, a more thorough search (and one beyond the scope of this paper) is needed. An initial perusal of news sources suggests that this statistic holds.

29. Such armchair Everest quarterbacking can be problematic—judging from afar climbers bundled from head to toe against the cold and UV light who commonly stop and rest on the way up and down, often speak different languages, and suffer from hypoxia. It can be difficult to know when someone truly is in need. Those in this situation may not even know it themselves.

30. Heil, *Dark Summit*, 4.

31. Elements of a report by the Japanese team cited in Rachel Nuwer, "The Tragic Tale of Mt Everest's Most Famous Dead Body," *BBC Future*, October 8, 2015, https://www.bbc.com/future/article/20151008-the-tragic-story-of-mt-everests-most-famous-dead-body, ¶6 under "Ethics at 8,000m." It should be noted that this is far from the only instance where supposedly healthy climbers failed to help others in need or have expressed the same ethos. For examples on Everest and other peaks, see Michael Kodas, *High Crimes: The Fate of Everest in an Age of Greed* (New York, NY: Hyperion, 2008), and *Everest: Beyond the Limit*, season 2, episode 3, "Judgment Day," produced by Dick Colthurst and Tomi Landis, aired November 13, 2007, on the Discovery Channel. In the latter, British climber David Tait—who fundraises to help abused children—says that, should an errant team member require aid at Camp IV or above, he would like to just step over him.

32. Jack Simmons, personal communication, May 15, 2020. Some wrestlers also have engaged in "social distancing" matches during the coronavirus pandemic. Oliver Browning, "WWE News: Wrestlers Are Having 'Social Distancing Matches' and the Results Are Brilliant," *GiveMeSport*, March 23, 2020, https://www.givemesport.com/1557209-wwe-news-wrestlers-are-having-social-distancing-matches-and-the-results-are-brilliant.

33. Aitor Hernández-Morales, "Germany Confirms That Trump Tried to Buy Firm Working on Coronavirus Vaccine: CureVac Boss Was at the White House Last

Week to Discuss Its Vaccines Plans," *Politico*, March 15, 2020, updated March 19, 2020, https://www.politico.eu/article/germany-confirms-that-donald-trump-tried-to-buy-firm-working-on-coronavirus-vaccine/, ¶1–2. But, cf., Hans Von Der Burchard, "German Firm Insists Trump Didn't Try to Buy Coronavirus Vaccine: Pharma Company Contradicts Both German Government and Its Main Investor," *Politico*, March 17, 2020, updated March 18, 2020, https://www.politico.eu/article/trump-coronavirus-vaccine-germany-curevac/, and Phil Taylor, "Did Trump Offer CureVac $1bn for COVID-19 Vaccine Rights? Media Reports Claim Trump Administration Tried to Secure Exclusive Rights," *PMLive*, March 16, 2020, http://www.pmlive.com/pharma_news/did_trump_offer_curevac_$1bn_for_covid-19_vaccine_rights_1329233, ¶6: "Some German lawmakers dismissed the claims as electioneering by Trump, while the official US line is that the case has been exaggerated and the government has been negotiating with dozens of companies around the world working on COVID-19 vaccines, many of whom have been granted federal seed funding."

34. This is not a good idea for many reasons, least of all that the Constitution does not allow it. Amber Phillips, "Why Congress Probably Isn't Going to Let States Go Bankrupt," *The Washington Post*, April 30, 2020, https://www.washingtonpost.com/politics/2020/04/30/state-bankruptcy/.

35. Zolan Kanno-Youngs and Jack Nicas, "'Swept Up by FEMA': Complicated Medical Supply System Sows Confusion," *The New York Times*, April 6, 2020, https://www.nytimes.com/2020/04/06/us/politics/coronavirus-fema-medical-supplies.html.

36. Molly Ball, "Trump Told America's Governors They Were on Their Own. So Maryland's Larry Hogan Is Taking Charge," *Time*, April 30, 2020, https://time.com/5829777/governors-reopening-coronavirus/.

37. "'He didn't understand too much about what was going on,' Trump said of Hogan on April 20" in relation to federal testing capacity. Ball, "Trump Told America's Governors They Were on Their Own," ¶25.

38. Amy Brittain, Isaac Stanley-Becker, and Nick Miroff, "White House's Pandemic Relief Effort Project Airbridge Is Swathed in Secrecy and Exaggerations," *The Washington Post*, May 8, 2020, https://www.washingtonpost.com/investigations/white-house-pandemic-supply-project-swathed-in-secrecy-and-exaggerations/2020/05/08/9c77efb2-8d52-11ea-a9c0-73b93422d691_story.html, ¶5.

39. Stephanie Mencimer, "Jared Kushner Had One Job: Solve America's Supply Crisis. He Helped Private Companies Instead," *Mother Jones*, May 20, 2020, https://www.motherjones.com/politics/2020/05/jared-kushner-had-one-job-solve-americas-supply-crisis-he-helped-private-companies-instead/.

40. It is evident, whether one reads books about Everest climbs or views television programs, that a lack of coordination between teams and lax regulations put people and limbs at risk. *Everest: Beyond the Limit*, "The Final Cost."

41. Quint Forgey, "Strategic National Stockpile Description Altered Online After Kushner's Remarks," *Politico*, April 3, 2020, https://www.politico.com/news/2020/04/03/strategic-national-stockpile-description-altered-after-kushners-remarks-163181.

42. White House, "Remarks by President Trump, Vice President Pence, and Members of the Coronavirus Task Force in Press Briefing," *White House*, April 3,

2020, https://www.whitehouse.gov/briefings-statements/remarks-president-trump-vice-president-pence-members-coronavirus-task-force-press-briefing-17/, ¶506.

43. Thanks to a reviewer for this insight (and several of those that follow) and the suggestion to further analyze Kushner's statement and President Trump's response.

44. Transcribed from the video of Trump's press briefing associated with Phil Thomas, "Coronavirus: Trump Hits Out at 'Nasty' Question Over Jared Kushner's Stockpile Gaffe," *The Independent*, April 4, 2020, https://www.independent.co.uk/news/world/americas/us-politics/trump-coronavirus-jared-kushner-stockpile-question-a9447366.html.

45. The original language on the Strategic National Stockpile's website. Cited in Forgey, "Strategic National Stockpile Description Altered," ¶3–4.

46. Trump cited in Thomas, "Coronavirus: Trump Hits Out at 'Nasty' Question," ¶9.

47. Mencimer, "Jared Kushner Had One Job," ¶4.

48. On the other hand, Trump turns real people into fake persons to deny information leaking from the White House. In the April 3 Coronavirus Task Force briefing, a reporter states that "unnamed White House officials have described [Kushner's] role as being something of running a shadow task force" behind that of Vice President Pence. While Kushner responds that these sources are "probably not informed as to what's going on," Trump interrupts to say, "Or they don't exist. . . . They're fake persons, okay? A lot of fake sources out there. They don't exist." These "fake persons," who are very likely real, are not to be believed, while the very unreal "our" should be. White House, "Coronavirus Task Force in Press Briefing," April 3, 2020, ¶512–18.

49. Wesley Newcomb Hohfeld, *Fundamental Legal Conceptions as Applied in Judicial Reasoning* (Union, NJ: The Lawbook Exchange, Ltd., 2002).

50. Cited in Manny Fernandez, "Conservatives Fuel Protests Against Coronavirus Lockdowns," *The New York Times*, April 18, 2020, https://www.nytimes.com/2020/04/18/us/texas-protests-stay-at-home.html, ¶9.

51. Holly Yan, "Protests Erupt Again Over Coronavirus Shelter-in-Place Orders. Here's Why Some Governors Aren't Budging," *CNN*, April 20, 2020, https://www.cnn.com/2020/04/20/us/protests-coronavirus-stay-at-home-orders/index.html, ¶13–14.

52. Ibram X. Kendi, "We're Still Living and Dying in the Slaveholders' Republic: The Pandemic Has Brought the Latest Battle in the Long American War Over Communal Well-Being," *The Atlantic*, May 4, 2020, https://www.theatlantic.com/ideas/archive/2020/05/what-freedom-means-trump/611083/.

53. Thomas Hobbes, *Leviathan* (Cambridge: Cambridge University Press, 1904), 84. Additionally, in Hobbes' contract theory and most concepts of democracy, there is no inherent "right" to disobey the law; not performing the contract is defined as "unjust." The notion of "civil disobedience" entails consciously accepting the consequences of defying whatever law(s) with which one disagrees and thus returning to a "state of war." "It is not freedom from legal restrictions," per se, "but accepting that the penalty is less onerous than compliance" (with thanks to a reviewer for these additions).

54. Hohfeld, *Fundamental Legal Conceptions*, 26.

55. A principle applied in law and health care that a state or medical authority should prioritize whatever intervention achieves the desired end(s) with the least possible infringement on an individual's liberties. See *Shelton v. Tucker*, 364 U.S. 479 (1960) and Mark R. Munetz and Jeffrey L. Geller, "The Least Restrictive Alternative in the Postinstitutional Era," *Hospital and Community Psychiatry* 44, no. 10 (October 1993): 967–73.

56. Tweet cited in Ann Schmidt, "Costco's Coronavirus Mask Policy Sparks Backlash on Social Media: Costco Created the Policy in Alignment With CDC Guidelines," *Fox Business*, May 7, 2020, https://www.foxbusiness.com/lifestyle/costco-coronavirus-mask-policy-backlash.

57. James Bartholomew, "Easy Virtue: Want to Be Virtuous? Saying the Right Things Violently on Twitter Is Much Easier Than Real Kindness," *The Spectator*, April 18, 2015, https://www.spectator.co.uk/article/easy-virtue.

58. See Stacy G. Ulbig, "Dealing With the Devil: Objectification of Counter-Partisans and Political Compromise," in *The Twenty-First Century and Its Discontents: How Changing Discourse Norms Are Changing Culture*, ed. by Jack Simmons, 167–203 (Lanham, MD: Lexington Books, 2020) in this volume regarding the vitriol between in-groups and out-groups.

59. And, in particular, those who are the "first" in some sort of category (e.g., the first ever, the first without supplemental oxygen, the first with no guides, the first with no sight, the first with no legs, etc.). It also is interesting that Sherpas may be overlooked for their feats, despite the fact that some may summit in one day (while transporting equipment and fixing ropes) or more than once in a season. In *Everest: Beyond the Limit*, "Judgment Day," David Tait explains how he intends to be the first person to do a double traverse (summiting once from the south side and turning around to summit again from the north), but then qualifies, "Western person, I mean."

60. Mario Ricca, "Don't Uncover that Face! Covid-19 Masks and the Niqab: Ironic Transfigurations of the ECtHR's Intercultural Blindness," *International Journal for the Semiotics of Law*, published ahead of print, April 30, 2020, doi:10.1007/s11196-020-09703-y.

61. Zack Beauchamp, "The Partisan Culture War Over Masks," *Vox*, May 13, 2020, https://www.vox.com/2020/5/13/21257181/coronavirus-masks-trump-republicans-culture-war.

62. See John Fritze and Michael Collins, "As Trump Touts Increased Production, Coronavirus Swabs Made During His Maine Factory Tour Will Be Tossed in the Trash," *USA Today*, June 5, 2020, https://www.usatoday.com/story/news/politics/2020/06/05/trump-maine-puritan-throw-away-coronavirus-swabs/3153622001/; Melissa Macaya, Maegan Vazquez, Joe Ruiz, and Kyle Blaine, "Trump Holds Rally in Tulsa, Oklahoma," *CNN*, June 21, 2020, https://www.cnn.com/politics/live-news/trump-rally-tulsa-oklahoma/h_f64883b09b329l0d3fb4481c72592309; and Jessica Boehm, "Trump Barely Mentions COVID-19 to Crowd of Mostly Unmasked Supporters in Phoenix," *Arizona Republic*, June 23, 2020, https://www.azcentral.com/story/news/local/phoenix/2020/06/23/phoenix-rally-president-donald-trump-barely-mentions-covid-19-crowd-mostly-unmasked-supporters/3239570001/.

63. Aaron Blake, "Trump's Dumbfounding Refusal to Encourage Wearing Masks," *The Washington Post*, June 25, 2020, https://www.washingtonpost.com/politics/2020/06/25/trumps-dumbfounding-refusal-encourage-wearing-masks/, ¶12.

64. Krakauer, *Into Thin Air*, 245.

65. Ibid. For example, Krakauer recognized too late instances where he could have intervened when Andy Harris "was acting irrationally [at the South Summit] and had plainly slipped well beyond routine hypoxia" or with a fellow climber, Beck Weathers, who lost his eyesight and was waiting in place for Rob Hall to return. Krakauer notes that he and Andy "were very similar in terms of physical ability and technical expertise; had we been climbing together in a nonguided situation as equal partners, it's inconceivable to me that I would have neglected to recognize his plight. . . . The thought never entered my crippled mind that Andy might in fact be in terrible straits—that a guide might urgently need help from me." That evening, Harris went missing, never to be heard from again, and Weathers was twice left for dead despite eventually making it off the mountain. For Weathers' own perspective, see Beck Weathers and Stephen G. Michaud, *Left for Dead: My Journey Home From Everest* (New York, NY: Villard, 2000).

66. Krakauer, *Into Thin Air*, 228. Fixed lines are a safeguard for each climber and also prevent traffic jams by expediting the progress of the various groups trying to summit Everest at the same time.

67. Ibid., 228–29.

68. With today's greater emphasis on team-based care in medicine, this has been changing—although nurses and many allied health professionals still have less capital (in all senses) than doctors. For an evolving understanding of moral distress, see Andrew Jameton, "The Nurse: When Roles and Rules Conflict," *The Hastings Center Report* 7, no. 4 (August 1977): 22–23; Andrew Jameton, *Nursing Practice: The Ethical Issues* (Englewood Cliffs, NJ: Prentice-Hall, 1984); and Andrew Jameton, "A Reflection on Moral Distress in Nursing Together With a Current Application of the Concept," *Journal of Bioethical Inquiry* 10, no. 3 (October 2013): 297–308.

69. Ann B. Hamric, Walter S. Davis, and Marcia Day Childress, "Moral Distress in Health Care Professionals: What Is It and What Can We Do About It?" *Pharos* 69, no. 1 (Winter 2006): 16–23, 18.

70. Ibid.

71. For Krakauer, he was merely trying to be a team player per the rules his leader set; in not speaking up, he didn't fear for his job but, ironically, the lives of his mates, believing the guides knew best. He also was a part of the team through an arrangement with *Outside* magazine and, thus, was in a professional role as a representative of the publication and not (truly) climbing for himself. His job was to tell the story, not to question the approach of Rob Hall, who was a respected and successful mountaineer and Everest guide.

72. Noam Scheiber and Brian M. Rosenthal, "Nurses and Doctors Speaking Out on Safety Now Risk Their Job," *The New York Times*, April 9, 2020, updated April 27, 2020, https://www.nytimes.com/2020/04/09/business/coronavirus-health-workers-speak-out.html, ¶11.

73. Suspended nurse "'Mr. [Adam] Witt is not allowed on property at [Jersey Shore University Medical Center],' the [posted flyer] said, beneath a picture of him looking tired and pained. 'If he is seen on property please contact your supervisor immediately'." Scheiber and Rosenthal, "Nurses and Doctors Speaking Out on Safety Now Risk Their Job," ¶2.

74. Helene Cooper, Eric Schmitt, and Thomas Gibbons-Neff, "Navy May Reinstate Fired Captain to Command of Roosevelt," *The New York Times*, April 15, 2020, https://www.nytimes.com/2020/04/15/us/politics/coronavirus-navy-roosevelt-crozier.html, ¶1.

75. Per his whistleblower complaint. Yasmeen Abutaleb and Laurie McGinley, "Ousted Vaccine Official Alleges He Was Demoted for Prioritizing 'Science and Safety'," *The Washington Post*, May 5, 2020, https://www.washingtonpost.com/health/2020/05/05/rick-bright-hydroxychloroquine-whistleblower-complaint/, ¶1.

76. Dan Diamond, "Ousted Vaccine Expert Battles With Trump Team Over His Abrupt Dismissal," *Politico*, April 22, 2020, https://www.politico.com/news/2020/04/22/hhs-ousts-vaccine-expert-as-covid-19-threat-grows-201642, ¶10. Also, many thanks to another reviewer whose suggestions strengthened the analysis in this section.

77. U.S. Department of State, *Deborah L. Birx, M.D.*, U.S. Department of State, no date, https://www.state.gov/biographies/deborah-l-birx-md/, ¶1.

78. White House, "Remarks by President Trump," ¶106 and ¶108.

79. Cited in Madeleine Carlisle, "'When He Gets New Information, He Likes to Talk That Through Out Loud,' Dr. Birx Says of Trump's Comments on Ultraviolet Light, Disinfectants as COVID-19 Treatments," *Time*, April 25, 2020, https://time.com/5827448/birx-trump-disinfectant-sunlight/, ¶2. Birx also admonished the press for not moving on: "It bothers me that this is still in the news cycle, because I think we're missing the bigger pieces of what we need to be doing as an American people to continue to protect one another." Cited in Connor O'Brien, "'It Bothers Me That This Is Still in the News Cycle,' Birx Says of Trump's Disinfectant and Light Comments," *Politico*, April 26, 2020, https://www.politico.com/news/2020/04/26/birx-trump-disinfectant-coronavirus-209063, ¶5.

80. Helene Cooper, "Milley Apologizes for Role in Trump Photo Op: 'I Should Not Have Been There'," *The New York Times*, June 11, 2020, updated June 12, 2020, https://www.nytimes.com/2020/06/11/us/politics/trump-milley-military-protests-lafayette-square.html, ¶2, ¶10, ¶12, and ¶14. Defense Secretary Mark Esper also broke with Trump over the incident. Ryan Pickrell, "Defense Secretary Mark Esper Says He 'Didn't Know' Where He Was Going When He Walked With Trump Through a Park Aggressively Cleared of Protesters Moments Before," *Business Insider*, June 2, 2020, https://www.businessinsider.com/esper-says-didnt-know-about-trump-church-photo-op-plans-2020-6.

81. In Discovery's *Everest: Beyond the Limit*, most of the clients who are a part of Russell Brice's commercial team talk about how climbing Everest is

a lifelong "dream." While doing so does take physical and mental endurance, this highlights a Western individualist perspective where a goal that primarily serves oneself, requires significant financial wherewithal, and creates more negative than positive externalities trumps other purposes that could have a greater impact.

82. Cathy O'Dowd cited in Heil, *Dark Summit*, 167–68, who added, "Don't pillory my companions for my choices."

83. Heil, *Dark Summit*, 243. In 2019, new rules also were proposed in Nepal's parliament that would require climbers and guides to have a certain level of experience in order to be eligible for a permit. Bhadra Sharma and Kai Schultz, "New Everest Rules Could Significantly Limit Who Gets to Climb," *The New York Times*, August 14, 2019, https://www.nytimes.com/2019/08/14/world/asia/everest-climbing-rules.html.

84. See Kodas's discussion in *High Crimes*, 332–33, of the poverty in the regions around Everest and the shooting of Tibetan refugees fleeing to Nepal via the Nangpa La Pass.

85. Ed Yong, "America's Patchwork Pandemic Is Fraying Even Further," *The Atlantic*, May 20, 2020, https://www.theatlantic.com/health/archive/2020/05/patchwork-pandemic-states-reopening-inequalities/611866/.

86. Trump cited in Philip Bump, "What Trump Did About Coronavirus in February: For the Most Part, He Downplayed the Threat," *The Washington Post*, April 20, 2020, https://www.washingtonpost.com/politics/2020/04/20/what-trump-did-about-coronavirus-february/, ¶2 under "Feb. 10."

87. Ezra Klein, "The President's Job Is to Manage Risk. But Trump Is the Risk. Trump Was a Gamble. It's Not Paying Off," *Vox*, May 18, 2020, https://www.vox.com/2020/5/18/21251370/donald-trump-risk-coronavirus-2020-reelection-nuclear-china, ¶6.

88. This is not to say that public health and health care funding should only be based on their economic impact, just that something is needed to overcome the U.S. lobbying-based inertia that has gotten us here (since human well-being and various other arguments haven't done the trick).

89. Li Zhou, "'Leave No Vacancy Behind': Mitch McConnell Remains Laser-Focused on Judges Amid Coronavirus," *Vox*, May 4, 2020, https://www.vox.com/2020/5/4/21246313/federal-judges-mitch-mcconnell-senate-coronavirus-pandemic.

90. Cassie Miller, "Protests Against State-Imposed Stay-at-Home Orders Have Exploded Across the Country and Attracted a Wide Array of Right-Wing Supporters, Including the Proud Boys," *Southern Poverty Law Center*, April 27, 2020, https://www.splcenter.org/hatewatch/2020/04/27/anti-lockdown-rallies-are-providing-opening-proud-boys-and-other-far-right-extremists.

91. Laurie Sobel, Amrutha Ramaswamy, Brittni Frederiksen, and Alina Salganicoff, "State Action to Limit Abortion Access During the COVID-19 Pandemic," *Kaiser Family Foundation*, May 1, 2020, https://www.kff.org/womens-health-policy/issue-brief/state-action-to-limit-abortion-access-during-the-covid-19-pandemic/.

92. Texas Lieutenant Governor Dan Patrick cited in Doha Madani, "Dan Patrick on Coronavirus: 'More Important Things Than Living'," *NBC News*, April 21, 2020, https://www.nbcnews.com/news/us-news/texas-lt-gov-dan-patrick-reopening-economy-more-important-things-n1188911, ¶3.

93. Indiana Representative Trey Hollingsworth cited in the subtitle of Dennis Romero, "Indiana Congressman Says He's Willing to Let More Americans Die to Save Economy," *NBC News*, April 14, 2020, https://www.nbcnews.com/news/us-news/indiana-congressman-says-he-s-willing-let-more-americans-die-n1184036. Hollingsworth also stated (in ¶9), "We are going to have to look Americans in the eye and say, 'We are making the best decisions for the most Americans possible,' and the answer to that is to get Americans back to work, to get Americans back to their businesses"—failing to recognize that some women and their partners seek abortions because it is what's best for their families. This especially was the case during the Great Depression, when women were fired from jobs once they became pregnant even if they were the sole breadwinners in their households. See Leslie J. Reagan, *When Abortion Was a Crime: Women, Medicine, and Law in the United States, 1867–1973* (Berkeley, CA: University of California Press, 1997).

94. Kodas, *High Crimes*, 336.

95. Heil, *Dark Summit*, 234–35.

96. Sir Edmund Hillary, who was the first to summit Everest with Tenzing Norgay on May 29, 1953, has said that "[h]uman life is far more important than just getting to the top of a mountain. . . . It [is] wrong, if there [is] a man suffering altitude problems and huddled under a rock, just to lift your hat, say 'good morning' and pass on by." Kodas, *High Crimes*, 6 and 318.

97. Heil, *Dark Summit*, 218.

98. Ibid., 219. Sadly, while Dan Mazur and his two clients were crowned heroes, the latter told Mazur they "were 'pissed' at having to turn around, and he didn't think they would hire him as a guide again." Kodas, *High Crimes*, 319. For Hall's take, see Lincoln Hall, *Dead Lucky: Life After Death on Mount Everest* (New York, NY: Penguin, 2007).

99. Escalation of commitment is a bias defined in organizational theory where a leader or "manager continues to allocate more resources to a losing proposition," often because a company and/or its personnel have already sunk so much time and investment that to turn back or "make midcourse corrections" seems wrong. The phrases "in too deep" and "throwing good money after bad" are common notions of this idea. Nancy Borkowski, *Organizational Behavior, Theory, and Design in Health Care*, 2nd edition (Burlington, MA: Jones & Bartlett Learning, 2016), 298–99. As on Everest, doing so can lead to disastrous results, and it typically is more profitable to accept a loss earlier and develop a new path. In *Everest: Beyond the Limit*, "The Final Cost," one climber on Russell Brice's team lost parts of every finger and toe to frostbite, while another—the first person with double-leg amputations to summit—spent six weeks recovering in hospital, where additional tissue had to be removed from his limbs.

100. See Kodas, *High Crimes*, 20, for a description of how one climber and his guide were not willing to retreat even after an experienced Sherpa "had repeatedly

tried to turn the team around." The climber later was left to die on the mountain. Additionally, the cost of a trek varies depending on how much support one desires and which side is used to approach Everest. From Nepal, permits are so expensive that climbers may need such high amounts, while in Tibet, expeditions may run $10,000 or less. As Kodas explains on page 10, the Tibet side has thus been called "the Everest climber's Wal-Mart."

101. For example, Tim Medvetz, who is featured in the first two seasons of *Everest: Beyond the Limit*, underscores more than once that he is paying Russell Brice between $45,000 and $50,000 (his description changes) to climb Everest, while Brice and others remark how Medvetz is frequently late and repeatedly refuses to follow directions. Like the man tweeting about Costco, the intimation here is that Brice works for Medvetz, regardless if Medvetz's actions put others at risk.

102. For example, this enabled one Sherpa "to move his family to Kathmandu and send his two daughters to school." Kodas, *High Crimes*, 18.

103. Ibid., 11.

104. David A. Graham, "Why Trump Was Deaf to All the Warnings He Received: The President's Incuriosity and Paranoia Hobbled His Response," *The Atlantic*, April 29, 2020, https://www.theatlantic.com/ideas/archive/2020/04/how-many-warnings-did-trump-ignore/610846/. For an example of a Trump-like Everest guide, see Kodas, *High Crimes*, 338, and the author's descriptions of Gustavo Lisi, whose self-centered interests and mendacity cost the life of climber Nils Antezana in 2004. (Antezana's own escalation of commitment, however, may have played a role. As Antezana's daughter noted after investigating the guide's lack of experience, "How could [her father's] pride keep him pushing on into such an obvious disaster?")

105. Bob Ortega, Scott Bronstein, Curt Devine, and Drew Griffin, "How the Government Delayed Coronavirus Testing," *CNN*, April 9, 2020, https://www.cnn.com/2020/04/09/politics/coronavirus-testing-cdc-fda-red-tape-invs/index.html. See also Caitlin Oprysko, "'I Don't Take Responsibility at All': Trump Deflects Blame for Coronavirus Testing Fumble," *Politico*, March 13, 2020, https://www.politico.com/news/2020/03/13/trump-coronavirus-testing-128971.

106. Aaron Rupar, "Rudy Giuliani Doesn't Get How Coronavirus Works. Fox News Showcased His Misinformation Anyway," *Vox*, April 24, 2020, https://www.vox.com/2020/4/24/21234340/laura-ingraham-rudy-giuliani-coronavirus-contact-tracing. See also Andrey Simonov, Szymon K. Sacher, Jean-Pierre H. Dubé, and Shirsho Biswas, "The Persuasive Effect of Fox News: Non-Compliance With Social Distancing During the COVID-19 Pandemic," *National Bureau of Economic Research, Working Paper 27237*, May 2020, revised June 2020: 1–67, http://www.nber.org/papers/w27237, and Leonardo Bursztyn, Aakaash Rao, Christopher P. Roth, and David H. Yanagizawa-Drott, "Misinformation During a Pandemic," *National Bureau of Economic Research, Working Paper 27417*, June 2020: 1–116, http://www.nber.org/papers/w27417, who note (on page 1) that Fox News is "the most-watched cable network in the United States."

107. Thanks to a reviewer for this insight.

108. Hegel, *Lectures on the Philosophy of History*, 6.

BIBLIOGRAPHY

Abbey, Edward. *Desert Solitaire: A Season in the Wilderness*. New York, NY: McGraw-Hill, 1968.

Abutaleb, Yasmeen, and Laurie McGinley. "Ousted Vaccine Official Alleges He Was Demoted for Prioritizing 'Science and Safety'." *The Washington Post*, May 5, 2020. https://www.washingtonpost.com/health/2020/05/05/rick-bright-hydroxychloroquine-whistleblower-complaint/.

Ball, Molly. "Trump Told America's Governors They Were on Their Own. So Maryland's Larry Hogan Is Taking Charge." *Time*, April 30, 2020. https://time.com/5829777/governors-reopening-coronavirus/.

Bartholomew, James. "Easy Virtue: Want to Be Virtuous? Saying the Right Things Violently on Twitter Is Much Easier Than Real Kindness." *The Spectator*, April 18, 2015. https://www.spectator.co.uk/article/easy-virtue.

Bastian, Frank. "Defoe's *Journal of the Plague Year* Reconsidered." *The Review of English Studies* 16, no. 62 (May 1965): 151–173.

Beauchamp, Zack. "The Partisan Culture War Over Masks." *Vox*, May 13, 2020. https://www.vox.com/2020/5/13/21257181/coronavirus-masks-trump-republicans-culture-war.

Blake, Aaron. "Trump's Dumbfounding Refusal to Encourage Wearing Masks." *The Washington Post*, June 25, 2020. https://www.washingtonpost.com/politics/2020/06/25/trumps-dumbfounding-refusal-encourage-wearing-masks/.

Boehm, Jessica. "Trump Barely Mentions COVID-19 to Crowd of Mostly Unmasked Supporters in Phoenix." *Arizona Republic*, June 23, 2020. https://www.azcentral.com/story/news/local/phoenix/2020/06/23/phoenix-rally-president-donald-trump-barely-mentions-covid-19-crowd-mostly-unmasked-supporters/3239570001/.

Borkowski, Nancy. *Organizational Behavior, Theory, and Design in Health Care*, 2nd ed. Burlington, MA: Jones & Bartlett Learning, 2016.

Brittain, Amy, Isaac Stanley-Becker, and Nick Miroff. "White House's Pandemic Relief Effort Project Airbridge Is Swathed in Secrecy and Exaggerations." *The Washington Post*, May 8, 2020. https://www.washingtonpost.com/investigations/white-house-pandemic-supply-project-swathed-in-secrecy-and-exaggerations/2020/05/08/9c77efb2-8d52-11ea-a9c0-73b93422d691_story.html.

Browning, Oliver. "WWE News: Wrestlers Are Having 'Social Distancing Matches' and the Results Are Brilliant." *GiveMeSport*, March 23, 2020. https://www.givemesport.com/1557209-wwe-news-wrestlers-are-having-social-distancing-matches-and-the-results-are-brilliant.

Bump, Philip. "What Trump Did About Coronavirus in February: For the Most Part, He Downplayed the Threat." *The Washington Post*, April 20, 2020. https://www.washingtonpost.com/politics/2020/04/20/what-trump-did-about-coronavirus-february/.

Bursztyn, Leonardo, Aakaash Rao, Christopher P. Roth, and David H. Yanagizawa-Drott. "Misinformation During a Pandemic." *National Bureau of Economic Research, Working Paper 27417*, June 2020: 1–116. http://www.nber.org/papers/w27417.

Carlisle, Madeleine. "'When He Gets New Information, He Likes to Talk That Through Out Loud,' Dr. Birx Says of Trump's Comments on Ultraviolet Light, Disinfectants as COVID-19 Treatments." *Time*, April 25, 2020. https://time.com/5827448/birx-trump-disinfectant-sunlight/.

Cooper, Helene. "Milley Apologizes for Role in Trump Photo Op: 'I Should Not Have Been There'." *The New York Times*, June 11, 2020, updated June 12, 2020. https://www.nytimes.com/2020/06/11/us/politics/trump-milley-military-protests-lafayette-square.html.

Cooper, Helene, Eric Schmitt, and Thomas Gibbons-Neff. "Navy May Reinstate Fired Captain to Command of Roosevelt." *The New York Times*, April 15, 2020. https://www.nytimes.com/2020/04/15/us/politics/coronavirus-navy-roosevelt-crozier.html.

Creighton, Charles. *A History of Epidemics in Britain, Vol. 1: From A.D. 664 to the Extinction of Plague*. London: Cambridge University Press, 1891.

Defoe, Daniel. *A Journal of the Plague Year*. London: Cassell and Company, 1909.

Diamond, Dan. "Ousted Vaccine Expert Battles With Trump Team Over His Abrupt Dismissal." *Politico*, April 22, 2020. https://www.politico.com/news/2020/04/22/hhs-ousts-vaccine-expert-as-covid-19-threat-grows-201642.

Dundruk, Master Kungga. "Everest Base Camp Weather: A Detailed Guide to Climate and Weather of Everest Base Camp in Tibet." *Tibet Vista*, November 18, 2019. https://www.tibettravel.org/tibet-travel-advice/climate-and-temperature-of-ebc.html.

Everest: Beyond the Limit. Season 1, episode 6, "The Final Cost." Produced by Dick Colthurst and Tomi Landis. Aired December 19, 2006, on the Discovery Channel.

Everest: Beyond the Limit. Season 2, episode 3, "Judgment Day." Produced by Dick Colthurst and Tomi Landis. Aired November 13, 2007, on the Discovery Channel.

Fernandez, Manny. "Conservatives Fuel Protests Against Coronavirus Lockdowns." *The New York Times*, April 18, 2020. https://www.nytimes.com/2020/04/18/us/texas-protests-stay-at-home.html.

Forgey, Quint. "Strategic National Stockpile Description Altered Online After Kushner's Remarks." *Politico*, April 3, 2020. https://www.politico.com/news/2020/04/03/strategic-national-stockpile-description-altered-after-kushners-remarks-163181.

Fritze, John, and Michael Collins. "As Trump Touts Increased Production, Coronavirus Swabs Made During His Maine Factory Tour Will Be Tossed in the Trash." *USA Today*, June 5, 2020. https://www.usatoday.com/story/news/politics/2020/06/05/trump-maine-puritan-throw-away-coronavirus-swabs/3153622001/.

Garrett, Laurie. *The Coming Plague: Newly Emerging Diseases in a World Out of Balance*. New York, NY: Farrar, Straus and Giroux, 1994.

Graham, David A. "Why Trump Was Deaf to All the Warnings He Received: The President's Incuriosity and Paranoia Hobbled His Response." *The Atlantic*, April 29, 2020. https://www.theatlantic.com/ideas/archive/2020/04/how-many-warnings-did-trump-ignore/610846/.

Hall, Lincoln. *Dead Lucky: Life After Death on Mount Everest*. New York, NY: Penguin, 2007.

Hamric, Ann B., Walter S. Davis, and Marcia Day Childress. "Moral Distress in Health Care Professionals: What Is It and What Can We Do About It?" *Pharos* 69, no. 1 (Winter 2006): 16–23, 18.

Hegel, Georg W. F. *Lectures on the Philosophy of History*, 3rd ed., translated by J. Sibree. London: Henry G. Bohn, 1861.

Heil, Nick. *Dark Summit: The True Story of Everest's Most Controversial Season*. New York, NY: Holt Paperbacks, 2008.

Hernández-Morales, Aitor. "Germany Confirms That Trump Tried to Buy Firm Working on Coronavirus Vaccine: CureVac Boss Was at the White House Last Week to Discuss Its Vaccines Plans." *Politico*, March 15, 2020, updated March 19, 2020. https://www.politico.eu/article/germany-confirms-that-donald-trump-tried-to-buy-firm-working-on-coronavirus-vaccine/.

Hobbes, Thomas. *Leviathan*. Cambridge: Cambridge University Press, 1904.

Hohfeld, Wesley Newcomb. *Fundamental Legal Conceptions as Applied in Judicial Reasoning*. Union, NJ: The Lawbook Exchange, Ltd., 2002.

Jameton, Andrew. "A Reflection on Moral Distress in Nursing Together With a Current Application of the Concept." *Journal of Bioethical Inquiry* 10, no. 3 (October 2013): 297–308.

Jameton, Andrew. *Nursing Practice: The Ethical Issues*. Englewood Cliffs, NJ: Prentice-Hall, 1984.

Jameton, Andrew. "The Nurse: When Roles and Rules Conflict." *The Hastings Center Report* 7, no. 4 (August 1977): 22–23.

Kanno-Youngs, Zolan, and Jack Nicas. "'Swept Up by FEMA': Complicated Medical Supply System Sows Confusion." *The New York Times*, April 6, 2020. https://www.nytimes.com/2020/04/06/us/politics/coronavirus-fema-medical-supplies.html.

Kendi, Ibram X. "We're Still Living and Dying in the Slaveholders' Republic: The Pandemic Has Brought the Latest Battle in the Long American War Over Communal Well-Being." *The Atlantic*, May 4, 2020. https://www.theatlantic.com/ideas/archive/2020/05/what-freedom-means-trump/611083/.

Klein, Ezra. "The President's Job Is to Manage Risk. But Trump Is the Risk. Trump Was a Gamble. It's Not Paying Off." *Vox*, May 18, 2020. https://www.vox.com/2020/5/18/21251370/donald-trump-risk-coronavirus-2020-reelection-nuclear-china.

Kodas, Michael. *High Crimes: The Fate of Everest in an Age of Greed*. New York, NY: Hyperion, 2008.

Krakauer, Jon. *Into Thin Air: A Personal Account of the Mount Everest Disaster*. New York, NY: Anchor Books, 1998.

Macaya, Melissa, Maegan Vazquez, Joe Ruiz, and Kyle Blaine. "Trump Holds Rally in Tulsa, Oklahoma." *CNN*, June 21, 2020. https://www.cnn.com/politics/live-news/trump-rally-tulsa-oklahoma/h_f64883b09b32910d3fb4481c72592309.

Madani, Doha. "Dan Patrick on Coronavirus: 'More Important Things Than Living'." *NBC News*, April 21, 2020. https://www.nbcnews.com/news/us-news/texas-lt-gov-dan-patrick-reopening-economy-more-important-things-n1188911.

Mencimer, Stephanie. "Jared Kushner Had One Job: Solve America's Supply Crisis. He Helped Private Companies Instead." *Mother Jones*, May 20, 2020. https://ww

w.motherjones.com/politics/2020/05/jared-kushner-had-one-job-solve-americas-supply-crisis-he-helped-private-companies-instead/.

Miller, Cassie. "Protests Against State-Imposed Stay-at-Home Orders Have Exploded Across the Country and Attracted a Wide Array of Right-Wing Supporters, Including the Proud Boys." *Southern Poverty Law Center*, April 27, 2020. https://www.splcenter.org/hatewatch/2020/04/27/anti-lockdown-rallies-are-providing-opening-proud-boys-and-other-far-right-extremists.

Munetz, Mark R., and Jeffrey L. Geller. "The Least Restrictive Alternative in the Postinstitutional Era." *Hospital and Community Psychiatry* 44, no. 10 (October 1993): 967–973.

National Center for Immunization and Respiratory Diseases (NCIRD). "1918 Pandemic (H1N1 Virus)." *Centers for Disease Control and Prevention*, March 20, 2019. https://www.cdc.gov/flu/pandemic-resources/1918-pandemic-h1n1.html.

Nuwer, Rachel. "The Tragic Tale of Mt Everest's Most Famous Dead Body." *BBC Future*, October 8, 2015. https://www.bbc.com/future/article/20151008-the-tragic-story-of-mt-everests-most-famous-dead-body.

O'Brien, Connor. "'It Bothers Me That This Is Still in the News Cycle,' Birx Says of Trump's Disinfectant and Light Comments." *Politico*, April 26, 2020. https://www.politico.com/news/2020/04/26/birx-trump-disinfectant-coronavirus-209063.

Oprysko, Caitlin. "'I Don't Take Responsibility at All': Trump Deflects Blame for Coronavirus Testing Fumble." *Politico*, March 13, 2020. https://www.politico.com/news/2020/03/13/trump-coronavirus-testing-128971.

Ortega, Bob, Scott Bronstein, Curt Devine, and Drew Griffin. "How the Government Delayed Coronavirus Testing." *CNN*, April 9, 2020. https://www.cnn.com/2020/04/09/politics/coronavirus-testing-cdc-fda-red-tape-invs/index.html.

O'Toole, Fintan. "The Lie That Poverty Is a Moral Failing Was Buried a Century Ago. Now It's Back." *The Guardian*, October 18, 2017. https://www.theguardian.com/commentisfree/2017/oct/18/george-bernard-shaw-poverty-moral-myth.

Phillips, Amber. "Why Congress Probably Isn't Going to Let States Go Bankrupt." *The Washington Post*, April 30, 2020. https://www.washingtonpost.com/politics/2020/04/30/state-bankruptcy/.

Pickrell, Ryan. "Defense Secretary Mark Esper Says He 'Didn't Know' Where He Was Going When He Walked With Trump Through a Park Aggressively Cleared of Protesters Moments Before." *Business Insider*, June 2, 2020. https://www.businessinsider.com/esper-says-didnt-know-about-trump-church-photo-op-plans-2020-6.

Plato. *Cratylus*, translated by C. D. C. Reeve. Indianapolis, IN and Cambridge: Hackett Publishing Company, Inc., 1998.

Reagan, Leslie J. *When Abortion Was a Crime: Women, Medicine, and Law in the United States, 1867–1973*. Berkeley, CA: University of California Press, 1997.

Reynolds, Barbara, Julia Hunter Galdo, and Lynn Sokler. *Crisis and Emergency Risk Communication*. Atlanta, GA: Centers for Disease Control and Prevention, 2002.

Ricca, Mario. "Don't Uncover that Face! Covid-19 Masks and the Niqab: Ironic Transfigurations of the ECtHR's Intercultural Blindness." *International Journal for the Semiotics of Law*, published ahead of print, April 30, 2020. doi:10.1007/s11196-020-09703-y.

Romero, Dennis. "Indiana Congressman Says He's Willing to Let More Americans Die to Save Economy." *NBC News*, April 14, 2020. https://www.nbcnews.com/news/us-news/indiana-congressman-says-he-s-willing-let-more-americans-die-n1184036.

Rupar, Aaron. "Rudy Giuliani Doesn't Get How Coronavirus Works. Fox News Showcased His Misinformation Anyway." *Vox*, April 24, 2020. https://www.vox.com/2020/4/24/21234340/laura-ingraham-rudy-giuliani-coronavirus-contact-tracing.

Saunders-Hastings, Patrick R., and Daniel Krewski. "Reviewing the History of Pandemic Influenza: Understanding Patterns of Emergence and Transmission." *Pathogens* 5, no. 4 (December 2016): 66. doi:10.3390/pathogens5040066.

Scheiber, Noam, and Brian M. Rosenthal. "Nurses and Doctors Speaking Out on Safety Now Risk Their Job." *The New York Times*, April 9, 2020, updated April 27, 2020. https://www.nytimes.com/2020/04/09/business/coronavirus-health-workers-speak-out.html.

Schmidt, Ann. "Costco's Coronavirus Mask Policy Sparks Backlash on Social Media: Costco Created the Policy in Alignment With CDC Guidelines." *Fox Business*, May 7, 2020. https://www.foxbusiness.com/lifestyle/costco-coronavirus-mask-policy-backlash.

Schwartz, Thomas F. "Lincoln Never Said That." *For the People* 1, no. 1 (Spring 1999): 4–6. http://www.abrahamlincolnassociation.org/Newsletters/1-1.pdf.

Sharma, Bhadra, and Kai Schultz. "New Everest Rules Could Significantly Limit Who Gets to Climb." *The New York Times*, August 14, 2019. https://www.nytimes.com/2019/08/14/world/asia/everest-climbing-rules.html.

Shaw, George Bernard. *Major Barbara*. Auckland: The Floating Press, 2009.

Simonov, Andrey, Szymon K. Sacher, Jean-Pierre H. Dubé, and Shirsho Biswas. "The Persuasive Effect of Fox News: Non-Compliance With Social Distancing During the COVID-19 Pandemic." *National Bureau of Economic Research, Working Paper 27237*, May 2020, revised June 2020: 1–67. http://www.nber.org/papers/w27237.

Slavsky, Bennett. "How Climate Change is Making Mount Everest More Dangerous: Though Overcrowding Was a Deadly Factor on Mount Everest This Year, Climate Change Might Prove More Devastating in the Long Run." *Climbing*, May 29, 2019. https://www.climbing.com/news/climate-change-on-mount-everest-old-bodies-and-new/.

Sobel, Laurie, Amrutha Ramaswamy, Brittni Frederiksen, and Alina Salganicoff. "State Action to Limit Abortion Access During the COVID-19 Pandemic." *Kaiser Family Foundation*, May 1, 2020. https://www.kff.org/womens-health-policy/issue-brief/state-action-to-limit-abortion-access-during-the-covid-19-pandemic/.

Spellberg, Brad, and Bonnie Taylor-Blake. "On the Exoneration of Dr. William H. Stewart: Debunking an Urban Legend." *Infectious Diseases of Poverty* 2, no. 1 (February 2013): 3. doi:10.1186/2049-9957-2-3.

Starr, Paul. *The Social Transformation of American Medicine: The Rise of a Sovereign Profession and the Making of a Vast Industry*. New York, NY: Basic Books, 1982.

Taylor, Phil. "Did Trump Offer CureVac $1bn for COVID-19 Vaccine Rights? Media Reports Claim Trump Administration Tried to Secure Exclusive Rights." *PMLive*, March 16, 2020. http://www.pmlive.com/pharma_news/did_trump_offer_curevac_$1bn_for_covid-19_vaccine_rights_1329233.

The Associated Press. "Khumbu Icefall: Unsteady & Deadly." *The Denver Post*, April 22, 2014, updated April 27, 2016. https://www.denverpost.com/2014/04/22/khumbu-icefall-unsteady-deadly/.

Thomas, Phil. "Coronavirus: Trump Hits Out at 'Nasty' Question Over Jared Kushner's Stockpile Gaffe." *The Independent*, April 4, 2020. https://www.independent.co.uk/news/world/americas/us-politics/trump-coronavirus-jared-kushner-stockpile-question-a9447366.html.

Ulbig, Stacy G. "Dealing With the Devil: Objectification of Counter-Partisans and Political Compromise." In *The Twenty-First Century and Its Discontents: How Changing Discourse Norms Are Changing Culture*, edited by Jack Simmons, 167–203. Lanham, MD: Lexington Books, 2020.

U.S. Department of State. *Deborah L. Birx, M.D.* U.S. Department of State, no date. https://www.state.gov/biographies/deborah-l-birx-md/.

U.S. Food and Drug Administration. "Coronavirus Update: FDA and FTC Warn Seven Companies Selling Fraudulent Products that Claim to Treat or Prevent COVID-19." *FDA*, March 9, 2020. https://www.fda.gov/news-events/press-announcements/coronavirus-update-fda-and-ftc-warn-seven-companies-selling-fraudulent-products-claim-treat-or.

Von Der Burchard, Hans. "German Firm Insists Trump Didn't Try to Buy Coronavirus Vaccine: Pharma Company Contradicts Both German Government and Its Main Investor." *Politico*, March 17, 2020, updated March 18, 2020. https://www.politico.eu/article/trump-coronavirus-vaccine-germany-curevac/.

Watson, Crystal, Anita Cicero, James Blumenstock, and Michael Fraser. "A National Plan to Enable Comprehensive COVID-19 Case Finding and Contact Tracing in the US." *Johns Hopkins Center for Health Security*, April 10, 2020. https://www.centerforhealthsecurity.org/our-work/pubs_archive/pubs-pdfs/2020/200410-national-plan-to-contact-tracing.pdf.

Weathers, Beck, and Stephen G. Michaud. *Left for Dead: My Journey Home from Everest*. New York, NY: Villard, 2000.

White House. "Remarks by President Trump, Vice President Pence, and Members of the Coronavirus Task Force in Press Briefing." *White House*, April 3, 2020. https://www.whitehouse.gov/briefings-statements/remarks-president-trump-vice-president-pence-members-coronavirus-task-force-press-briefing-17/.

White House. "Remarks by President Trump, Vice President Pence, and Members of the Coronavirus Task Force in Press Briefing." *White House*, April 23, 2020. https://www.whitehouse.gov/briefings-statements/remarks-president-trump-vice-president-pence-members-coronavirus-task-force-press-briefing-31/.

Yan, Holly. "Protests Erupt Again Over Coronavirus Shelter-in-Place Orders. Here's Why Some Governors Aren't Budging." *CNN*, April 20, 2020. https://www.cnn.com/2020/04/20/us/protests-coronavirus-stay-at-home-orders/index.html.

Yong, Ed. "America's Patchwork Pandemic Is Fraying Even Further." *The Atlantic*, May 20, 2020. https://www.theatlantic.com/health/archive/2020/05/patchwork-pandemic-states-reopening-inequalities/611866/.

Zhou, Li. "'Leave No Vacancy Behind': Mitch McConnell Remains Laser-Focused on Judges Amid Coronavirus." *Vox*, May 4, 2020. https://www.vox.com/2020/5/4/21246313/federal-judges-mitch-mcconnell-senate-coronavirus-pandemic.

Chapter 9

Strategic Discourse in the Time of the Coronavirus

Robert Gressis

Since January of 2020, I've seen a lot of insincerity. Don't get me wrong, insincerity is part of the warp and woof of humanity, but never before have I seen groups of people, credentialed experts, institutional agents, and representatives of political movements, act so much like schools of fish, turning *en masse* on a dime. Every week, it seems, offers us a new Molotov-Ribbentrop pact.

This is the time of the coronavirus. The coronavirus has revealed deep problems in American institutions, so, not surprisingly, those institutions try to defend themselves, pass the buck, make strategic alliances, and, well, lie. Thus, though the problems with our institutions run far deeper than in how they express themselves, it's also true that how they express themselves—their discourse—reveals important truths about them.

In this chapter, I'm going to discuss discourse in the time of the coronavirus.

COMMUNICATIVE AND STRATEGIC DISCOURSE

As background, though, I begin with an explanation of how I understand two designations: "communicative discourse" and "strategic discourse."

Roughly, "communicative discourse" is discourse aimed at communicating or understanding the truth, independent of the consequences, while "strategic discourse" is discourse aimed at bringing about certain consequences, independent of the truth. I cannot give necessary and sufficient conditions for strategic and communicative discourse, any more than I can for any concept that emerges from ordinary language or reflections thereupon. However, I offer an example to render the contrast intuitive.

Imagine you're my student and you ask me why your paper got a "B." I ask you, "why are you asking me this?" and you reply, "because I want to know how to improve my work in the future." If you genuinely want to understand how to improve your future work, then you're engaging in communicative discourse with me. Alternatively, if you don't care at all about how to improve your performance, but just want a higher grade, then you're engaging in strategic discourse.

The rest of our conversation will reveal to me (and perhaps even to you) which kind of discourse you're engaging in. If, during the rest of the conversation, you don't ask for a higher grade (or even ask for a lower grade, on the grounds you think that you didn't meet my "B" standards), then you were probably engaging in communicative discourse all along. But if this meeting turns into a protracted argument where it becomes clear to me that you will use any tool in your argumentative arsenal to get yourself a higher grade (e.g., by appealing to principles that I know you reject in other contexts), then you were probably engaging in strategic discourse all along.

With that out of the way, let's talk about discourse in the time of the coronavirus.

THE POLITICAL LANDSCAPE

If you want to understand when and how someone engages in strategic discourse, you have to have a sense of their aims. Unless you know what they'd like to bring about, you won't be able to understand what their strategies are or when they are employing them. That's why I begin with politics.

Broadly speaking, there are four "teams" dominating the American political landscape: on the right, there are populists and libertarians, and on the left, progressives and technocrats. Each of these teams contains multitudes,[1] but I'm going to oversimplify for ease of exposition.

As populists see things, there is an elite class in the United States that forms part of a larger, "globalist" class. These people go to the same selective schools and universities, work in similar kinds of (mostly intellectual or white collar) jobs, marry each other, and have a great deal of authority over the culture at large.[2] These shared experiences give rise to a shared, cosmopolitan culture, such that a member of this elite who was born and raised in Boston and went to Princeton would have more in common with a Frenchman born and raised in Marseilles who went to the Sorbonne than she would with a plumber born and raised in Boston who went to a trade school.

Because this global elite both shares a worldwide culture and has authority over the direction their nation's institutions take, they drive those institutions to benefit themselves at the expense of their native populations. They favor free trade, open borders, lower taxes, international financial institutions, and so on, not for their stated reasons (e.g., that free trade and open borders massively improve the prospects of the world's poorest people), but rather because these policies end up enriching the globalists themselves. Overall, then, populists see the world as us-versus-them: globalists versus natives.

There are two kinds of libertarians: rugged individualists who don't like being told what to do and want as much freedom from government interference as possible (think: Ron Swanson from *Parks and Recreation*), and intellectuals who strongly value negative liberty and who believe both that society is too complex to benefit much from expert guidance while also believing that spontaneous orders arising in market contexts will tend to produce the best solutions to social problems. Whereas the former will share a lot of overlap with the populists (populists don't like *globalists* telling them what to do; rugged individualists don't like *anyone* telling them what to do), the latter are themselves of that globalist class whom the populists hate.

Progressives think that American society is fundamentally kyriarchical: it is racist, sexist, homophobic, transphobic, classist, ableist, you name it. Consequently, many of its institutions—the police, military, and legal and financial systems—are tainted to their core. Progressives, like populists, have a distrust of many institutional authorities, but unlike populists, progressives have a high opinion of certain institutions, namely academia and the media (progressivism's idea-generators and -disseminators, respectively), while having a lower opinion of the typical American, whom they see as shaped by racist, sexist, ways of thinking.

Finally, the technocrats are, probably more than any other group, the target of all the other groups' ire. This is not surprising, for technocrats, though not particularly numerous, run many of society's most important institutions—medicine, technology, finance, and much of the federal government. Perhaps because of their positions, they tend to see politics as a set of problems requiring technology or expertise to solve. Issues of liberty or justice are not usually foremost in their thinking, as they are with libertarians and progressives. Instead, they tend to worry about stability and keeping the system running. Consequently, technocrats make up the political center of American discourse. However, as we shall see, they are clearly more concerned about impressing progressives than they are about pleasing libertarians or populists.

THE CORONAVIRUS ARRIVES

First to worry about the coronavirus were elements of the technocracy, in particular some Internet entrepreneurs ("tech-bros," as they're derisively labeled by progressives), journalists, and epidemiologists. At first, progressives, populists, and libertarians reacted to worries about the coronavirus with either skepticism or scorn. Progressives heard talk of a potentially devastating virus coming to the United States from China and, given the source of this talk, didn't worry about the virus, but instead about how action against the coronavirus would lead to racism against Asians.[3] Populists and libertarians weren't scornful, but they were skeptical. Most notable among the populists was President Trump himself. Thanks to his director of Trade and Manufacturing Policy, the China hawk Peter Navarro, he at first reacted to reports of the coronavirus with somewhat restrictive measures meant to reduce travel from China, though, because he thought harsher restrictions would damage the economy, he later minimized the threat the virus posed.[4] Many libertarians were also skeptical, both because they thought that experts didn't know enough to justifiably believe that the coronavirus would devastate America (see libertarian law professor Richard Epstein's infamous prediction that the coronavirus would kill no more than 500 Americans, which he later revised upwards to 5,000 Americans[5]), and because they thought that private responses to the virus would turn out to be more effective, should the worst coronavirus fears turn out to be true.

In other words, before they knew much about the coronavirus, progressives, populists, and libertarians treated it as they treated every other issue: as confirming what they already believed. That is, they viewed the claims of epidemiologists, tech entrepreneurs, and health journalists, not mainly as sincere attempts to communicate the truth, but rather as emanating from racist priors, hostility to American citizens, or a desire to manage people's behavior. That is, these disparate groups interpreted coronavirus alarmists' communicative discourse as strategic.

Eventually, this all changed: by mid-March, thanks to events like the NBA shutting down its season and Tom Hanks coming forward as a coronavirus patient, Americans of all political persuasions began to take the coronavirus seriously (a libertarian would say: the market convinced people more effectively than the government). Progressives no longer thought worrying about the coronavirus was racist; instead, they began to say that not worrying *enough* was racist (witness their concerns about the virus' disproportionate impact on blacks and Hispanics). And populists and libertarians who had formerly claimed that the coronavirus was not something to worry about now said nothing, or claimed it was very serious, either because of Democratic mismanagement or because of failures of the regulatory state.[6]

Meanwhile, public health experts like Anthony Fauci, Scott Gottlieb, Mark Lipsitch, and others ascended to prominence. Their deliverances were treated as gospel truth by most Americans, many of whom would treat any deviation from expert advice as evidence of moral turpitude. Because you can have and transmit the coronavirus without knowing you have it, and because it's so deadly, you should stay home as much as you can. Indeed, governments should impose lockdowns on their citizenry in order to "flatten the curve."[7] In fact, we can be so sure of the accuracy of public health experts' advice that we can safely conclude that anyone who violates public guidelines is a self-centered jerk, and that anyone who questions official medical wisdom is a threat to public health: sowing doubt at a time like this could get people killed, so people who try to raise doubts should be shouted down (on social media, at least), if not silenced altogether (by having their posts taken down from Medium[8]).

If you think that questioning expert commentary on the coronavirus is dangerous and should be yelled at or removed, then it seems to me that you probably endorse the following beliefs: some people are selfish, and just want to do whatever they want, even if it endangers others; and some people are impressionable, willing to believe any knave who tries to sell them a bill of goods, especially if it promises to make their lives easier. This means that we should be very careful regarding how we talk about the coronavirus, because there are selfish people trying to sow confusion, and there are impressionable bystanders, susceptible to being confused. These sowers of confusion aren't engaging in communicative discourse: instead, they are asking questions strategically—they want to justify reopening their businesses, or keeping the economy as strong as possible, to help the Republicans. But if that's right, then there's no point in trying to reason with them, no point in treating their strategic discourse as communicative. All that does is legitimate their point of view and confuse bystanders. So, you must respond to those throwing smoke in the air by pushing them away.

In other words, because *they*, the hucksters, engage in strategic discourse, and because bystanders are gullible, *we*, those who follow science, have to engage in strategic discourse ourselves: *we* must attack *them*, because that will convince the benighted masses not to believe the hucksters. The fact that the people most vocally skeptical of public health advice tended to be populists and libertarians, and the fact that people most supportive of it tended to be technocrats and progressives, helped to fuel this outlook. After all, this was already the approach progressives used to deal with non-progressives, so it was easy to transfer to discussions about the coronavirus.

Americans' confidence in public health experts eventually declined, though, because public health recommendations changed quickly enough for people to notice. First, experts downplayed the virus: they didn't want to alarm us, so they downplayed the virus' threat. Second, once they realized that the virus was beyond containment, they wanted to alarm the public, so they told Americans to wash their hands constantly, wipe down surfaces, and to stay home. In addition, they told Americans *not* to wear masks, on the grounds that medical personnel needed them, only N95 masks would work, and most Americans wouldn't be able to figure out how to properly wear N95 masks. Finally, they said the surest signs of having the coronavirus was a fever, shortness of breath, and a deep, dry cough.

The third iteration of public health guidance repudiated its earlier advice: it turns out that surfaces were not the main medium of transfer; instead, droplets were. Consequently, people *should* wear masks, pretty much any kind of mask.[9] In addition, it's really hard to get the coronavirus if you're outside, so what you should most avoid is staying indoors for prolonged periods of time talking to people who may, unbeknownst to anyone, have the coronavirus. Finally, the coronavirus's symptoms multiplied: yes, fever was often a sign, but so were digestive issues. Shortness of breath remained a common symptom, but now we also had to contend with sudden lack of smell and COVID-toes. After a while, it seemed like anything could be a sign of the virus.

Though constantly shifting advice probably shook Americans' confidence in their public health establishment, I suspect that what happened next shattered it, at least among conservatives.[10]

THE BLACK LIVES MATTER PROTESTS

The murder of George Floyd led to massive, lasting, nationwide protests against police brutality and systemic racism. These protests, which I'll call the Black Lives Matter (BLM) protests, brought hundreds of thousands of people, mostly masked, but often singing or chanting, into close, prolonged contact with each other. While some public health experts (e.g., Fauci) quietly worried about these protests leading to coronavirus outbreaks, most prominent public health experts supported them, for a variety of reasons.

The most common explanation given (by, e.g., Johns Hopkins epidemiologist Jennifer Nuzzo) was the following: racism is a public health issue; since it is a public health issue, protesting it is a good idea, *even* from a public health point of view; consequently, the BLM protests were helping public health.[11]

This kind of explanation raised eyebrows, to put it mildly. There is first of all the problem of calling racism a public health crisis; once racism counts as a public health crisis, what doesn't? Surely there are similar cases to be made for crime, police brutality, overly permissive speed limits, financial inequality, and perhaps even capitalism itself being public health crises.

Second, this explanation assumes that protesting is good way to address racism. It may or may not be, but what reason do we have for thinking that public health training gives public health experts the ability to make defensible predictions about their efficacy?

Third, and, from the public's perspective, most salient, many of the public health experts praising the BLM protests unreservedly condemned earlier anti-lockdown protests, many of whom justified themselves by pointing out all the negative psychological and health consequences a months-long lockdown posed. Why were the anti-lockdown protests bad from a public health perspective, while the BLM protests were good from a public health perspective?

The Kent State University epidemiologist Tara Smith offered a blunt answer to this last question. According to Smith, the BLM protests were simply morally better than the anti-lockdown protests. The cause of the BLM protests was righteous, while the cause of the anti-lockdown protests was iniquitous. Consequently, public health experts should support the former while condemning the latter.[12]

This answer, though, raised questions about the discipline of public health: is it foundational to public health research that it, qua *public health research*, presupposes particular stances on controversial moral questions to be correct? If so, what in their training as public health officials justifies public health officials in thinking that these stances are correct?

Here the University of Washington epidemiologist Carl Bergstrom admitted that he supported the BLM protests not as a public health expert, but as a citizen.[13] Fair enough. But that just raised the questions: when do public health experts make claims *qua* public health experts and when do they make claims *qua* citizen? Do they tell us when? And if Bergstrom's support of BLM was as a citizen, what are we to make of those 1,000+ public health experts who signed an open letter[14] telling us that they were supporting the Black Lives Matter protests *as a matter of public health*?[15]

I wager that epidemiologists' (obviously) politically motivated reasoning surrounding the BLM protests convinced the public, more than any coronavirus skepticism, that public health experts' communications are as much strategic as they are communicative. Obviously, public health experts' advice before the BLM protests kept on shifting because our knowledge of the coronavirus quickly grew. Experts thought that the coronavirus operated in one way, and then more experimentation and observation convinced them that it operated in another way. However, the fact that each iteration of epidemiological consensus was accompanied by hectoring certainty from their online and politician supporters moved at least some of us into thinking that perhaps our appointed experts don't have as much of a handle on this whole coronavirus thing as we thought they had. Add to this the fact that condemnations of the use of hydroxychloroquine—which just happened to be the drug that Donald Trump (seemingly, quite baselessly) repeatedly hyped—were based on studies in the *Lancet* and the *New England Journal of Medicine* that had to be retracted,[16] and many people began to see epidemiological advice as serving the goal of removing Trump just as much as protecting the public. (Though, in public health experts' defense, perhaps removing Trump was an urgent matter of public health?)

KNOWING YOU'RE NEVER GOING TO KNOW

One of the troubling things about the coronavirus is that it's possible to have it without knowing it. This is true in one obvious way: you can have it but be asymptomatic, and so not even realize you ever carried it. But it can be true in another, more troubling way: you can have it, and even have symptoms consistent with it, but test negative for it. In such a situation, what should you conclude: that you had it, but that the test gave you a false negative? Or that you never had it, despite what your body was telling you? In other words, should you trust the science or your senses?

We'll have similar problems with regard to the coronavirus. There will be outbreaks a few weeks after the protests started; indeed, as I write this, on June 19, 2020, this has already started to happen. But, unsurprisingly, there is a lot of disagreement about their source. Libertarians and, especially, populists, blame the BLM protests for spikes in infections. Progressives and technocrats blame either the police (for using tear gas, trapping people like sardines in jail, and corralling demonstrators into each other) or entitled Americans going back to salons, restaurants, and casinos, for the spiking infection rate. And at this point, because public health experts have lost credibility, libertarians and conservatives won't believe them when they say (as they probably will) that the main sources of the outbreaks are police misconduct and the failure of vigilance in everyday Americans. So, I predict that people will look at the messy aftermath of the second wave of coronavirus infections and conclude that any bad news is the other teams' fault. It will be very difficult to know where the fault actually lies.

There is lots of blame to go around. The protests almost assuredly increased the case count, as did police behavior and economies reopening. Moreover, Republicans in Congress were dead-set against giving working people any more government income, thereby forcing them to go back to the economy. Perhaps Republicans did this because they honestly believed that government had done enough, but I suspect their behavior was undertaken for two reasons: first, not giving people money would force the economy to reopen, which would help their and Trump's reelection chances. And second, giving people free money would allow them to protest for longer, thereby forcing the government to give in to more and more protester demands, not to mention allowing the formation of a sticky, left-wing movement.

So, I'm viewing Republicans' behavior strategically. But how do I explain the behavior of public health experts?

I have two complementary theories. First, public health experts were already unpopular with conservatives: many polls showed that Republicans weren't as worried about the coronavirus as Democrats, and that whites weren't as worried about the coronavirus as much as blacks and Hispanics were (as for Asians: apparently no one cares to know what they think). Consequently, if you want to maintain as much influence as possible, you should side with the most powerful group that will believe you, and that's the progressives.

My second theory is that most of the public health experts who supported the protests really did believe that, from a public health point of view, the protests were a good thing. When you think about it, this fits public health experts' track record: they sincerely and wrongly believed that masks didn't work, despite having masses of evidence of their success in Asian countries. And they sincerely and wrongly assured us that quarantines don't work, even as China, apparently unconcerned about state-of-the-art epidemiology, showed the world that quarantines could indeed work.

If I'm right that public health experts are sincere, then this is pretty good evidence against what I wrote in my other contribution to this volume. There I wrote of my skepticism regarding the idea that the Western world is transitioning from a duty culture to a victimhood culture. I reasoned that 8 percent of the public was sincere in holding their social justice worldview, while the 67 percent of the populace that was neither conservative nor progressive was merely mouthing platitudes without acting on them. But I think that, for whatever reason, victimhood culture really is winning out. As the conservative blogger Andrew Sullivan put it, "We All Live on Campus Now."[17]

I'll close with a small reflection on a big subject, sincerity. I began this chapter by mentioning that I've never seen so much insincerity, and I'm closing it by expressing surprise at the possibly sincere social justice worldview of public health experts. The insincerity I see is whenever any group of people confesses allegiance to any principle. The sincerity I see is favoring one's ingroup. If someone says to me, "I favor individual rights" or "I favor justice for the oppressed," I now add, in my mind, an elliptical ". . . for my ingroup." The talk of principles is mostly a smokescreen; there are, of course, honorable exceptions. But most people basically just like some people and hate others. They will support whatever principles they need to justify harming their enemies and helping their friends.

Few people come out and say that, of course. As a culture, Americans have gotten much better about being sly. The propaganda that convinced us to go to war in World War I looks cartoonish and childlike compared to the propaganda we see today. The fact that propaganda has to be undertaken in a much more roundabout matter than it was done in the past means that it takes more effort to appeal to our atavistic parts. So, we probably have improved, despite the politicization of everything. And that's a good thing. Believe me.

NOTES

1. One notable group left out of my taxonomy is what you might call the "class justice" left. I'm thinking here of Marxist academics like Adolph Reed Jr., left-wing journalists like Glenn Greenwald, and socialist political figures like Bernie Sanders. In addition, there is a large number of Americans who probably fall into *none* or *more than one* of these groups. As I imagine things, these Americans are probably closest in their outlook to technocrats, though without having the knowledge or inclinations of the technocrats.

2. See Bill Bishop, *The Big Sort: Why the Clustering of Like-Minded America is Tearing Us Apart* (New York, NY: Mariner Books, 2009). Bishop points out that Americans have been increasingly sorting themselves into like-minded communities. Thus, one of the effects of there being a worldwide cosmopolitan class that likes to associate mainly with itself is the corresponding growth of an increasingly more homogeneous provincial class.

3. See, for example, Regina Rini, "Virulent Attitudes," *TLS*, https://www.the-tls.co.uk/articles/coronavirus-virulent-attitudes-morals-story-rini/, accessed June 19, 2020.

4. Navarro is a populist in the Tucker Carlson and Steve Bannon mode, both of whom were among the earliest worriers about the coronavirus. The cases of Navarro, Carlson, and Bannon raise the hypothetical possibility that populists could have been the ones most alarmed about the coronavirus, on the grounds that it's one more bad thing that comes from globalization, migration, international trade, and so on. It's worth wondering how progressives and the public health community would have treated the coronavirus if Trump had taken a strong, pro-lockdown stance.

5. Richard A. Epstein, "Coronavirus Perspective," *Hoover Institution*, March 16, 2020, https://www.hoover.org/research/coronavirus-pandemic, accessed June 19, 2020.

6. The libertarian-adjacent blog *Marginal Revolution* has a whole series of posts each of which is entitled, "Our regulatory state is failing us." One of the blog's proprietors, Tyler Cowen, posted an entry by that name on April 6, May 13, May 26, June 8, June 19, and had other posts going under different titles, but making the same point, on April 2, April 30, May 5, May 15, and May 30, all of 2020. It should be noted that neither of the two economists running *Marginal Revolution*, Tyler Cowen and Alex Tabarrok, were coronavirus skeptics.

7. It was around this point that the film *Plandemic*, which propounded a conspiracy theory according to which the government was going to use a phony coronavirus scare to institute its plan to put a tracking chip in all American citizens, came out and become popular among certain, mostly right-wing (or at least that's how I'd bet), groups.

8. See Chris White, "Medium Removes Post Imploring Americans To Consider Evidence Over Hysteria On Coronavirus Panic," *Daily Caller*, March 22, 2020, https://dailycaller.com/2020/03/22/twitter-medium-coronavirus-hysteria-aaron-ginn/, accessed June 19, 2020.

9. Relying on my own subjective impressions, it seems to me that the changing public health guidance on masks was the first chip in public health experts' armor. I heard numerous smart, well-informed people take the changing advice to be evidence that the public health establishment knew about the effectiveness of masks all along, but wanted to prevent the public from buying them up so that medical personnel wouldn't run out. This, though, is almost certainly not true, as the WHO has been bearish on masks since at least 2009 (see Scott Alexander, "Face Masks: Much More Than You Wanted to Know," *Slate Star Codex*, March 23, 2020, https://slatestarcodex.com/2020/03/23/face-masks-much-more-than-you-wanted-to-know/, accessed June 19, 2020). This is a case, I think, where people were interpreting communicative discourse that was simply inaccurate as being strategic.

10. Unfortunately, as of June 19, 2020, I could not find any polls of Americans' trust in public health officials, let alone polls divided along political lines. I cannot help but to find that suspicious, though perhaps I am explaining a lack of information as resulting from strategy on the part of pollsters, rather than as resulting from a lack of money.

11. See Dan Diamond, "Suddenly, Public Health Officials Say Social Justice Matters More Than Social Distance," *Politico*, June 4, 2020, https://www.politico.com/news/magazine/2020/06/04/public-health-protests-301534, accessed June 19, 2020.

12. Tara Smith, "From Several Commenters . . . ," *Twitter*, May 31, 2020, https://twitter.com/aetiology/status/1267104914951540736, accessed June 19, 2020.

13. Carl T. Bergstrom, "1. Many people . . . ," *Twitter*, June 5, 2020, https://twitter.com/CT_Bergstrom/status/1269034455810727936, accessed June 19, 2020.

14. "Open Letter Advocating for an Anti-Racist Public Health Response to Demonstrations Against Systemic Injustice Occurring During the COVID-19 Pandemic," https://drive.google.com/file/d/1Jyfn4Wd2i6bRi12ePghMHtX3ys1b7K1A/view, accessed June 19, 2020.

15. Tyler Cowen raised such questions in his blog post, "Rescheduling for Thee, But Not for Me," *Marginal Revolution*, June 7, 2020, https://marginalrevolution.com/marginalrevolution/2020/06/rescheduling-for-thee-but-not-for-me.html, accessed June 19, 2020.

16. Jason Silverstein, "Authors Retract Hydroxychloroquine Study that Raised Global Concern about Drug's Use for Coronavirus," *CBS News*, June 4, 2020, https://www.cbsnews.com/news/the-lancet-retracts-hydroxychloroquine-studies-covid-19/, accessed June 19, 2020.

17. Andrew Sullivan, "We All Live on Campus Now," *New York Magazine*, February 9, 2018, https://nymag.com/intelligencer/2018/02/we-all-live-on-campus-now.html, accessed June 19, 2020.

Index

abortion, 67, 81–83, 85, 242
actively open-minded thinking (AOT), 184
affective polarization, 170
AMA *Code of Ethics*, 70, 91, 100
American Dream, 205
American Hospital Association, 85
American Medical Association, 31, 33, 36, 70, 83
anti-vaccine movement, 242
Aquinas, Thomas, 113
Augustine of Hippo, 112
autonomy, 31

Bannon, Steve, 272
base camp, 242
Beauchamp, Tom, 66, 67, 74–78, 82, 83, 85, 87, 88
Beauvoir, Simone de, 212
The Belmont Report, 66, 67, 88
Bergstrom, Carl, 269
Biomedical Advanced Research and Development Authority, 240
The Birth of the Clinic (Michel Foucault), 69
Birx, Deborah, 240, 241
Black Lives Matter/BLM, 206, 268–70
blasphemy laws, 49
Boccaccio, 233

bodily integrity, 72
Bright, Rick, 240
Brundage, James, 114, 119–21

Camp IV, 239
Campbell, Bradley, 144, 146–49
Canterbury v. Spence, 464 F.2d 772 (D.C. Cir. 1972), 73, 74
Capron, Alexander, 51, 72
Cardozo, Benjamin, 72, 73
Carlson, Tucker, 272
Centers for Disease Control and Prevention (CDC), 243
Charcot, Jean-Martin, 71
Childress, James, 67, 74–78, 82, 83, 85, 87, 88
Christie, Chris, 239
Clinton, Hillary, 145, 152
Cobbs v. Grant, 8 Cal. 3d 229 (1972), 74–76, 87
Codevilla, Angelo, 144–47, 149
Collins, Patricia Hill, 207, 215, 219
communicative action, 65, 67, 69, 70, 74, 76, 78, 81
compromise, willingness to, 179
consent, 2, 7–8, 24, 65–68, 70–88; consent form, 24, 66; informed consent, 8, 24, 65–68, 73–88; sexual consent, 107, 109–11, 114–25

contact tracing, 235, 243
contract law, 72, 83–85, 236, 238
coronavirus, 231, 233, 236, 240–43, 263–71
corporate personhood, 27–29
Costco, 238
Court of Appeals of California, First District, 73
Court of Appeals of New York, 72
COVID–19, 99, 231–33, 241
Crenshaw, Kimberle, 215
Crisis Pregnancy Center, 97
critique, ideology, 140–42
Crozier, Brett, 240
culture, 140, 141; dignity, 146, 154–55, 271; honor, 146, 147; moral, 146; victimhood, 146–47, 150, 154–55, 271

Dark Summit (Nick Heil), 241
death zone, 231, 235, 237, 243
Decameron (Boccaccio), 233
Defoe, Daniel, 233
difficulty claim, 138, 139, 143, 149, 150
discourse ethic, 3, 117, 136, 139, 142, 149, 136, 139, 142–44, 149–51, 154; communicative discourse, 263–64, 267; discourse theory, 6, 107; social justice discourse, 9–10, 40, 43–44, 135–39, 141–56, 271; strategic discourse, 263–64, 267. *See also* ethics
dominance theory, 110–11
Dorje, Ang, 239
DuBois, W. E. B., 208, 211
Dworkin, Andrea, 107, 110–12

Eberhardt, Jennifer, 150
effects over intent, 143, 144, 149, 151, 154
elite theory, 142
enlightenment humanism, 218
enlightenment, 74, 88, 90
epidemic, 232, 234
epistemological diversity, 39, 42–43, 46, 57
Epstein, Richard, 266

escalation of commitment, 243
ethics, 3, 7, 15–20, 23–26, 29–32, 67, 70, 74, 77, 78, 83, 85; ethical equivocation, 26, 31; professional ethics, 16, 31; system-internalization of ethics, 32–33. *See also* discourse ethics
Europe, 233

Fairness Claim, 138, 143, 149, 151
Fauci, Anthony, 266, 268
Federal Emergency Management Agency (FEMA), 236
fee-for-service care, 85
feminism, 108, 112, 123–24; black feminism, 207, 215, 219
Fink, Sheri, 16
Fissell, Mary, 72, 74
Flax, Jane, 1–3, 125, 197
Floyd, George, 241, 268
flu (influenza), 232, 234
Foreman, Eric (fictional character), 66, 86–88
for-profit care, 85
Foucault, Michel, 45, 60, 69, 70
Fox News, 243
free speech, 51, 82, 85, 238; by class rank, 51; by class rank and race/ethnicity, 52; college campus speech codes, 48; compelled speech, 65, 67, 81, 82, 83, 85; derogatory speech, 48; First Amendment, 4, 48–50, 58, 82, 238; hate speech, 49; index measurement of, 50

Garrett, Laurie, 232, 243
Gernot Bohme, 17–18
al-Gharbi, Musa, 153
Goldberg, Jonah, 150
Gottlieb, Scott, 266
Gramsci, Antonio, 145
Gratian, 108, 113–15, 117–19, 121
Greenwald, Glenn, 272
Groom, Mike, 239
group threat, 171

Index 277

H_1N_1, 232
H_2N_2, 234
Habermas, Jürgen, 3, 7, 65, 67–70, 74, 76, 78, 82, 85, 87, 107, 109, 117, 168
Hajdin, Mane, 115
Hall, Lincoln, 243
Halley, Janet, 111, 116, 123
Hanks, Tom, 266
Harris, Andy, 239
Hartmann, Thom, 28
Haslanger, Sally, 140, 150
Hegel, Georg, 88, 232, 243
Heil, Nick, 235, 241
Heraclitus, 232
Hetey, Rebecca, 150
Hillary, Edmund, 254
Hippocrates, 72
Hippocratic Oath, 70, 71
Hobbes, Thomas, 25
Hogan, Larry, 236
House M.D. (TV show), 66, 86–88
House, Gregory (fictional character), 86, 87
Huemer, Michael, 148, 154
hydroxychloroquine, 241
hysterectomy, 68, 73, 77

identity, 179, 180, 182; dehumanization, 175; group diversity, 39, 45–46, 53, 60–61; identity theory, 170–71; partisan polarization, 171; political compromise, 173; political ideology, 171–72; political partisanship, 171; prejudice, 170; symbolic issues, 176; 2020 presidential election, 172
Ihde, Don, 33
informed consent, 8, 24, 65–68, 73–88
In re Quinlan, 70 N.J. 10, 355 A.2d 647 (1976), 93
Into Thin Air (Jon Krakauer), 231, 235

Jameton, Andrew, 240
The Johns Hopkins Center for Health Security, 232

A Journal of the Plague Year (Daniel Defoe), 233
Justin II, 72

Krakauer, Jon, 231–33, 235, 238–40
Kushner, Jared, 236

Lafayette Square, 241
Landes, Joan, 117
Last Week Tonight with John Oliver, 84
Lectures on the Philosophy of History (Georg Hegel), 232
Left for Dead (Beck Weathers), 251
Lenin, Vladimir, 145
le regard (Michel Foucault), 70, 76
Leviathan (Thomas Hobbes), 249
Lewis, C. S., 113
liberal education, 41–46, 52, 54, 60–61
liberalism, 148
libertarians, 264–67, 270
Lipsitch, Mark, 266
Lombard, Peter, 108, 112
Lombardo, Paul A., 68
Lorenzini, Carlo, 15

Manne, Kate, 152–53
Manning, Jason, 144, 146–49, 155
Marcuse, Herbert, 222
Martha Nussbaum, 22
Marx, Karl, 145
Marxism, 139–40, 144–45
Masks, 236–39, 267–68, 271
McConnell, Mitch, 236
McKinnon, Catherine, 107, 110–11, 123
Men in Black (film), 233
methodological reason, 16–18, 20–23
microaggression, 147, 149
Milley, Mark, 241, 252, 257
minority rule (Nicholas Nassim Taleb), 155
Mohr v. Williams, 95 Minn. 261 (1905), 72
moral agency, 28, 32–33; moral compromise, 180; moral devices, 19; moral distress, 233, 240, 241, 251,

258; moral judgment, 175, 183; moral partisanship, 177–78; moral pluralism, 39, 45–46, 53, 60–61; progressive moral realism (Michael Huemer), 144, 148, 149, 151; virtue (arete), 23–24
Mount Everest, 232–33, 235–39, 241–43

National Institutes of Health, 240
National Research Act in, 1974, 66
National Security Council's Pandemic Response Team, 231
Navarro, Peter, 266
Niccolo Machiavelli, 25
Nordenhaug, Erik, 87
Nuzzo, Jennifer, 268

Obama, Barack, 205
Oliver, John, 84
oppression, repressive, 140; dogmatism about oppression, 143, 144, 149, 151, 154; ideological oppression (Sally Haslanger), 140–44, 149, 151; reverence for the oppressed, 142, 143, 149–51, 154
Orentlicher, David, 82
Outlaw, Lucius, 210–12, 218
overstratification (Bradley Manning and Jason Campbell), 147

pandemic, 231–34, 236–38, 240–43
parens patriae, 81
party line voting, 169
patient financial responsibility, 8, 68, 81, 83, 85
Patient Protection and Affordable Care Act of 2010, 29, 234
Pence, Mike, 239
personal protective equipment (PPE), 237
Pineau, Lois, 107, 115–16, 124
plague (the disease), 232–34
Planned Parenthood of Southeastern Pennsylvania v. Casey, 505 U.S. 833 (1992), 81–83
Plato, 22–24, 72, 88, 112

populists, 264–67, 270
Porter, Katie, 84
power claim, 138, 144–51
Pratt v. Davis, 224 Ill. 300 (1906), 68–72, 77
prejudice, 47
primary prevention, 242
Principles of Biomedical Ethics (Tom L. Beauchamp and James F. Childress), 67, 74, 78, 85, 87, 88
privilege, cognitive, 150, 153
progressives, 264–67, 270
Project Airbridge, 236, 237, 248, 256
pro-life movement, 152
protest, 237, 238, 241, 242; campus protest, 47; laws, 48–49

racism, 1, 3–6, 10, 77, 140, 143–45, 151, 205–7, 209, 211, 213–15, 217–21, 266, 268; prejudice, 47. *See also* white supremacy
reason, 6–7; externalized, 22–23, 25–26; means-end, 6, 9–10, 116, 123–24
Reed, Jr., Adolph, 144–47, 149, 151
remdesivir, 241
rescue, 235, 241, 243
rights, 66, 72, 75, 81–82, 232–33, 236–38, 241
risk, 65, 72–74, 77, 79–85, 232, 235, 237–38, 241, 243
Rob Hall, 239
Roe v. Wade, 410 U.S. 113 (1973), 81

Salgo v. Leland Stanford Jr. University Board of Trustees, 154 Cal.App.2d 560 (1957), 73, 74, 76
Sanders, Bernie, 145
SARS-CoV-2, 231, 233, 236, 241
Sartre, Jean-Paul, 216–18
Schloendorff v. The Society of the New York Hospital, 211 N.Y. 125 (1914), 72, 73
science fiction, 231
self-categorization theory (SCT), 173
Sewell, William, 140

Shaw, George Bernard, 244, 260
sherpa, 235, 239, 242, 243
Simmons, Jack, 78
smallpox, 232
Smith, Tara, 269
The Social Transformation of American Medicine (Paul Starr), 246
standpoint epistemology, 207
Stanley, Jason, 153–54
Stanley, Manfred, 153–54
Starr, Paul, 246
Stewart, Cameron, 29
Stewart, William H., 246
strategic action, 68, 69, 72, 74, 76, 81
strategic disagreement, 168
Strategic National Stockpile, 236, 237
Sullivan, Andrew, 271
Superintendent of Belchertown State School v. Saikewicz, 373 Mass. 728 (1977), 94
Supreme Court of California, 73
Supreme Court of Illinois, 71
Supreme Court of Minnesota, 72
Supreme Court of New Jersey, 93
Supreme Court of the United States, 81, 82, 152
surprise medical billing, 84, 85

table top exercise, 232
Taleb, Nicholas Nassim, 155
teamsmanship, 167–68
technocrats, 264–67, 270
technology, 33
tertiary prevention, 235, 242
testing, 234, 236, 243
Theodore Roosevelt (naval ship), 240
The Theory of Communicative Action (Jürgen Habermas), 67
Tibet, 244, 253, 255
Title IX, 8, 109–10, 113–15, 117, 119–25

Trump, Donald, or the Trump Administration, 84–85, 152, 206–7, 266, 269–70
Tuskegee syphilis study, 66
Twitter or tweet, 238

U.S. Congress, 66, 84, 85; incivility, 167
U.S. Court of Appeals for the D.C. Circuit, 73, 74
U.S. Court of Appeals for the Eighth Circuit, 81, 82
U.S. Department of Health and Human Services, 99
U.S. Department of Justice, 236
U.S. Department of State, 252
U.S. Federal Trade Commission, 245
U.S. Food and Drug Administration, 245
U.S. Senate, 236
Ultimate Survival: Everest (TV show), 244
underdiversity (Bradley Manning and Jason Campbell), 147
Union Pacific Railway Company v. Botsford, 141 U.S. 250 (1891), 92

vaccine, 231, 234, 236, 240, 241
value claim, 138, 143, 144, 149, 151
Verbeek, Peter-Paul, 32
viewpoint diversity, 47

Weathers, Beck, 251
Weber, Max, 78
Weinberg, Alvin, 18
White House, 236, 241
White House Coronavirus Task Force, 236, 240
white supremacy, 206–7
World Health Organization, 231

About the Contributors

Elizabeth Butterfield is an associate professor of philosophy at Georgia Southern University. She is the author of *Sartre and Post-Humanist Humanism*, which uses the tools of Sartre's later Marxist-Existentialism, in combination with feminism, critical race theory, and Frankfurt School critical theory, to seek a new approach to understanding human identity as well as race, class, and gender, within the framework of a politics of difference. She has also authored several articles on existentialism, Marcuse, and pop culture. She is the past president of the North American Sartre Society, and she regularly teaches courses on Ethics, Existentialism, Philosophy of Religion, Happiness and the Meaning of Life, and Race, Class, and Gender.

Robert Gressis received his PhD in philosophy in 2007, where he wrote his dissertation on Kant's theory of evil. Currently, he is a professor of philosophy at California State University, Northridge, where he has been teaching since 2008. His primary research focus has been on Kant's religious and ethical philosophy, but he has also written articles on Hume's philosophy of religion, in experimental philosophy, and on the epistemology of disagreement. His current research focuses on metaphilosophy, specifically the questions of what it takes for philosophy to count as good philosophy, and on what motivations a mediocre philosopher can or should have for doing philosophy. In addition, he writes popular philosophy articles for the website The Electric Agora, and he regularly appears on bloggingheads.tv. He is also writing a textbook on critical thinking.

Kenneth B. McIntyre is professor of political science at Sam Houston State University, USA. He is the author of *The Limits of Political Theory: Michael Oakeshott on Civil Association* (2004), *Herbert Butterfield: History, Providence,* *and Skeptical Politics* (2011), *Nomocratic Pluralism: Plural Values, Negative Liberty, and the Rule of Law* (2021), and coeditor of *Critics of Enlightenment Rationalism* (2020). He has also written essays on a variety of subjects including the philosophy of history and social science, ordinary language philosophy, American constitutionalism, and international relations theory.

Erik Nordenhaug is an associate professor of philosophy on the Armstrong Campus of Georgia Southern University where he has been an active in faculty governance since 1995. He is a founding member of Teaching Ethics Across the Curriculum Society (2000) and a long-standing member of the Jacques Ellul International Society. He completed his PhD at Emory University and his area of specialization focuses on the technological enframement of philosophy, ethics and all human relations. His writings observe technological systems and the corresponding technological rationality that fuels them steadily transforming and marginalizing the humanities as academic disciplines and human qualities in our daily interactions.

Leigh E. Rich is a professor of health administration at Georgia Southern University in Savannah, Georgia, where she teaches courses in bioethics, health law and policy, and social theory and is developing a philosophy-based course called "Health Care on Television." A longtime "culture critic," she has a background in cultural and medical anthropology and has worked as a journalist and an editor, including six years as editor in chief of the *Journal of Bioethical Inquiry*. She is an award-winning writer of editorials, news and feature stories, and reviews and is the host of the weekly radio programs *Listening to Literature* and *The Common Good* on Savannah's WRUU 107.5 FM. Her research focuses on the anthropology of the body and the philosophy and history of medicine, and she currently is working on a socio-legal book titled *Bodies and Body Boundaries in the Age of Biotechnology*.

Jack Simmons is a professor of philosophy at Georgia Southern University in Savannah, where he teaches twentieth-century philosophy, philosophy of film, postmodernism, and contemporary philosophy. His research focuses on the application of discourse theory and hermeneutics to science, technology, mass media, and ethics, including recent publications on Heidegger's critique of modernity, and an analysis of euthanasia and suicide from the perspective of prominent Continental philosophers. He is also a playwright and novelist, and recently published a philosophical novel entitled *Three Dashes Bitters*. A cofounder of the Savannah Clemente Course, a free course in the liberal arts designed to benefit the poor, he believes that a liberal education provides students with the tools to better their lives, regardless of their economic situation.

Dr. Stacy G. Ulbig currently serves as professor of political science at Sam Houston State University, where she specializes in the study of political attitude formation and the mass electoral behavior. She is the author of *Vice Presidents, Presidential Elections, and the Media* and coauthor of *The Resilient Voter: Stressful Polling Places and Voting Behavior.* Her latest book *Angry Politics: Partisan Hatred and Political Polarization among College Students* is available at the University Press of Kansas. Ulbig received her PhD from Rice University, where she served as a survey research coordinator in the Behavioral Research Lab, and has previously served as an assistant professor at Missouri State University and distinguished visiting professor at the U.S. Air Force Academy.

www.ingramcontent.com/pod-product-compliance
Lightning Source LLC
Chambersburg PA
CBHW070826300426
44111CB00014B/2472